ADDISON-WESLEY PUBLISHING COMPANY
Reading, Massachusetts • Menlo Park, California
London • Amsterdam • Don Mills, Ontario • Sydney

PASCAL:
A
PROBLEM
SOLVING
APPROACH

ELLIOT B. KOFFMAN
Temple University

The Cover: Marshall Henrichs, photographer.

The Apple II* microcomputer shown in a typical home setting.

*a registered trademark of Apple Computer, Inc.

This book is in the

Addison-Wesley Microbooks

Popular Series

Library of Congress Cataloging in Publication Data

Koffman, Elliot B.
   Pascal, a problem solving approach.

   (Addison-Wesley series in joy of computing)
   Includes index.
   1. PASCAL (Computer program language)   I.   Title.
II.   Series.
QA76.73.P2K62   001.64′24   81-3647
ISBN 0-201-10341-9   AACR2

Copyright © 1982 by Addison-Wesley Publishing Company, Inc. Philippines
copyright 1982 by Addison-Wesley Publishing Company, Inc.

ISBN 0-201-10341-9
ABCDEFGHIJK-DO-8987654321

To my family—Caryn, Robin, Deborah, and Richard Koffman, for their constant love and understanding

To my parents—Edward and Leah Koffman, for all that they have given me

Preface

Why PASCAL?

One of the principal reasons for the design of PASCAL was to create a programming language that could be used to teach a careful, disciplined approach to programming and problem solving. The growing popularity of PASCAL as an instructional language in colleges and universities attests to the success of PASCAL in fulfilling this goal. Further, PASCAL is becoming increasingly important as a language for implementing program systems. The widespread availability of UCSD PASCAL has made PASCAL a useful language for developing applications programs on personal computers and microcomputers such as the Apple, TRS-80, LSI-11 and others.

Problem Solving

Besides providing a thorough coverage of all aspects of UCSD PASCAL, this book helps beginners and advanced programmers develop their problem solving skills. Unlike most programming books, which simply teach a programming language, the step-by-step design of algorithms is emphasized throughout the book. Over 30 problems are carefully analyzed and solved from beginning (problem formulation) to end (PASCAL program) using a process that has been thoroughly tested in three other programming language books. All told, there are approximately 100 complete program modules included.

Other Major Features

- This book should appeal to both beginners and experienced BASIC programmers. Beginners will learn good programming and problem solving principles from the start. Experienced BASIC programmers will learn the principles of "GOTO-free" or structured programming as well as PASCAL.

- A modular approach to the design of programming is stressed. Procedure and function blocks are introduced early in the book.
- There is complete coverage of all features of standard and UCSD PASCAL including arrays, records, strings, sets, sequential and random access files.
- Program style displays discuss important issues of programming style.
- Special display boxes summarize the syntactic form of each new language feature introduced.
- Self-check exercises are integrated with the text. Answers to approximately half of these are provided at the end of the book.
- Each chapter ends with a summary and a discussion of common programming errors. The latter material will help you to write error-free programs.
- Additional programming problems are listed at the end of each chapter. They are representative of the kinds of problems you should be able to solve.
- Appendices are provided that illustrate the differences between UCSD and standard PASCAL; special identifiers and operators of PASCAL; using UCSD PASCAL; and syntax diagrams of PASCAL statements. These appendices will be valuable for future reference.
- Other reference aids are indices to program style displays as well as programs, procedures and functions.

Acknowledgments

My thanks to Professor John Gannon (University of Maryland), Professor Lori Clarke and Charles Weems (University of Massachusetts), Professor Richard Sites (formerly University of California at San Diego, now Digital Equipment Corp.) and Professor Frank Friedman (Temple University). I am indebted to all of them for their insightful comments.

This book focuses on interactive programming in UCSD PASCAL. Paul Fessler (Computers Plus Inc., Alexandria, Va.) and Edward Carotty (Philadelphia High School of Engineering and Science, Philadelphia, Pa.) also provided valuable constructive criticism.

Anthony DeLacy, a student at Temple University, did an excellent job of testing and debugging most of the programs provided in the book. I would like to thank him for his assistance and the many improvements that he made to these programs.

Fran Palmer Fulton performed the difficult job of production management in a very professional manner. I am indebted to her for the many hours she spent in coordinating the production of this book. I would also like to thank Jeanne Griffith of International Computaprint Corporation, Fort Washington, Pa., who supervised the type composition of the book. Additionally, special thanks to William Gruener, Executive Editor of Computer Science at Addison-Wesley, for initiating this project and for all his support.

I would be remiss in not thanking my family for their patience with me during my involvement with this manuscript. I would also like to acknowledge my daughter, Robin Koffman, for her help with the index.

Special Acknowledgment

I would especially like to thank my friend and colleague at Temple University, Professor Frank Friedman, who shared in the development of many of the ideas and pedagogy presented in this book during our earlier collaborations on *Problem Solving and Structured Programming in FORTRAN* and *Problem Solving and Structured Programming in BASIC.*

E.B.K.
Marion, MA
August, 1981

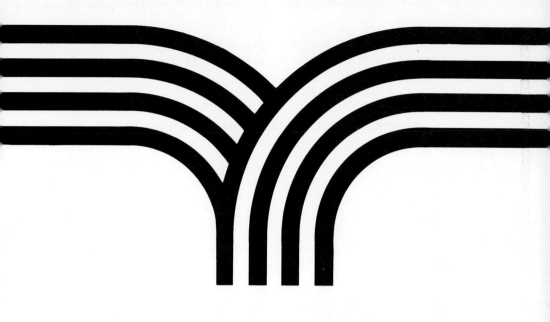

CONTENTS

APPENDICES

INTRODUCTION TO COMPUTERS AND PROGRAMMING

1

1.1 INTRODUCTION

This chapter will describe the general organization of computers and also discuss languages used for communicating with computers (programming languages). We shall see that all computers consist of four basic components— memory, central processor, input devices and output devices—and learn how information is represented in the memory of a computer and how it is manipulated.

An introduction to programming languages will be provided as well. Two kinds of programming languages will be discussed: machine language and high-level language. We shall introduce one high-level language, PASCAL, and give examples of how to specify some basic computer operations in PASCAL.

1.2 COMPUTER ORGANIZATION

1.2.1 Introduction

A computer is a tool for representing and manipulating information. There are many different kinds of computers, ranging in size from hand-held calculators

Fig. 1.1 Apple computer. (Photo courtesy of Caryn Koffman and the Philadelphia High School of Engineering and Science.)

to large and complex computing systems filling several rooms or entire buildings. In the recent past, computers were so expensive that they could be used only for business or scientific computations; now there are personal computers available for use in the home (see Fig. 1.1).

The size and cost of a computer is generally dependent upon the amount of work it can turn out in a given time unit. Larger, expensive computers have the capability of carrying out many operations simultaneously, thus increasing their work capacity. They also have more devices attached to them for performing special functions, all of which increase their capability and cost.

1.2.2 Components of a Computer

Despite large variation in cost, size and capabilities, modern computers are remarkably similar in a number of ways. Basically, a *computer* consists of four components as shown in Fig. 1.2. (The lines connecting the various units represent possible paths of information flow. The arrows show the direction of information flow.)

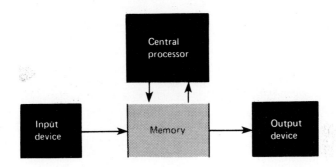

Fig. 1.2   Diagram of the basic components of a computer.

All information that is to be processed by the computer must first be entered into the computer memory via an input device. The information in memory is manipulated by the central processor and the results of this manipulation are also stored in the memory of the computer. Information in memory can be displayed through the use of appropriate output devices. These components and their interaction are described in more detail in the following sections.

1.2.3 The Computer Memory

The memory of a computer may be pictured as an ordered sequence of storage locations called *memory cells*. Each cell has associated with it a distinct *address*, which indicates its relative position in the sequence. Figure 1.3 depicts a computer memory consisting of 1000 cells numbered consecutively from 0 to 999. Some large-scale computers have memories consisting of millions of cells.

The memory cells of a computer are used to *represent* information. All types of information—numbers, names, lists, and even pictures—may be represented in the memory of a computer. The information that is stored in a memory cell is called the *contents* of the memory cell. Every memory cell contains some information—no cell is ever empty. Furthermore, no cell can ever contain more than one data item. Whenever a data item is placed into a memory cell, any information already there is destroyed and cannot be retrieved. In Figure 1.3, the contents of memory cell 3 is the number −26, and the contents of memory cell 4 is the number 12.5.

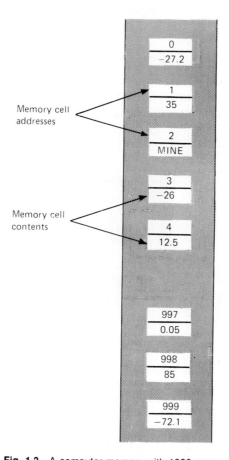

Fig. 1.3   A computer memory with 1000 memory cells.

It is important to realize that the actual instructions for manipulating data are also stored in the memory of the computer. These instructions are examined and carried out by the central processor unit, described next.

Exercise 1.1:   What are the contents of memory cells 0, 2, and 997 shown in Fig. 1.3?

1.2.4   The Central Processor Unit

The information representation capability of the computer would be of little use to us by itself. Indeed, it is the *manipulative* capability of the computer that enables us to study problems that would otherwise be impossible because of their computational requirements. With appropriate directions, modern computers can generate large quantities of new information from old, solving many otherwise impossible problems, and providing useful insights into others; and they can do so in exceptionally short periods of time.

The heart of the manipulation capability of the computer is the *central processor unit* (CPU). The CPU can retrieve information from the memory unit. This information may be either data or instructions for manipulating data. The CPU can also store the results of manipulations back into the memory unit for later reference.

The CPU coordinates all activities of the various components of the computer. It determines which operations should be carried out and in what order. The transmission of coordinating control signals and commands is the function of the *control unit* within the central processor.

Also found within the central processor is the *arithmetic-logic unit.* The *arithmetic* portion consists of electronic circuitry that performs a variety of arithmetic operations, including addition, subtraction, multiplication and division. The time in which it can perform these operations is on the order of a millionth of a second. The *logic* unit consists of electronic circuitry to compare information and to make decisions based upon the results of the comparison. It is this feature, together with its powerful storage facility (the memory), that distinguishes the computer from the simple, hand-held calculators that many of us have used. Most of these calculators can be used only to perform arithmetic operations on numbers; they cannot compare these numbers, make decisions, or store large quantities of numbers.

1.2.5   Input and Output Devices

The manipulative skills of the computer would be of little use to us if we were unable to communicate with the computer. Specifically, we must be able to enter information into the computer memory, and display information (usually the results of a manipulation) stored in the computer memory. The input devices are used to *enter* data into the computer memory; the output devices are used to *display* results in a readable form.

Most personal computers use a keyboard for input and a television-like monitor for output as shown in Fig. 1.1. In addition, game paddles or joysticks are sometimes used to enter information. A printer may be available to provide a permanent record of the computational results.

In personal computer systems, a disk may be used to provide additional capability for information storage and retrieval. A much larger quantity of information may be stored on a disk platter (or diskette) than can fit in memory at one time. During a computer session, information saved previously is retrieved from a disk as needed and entered into the main memory where it is manipulated. Also, new information can be saved for future retrieval and use.

1.3   PROGRAMS AND PROGRAMMING LANGUAGES

1.3.1   Introduction

The computer is quite a powerful tool. Information (*input data*) may be stored in its memory and manipulated at exceptionally high speed to produce a result (*program output*). We can describe a data manipulation task to the computer by presenting it with a list of instructions (called a *program*) that are to be carried out. Once this list has been provided to the computer, it can then carry out (*execute*) these instructions.

The process of making up a list of instructions (writing a program) is called *programming*. Writing a computer program is very similar to describing the rules of a game to people who have never played the game. In both cases, a language of description understood by all parties involved in the communication is required. For example, the rules of the game must be described in some language, and then read and carried out. Both the inventor of the game and those who wish to play must be familiar with the language of description used.

Languages used for communication between man and the computer are called *programming languages*. All instructions presented to a computer must be represented and combined (to form a program) according to the *syntactic rules* (grammar) of the programming language. There is, however, one significant difference between a programming language and a language such as French, English or Russian. The rules of a programming language are very precise and have no "exceptions" or "ambiguities." The reason for this is that a computer cannot think! It can only follow instructions exactly as given. It cannot interpret these instructions to figure out, for example, what the program writer (*programmer*) meant it to do. An error in writing an instruction will change the meaning of a program and cause the computer to perform the wrong action.

In this book, we shall concentrate on the PASCAL programming language. PASCAL is a relatively new programming language developed in 1970 by Professor Niklaus Wirth of Zurich, Switzerland. It contains many advanced features to facilitate writing programs in a variety of different applications areas.

We shall focus on a special version of PASCAL called UCSD PASCAL.(TM) UCSD PASCAL was developed at the University of California at San Diego by Professor Kenneth Bowles especially for use on microcomputers. It has some features that are different from those of standard PASCAL. We shall point out these differences where they occur; they are also summarized in Appendix 1.

Most computers cannot execute PASCAL programs directly. They must first be translated into the language understood by the computer, *machine language*.

Instructions in machine language are specified using a numeric code for operations and numeric addresses for data. The translation into machine language is performed by a special program called a *compiler.* If the translation is successful, the machine language version of the program is stored, ready to be brought into memory and carried out or *executed.*[1] After compilation, the program can be executed as often as desired without compiling again, provided no changes are made in the text of the program. This process is illustrated in Fig. 1.4.

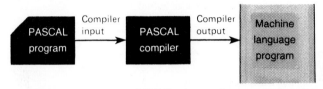

Fig. 1.4   Preparing a PASCAL program for execution.

There are two major advantages to programming in a *high-level language* like PASCAL rather than machine language. First, PASCAL is much closer to our own language than is machine language; hence, it is much easier to write PASCAL programs. Second, PASCAL programs are highly *portable;* a PASCAL program written for one computer can often be executed on a variety of computers. On the other hand, a machine language program written for one computer will not normally execute on a different type of computer.

We will discuss a few of the fundamental features of the PASCAL language in Section 1.4. Others will be introduced throughout the rest of the text.

1.3.2   Executing a Program

In order to execute a program, the central processor examines each program instruction in memory, starting with the first, and sends out the command signals appropriate for carrying out the instruction. Normally, the instructions are executed in sequence; however, as we shall see later, it is possible to have the computer skip over some instructions or execute some instructions more than once.

During execution, data may be entered into the memory of the computer, and the results of the manipulations performed on this data may be displayed. Of course, these things will happen only if the program contains instructions telling the computer to enter or display the appropriate information.

Figure 1.5 shows the relationship between a program for computing a payroll and its input and output, and indicates the *flow of information* through the computer during execution of the program. The data to be manipulated by the program (employee time cards) must first be entered into the computer memory

---

[1]Technically speaking, PASCAL compiles into a hypothetical machine language called P-code. P-code is then interpreted on the actual machine.

(Step 1 in Fig. 1.5). As directed by the program instructions, the central processor unit manipulates the data in memory, and places the results of these computations back into memory (Steps 2-4). When the computation process is complete, the final results can be output from the memory of the computer (Step 5) in the desired forms (as employee checks and payroll reports).

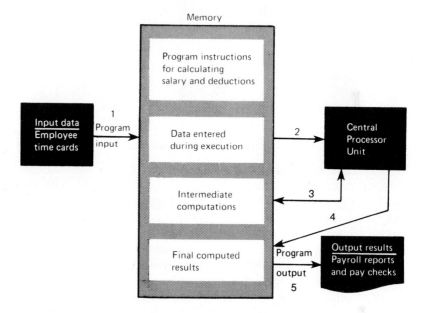

Fig. 1.5   The flow of information through the computer.

1.4   INTRODUCTION TO PASCAL

1.4.1   Use of Symbolic Names in PASCAL

One of the most important features of a high level language such as PAS-CAL is that it permits us to reference data stored in memory by descriptive names (called *variable names* or, simply, *variables*) rather than by numeric memory-cell addresses. The compiler allocates (assigns) one or more memory cells for each variable name used in our program. We need not be concerned with addresses. We simply tell the compiler the name of each variable we want to use and let the compiler determine the address of the cell associated with that variable.

Only valid PASCAL *identifiers* may be used as variable names. Identifiers are described next.

Identifiers

1. May contain only combinations of letters (A–Z), and the digits (0–9).
2. Must always begin with a letter (A–Z).

Although there is no specified limit to the length of an identifier, the UCSD PASCAL compiler only uses the first eight characters of an identifier to distinguish it from other identifiers. This means that both DISTANCE1 and DISTANCE2, for example, cannot be used as identifiers in the same program.

It is a good idea to use identifiers that describe what each variable represents. For the payroll problem, we might use the variable HOURS (for hours worked), RATE (for hourly rate), GROSS (for gross salary), and NET (for net pay). These are pictured in Fig. 1.6. The question mark in each box indicates that we have no idea of the current values of these variables (although variables always have values).

Fig. 1.6 Using meaningful variable names to designate memory cells.

The PASCAL statement used to inform the compiler that these variable names will designate the memory cells used in a program is:

```
VAR HOURS, RATE, GROSS, NET : REAL
```

This statement is called a *variable declaration statement*. Note that each variable name is separated from the next one in the list by a comma.

The word REAL indicates the *data type* (or *type*) of these variables. A type REAL variable is used for the storage of real numbers. In PASCAL, real numbers contain a decimal point and there must be at least one digit before and after the decimal point (examples of real numbers: 3.14, 0.005, −35.0, 0.0).

The data type of a variable indicates to the compiler what kind of data may be stored in that variable and the operations that may be performed on it. Consequently, we must know precisely how a variable will be used before we can declare its type. Once declared, the type of a variable cannot be changed.

A declaration statement similar in form to the previous one, but ending with the word INTEGER, indicates to the PASCAL compiler the names of variables used for the storage of integers. Numbers without decimal points are called whole numbers or *integers* (examples of integers: −99, 35, 0, 1). We will use only real numbers in this chapter. Different data types will be discussed in more detail in Section 1.7. The variable declaration statement is described in the next display.

Variable Declaration Statement

VAR *variable list* : *type*

Interpretation: A memory cell is allocated for each variable (an identifier) in the *variable list*. The *type* of data (REAL, INTEGER, etc.) to be stored in each variable is specified following the ":". Commas are used to separate the identifiers in the *variable list*.

There is no specific limit on the length of an identifier. However, one restriction is that certain *reserved words* in PASCAL have special meaning to the compiler and cannot be used as identifiers. The word VAR is a reserved word; other reserved words that we shall see in this chapter are CONST, PROGRAM, BEGIN and END. Appendix 2 provides a list of PASCAL reserved words.

There are also *standard identifiers* in PASCAL. These identifiers are predefined in PASCAL and have special meaning, but they are not reserved. This means that they may be redefined by the programmer, although we do not recommend your doing so. The words REAL and INTEGER fall into this category. A list of standard identifiers is also given in Appendix 2.

Exercise 1.2:   Which of the following "strings" of characters can be used as legal variable names in PASCAL? Indicate the errors in the strings that are illegal.

1) ARK	2) MICHAEL	3) ZIP12	4) 12ZIP
5) ITCH	6) P3$	7) CONST	8) X123459
9) NINE$T	10) GROSS	11) PROGRAM	

1.4.2   Some Computer Operations and Their PASCAL Descriptions

There are a large number of computers available today and each has a unique set of operations that it can perform. These operations generally fall into three categories:

> Input and output operations
> Data manipulation and comparison
> Control operations

Despite the large variety of operations in these categories, there are a few operations in each that are common to most computers. These operations are summarized below.

Input/Output Operations

> Read
> Write

Data Manipulation and Comparison

Add	Subtract	Multiply	Divide
Negate	Copy	Compare	

Control Operations

> Transfer control
> Conditional execution

In the remainder of this chapter, we will describe some of these operations by showing how they are written in PASCAL. We will do this by way of example, using a payroll processing problem.

Problem 1.1:   Compute the gross salary and net pay for an employee of a company, given the employee's hourly rate, the number of hours worked, and the tax deduction amount.

1.4.3   Simple Data Manipulation—Assignment Statements

We will choose variables named HOURS and RATE to represent the number of hours worked and the hourly wage rate, respectively. The variables GROSS and NET will be used to represent the computed gross and net salary, respectively. The variable TAX will represent the amount of tax to be withheld from the paycheck. For simplicity, we will assume the withholding tax amount to be \$25 regardless of an employee's gross salary. (A more realistic tax schedule would calculate the amount of tax withheld by using a table of varying percentages based on the employee's gross salary.)

Our problem is to perform the following two computations:
Compute gross salary as the product of hours worked and hourly rate;
Find net pay by deducting the tax amount from the gross salary.

We need to learn how to write PASCAL instructions to tell the computer to perform these computations. This can be done using the PASCAL *assignment statements*

$$\text{GROSS} := \text{HOURS} * \text{RATE}$$
$$\text{NET} := \text{GROSS} - \text{TAX}$$

These data manipulation statements are called assignment statements because they specify an assignment of value to a given variable. For example, the statement

$$\text{GROSS} := \text{HOURS} * \text{RATE}$$

specifies that the variable GROSS will be assigned the result of the multiplication of the values of the variables HOURS and RATE (* means "times") The right hand side of an assignment statement (e.g. HOURS * RATE) is called an *expression*. Figure 1.7 illustrates the effect of the two assignment statements used for calculating net salary.

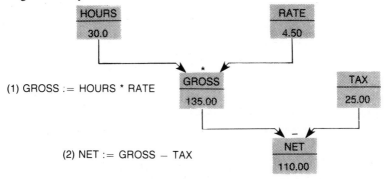

Fig. 1.7   Effect of assignment statements.

The effect of the first statement is to cause the value of the variable **GROSS** to be replaced by the product of the values of the variables **HOURS** and **RATE**, or 135.00. The second statement causes the value of the variable **NET** to be replaced by the difference between the values of the variables **GROSS** and **TAX**, or 110.00. We are assuming, of course, that meaningful data items are already present in the variables **HOURS**, **RATE**, and **TAX**. Only the contents of **GROSS** and **NET** are changed by this sequence of arithmetic operations.

Example 1.1: In PASCAL, it is perfectly permissible to write assignment statements of the form

```
SUM := SUM + ITEM
```

where the variable **SUM** is used on both sides of the assignment operator (:=). This is obviously not a mathematical equation, but it illustrates something that is often done in PASCAL. This statement instructs the computer to add the value of the variable **SUM** to the value of the variable **ITEM** and assign the result as the new value of the variable **SUM**. The previous value of **SUM** is lost in the process as shown next.

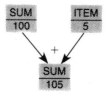

Example 1.2: Assignment statements can also be written with a single operand. The statement

```
NEWX := X
```

instructs the computer to *copy* the value of the variable **X** into **NEWX**. The statement

```
NEWX := -X
```

instructs the computer to *negate* the value of the variable **X** and store the result in **NEWX**. Neither of these statements affects the contents of the variable **X**. Negating a number is equivalent to multiplying it by -1. Thus, if the variable **X** contains -3.5, then the statement

```
NEWX := -X
```

will cause 3.5 to be stored in the variable **NEWX**.

In Chapter 4, we will discuss more complex examples of assignment statements involving the use of multiple operators and more than two operands. The simple assignment statements discussed so far are summarized in the next display.

Simple Assignment Statements

$result := operand_1$ *arithmetic-operator* $operand_2$
$result := operand_1$
$result := -operand_1$

Interpretation: $Operand_1$ and $operand_2$ represent the quantities being manipulated; *arithmetic-operator* indicates the manipulation to be performed. The operands may be either variable names or numbers. The *arithmetic-operator* is any of the symbols given in Table 1.1. The name of the variable that will be assigned a new value is specified by *result*. The previous value of *result* is destroyed when the new value is stored; however, the values of the operands are unchanged.

Arithmetic operator	Meaning
+	Addition
−	Subtraction
*	Multiplication
/	Division

Table 1.1   PASCAL Arithmetic Operators

1.4.4   Storing Data in Memory—Program Constants and Variables

Information cannot be manipulated by the computer unless it is first placed in memory. There are two ways of initially placing data into memory: (1) by use of a *constant definition statement,* or (2) by reading the data into memory during the execution of the program. Normally, the first approach is taken for a data item that is a *program constant* and does not change from one use of the program to the next. The second approach is taken for data that are likely to vary. In the payroll problem, the withholding-tax amount is always 25.00 regardless of which employee's net pay is to be computed. This value, therefore, may be associated with the constant identifier TAX through the use of the constant definition statement

$$\text{CONST TAX} = 25.00$$

Constant Definition Statement

$$\text{CONST } constant = value$$

Interpretation: The specified *value* is associated with the identifier *constant*. The value of *constant* cannot be changed by any subsequent program statements.

The definition of a program constant is permanent in the sense that the designated constant always has the value specified. Unlike a variable, a constant cannot have its value changed during program execution.

The *data type* of a constant identifier is implied by its associated value. Hence, if the value is a number containing a decimal point, then the constant is type REAL; if the value is a number without a decimal point, then the constant is type INTEGER.

In the following section, we describe how data that are likely to vary with each execution of a program may be entered into computer memory.

1.4.5   The READLN Statement

Since each employee of a company may work a different number of hours per week at his or her own hourly rate, the values of HOURS and RATE are frequently changing. Consequently, their values should be entered into memory during program execution. This operation must be done prior to performing the calculations described earlier (Section 1.4.3).

The statement

           READLN (HOURS, RATE)

causes the computer to wait for two data items to be typed. The first data item is stored in the variable HOURS; the second data item is stored in the variable RATE. (The previous values of these variables are lost.) The program resumes execution when the carriage return key is pressed. The READLN statement is illustrated below and described in the next display.

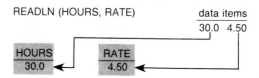

READLN Statement

                        READLN (*input list*)

Interpretation: Data are entered into each variable specified in the *input list.* Commas are used to separate the variable names in the *input list.* (The data items are typed in during program execution.)

The statement used to display or print out the value of a variable is described in the next section.

1.4.6   The WRITELN Statement

Thus far, we have discussed the PASCAL instructions required for the entry of employee hours and wage rate, and the computation of gross salary and net pay. The computational results have been stored in the variables GROSS and NET, respectively. Yet all of this work done by the computer is of little use to us since we cannot physically look into a memory cell to see what is there. We must, therefore, have a way to instruct the computer to display or print out the value of a variable.

The PASCAL instruction

WRITELN (GROSS, NET)

would cause the values of the variables GROSS and NET to be printed on a line of program output (Fig. 1.8). The values of GROSS and NET are not altered by this operation.

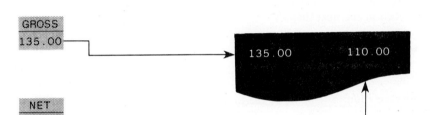

Fig. 1.8   Effect of WRITELN Statement

The WRITELN statement is described in the next display.

WRITELN Statement

WRITELN (*output list*)

Interpretation: The value of each variable in the *output list* is printed in sequence. Commas are used to separate items in the *output list*.

(The READLN and WRITELN operations are predefined procedures in PASCAL. The variables appearing in an input or output list are called parameters of the procedure. We shall discuss procedures and parameters in Chapter 5.)

1.4.7   The Payroll Program

We can now collect all of the instructions that have been discussed, and order them to produce a complete PASCAL program for Problem 1.1 (Fig. 1.9).

```
PROGRAM PAYROLL;

CONST
  TAX = 25.00;

VAR
  HOURS, RATE, GROSS, NET : REAL;

BEGIN
  READLN (HOURS, RATE);
  GROSS := HOURS * RATE;
  NET := GROSS - TAX;
  WRITELN (GROSS, NET)
END.
```

Fig. 1.9 The payroll program in PASCAL

The first statement in Fig. 1.9 is used to specify the name, PAYROLL, of the program. Every PASCAL program must begin with a *program statement* as described in the next display.

Program Statement

PROGRAM *prog-name*

Interpretation: The name of the program is indicated by *prog-name.*

The next two statements represent the *declaration part* of this PASCAL program. The declaration part consists of the constant definition statement followed by the variable declarations.

A statement may be continued from one line to the next. We have written the reserved words CONST and VAR on separate lines. Each declaration statement is completed on the next line.

The reserved word BEGIN indicates the start of the *program body,* the statements that perform the actual data manipulation. The first statement in the program body causes the values of the variables HOURS and RATE to be entered. The assignment statements compute values for GROSS and NET, which are then displayed. The last statement of the program body is always followed by the reserved word END and a period.

The semicolon (;) is used in PASCAL as a separator between statements. The semicolon following each statement is used to separate that statement from the next one in the program. Note that semicolons are not used after BEGIN or before END.

If the two numbers 30.0 and 4.50 were typed in as data, the payroll program would generate the output line

$$1.35000E+2 \quad 1.10000E+2$$

The numbers shown are the values computed for GROSS and NET.

These numbers are printed in *scientific* or *exponential notation* as indicated by the letter E. The two-digit number following the letter E specifies how many positions to shift the decimal point; the sign after the letter E indicates the direction (+ right, − left). The numbers printed are equivalent to the real numbers 135.0 and 110.0.

Program Style

Use of blank space

Program style is a very important considēration in programming. A program that "looks good" is easier to read and understand than a sloppy one. Most programs, at some time or another, will be examined or studied by someone else. It is certainly to everyone's advantage if a program is neat and its meaning is clear.

The consistent and careful use of blanks can significantly enhance the style of a program. A blank space is required between words in a program (e.g., between **PROGRAM** and **PAYROLL** in the program statement). However, extra blanks in PASCAL programs are ignored by the compiler and may be inserted as desired to improve the style and appearance of a program.

As shown in Fig. 1.9, we shall always leave a blank space after a comma and before and after operators such as *, −, and :=. In addition, we shall indent each statement in the program body. We shall also write the reserved words, CONST, VAR, BEGIN and END by themselves on a line so that they stand out. Finally, we shall use blank lines to separate the declaration part from the rest of the program.

All of these measures are taken for the sole purpose of improving the style and, hence, the clarity of the program. They have no effect whatsoever on the meaning of the program.

(Due to differences in type styles an asterisk will appear as * in text copy and as * in programs.)

Exercise 1.3: Can any of the statements in the program in Fig. 1.9 be moved without altering the results of the program? Which statements can be moved? Which cannot be moved? Why?

Exercise 1.4: What values will be printed by the Payroll Program for the alternate pair of data items 35.0 and 3.80?

Exercise 1.5: Let H, R, and T be the names of memory cells containing the information shown below:

H	R	T
40.0	16.25	0.18

What values will be printed following the execution of this sequence of instructions?

```
G := H * R;
T := G * T;
N := G - T;
WRITELN (H, R, G, T, N)
```

1.4.8   General Form of a Program

The general form of a PASCAL program is shown in Fig. 1.10. Every identifier used in a program must be declared exactly once in the declaration part unless it is a reserved word or standard identifier. This means that the same identifier cannot be used as both the name of a constant and the name of a variable. The reserved words CONST and VAR also appear exactly once in the declaration part in the order shown. All constant definitions come after CONST and all variable declarations after VAR. There may be more than one constant definition or variable declaration statement. Every statement in either the declaration part or program body should be separated from the statement following it by a semicolon.

Each variable must be initialized in the program body through a read or assignment before it can be manipulated in an expression or printed.

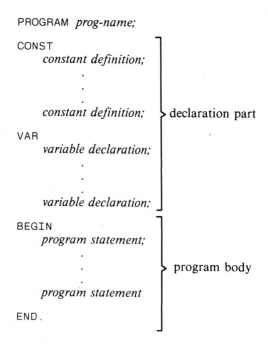

```
PROGRAM prog-name;

CONST
    constant definition;       ┐
         .
         .
    constant definition;       ├ declaration part
VAR
    variable declaration;      │
         .
         .
    variable declaration;      ┘

BEGIN
    program statement;         ┐
         .
         .                     ├ program body
    program statement          │
END.                           ┘
```

Fig. 1.10   General form of a program.

Exercise 1.6:   Correct all the errors in the program below.

```
PROGRAM
VAR
  X, Y := REAL:
CONST
  X := 3.5;
  A := 2.2 + X;
BEGIN
  Y := X + Z
  WRITELN (A, X, Y);
END;
```

1.5   USING THE COMPUTER

Once your program is written, it must be entered in the computer and translated by the PASCAL compiler before it can be executed. In UCSD PASCAL, this is done by creating a *workfile* on disk containing your program. The *editor* is used to create this workfile. Once you are satisfied with your program, you can instruct the UCSD PASCAL system to compile and run your program. If there are no *syntax errors* in the PASCAL statements, your program will be translated successfully and stored in memory in executable form (machine language). During the actual execution of the program, you would type in any data that may be required.

The details of creating a workfile and saving this workfile on disk for later use are described in Appendix 3.

1.6   ADDITIONAL INPUT AND OUTPUT FEATURES

1.6.1   Annotated Output

The printout for our payroll program consists of two numbers only, with no indication of what these numbers mean. In this section, we shall learn how output values may be annotated using *quoted strings* (or strings) to make it easier for us to identify the variable values they represent. We will learn more about the use of strings, but for the present it would be useful to know how to use them to clarify program output.

A *string* is a sequence of symbols enclosed in single quotes or apostrophes. We can insert strings directly into WRITELN statements in order to provide descriptive messages in the program output. The string will be displayed exactly as it is typed (with the quotes removed).

Example 1.3:   The Statement

```
WRITELN ('GROSS = $ ', GROSS, ' NET = $ ', NET)
```

generates the output line

```
GROSS = $ 1.35000E+2 NET = $ 1.10000E+2
```

The numbers 135.0 and 110.0 are now clearly associated with GROSS and NET, respectively.

1.6.2   Writing Prompting Messages

If you ran the program in Fig. 1.9, you noticed that nothing happened until you entered two data items. The computer did not indicate that it was waiting for data, and unless you had a copy of the program next to you, there would be no way of knowing what data were needed.

To avoid this problem, it is a good idea to precede each READLN statement with a WRITELN statement that prints a *prompting message*. This message should inform the program user that the computer is waiting for data and indicate the order in which the data items should be entered.

Example 1.4:   The statement pair

```
WRITELN ('ENTER HOURS WORKED AND RATE OF PAY');
READLN (HOURS, RATE)
```

would cause the line

```
            ENTER HOURS WORKED AND RATE OF PAY
```

to be printed before the computer pauses for data entry. The data requested can then be typed in as before. The revised program is shown in Fig. 1.11 along with a sample run. The input data are underlined. The next example provides another illustration of the use of string values in WRITELN statements.

```
PROGRAM PAYROLL;

CONST
  TAX = 25.00;

VAR
  HOURS, RATE, GROSS, NET : REAL;

BEGIN
  WRITELN ('ENTER HOURS WORKED AND RATE OF PAY');
  READLN (HOURS, RATE);
  GROSS := HOURS *  RATE;
  NET := GROSS - TAX;
  WRITELN ('GROSS = $ ', GROSS, ' NET = $ ', NET)
END.

ENTER HOURS WORKED AND RATE OF PAY
30.0       4.50
GROSS = $ 1.35000E+2 NET = $ 1.10000E+2
```

Fig. 1.11 Revised payroll program and sample run.

Example 1.5: The program in Fig. 1.12 computes the estimated time and cost of an automobile trip using the formulas below:

(1) time = distance/speed
(2) gallons used = distance/miles per gallon
(3) cost of trip = gallons used × cost per gallon

There are four input data items for this program; trip distance (DIS-TANCE), average speed (SPEED), number of miles travelled on a gallon of gas (MILESPERGAL), and cost of a gallon (GALCOST). The program computes the estimated time of the trip (TIME) and the total cost of gasoline (TOTALCOST).

```
PROGRAM TRIPPLAN;

VAR
   DISTANCE, SPEED, TIME, GALCOST,
   MILESPERGAL, GALUSED, TOTALCOST :   REAL;

BEGIN
   WRITELN ('COMPUTE TRIP TIME AND COST');
   WRITE ('DISTANCE (IN MILES) = ');
   READLN (DISTANCE);
   WRITE ('SPEED (MILES PER HOUR) = ');
   READLN (SPEED);
   TIME := DISTANCE / SPEED;
   WRITELN ('TIME OF TRIP =', TIME :8:2, ' HOURS');
   WRITELN;

   WRITE ('MILEAGE (MILES PER GALLON) = ');
   READLN (MILESPERGAL);
   WRITE ('PRICE OF GAS = $');
   READLN (GALCOST);
   GALUSED := DISTANCE / MILESPERGAL;
   TOTALCOST := GALUSED * GALCOST;
   WRITELN ('ESTIMATED TRIP COST = $', TOTALCOST :8:2)
END.
```

Fig. 1.12 Use of strings to annotate output.

There are no constants needed for this program. The variable list in the variable declaration statement is written on two lines as it is too large to fit on just one line.

The computations performed by this program are quite simple. There is an assignment statement corresponding to each of the equations (1), (2) and (3) above. The remaining statements in the program body are used for data entry and display.

A sample run of the program follows.

```
COMPUTE TRIP TIME AND COST
DISTANCE (IN MILES) = 600
SPEED (MILES PER HOUR) = 55
TIME OF TRIP =   10.91 HOURS

MILEAGE (MILES PER GALLON) = 23
PRICE OF GAS = $1.75
ESTIMATED TRIP COST =   $   40.43
```

The first line above is generated by the initial **WRITELN** statement which prints a message indicating the program's purpose. The second line is generated by the statement pair

```
WRITE ('DISTANCE (IN MILES) = ');
READLN (DISTANCE);
```

Unlike the **WRITELN** statement, the current output line is not terminated by execution of a **WRITE** statement; consequently, the data item (600) may be typed on the same line as the prompt. The blank output line is generated by the **WRITELN** statement without an output list.

The two program results are printed in a much more familiar form than before. That is because each variable in an output list is followed by the symbols :8:2. These symbols specify the total width of the field in which the number is to be printed (8) and the number of digits after the decimal point (2). Since one space is always reserved for the sign and one space is used for the decimal point, the largest number that could be printed in the specified field is 9999.99. A number with fewer digits would be printed at the right of the field, preceded by blanks (*right-justified*).

Program Style

Blank lines in programs

We have left a blank line in the middle of the program in Fig. 1.12 to separate the two sections of the program body. We will continue this practice throughout the text.

Exercise 1.7:   Redo the payroll program in Fig. 1.11 so that separate **READLN** statements are used to enter each data item. The data item and its prompt should appear on the same line. Also, print the values of GROSS and NET accurate to two decimal places.

Exercise 1.8:   Give the seven **WRITELN** statements needed to print the TIC-TAC-TOE board configuration shown below.

```
        I     I
   X  I     I
  --- I --- I ---
      I  O  I  X
  --- I --- I ---
      I  O  I
      I     I
```

1.7   INTRODUCTION TO DATA TYPES

This chapter provides a brief introduction to programming in PASCAL. One of the most important features of PASCAL is that it offers the programmer a variety of *standard data types* (REAL, INTEGER, BOOLEAN, CHAR) and even allows the programmer to define new data types. The type of every variable used in a PASCAL program must be declared.

As we shall see when we study these data types in Chapter 4, the operations that can be performed on a data item are dependent on its type. If we attempt to manipulate a data item in a way that is inconsistent with its type, the compiler will inform us of our error by printing an *error diagnostic message.*

Only one data type was manipulated—type REAL. We manipulated real variables and values using the arithmetic operators (+ ,−,*,/) and the assignment operator (:=). These operators can also be used with the data type INTEGER although we have not done so as yet. Appendix 2 lists the operators.

The basic distinction between these two types is that real variables may be used to store a number containing a decimal point, whereas integer variables cannot. Hence, real variables must be used to represent quantities that are likely to have a fractional part (e.g., hourly salary, average speed). Integer variables are often used to represent a count of items since we usually use whole numbers for counting.

We also manipulated strings of characters. These strings were inserted in WRITE(LN) statements and used as prompting messages and for annotating output. In UCSD (but not standard) PASCAL, there is also a data type STRING that can be used for storage of string data. Although we cannot perform numerical operations on string data, we can manipulate strings in other ways. (This will be illustrated in Chapters 4 and 6.)

Example 1.6: The program in Fig. 1.13 illustrates the use of a string constant (COMPUTER — value 'APPLE ') and a string variable (NAME).

When the statement

```
READLN (NAME);
```

in Fig. 1.13 is executed, the computer pauses for data entry. All characters typed on the current input line (up to the carriage return) are stored in the string variable NAME. The program resumes execution when the carriage return is pressed. No apostrophes are required around a string when entered as a data item.

The statements

```
WRITE ('HELLO! I AM YOUR FRENDLY ');
WRITELN (COMPUTER, 'COMPUTER');
```

cause the message

```
HELLO! I AM YOUR FRIENDLY APPLE COMPUTER
```

to be printed. Make sure you understand the difference between the use of the constant COMPUTER (value of 'APPLE ') and the string 'COMPUTER' in the WRITELN statement above.

```
PROGRAM WELCOME;

CONST
  COMPUTER = 'APPLE ';

VAR
  NAME : STRING;

BEGIN
  WRITE ('HELLO! I AM YOUR FRIENDLY ');
  WRITELN (COMPUTER, 'COMPUTER');
  WRITE ('WHAT IS YOUR NAME? ');
  READLN (NAME);
  WRITELN ('I AM PLEASED TO MEET YOU ', NAME)
END.

HELLO! I AM YOUR FRIENDLY APPLE COMPUTER
WHAT IS YOUR NAME? HARRY
I AM PLEASED TO MEET YOU HARRY
```

Fig. 1.13 Introducing the computer.

In the next chapter, we shall see examples of expressions that evaluate to TRUE or FALSE. These values are associated with the BOOLEAN data type in PASCAL.

The last standard data type in PASCAL is type CHAR. A value of type CHAR is a string consisting of a single character, e.g. '*' or 'A'. We can assign character values to character variables or read a single character into a character variable; however, it makes no sense to perform arithmetic operations on character data and this, in fact, is illegal in PASCAL.

Example 1.7: The program in Fig. 1.14 reads three consecutive characters and prints them in reverse order enclosed in asterisks. Each character is stored in a variable of type CHAR; the character value '*' is associated with the constant identifier BORDER. The data entry HAT would be printed as *TAH*.

```
PROGRAM BACKWARDS;

CONST
  BORDER = '*';

VAR
  FIRST, SECOND, THIRD : CHAR;

BEGIN
  WRITELN ('ENTER 3 CHARACTERS');
  READLN (FIRST, SECOND, THIRD);
  WRITELN (BORDER, THIRD, SECOND, FIRST, BORDER)
END.
```

Fig. 1.14 Reading and printing characters.

Exercise 1.7:   Modify the payroll program in Fig. 1.11 so that the employee's name is also entered as a data item. If the employee's name is SALLY SMITH, the output generated should be

```
FOR SALLY SMITH
GROSS = $135.00 NET = $110.00
```

1.8 SUMMARY

You have been introduced to the basic components of the computer: the memory, the central processor unit, and the input and output units. A summary of important facts about computers that you should remember follows.

1. A memory cell is never empty, but its initial contents may be meaningless to your program.
2. The current contents of a memory cell are destroyed whenever new information is placed in that cell (via an assignment or read statement).
3. Programs must first be placed in the memory of the computer before they can be executed.
4. Data may not be manipulated by the computer without first being stored in memory.
5. The computer cannot think for itself, and must be instructed to perform a task in a precise and unambiguous manner, using a programming language.
6. Programming a computer can be fun—if you are patient, organized and careful.

You have also seen how to use the PASCAL programming language to perform some very fundamental operations. You have learned how to instruct the computer to read information into memory, perform some simple computations and print the results of the computation. All of this has been done using symbols (punctuation marks, variable names and special operators such as *, − and +) that are familiar, easy to remember and easy to use. You do not have to know very much about the computer you are using in order to understand and use PASCAL.

In Table 1.2 we have provided a summary of all of the statements introduced in this chapter. An example of the use of each statement is also given. You should use these examples as guides to ensure that you are using the correct syntax in the program statements that you write.

The small amount of PASCAL that you have seen is sufficient to enable you to solve many problems using the computer. However, many problems cannot be solved with just this limited PASCAL subset. The more you learn about PASCAL, the easier it will be for you to write programs to solve more complicated problems on the computer.

In the remainder of the text we will introduce you to more of the features of the PASCAL language and provide precise descriptions of the rules for using these features. You must remember throughout that, unlike the rules of English, the rules of PASCAL are quite precise and allow no exceptions. The compiler will be unable to translate PASCAL instructions formed in violation of these rules. Remember to declare every identifier used as a variable or constant and to separate program statements with semicolons.

Statement	Effect
Program statement PROGRAM PAYROLL	Identifies PAYROLL as the name of the program.

Constant definition
 	
  CONST
    TAX = 25.00
	Associates the constant, TAX, with the real value 25.00

Variable declaration
 	
  VAR
    X, Y, Z : REAL
	Allocates memory cells named X, Y and Z for storage of real numbers.

Assignment Statement DISTANCE := SPEED * TIME	Assigns the product of SPEED and TIME as the value of DISTANCE.
READLN statement READLN (HOURS, RATE)	Enters data into the variables HOURS and RATE.
WRITE statement WRITE ('NET = ', NET :8:2)	Displays the string 'NET = ' followed by the value of NET rounded to two decimal places. This value is printed in a field of eight columns.
WRITELN statement WRITELN (X, Y)	Terminates the output line after the values of X and Y are printed.

Table 1.2 Summary of PASCAL Statements

You should find the mastery of the rules of PASCAL relatively easy. By far the most challenging aspect of your work will be the formulation of the logic and organization of your programs. For this reason, we will introduce you to a methodology for problem solving with a computer in the next chapter and continue to emphasize this methodology throughout the remainder of the book.

PROGRAMMING PROBLEMS

1.2   Write a program to read in the weight (in pounds) of an object, and compute and print its weight in kilograms and grams. (*Hint:* one pound is equal to 0.453592 kilograms or 453.59237 grams.)

1.3   A cyclist coasting on a level road slows from a speed of 10 miles/hr. to 2.5 miles/hr. in one minute. Write a computer program that calculates the cyclist's constant rate of acceleration and determines how long it will take the cyclist to come to rest, given an initial speed of 10 miles/hr. (*Hint:* Use the equation

$$a = \frac{v_f - v_i}{t}$$

where a is acceleration, t is time, v_i is initial velocity, and v_f is the final velocity.)

1.4   Write a program to read three data items into variables X, Y, and Z, and find and print their product and sum.

1.5   Eight track stars entered the mile race at the Penn Relays. Write a program that will read in the race time in minutes (MINUTES) and seconds (SECONDS) for each of these runners, and compute and print the speed in feet per second (FPS) and in meters per second (MPS). (*Hints:* There are 5,280 feet in one mile and one kilometer equals 3,282 feet.) Test your program on one of the times (minutes and seconds) given below.

3.0 minutes 52.83 seconds	3.0 minutes 56.22 seconds	3.0 minutes 59.83 seconds
4.0 minutes 00.03 seconds	4.0 minutes 16.22 seconds	4.0 minutes 19.00 seconds
4.0 minutes 19.89 seconds	4.0 minutes 21.21 seconds	

1.6   You are planning to rent a car to drive from Boston to Philadelphia. Cost is no consideration, but you want to be certain that you can make the trip on one tankful of gas. Write a program to read in the miles-per-gallon (MPG) and tank size (TANKSIZE) in gallons for a particular rent-a-car, and print out the distance that can be travelled on one tank. Test your program for the following data:

miles-per-gallon	tank size (*gallons*)
10.0	15.0
40.5	20.0
22.5	12.0
10.0	9.0

1.7   Write a program that prints your initials in large block letters. (*Hint:* Use a 6×6 grid for each letter and print six messages. Each message should consist of a row of *'s interspersed with blanks.)

1.8   Write a program that reads and prints your name.

PROBLEM SOLVING WITH THE COMPUTER

2

2.1 INTRODUCTION

In this chapter, we shall develop a methodology for solving problems. The data table will be introduced as a means of identifying and describing the use of each variable needed in the problem solution. The general outline, or algorithm, for solving a problem will consist of a list of subtasks. We shall add detail to the algorithm through a process called stepwise refinement.

The Boolean condition has a value of true or false. Conditions will be used to formulate decision steps in algorithms. A decision step enables the algorithm to choose between two alternative execution paths. In addition, we shall learn how to specify the repetition of a group of operations through the use of a loop. Finally, we shall illustrate how to trace through an algorithm to verify that it is correct and how to implement simple decision steps and loops in PASCAL.

2.2 PROBLEM ANALYSIS

2.2.1 Problem Subtasks

Now that you have been introduced to the computer—what it is, how it works and what it can do—it is time to turn our attention to learning how to use the computer to solve problems.

Using the computer for problem solving is similar to trying to put a man on the moon in the late 1950's and 1960's. In both instances, there is a problem to be solved and a final "program" for solving it.

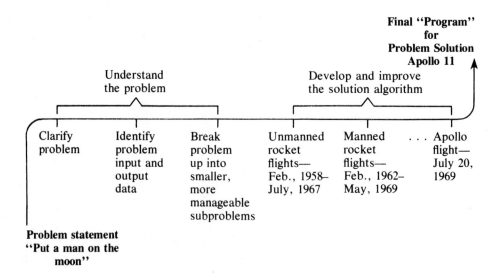

In the moon effort, the final goal was not achieved directly. Rather, it was brought about through the careful planning and organization of subtasks, each of which had to be completed successfully before the Apollo 11 flight could even be attempted.

Programming also requires careful planning and organization. It is rare, indeed, to see an error-free computer program written directly from the original statement of a problem. Usually, the final program is achieved only after a number of steps have been followed. These steps are the subject of this chapter.

2.2.2 Representation and Manipulation of Data

We stated earlier that the computer is a tool that can be used to represent and to manipulate data. It is, therefore, not too surprising that the first two tasks in solving a problem on the computer require the definition of the data to be represented in the computer memory, and the formulation of an *algorithm*—a list of steps that describe the desired manipulation of these data.

These two tasks are not entirely unrelated. Decisions that we make in defining the data may be changed when we formulate the algorithm. Nevertheless, we should perform the data definition as completely and carefully as possible before constructing the algorithm. Careless errors, or errors in judgment in deciding what information is to be represented, and what form this information is to take, can result in numerous difficulties later. Such mistakes can make the algorithm formulation extremely difficult, and sometimes even impossible.

Once the definition of the information to be represented in the computer has been made, and a precise statement of the problem is available, the algorithm for solving the problem can be formulated.

2.2.3 Understanding the Problem

The definition of the data to be represented in the computer memory requires a clear understanding of the stated problem. First, we must determine what information is to be computed and printed by the computer. Then it is necessary to identify the information that is to be given as input to the computer. Once the input and output data have been identified, we must ask if sufficient information is available to compute the required output from the given input. If the answer to this question is no, we must determine what additional information is needed and how this information can be provided to the program.

When identifying the data items associated with the problem, it is helpful to assign to each item a descriptive variable name that can be used to represent the computer memory cell containing the data item. Recall from Chapter 1 that we do not have to be concerned with the actual memory cell associated with each variable name. The compiler will assign a unique memory cell to each variable name and it will handle all bookkeeping details necessary to retain this correspondence.

To see how this process works, we will apply it to a specific problem.

Problem 2.1: Write a program to compute and print the sum and average of two numbers.

Discussion: The first step is to make certain that we understand the problem and to identify the input and output data for the problem. Then we can obtain a more precise formulation of the problem in terms of these input and output items.

All items of information to be used to solve a given problem should be listed in a *data table,* along with a description of the variable used to represent each data item. The data table for Problem 2.1 is given next. The entries shown describe the input and output data for the problem.

Data Table for Problem 2.1

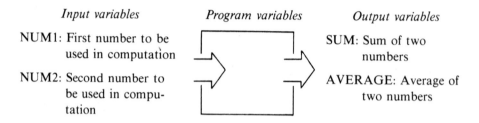

Input variables	*Program variables*	*Output variables*
NUM1: First number to be used in computation		SUM: Sum of two numbers
NUM2: Second number to be used in computation		AVERAGE: Average of two numbers

There are clearly two items of information required as output for this problem. They are the sum and the average of two numbers. In order to compute these values, we must first enter and store the data items to be summed and averaged in the memory of the computer. In this example, we will use the variables NUM1 and NUM2 to represent these two input data items.

The table form just illustrated will be used for all data tables in the text. Variables whose values are entered through read statements are listed as input variables; variables whose values represent final computational results required by the problem statement are listed as output variables. Other variables which may be used to store intermediate computational results are listed as program variables. Often, program variables are added to the data table as the algorithm develops. There are no program variables as yet in the data table for Problem 2.1. In all cases, it is important to include in the data table a short, concise description of how each variable is to be used in the program.

The data table is valuable not only during algorithm development but also as a piece of *program documentation.* It is a convenient reference document for associating variable names and their uses in the program. You should always prepare a data table, pay close attention to it during the algorithm development process, and save it along with your program listing. The data table may subsequently turn out to be your only reminder of how the variables in your program are being used.

A more precise formulation of Problem 2.1 is now possible: we must read two data items into the variables NUM1 and NUM2, find the sum and the average of these two items, and print the values of the sum and the average.

2.3 DESCRIPTION OF THE PROBLEM SOLUTION

2.3.1 Developing an Algorithm

At this point we should have a clear understanding of what is required for the solution of Problem 2.1. We can now proceed to organize the problem formulation into a carefully constructed list of steps—the algorithm—that will describe the sequence of manipulations to be performed in carrying out the problem solution.

Algorithm for Problem 2.1 (Level One)

Step 1   Read the data items into the variables NUM1 and NUM2 and print the data.

Step 2   Compute the sum of the data items in NUM1 and NUM2 and store the result in the variable SUM.

Step 3   Compute the average of the data items in NUM1 and NUM2 and store the result in the variable AVERAGE.

Step 4   Print the values of the variables SUM and AVERAGE.

2.3.2 Algorithm Refinement

Note that this sequence of events closely mirrors the problem formulation given earlier. This is as it should be! If the problem formulation is complete, it should provide us with a general outline of what must be done to solve the problem. The purpose of the algorithm formulation is to provide a detailed and precise description of the individual steps to be carried out by the computer in solving the problem. The algorithm is essentially a *refinement* of the general outline provided by the original problem formulation. It is often the case that several *levels of refinement* of the general outline are required before the algorithm is complete.

The key question in deciding whether or not further refinement of an algorithm step is required is this:

Is it clear precisely what PASCAL instructions are necessary in order to tell the computer how to carry out the step?

If it is not immediately obvious what the PASCAL instructions are, then the algorithm step should be further refined.

What is obvious to some programmers may not be at all clear to others. The refinement of an algorithm is, therefore, a personal matter to some extent. As you gain experience in developing algorithms and converting them to PASCAL programs, you may discover that you are doing less and less algorithm refinement. This may also happen as you become more familiar with the **PASCAL** language.

If we examine the level one algorithm for Problem 2.1, we see that only Step 3 may require further refinement. We already know how to write **PASCAL** instructions for reading, printing and adding two numbers. However, we may not know how to tell the computer to find the average of two numbers.

Refinement of Step 3

Step 3.1   Divide the sum (stored in SUM) by the number of items (2) used to compute the sum.

We now have an algorithm that is refined to a level of detail that is sufficient for us to write the **PASCAL** representation of the steps required to solve Problem 2.1 (see Fig. 2.1). We do this by implementing the algorithm on a step-by-step basis, using the variable names provided in the data table.

In writing the program, we have first incorporated the information in the data table in the declaration part. The program body consists of the **PASCAL** implementation of each of the algorithm steps in sequence. If an algorithm step is refined, then the refinement is implemented.

```
PROGRAM ADDTWO;
(* COMPUTES THE SUM AND AVERAGE OF TWO NUMBERS *)

VAR
  NUM1, NUM2, SUM, AVERAGE : REAL;

BEGIN
  (* READ NUM1 AND NUM2 *)
  WRITE ('FIRST NUMBER = ');
  READLN (NUM1);
  WRITE ('SECOND NUMBER = ');
  READLN (NUM2);

  (* COMPUTE THE SUM OF NUM1 AND NUM2 *)
  SUM := NUM1 + NUM2;

  (* COMPUTE THE AVERAGE OF NUM1 AND NUM2 *)
  AVERAGE := SUM / 2;

  (* PRINT SUM AND AVERAGE *)
  WRITELN ('SUM = ', SUM :9:2, ' AVERAGE = ', AVERAGE :9:2)
END.

FIRST NUMBER = 35.45
SECOND NUMBER = 65.45
SUM =    100.90   AVERAGE =      50.45
```

Fig. 2.1 PASCAL program for Problem 2.1.

Program Style

Use of comments

The statements in Fig. 2.1 enclosed by the symbols (* and *) are descriptive comments. They are ignored by the compiler during translation and are listed with the program statements to aid the programmer in identifying or documenting the purpose of each step of the program body. (We have left a blank line between steps.)

Each comment describes the purpose of the program statements that follow it. There should be enough comments to clarify the intent of each step of your program; however, too many comments can clutter the program and make it difficult to read. A good rule of thumb is to use a comment to identify the PASCAL implementation of each step in the level one algorithm as well as any other steps requiring further refinement. In this way, the correspondence between the algorithm and its PASCAL implementation becomes obvious.

Comments should be carefully worded. One suggestion is to use an abbreviated form of the corresponding algorithm step description. For example, the comment

```
(* COMPUTE THE AVERAGE OF NUM1 AND NUM2 *)
```

precedes the implementation of algorithm step 3 (see section 2.3.1). This comment conveys more information and hence is better than the comment

```
(* DIVIDE SUM BY 2 AND ASSIGN RESULT TO AVERAGE *)
```

which is simply an English version of the PASCAL statement

```
AVERAGE := SUM / 2;
```

that follows the comment.

Comments (along with the data table) can also aid in identifying the use of the important variables in each program segment. At least one comment should appear at the beginning of a program to summarize the program purpose.

Note: On some systems, comments are bracketed by the symbols {and}.

Exercise 2.1: Write a data table and an algorithm to compute the sum and average of four numbers.

2.3.3 Problem Solving Principles

Up to now we have presented a few suggestions for solving problems on the computer. These suggestions are summarized below.

1. Understand what you are being asked to do.
2. Identify all problem input and output data. Assign a variable name to each input or output item and list it in the data table.

3. Formulate a precise statement of the problem in terms of the input and output data and make certain there are sufficient input items provided to complete the solution.
4. State clearly the sequence of steps necessary to produce the desired problem output through manipulation of the input data; i.e., develop the level one algorithm.
5. Refine this algorithm until it can be easily implemented in the programming language to be used. List any additional variables required as program variables in the data table.
6. Transform the algorithm to a program.

Steps 4 and 5 are really the most difficult of the steps listed; they are the only truly creative part of this process. People differ in their ability to formulate solutions to problems. Some find it easy to develop algorithms for the most complex problem, while others must work diligently to produce an algorithm for solving a simple problem.

The ability to solve problems is fundamental to computer programming. The transformation of the refined algorithm to a working program (Step 6) is a highly skilled clerical task that requires a thorough knowledge of the programming language available. This detailed knowledge can normally be acquired by anyone willing to devote the necessary effort. However, a refined algorithm that correctly represents the necessary problem-solving operations and their relationship must first be developed.

This book will provide many detailed solutions to sample problems. Examining these solutions carefully should enable you to become more adept at formulating your own solutions, because the techniques used for one problem may frequently be applied in a slightly different way to solve another. Often, new problems are simply expansions or modifications of old ones.

The process of outlining and refining problem solutions can be used to break a complex problem up into more manageable subtasks (algorithm steps) that can be solved individually. This technique will be illustrated in all of the problems solved in the text. We suggest you practice it in developing your own solutions to programming problems.

2.4 ALGORITHMS INVOLVING DECISIONS

2.4.1 Decision Steps and Conditions

Normally, the steps of an algorithm are performed in the order in which they are listed. In many algorithms, however, the sequence of steps to be performed is determined by the input data. In such cases, decisions must be made, based upon the values of certain variables, as to which sequence of steps is to be performed. Such decisions require the evaluation of a condition that is expressed in terms of the relevant variables. The result of the evaluation determines which algorithm steps will be executed next.

The algorithm step that describes the condition is called a *decision step.* Each decision step involves the evaluation of a *Boolean expression*—that is, an expression that may have a value of either true or false.

In this chapter and the next, we shall use one form of Boolean expression or condition. A condition normally describes a particular relationship between a pair of variables or a variable and a constant. Examples of conditions are shown in Table 2.1.

Condition	PASCAL form
GROSS greater than MIN	GROSS $>$ MIN
X equal to Y	X = Y
X not equal to 0	X $<>$ 0
COUNT less than or equal to 10	COUNT $<=$ 10

Table 2.1 Examples of Conditions

For the time being, each condition will follow the pattern

$$operand_1 \;\; relational\text{-}operator \;\; operand_2$$

where *operand$_1$* is normally a variable and *operand$_2$* is a variable or constant. The *relational-operators* in PASCAL are described in Table 2.2. The value of a condition is true if the specified relationship holds for the current variable values; otherwise, the condition value is false. We will provide further details on the use of Boolean expressions in Chapter 4.

Relational-operator	Meaning
=	equal to
$<>$	not equal to
$<$	less than
$>$	greater than
$<=$	less than or equal to
$>=$	greater than or equal to

Table 2.2 PASCAL Relational-Operators

We will illustrate the decision step by studying a modified form of the payroll problem discussed in Chapter 1.

Problem 2.2: Compute the gross salary and net pay for an employee of a company, given the number of hours worked and the employee's hourly wage rate. Deduct a tax amount of $25 if the employee's gross salary exceeds $100.

The data table and algorithm for this problem are shown below. We have included two program constants in the data table.

Data Table for Problem 2.2

Constants

TAX = $25, tax amount
MINIMUM = $100, minimum salary for a tax deduction

| Input variables | Program variables | Output variables |

HOURS: Number of
    hours worked

RATE: Hourly wage
    rate

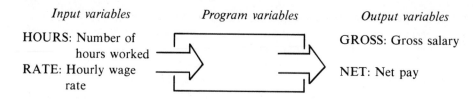

GROSS: Gross salary

NET: Net pay

Level One Algorithm for Problem 2.2

1. Read HOURS and RATE
2. Compute GROSS
3. Compute NET
4. Print GROSS and NET

The refinement of Step 3 should show that there are two alternative courses of action: either deduct TAX or do not deduct TAX. This is done below using a decision step.

Level Two Refinements

Step 3   *Compute NET*

    3.1 IF GROSS is greater than MINIMUM THEN
           3.2 NET := GROSS − TAX
       ELSE
           3.3 NET := GROSS

In numbering algorithm steps and their refinements, we will use a scheme that is analogous to the numbering of sections in this text. For example, refinements of Step 3 are numbered 3.1, 3.2, etc. If Step 3.2 were to be refined further, its refinements would be numbered 3.2.1, 3.2.2, etc. All steps in a level one algorithm will be numbered. Normally, only those refinement steps that require additional refinement or are referred to in the text narrative will be numbered.

The decision Step (3.1) describes the condition ("GROSS is greater than MINIMUM") that is evaluated in order to decide which algorithm step should be executed next. If the condition is true, Step 3.2 is performed next. Otherwise, step 3.3 is performed next. In either case, Step 4 will be carried out following the completion of the chosen step.

The decision step just discussed (3.1) involves a choice between two alternatives—a sequence of one or more steps to be executed if the condition is true (the True Statement) and a sequence to be executed if the condition is false (the False Statement). Such a decision step is called a *double alternative decision step.* The general form of the double alternative decision follows.

IF *condition* THEN
    True Statement
ELSE
    False Statement

Quite often, a double alternative decision step is represented using the *flow diagram* shown below.

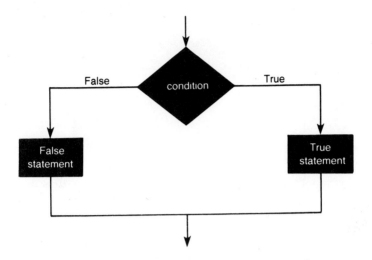

This diagram illustrates that either the *True Statement* or *False Statement* is executed, but not both. The particular statement executed is determined by the value of the *condition,* true or false.

The flow diagram for the refinement of Step 3 above is shown next.

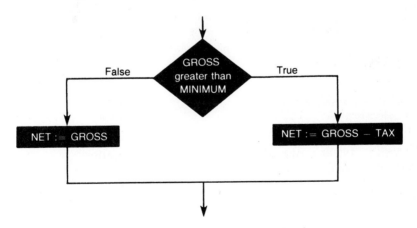

Sometimes a decision step in an algorithm will involve only one alternative: a sequence of one or more steps that will be carried out if the given condition is true, but skipped if the condition is false. The general form of this *single alternative decision* is shown below.

IF *condition* THEN
True Statement

The flow diagram below

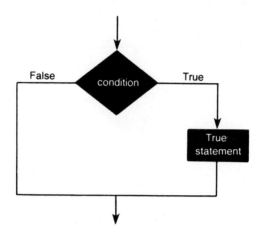

indicates that the *True Statement* is executed only when the *condition* evaluates to true; nothing is done when the *condition* evaluates to false.

2.4.2   More Algorithms with Decisions

Additional examples of algorithms with decision steps are provided next.

Problem 2.3:   Read an employee's salary and compute the social security tax due. The social security tax is 6.1 percent of an employee's gross salary. Only the first $19,000 earned is taxable. (This means that all employees earning $19,000 or more pay the same tax.)

Data Table for Problem 2.3

Constants

MAXSAL = 19000.00, the maximum salary for social security
TAXRATE = 0.061, the tax percentage as a fraction

Input variables	*Program variables*	*Output variables*
SALARY: Employee's salary		SOCIALTAX: Social Security tax

Level One Algorithm for Problem 2.3

1. Read SALARY
2. Compute SOCIALTAX
3. Print SOCIALTAX

In order to refine Step 2, a new variable, TAXSAL, is introduced to represent the portion of SALARY on which the Social Security tax will be computed. The additional data table entry and refinement of Step 2 follow.

Program variables

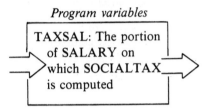

TAXSAL: The portion of SALARY on which SOCIALTAX is computed

Level Two Refinements

Step 2   *Compute SOCIALTAX*

    2.1   Compute TAXSAL
    2.2   Compute SOCIALTAX due on TAXSAL

TAXSAL should be defined as the smaller of MAXSAL and SALARY as shown in the refinement of Step 2.1 next.

Level Three Refinements

Step 2.1

    2.1.1   IF SALARY is less than MAXSAL THEN
            TAXSAL := SALARY
        ELSE
            TAXSAL := MAXSAL

Step 2.2

    2.2.1   SOCIALTAX := TAXRATE * TAXSAL

The next example uses both the single and double alternative decision steps.

Problem 2.4:   Read three numbers and find and print the largest number.

Data Table for Problem 2.4

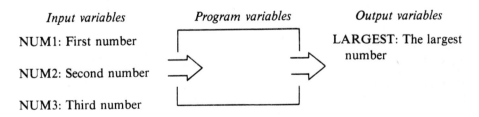

Input variables	*Program variables*	*Output variables*
NUM1: First number		LARGEST: The largest number
NUM2: Second number		
NUM3: Third number		

Level One Algorithm for Problem 2.4

1. Read NUM1, NUM2 and NUM3.
2. Store the larger of NUM1 and NUM2 in LARGEST.
3. Store the larger of NUM3 and the largest so far in LARGEST.
4. Print LARGEST.

Since only a pair of numbers can be compared at one time, the algorithm above uses two steps (Steps 2 and 3) to find LARGEST. Step 2 finds the larger of NUM1 and NUM2; Step 3 compares this value to NUM3.

Level Two Refinements

Step 2   *Store the larger of NUM1 and NUM2 in LARGEST*

    2.1   IF NUM1 is greater than NUM2 THEN
           LARGEST := NUM1
      ELSE
           LARGEST := NUM2

Step 3   *Store the larger of NUM3 and LARGEST in LARGEST*

    3.1   IF NUM3 is greater than LARGEST THEN
           LARGEST := NUM3

As shown above, the refinement of Step 2 is a double alternative decision, whereas the refinement of Step 3 is a single alternative decision. In Step 3, nothing is done if LARGEST already contains the largest of the three numbers.

Exercise 2.2:   Write decision steps to represent the following:

  a)   If a data item (ITEM) is not equal to 0, then multiply the product (PRODUCT) by ITEM. Otherwise, skip this step. In either case, then print the value of PRODUCT.

  b)   If ITEM exceeds LARGEST, store the value of ITEM in LARGEST. Otherwise, skip this step. In either case, then print the value of LARGEST.

  c) If X is larger than 0, add X to the positive sum (PLUSSUM). Otherwise, if X is smaller than 0, add X to the negative sum (MINUSSUM). Otherwise, if X is equal to 0, add one to the count of zeros (ZEROCOUNT).

Exercise 2.3:   What values would be printed by the algorithm for Problem 2.2 if HOURS is 37.5 and RATE is 3.75? If HOURS is 20 and RATE is 4? "Execute" the algorithm yourself to determine the results.

Exercise 2.4:   What happens in the algorithm for Problem 2.4 if NUM1 is equal to NUM2 or NUM3 is equal to LARGEST? Does the algorithm work for these cases?

Exercise 2.5:   Modify the algorithm for Problem 2.4 to find the smallest of four numbers.

Exercise 2.6:   Devise a new algorithm for Problem 2.4 using three double-alternative decision steps.

Exercise 2.7:   Write an algorithm that computes the absolute difference between two numbers. If X is greater than Y, the absolute difference is X-Y; if Y is greater than X, the absolute difference is Y-X.

2.4.3   Implementing Decision Structures in PASCAL

We can implement the algorithms in the previous section quite easily in PASCAL through the use of the IF statement. The IF statement will be discussed more formally in Chapter 3, but for the time being we will use the form

> IF *condition* THEN
> *True Statement*
> ELSE
> *False Statement*

to implement a double-alternative decision, and the form

> IF *condition* THEN
> *True Statement*

to implement a single-alternative decision. These forms are identical to the decision step patterns described earlier. For the time being, we will restrict ourselves to single statements only for the True Statement and False Statement.

The PASCAL implementation of the modified payroll program is shown in Fig. 2.2; the largest of three numbers problem is shown in Fig. 2.3. You should compare each PASCAL program with its corresponding algorithm.

```
PROGRAM PAYROLL2;
(* MODIFIED PAYROLL PROGRAM - TAX ON MINIMUM GROSS *)

CONST
   TAX = 25.00;
   MINIMUM = 100.00;

VAR
   HOURS, RATE, GROSS, NET : REAL;

BEGIN
   (* READ HOURS AND RATE *)
   WRITE ('HOURS WORKED = ');
   READLN (HOURS);
   WRITE ('HOURLY RATE = $');
   READLN (RATE);

   (* COMPUTE GROSS SALARY *)
   GROSS := HOURS * RATE;
```

(continued)

```
(* COMPUTE NET SALARY *)
IF GROSS >= MINIMUM THEN
   NET := GROSS - TAX
ELSE
   NET := GROSS;

(* PRINT RESULTS *)
   WRITELN ('GROSS = $', GROSS :8:2, '    NET = $', NET :8:2)
END

HOURS WORKED = 300
HOURLY RATE = $4.50
GROSS = $    135.00   NET = $    110.00
```

Fig. 2.2 Modified payroll program.

Program Style

Indenting True and False Statements

We have indented the True Statement and False Statement in all of the IF statements shown. This is not required; however, it is a good practice to follow as it clarifies the meaning of the IF statement and improves the readability of the program.

Program Style

Use of Constants

Notice that two constants (TAX, MINIMUM) have been defined in the constant declaration part of the modified payroll program. We could just as easily have inserted the constant values directly in the decision step and written

```
IF GROSS > 100.00 THEN
   NET := GROSS - 25.00
ELSE
   NET := GROSS;
```

There are two advantages to using constants. First, the decision step shown in Fig. 2.2 conveys what is happening more clearly than the one shown above. Instead of using two numbers, 100.00 and 25.00, which have no intrinsic meaning, it uses words like MINIMUM and TAX, which are quite descriptive. Second, if we wish to modify the value of the constants in Fig. 2.2, we need only modify the constant definition part of our program. If the values were inserted directly in the decision step, then we would have to redo the decision step and also change any other statements that manipulated these constant values as well. This can become a tedious task in a large program with multiple references to a constant value.

```
PROGRAM LARGESTTHREE;
(* FINDS THE LARGEST OF THREE NUMBERS *)

VAR
  NUM1, NUM2, NUM3, LARGEST : REAL;

BEGIN
  (* READ THREE NUMBERS *)
  WRITELN ('ENTER 3 NUMBERS - SEPARATED BY SPACES');
  READLN (NUM1, NUM2, NUM3);

  (* FIND THE LARGER OF NUM1 AND NUM2 *)
  IF NUM1 > NUM2 THEN
    LARGEST := NUM1
  ELSE
    LARGEST := NUM2;

  (* FIND THE LARGER OF NUM3 AND LARGEST SO FAR *);
  IF NUM3 > LARGEST THEN
    LARGEST := NUM3;
    '
  (* PRINT LARGEST *)
  WRITELN ('THE LARGEST NUMBER IS ', LARGEST :8:2)
END.
```

```
ENTER 3 NUMBERS - SEPARATED BY SPACES
17.5  87.2  -20.1
THE LARGEST NUMBER IS      87.2
```

Fig. 2.3   Largest of three numbers.

Exercise 2.8:   Provide the PASCAL form of the algorithm for Problem 2.3 and use it on your computer.

2.5   ALGORITHMS WITH LOOPS

In Section 2.3.1, we developed an algorithm for finding the sum and average of two numbers. Suppose, however, that we are asked to solve a slightly different problem.

Problem 2.5:   Write a program to compute and print the sum of all odd numbers between 1 and 99 inclusive.

Discussion: If we expand the solution to the original problem, we might come up with the algorithm below.

Level One Algorithm for Problem 2.5

1. Form the sum of the first and second odd numbers.
2. Add the third odd number to the sum.

3. Add the fourth odd number to the sum.
4. Add the fifth odd number to the sum.

.

.

.

Obviously, this algorithm is impractical and a new approach is needed. The essence of the problem is to find a way to form the sum without using separate instructions for the addition of each of the odd numbers. It would be ideal if we could write one step for adding an odd number to the sum accumulated so far, and then repeat this step for all of the odd numbers. This is possible only if we are able to reference each of the odd numbers using the same variable name.

The solution to the naming problem rests upon the following realization:

Once an odd number has been stored in the computer memory and added to the sum, it is no longer needed.

Thus, each odd number can be stored in the same variable, ODDS. After the value of ODDS is added to the sum, the next odd number can then be stored in ODDS. This, of course, destroys the previous odd number, but it is no longer needed for the computation.

To see how this works, consider what happens if we try to carry out an algorithm consisting solely of the repetition of the steps

1. Add the value of ODDS to the accumulated sum (SUM) and store the result in SUM.
2. Store the next odd number in the variable named ODDS.

To begin, the memory cells ODDS and SUM should appear as shown below

where ODDS contains the first odd number and the accumulated sum is zero. After steps (1) and (2) are performed the first time, the variables ODDS and SUM should be defined as follows:

Note that the odd number 1 has now been incorporated into the sum that we are computing, and is no longer required for this problem. After the second execution of (1) and (2), we have:

and upon completion of the third execution of (1) and (2), we obtain:

This process continues for all odd numbers. During each execution of steps (1) and (2), the current odd number is processed and is then replaced in ODDS by the next odd number. The next odd number is obtained by adding 2 to the previous one. With this solution in mind, the data table for Problem 2.5 is written below.

Data Table for Problem 2.5

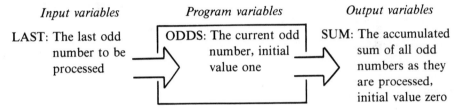

Input variables	*Program variables*	*Output variables*
LAST: The last odd number to be processed	ODDS: The current odd number, initial value one	SUM: The accumulated sum of all odd numbers as they are processed, initial value zero

The last odd number (99 in this case) is a data value that will be read into the input variable LAST. By specifying this one data value, we can use the algorithm to compute the sum of as many odd numbers as we want.

The variable ODDS is listed as a program variable. This is because we are neither reading in each odd number nor providing a list of odd numbers as program output.

A new level one version of the algorithm is shown below. This algorithm contains three phases: the *initialization phase* (Steps 1 and 2), the *data manipulation phase* (Step 3), and the *output phase* (Step 4).

Revised Level One Algorithm for Problem

1. Read in the last odd number (LAST).
2. Initialize SUM to zero and ODDS to one.
3. Compute the sum (SUM) of all odd numbers through LAST.
4. Print SUM.

From this algorithm, it is clear what is required in the initialization and output phases of the algorithm. However, part of the data manipulation phase (Step 3) requires further refinement before the program can be written.

In order to refine algorithm Step 3, we need to have a way to indicate that a sequence of steps should be repeated. Such a sequence is called a *loop*.

Level Two Refinements

Step 3   *Compute the sum of all odd numbers through LAST.*

3.1   Repeat the following sequence of steps:

    3.2   Add the value of ODDS to the accumulated sum (SUM) and store the result in SUM

    3.3   Store the next odd number in the variable named ODDS

How do we know when the loop is done? More importantly, how can we tell the computer when it has completed the execution of the loop? A person might do it 10 or 100 times and then ask, "Am I done yet?" However, we are developing an algorithm that will eventually take the form of a sequence of steps to be performed by a computer—and the computer cannot think!! Therefore, if we want to tell it to repeat a sequence of steps, it is not enough to tell it what those steps are. We must also tell the computer when to stop performing these steps and *exit* from the loop. This information is provided by the *loop control step.*

The general form of the loop control step is

WHILE *condition* DO

For this problem, the loop control step should specify that the loop should be repeated while the current odd number (ODDS) is less than or equal to the last odd number (LAST). The revised refinement of Step 3 follows. The words BEGIN and END bracket the *loop body,* the steps to be repeated.

Revised Level Two Refinements

Step 3   *Compute the sum of all odd numbers through LAST*

    3.1 WHILE ODDS is less than or equal to LAST DO
        BEGIN
                3.2 Add the value of ODDS to the accumulated sum (SUM) and store the result in SUM
                3.3 Store the next odd number in the variable named ODDS
        END

Level Three Refinements

Step 3.2

    3.2.1 SUM := SUM + ODDS

Step 3.3

    3.3.1 ODDS := ODDS + 2

The variable ODDS is often called a *loop control variable* since its value is used to control loop repetition. Normally, the three operations listed below must be performed on the loop control variable. The algorithm step corresponding to each operation is shown in parentheses.

    1. Initialize the loop control variable (Step 2)
    2. Test the loop control variable (Step 3.1)
    3. Update the loop control variable (Step 3.3)

Operation 1 must be performed before the loop is entered. Operation 2, the loop control step, must be performed before each execution of the loop body: depending on the result of this test, the loop will either be repeated—or exited. Operation 3 must be included as part of the loop body. Unless the loop control variable is updated in the loop body, its value cannot change and loop exit will never occur.

The loop pattern described in the refinement of Step 3 is called a *WHILE loop*. The flow diagram below is often used to represent a WHILE loop.

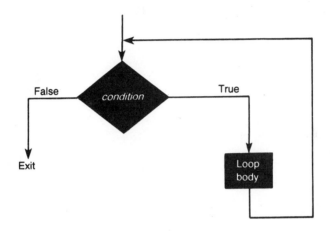

The flow diagram indicates that a *condition* is first evaluated (the loop control step). If the *condition* is true, the *loop body* is executed and the *condition* is reevaluated. Hence, the *loop body* is executed repeatedly until the *condition* evaluates to false, at which point the loop is exited and control is passed to the next algorithm step.

The flow diagram corresponding to Step 3 of our algorithm follows.

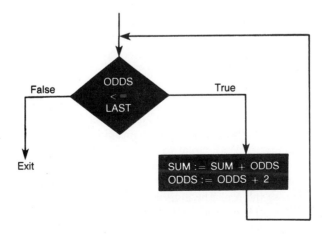

Exercise 2.9:   Modify the algorithm for Problem 2.5 to compute the sum of all even numbers less than or equal to 100.

Exercise 2.10:   Suppose you also wished to compute the average value of the numbers added together in Problem 2.5. Indicate what changes would be required to the algorithm.

Exercise 2.11:   Very often, more than one algorithm can be used to solve a problem. Develop a different algorithm that is based on the observation that the first and last odd numbers sum to the same value as the second and next-to-last odd numbers.

2.6   IMPLEMENTING THE ALGORITHM

2.6.1   Tracing an Algorithm

Once the algorithm and data table for a problem are complete, it is important to verify that the algorithm specifies the sequence of steps required to produce the desired results before writing the program. The algorithm verification can be carried out by manually *tracing* the sequence of steps indicated by the algorithm. Such traces can often lead to the discovery of a number of *logical errors* in the algorithm. The correction of these errors prior to writing the PASCAL instructions can save considerable effort during the final testing of the PASCAL program.

Algorithm traces must be done diligently, however, or they are of little use. The algorithm refinements must be traced carefully, on a step-by-step basis. Changes in variable values must be noted at each step and compared to the expected results. This should be done for at least one carefully chosen set of test data for which the final and intermediate results can easily be determined.

If the algorithm contains decision steps, then extra sets of test data should be provided to ensure that all "paths" through the algorithm are traced. For example, the algorithm that computes the largest of three numbers (Problem 2.4, Section 2.4.2) contains two decision steps. To trace all paths of this algorithm, at least four sets of test data are necessary. The data values N1, N2 and N3 should be chosen to satisfy the relations: N1 > N2 and N3 > N1 (both conditions TRUE); N1 > N2 and N3 <= N1 (first condition TRUE, second condition FALSE); N1 <= N2 and N3 > N2 (first condition FALSE, second condition TRUE); N1 <= N2 and N3 <= N2 (both conditions FALSE). An example of a test set which satisfies the first case described above would be N1 = 7.5, N2 = 5.0, N3 = 10.0 (7.5 > 5.0, 10.0 > 7.5).

We will now provide an illustration of a trace of the algorithm for Problem 2.5. It is clear that we cannot trace the algorithm for all odd numbers less than or equal to 99. However, we can perform a meaningful, informative test for the first three odd numbers (LAST equal to 5). If the algorithm works properly for this limited case, it should work for the original case as well.

The trace table is shown in Table 2.3. The variable names found in the data table are listed across the top. The algorithm step numbers are from Section 2.5. Each step is listed in the sequence in which it is executed. Steps 3.1, 3.2.1 and 3.3.1 (the loop) are listed more than once. If the algorithm step changes a variable value, the new value of this variable is shown to the right of the step; otherwise, the "effect" of the step is described (Step 3.1). The values of all variables after the execution of Step 1 are shown in the first line. (ODDS and SUM are still undefined.)

Algorithm Step	ODDS	SUM	LAST	Effect
1	?	?	5	
2	1	0		
3.1				1 < = 5 is true — execute loop
3.2.1		1		
3.3.1	3			
3.1				3 < = 5 is true — execute loop
3.2.1		4		
3.3.1	5			
3.1				5 < = 5 is true — execute loop
3.2.1		9		
3.3.1	7			
3.1				7 < = 5 is false — exit loop
4				print the value 9

Table 2.3 Trace of Algorithm

As shown in the trace table, the last execution of Step 3.3.1 assigns a value of 7 to ODDS. Since this number is greater than LAST (5 for this test case), the loop will be exited and the value of SUM (9) is printed by Step 4.

2.6.2 Implementing the Loop

The loop described in Section 2.5 can be implemented in a straight-forward manner in PASCAL using the WHILE statement

WHILE *condition* DO
loop body

where the condition corresponds to the loop control variable test (Step 3.1 of the algorithm). The loop body is the PASCAL statement or statements to be repeated. If the loop body contains more than one PASCAL statement, these statements should be preceded by the keyword BEGIN and followed by the keyword END. The ";" should be used to separate statements in the loop body. The implementation of the algorithm is shown in Fig. 2.4.

The data type INTEGER is used as the odd numbers are whole numbers. The operators + and := can, of course, be used with integer operands.

```
PROGRAM SUMODD;
(* COMPUTES THE SUM OF ODD NUMBERS THROUGH LAST *)

VAR
   ODDS, LAST, SUM : INTEGER;

BEGIN
   (* READ LAST ODD NUMBER *)
   WRITE ('LAST = ');
   READLN (LAST);
```

(continued)

```
(* INITIALIZE SUM AND ODDS *)
SUM := 0;
ODDS := 1;

(* COMPUTE SUM OF ODD NUMBERS THROUGH LAST *)
WHILE ODDS <= LAST DO
  BEGIN
     SUM := SUM + ODDS;
     ODDS := ODDS + 2
  END; (* WHILE *)

(* PRINT SUM *)
WRITELN ('SUM = ', SUM)
END.
```

Fig. 2.4 Program for sum of odds.

Program Style

Indenting the Loop Body

In Fig. 2.4, the loop body has been indented to clarify the structure of the program. The program lines starting with WHILE and continuing through the first END are all considered part of the WHILE statement. The comment (* WHILE *) is inserted after END to emphasize this fact. The semicolon preceding this comment separates the WHILE statement from the next program statement. Note that semicolons are not used after BEGIN and before END in the loop body.

Program Style

Writing General Programs

In Fig. 2.4, we have used a READ statement to define the value of LAST. Since the value of LAST is known to be 99, we could have used the assignment statement

LAST := 99;

or even defined LAST as a constant instead of a variable

CONST LAST = 99;

The READ statement is preferable because it allows us to use this program without modification to compute the sum of as many odd numbers as we desire. All we have to do is change the data item entered, not the program.

Programs should always be written in the most general form possible. This may take a little extra thought initially, but it will pay dividends if the program is likely to be reused with different sets of data.

The WHILE statement will be described formally in the next chapter. We will also describe the compound statement in PASCAL which is a group of statements bracketed by a BEGIN-END pair.

2.7 SUMMARY

In the first part of this chapter we outlined a method for solving problems on the computer. This method stressed six points:

1. Understand the problem.
2. Identify the input and output data for the problem as well as other relevant data in a data table.
3. Formulate a precise statement of the problem.
4. Develop an *algorithm*.
5. *Refine* the algorithm.
6. Implement the algorithm in PASCAL.

Algorithms normally consist of three phases: initialization of variables, manipulation of data and display of results. The data manipulation phase is most critical. This phase can be started once the input data and desired problem outputs have been clearly defined in a data table and a precise understanding of the problem has been achieved. The initialization of variable values that is required usually depends on the particular method chosen to perform the data manipulation.

Several guidelines for using program comments were discussed. Well-placed and carefully worded comments, combined with a complete and concise data table, can easily provide all of the documentation necessary for a program.

In the remainder of the chapter, we discussed the representation of the various steps in an algorithm and illustrated the step-wise development, or refinement, of algorithms.

We provided a convenient form of representation for the loop and decision steps of an algorithm. By using these forms we can maintain a clear separation between the relevant control information in a loop or decision structure and the steps to be carried out subject to this control. These forms and their flow diagrams are provided in Fig. 2.5.

The notion of a trace or simulation of an algorithm was also introduced in this chapter. These simulations, if carried out carefully, can often help uncover numerous algorithm logic errors even before a program is written.

We briefly introduced the IF and WHILE statements. In the next chapter we will describe how to implement general loop and decision structures in PASCAL. These statements will enable us to translate our algorithms into PASCAL programs with a minimum of effort. This will allow us to solve some relatively complex problems on the computer, using programs that reflect the careful planning and organization practiced in our algorithm development.

Double alternative Decision Step

```
IF  condition THEN
    True statement
ELSE
    False Statement
```

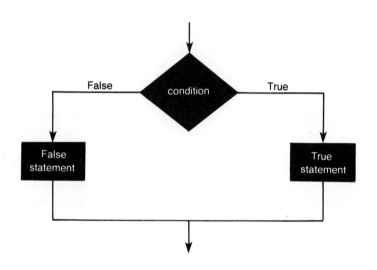

Single alternative Decision Step

```
IF  condition THEN
    True Statement
```

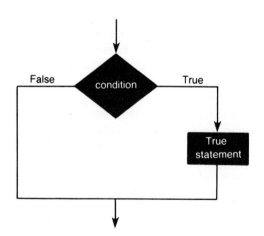

WHILE Loop

WHILE *condition* DO
   Loop Body

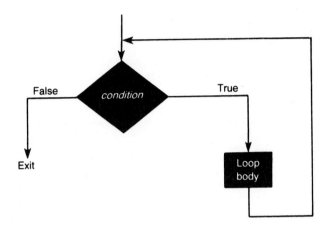

Fig. 2.5 Decision and loop steps.

PROGRAMMING PROBLEMS

For all problems, a data table and refined algorithm are required.

2.6   Given the bank balance in your checking account for the past month and all the transactions in your account for the current month, write an algorithm to compute and print your checking account balance at the end of the current month. You may assume that the total number of transactions for the current month is known ahead of time. (*Hint:* Your first data item should be your checking account balance at the end of last month. The second item should be the number of transactions for the current month. All subsequent items should represent the amount of each transaction for the current month.)

2.7   Write an algorithm to compute the factorial, N!, of a single arbitrary integer N. (N! = N × (N − 1) × . . . 2 × 1). Your program should read and print the value of N and print N! when done.

2.8   If N contains an integer, then we can compute X^N for any X, simply by initializing a variable to 1 and multiplying it by X a total of N times. Write an algorithm to read in a value of X and a value of N, and compute X^N via repeated multiplications. Check your algorithm for

$$X = 6.0, N = 4$$
$$X = 2.5, N = 6$$
$$X = -8.0, N = 5$$

2.9   Continuation of Problem 2.8:

    a)   How many multiplications are required in your algorithm for Problem 2.8 in order to compute X^9? Can you figure out a way of computing X^9 in fewer multiplications?

    b)   Can you generalize your algorithm for computing X^9 to compute X^N for any positive N?

    c)   Can you use your algorithm in part (b) to compute X^{-N} for any positive N? How?

2.10   Write an algorithm that will find the product of a collection of data values. Your algorithm should terminate when a zero is read.

2.11   Compute and print a table showing the first 15 powers of 2.

2.12   Redo the modified payroll program (Problem 2.2) so that a prespecified number of employees can be processed in a single run.

2.13   Redo Problem 1.5 so that all cases are processed in a single program run.

2.14   Redo Problem 1.6 so that all cases are processed in a single program run.

FUNDAMENTAL CONTROL STATEMENTS

3.1 INTRODUCTION TO CONTROL STATEMENTS

3.1.1 Control Statements

The control statements of a programming language enable the programmer to control the sequence and frequency of execution of segments of a program. In this chapter, we will examine three very important control statements of PAS-CAL: the IF statement, WHILE statement, and FOR statement.

Using these statements, we can easily implement the decision and loop steps discussed in the last chapter. We shall utilize the problem-solving methodology also outlined in that chapter to solve several example problems.

3.1.2 Compound Statements

Before describing the control statements of PASCAL, we shall introduce the concept of a compound statement. A *compound statement* is a sequence of one or more statements starting with BEGIN and ending with END. The ";" is used to separate statements in the sequence; there is no ";" after BEGIN or before the word END.

Example 3.1:   The statements below form a compound statement.

```
BEGIN
  WRITE ('HOW OLD ARE YOU NOW? ');
  READLN (AGE);
  NEXTAGE := AGE + 1;
  WRITELN ('YOU WILL BE ', NEXTAGE,' ON YOUR NEXT BIRTHDAY')
END
```

If the data value read is 20, the following will be printed.

```
HOW OLD ARE YOU NOW? 20
YOU WILL BE 21 ON YOUR NEXT BIRTHDAY
```

It is important to realize that the body of a program is itself a compound statement. The program body starts with BEGIN and ends with the word END followed by a period. The reserved words BEGIN and END serve to "bracket" the executable statements that make up a compound statement.

3.2 THE IF STATEMENT

3.2.1 Definition of the IF Statement

In chapter two, we introduced two forms of decision steps: the double alter-native decision step and the single alternative decision step. The IF statement may be used to implement these decisions as described next.

IF Statement (double alternative)

IF *condition* THEN
         True Statement
ELSE
         False Statement

Interpretation: If the specified *condition* evaluates to true, then the *True Statement* is executed; otherwise, the *False Statement* is executed. The *True Statement* and *False Statement* may either be single or compound PASCAL statements.

IF Statement (single alternative)

IF *condition* THEN
         True Statement

Interpretation: If the specified *condition* evaluates to true, the *True Statement* is executed; otherwise, it is skipped. The *True Statement* may either be a single or compound PASCAL statement.

To illustrate further the use of the IF statement, we next present solutions to two sample problems.

3.2.2   Applications of Decision Structures

In the first problem, we shall illustrate the use of the single alternative decision step.

Problem 3.1:   Read two numbers and compare them. Place the larger in X and the smaller in Y.

Discussion: We will read the two numbers into X and Y and rearrange them if necessary. The data table and algorithm follow.

Data Table for Problem 3.1

Input variables	*Program variables*	*Output variables*
X: First number		X: Larger number
Y: Second number		Y: Smaller number

Level One Algorithm for Problem 3.1

1. Read X and Y.
2. Store the larger number in X and the smaller in Y.
3. Print X and Y.

Only step 2 needs further refinement. We must exchange the values in X and Y if they are not in the desired order.

Level Two Refinements

Step 2   *Store the larger number in X and the smaller in Y*

   2.1   IF X < Y THEN
           2.2   Exchange the values in X and Y

In order to refine step 2.2, we will introduce a program variable TEMP that will be used to save the original value of X. The data table and algorithm are completed next; the PASCAL program is provided in Fig. 3.1.

Program variable

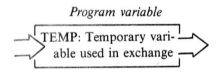

TEMP: Temporary variable used in exchange

Level Three Refinements

Step 2.2

   2.2.1   Save original value of X in TEMP
   2.2.2   Copy Y into X
   2.2.3   Copy TEMP into Y

To verify the need for TEMP, we will trace the algorithm for the data list 3.5, 7.2 in Table 3.1.

Algorithm Step	X	Y	TEMP	Effect
1	3.5	7.2	?	
2.1				3.5 < 7.2 is true - execute True Statement
2.2.1			3.5	
2.2.2	7.2			
2.2.3		3.5		
3				Print X (7.2) and Y (3.5)

Table 3.1 Trace of Algorithm for Problem 3.1

As indicated in the trace, the value 3.5 is no longer stored in X following the execution of step 2.2.2. Previously, saving this value in TEMP (step 2.2.1) prevents it from being lost.

The PASCAL program with sample output is shown in Fig. 3.1.

Another example of the use of the IF statement is shown in Problem 3.2.

```
PROGRAM LARGER;
(* FINDS THE LARGER OF TWO NUMBERS *)

VAR
  X, Y, TEMP : REAL;

BEGIN
  (* READ TWO NUMBERS *)
  WRITE ('X = ');
  READLN (X);
  WRITE ('Y = ');
  READLN (Y);

  (* STORE THE LARGER NUMBER IN X AND THE SMALLER IN Y *)
  IF X < Y THEN
    (* EXCHANGE X AND Y *)
    BEGIN
      TEMP := X;
      X := Y;
      Y := TEMP
    END;  (* IF *)

  (* PRINT X AND Y *)
  WRITELN ('LARGER (X) = ', X :8:2, ' SMALLER (Y) = ', Y:8:2)
END.

X = 25.5
Y = 37.1
LARGER (X) =      37.1    SMALLER (Y) =       25.5
```

Fig. 3.1 Larger of two numbers.

Problem 3.2:   Read two numbers and compute and print their quotient.

Discussion: This is a problem that looks quite straightforward, but it has the potential for disaster hidden between the lines of the problem statement. In this case, as in many others, the potential trouble spot is due to unanticipated values of input data—values for which one or more of the data manipulations required by the problem are not defined.

In this problem, the quotient is not defined mathematically if the divisor is zero. If we instruct the computer to perform the calculation in this case, it will either produce an unpredictable, meaningless result, or it will not even be able to complete the operation and will prematurely terminate or *abort* our program. In order to avoid the problem entirely, we will have our program test for a divisor of zero and print a message of its own if this situation should occur.

The data table and algorithm for this problem follow; the program is shown in Fig. 3.2.

Data Table for Problem 3.2

Input variables	*Program variables*	*Output variables*
DIVIDEND: Dividend		QUOTIENT: Quotient
		when defined
DIVISOR: Divisor		

Level One Algorithm for Problem 3.2

1. Read the dividend and divisor.
2. Compute and print the quotient if it is defined.

Level Two Refinements

Step 2   *Compute and print the quotient if it is defined*

2.1   IF DIVISOR $<>$ 0 THEN
           Compute and print QUOTIENT
       ELSE
           Print an error message

```
PROGRAM DIVIDE;
(* COMPUTES THE QUOTIENT OF TWO NUMBERS *)

VAR
  DIVIDEND, DIVISOR, QUOTIENT : REAL;

BEGIN
  (* READ THE DIVIDEND AND DIVISOR *)
  WRITE ('DIVIDEND = ');
  READLN (DIVIDEND);
  WRITE ('DIVISOR = ');
  READLN (DIVISOR);

  (* COMPUTE AND PRINT THE QUOTIENT IF DEFINED *)
  IF DIVISOR <> 0.0 THEN
    BEGIN
      QUOTIENT := DIVIDEND / DIVISOR;
      WRITELN ('QUOTIENT = ', QUOTIENT :8:2)
    END
  ELSE
    WRITELN ('DIVISOR IS 0.0, QUOTIENT IS UNDEFINED. ')
END.


DIVIDEND = -37.5
DIVISOR = 2.5
QUOTIENT =    -15.00
```

Fig. 3.2 PASCAL program for Problem 3.2.

Program Style

More on Indentation

In the programs shown in Figs. 3.1 and 3.2, we have indented the PASCAL statements that represent the True Statement and False Statement in order to clarify the structure of the program and to make it easier to read and understand. We have also followed the END terminating the single-alternative decision structure in Fig. 3.1 with the comment (* IF *) for the same reasons.

You should realize that the indentation by itself has no meaning. For example, if we mistakenly omitted the BEGIN – END pair bracketing the True Statement in Fig. 3.1 as shown below

```
            IF  X  <  Y  THEN
                TEMP  := X;
                X  := Y;
                Y  := TEMP;
```

then the True Statement would consist of the single statement

```
                TEMP  := X;
```

only. The next two statements would always be executed regardless of the value of the condition "X < Y".

Exercise 3.1:   Provide PASCAL program segments for the decisions stated below.

a)   Read a number into the variable N. If this number is positive, add one to the contents of POS. If the number is not positive, add one to the contents of NEG.

b)   Read a number into N. If N is zero, add one to the contents of ZERO.

c)   This is a combination of the above. Read a number into N. If N is positive, add one to POS; if N is negative, add one to NEG; and if N is zero, add one to ZERO.

Exercise 3.2:   The True Statement of Fig. 3.1 contains three statements and uses an additional variable TEMP. Could we have accomplished the same task with either set of statements below?

```
    a) BEGIN              or        b) BEGIN
           X  := Y;                        TEMP  := Y;
           Y  := X                         X  := TEMP;
       END                                 Y  := X
                                       END
```

What values would be stored in X and Y after each set of statements executes? Modify statement group (b) so that it works properly.

Exercise 3.3:   Represent the following English descriptions as algorithm steps and PASCAL statements.

a)   If the remainder (REM) is equal to zero, then print N.
b)   If the product (PRODUCT) is equal to N, then print the contents of the variable TEST and read a new value into N.
c)   If the number of traffic lights (LIGHTS) exceeds 25, then compute the gallons required (GALLONS) as total miles (MILES) divided by 14. Otherwise, compute GALLONS as MILES divided by 22.5.

3.3   THE WHILE STATEMENT

The algorithm representation for a *WHILE loop* was introduced in Chapter 2 (see Section 2.5). This loop may be implemented using the WHILE statement described in the next display.

WHILE Statement

> WHILE *condition* DO
>   *loop body*

Interpretation: If the specified *condition* is true, the *loop body* is executed and the *condition* is retested. The *loop body* is repeated as long as the *condition* is true. When the *condition* is retested and found to be false, the loop is exited and the first statement following the *loop body* is then executed. The *loop body* may be either a single or compound PASCAL statement.

Note: If the *condition* evaluates to false the first time it is tested, the *loop body* will be skipped and not executed.

Example 3.2:   The WHILE loop in Fig. 3.3 computes and prints all powers of two that are less than 1000, starting with 2^0 or 1. The last value assigned to POWER would be 1024; however, the last value printed would be 512.

```
POWER := 1;
WHILE POWER < 1000 DO
   BEGIN
      WRITELN (POWER);
      POWER := POWER * 2
   END (* WHILE *)
```

Fig. 3.3 Printing powers of two.

In Fig. 3.3, the variable POWER is used as the loop control variable; its value controls the loop repetition process. The three operations below are performed on the loop control variable.

- POWER is set to an initial value (POWER := 1)
- POWER is tested before each loop repetition (POWER < 1000)
- POWER is updated during each repetition (POWER := POWER * 2)

It is important to realize that the loop is not exited at the exact instant that POWER is assigned the value 1024. If there were more statements following the assignment in the loop body, they would be executed. Loop exit does not occur until the loop repetition test is reevaluated at the top of the loop.

In Section 3.4 we shall illustrate the design and implementation of algorithms involving the use of the WHILE loop. Two completely solved problems are presented.

Exercise 3.4:   What values would be printed if the order of the two statements in the loop body of Fig. 3.3 is reversed?

Exercise 3.5:   Write a WHILE loop that contains statements to read a number into the variable N, multiply each value of N by the next power of 2 (POWER), and print POWER, N, and the computed result. (The first value of N is to be multiplied by 2^0; the second value by 2^1, the third by 2^2, and so on.) Repeat the loop as long as the result is less than 10,000.

Exercise 3.6:   Write an algorithm and program for a loop that finds the largest cumulative product of the numbers 1, 2, 3, 4, . . . that is smaller than 10,000.

3.4   APPLICATION OF CONTROL STATEMENTS

3.4.1   Controlling Loop Repetition with Computational Results

The WHILE loop structure is well suited for loops in which the repetition condition involves a test of values that are computed in the loop body. For example, in processing checking account transactions, we might want to continue processing transactions as long as the account balance is positive or zero, and stop and print a message when the balance becomes negative.

In problems of this sort, the loop control variable serves a dual purpose: it is used for storage of a computational result as well as for controlling loop repetition. Occasionally, more than one computed value will be involved in the repetition test as illustrated in the following problem.

Problem 3.3:   Two cyclists are involved in a race. The first has a headstart because the second cyclist is capable of a faster pace. We will write a program to print out the distance from the starting line that each cyclist has travelled. These distances will be printed for each half hour of the race, beginning when the second cyclist departs, and continuing as long as the first cyclist is still ahead.

Discussion: This problem illustrates the use of the computer to simulate what would happen in a real world situation. We can get an estimate of the progress of the cyclists before the race even begins and perhaps use this information to set up monitoring or aid stations. We will make use of the formula

$$\text{distance} = \text{speed} \times \text{elapsed time}$$

in the computation of distance travelled.

The data table and algorithm are provided next.

Data Table for Problem 3.3

Constants

INTERVAL = 0.5, time interval between measurements in hours

Input variables	*Program variables*	*Output variables*

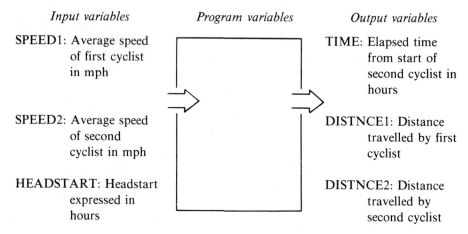

SPEED1: Average speed
of first cyclist
in mph

TIME: Elapsed time
from start of
second cyclist in
hours

SPEED2: Average speed
of second
cyclist in mph

DISTNCE1: Distance
travelled by first
cyclist

HEADSTART: Headstart
expressed in
hours

DISTNCE2: Distance
travelled by
second cyclist

Level One Algorithm

1. Read SPEED1, SPEED2, and HEADSTART.
2. Initialize DISTNCE2 and TIME to 0.
3. Compute headstart of first cyclist in miles (DISTNCE1).
4. Compute and print distances and elapsed time each half-hour while first cyclist is still ahead.

Level Two Refinements

Step 3   *Compute headstart of first cyclist in miles*

    3.1   DISTNCE1 := SPEED1 * HEADSTART

Step 4   *Compute distances and time while first cyclist is ahead*

    4.1   WHILE DISTNCE1 is greater than DISTNCE2 DO
        BEGIN
                4.2 Print elapsed time and distance travelled by each cyclist
                4.3 Increase TIME by INTERVAL
                4.4 Update DISTNCE1 and DISTNCE2
    END (* WHILE *)

As shown above, the initial value of DISTNCE1 (first cyclist's headstart) is computed as the product of speed (SPEED1) and the duration of the headstart (HEADSTART). DISTNCE2 is initially zero. The loop-repetition test involves a comparison of the two output variables DISTNCE1 and DISTNCE2, both of which are updated at the end of the loop (Step 4.4).

To refine Step 4.4, we must compute the incremental distance travelled in each time interval and add it to the distance traveled prior to the current time interval. This computation can be described as

$$\text{distance} = \text{distance} + \text{incremental distance}$$

where

$$\text{incremental distance} = \text{speed} \times \text{time interval}$$

To carry out these computations for each cyclist, we will introduce two new program variables: INCRMNT1 and INCRMNT2.

Program variables

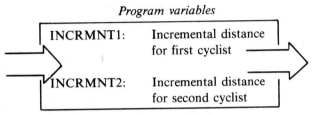

| INCRMNT1: | Incremental distance for first cyclist |
| INCRMNT2: | Incremental distance for second cyclist |

Given these variables, we can refine Step 4.4 as follows:

Level Three Refinements

Step 4.4

4.4.1   INCRMNT1 := SPEED1 * INTERVAL
4.4.2   DISTNCE1 := DISTNCE1 + INCRMNT1
4.4.3   INCRMNT2 := SPEED2 * INTERVAL
4.4.4   DISTNCE2 := DISTNCE2 + INCRMNT2

The final program is shown in Fig. 3.4 along with a sample run.

Program Style

Removing nonvarying computations from a loop

It is worthwhile recognizing that the values of INCRMNT1 and INCRMNT2 cannot vary while the loop is repeated. They remain the same because SPEED1 and SPEED2 never change and INTERVAL is a program constant. There is consequently no reason to recompute the values of INCRMNT1 and INCRMNT2 for each execution of the loop. This pair of computations (Steps 4.4.1 and 4.4.3) should be removed from the loop and performed prior to loop entry rather than in Step 4.4.

This change in the algorithm is reflected in the final program for Problem 3.3 shown in Fig. 3.4. The computation of INCRMNT1 and INCRMNT2 immediately follows the definition of the variables SPEED1 and SPEED2.

Removing these computations from the body of a loop yields a faster-executing program because the multiplications required to compute INCRMNT1 and INCRMNT2 are performed only once, instead of many times. In general, any computation producing the same result for each repetition of a loop should be removed from the loop in this manner.

```
PROGRAM CYCLERACE;
(* CYCLE RACE PROGRAM *)

CONST
  INTERVAL = 0.5;

VAR
  HEADSTART, DISTNCE1, DISTNCE2, TIME,
  INCRMNT1, INCRMNT2, SPEED1, SPEED2 : REAL;

BEGIN
  (* READ SPEED1, SPEED2, AND HEADSTART *)
  WRITE ('FIRST CYCLIST SPEED (MPH) = ');
  READLN (SPEED1);
  WRITE ('SECOND CYCLIST SPEED (MPH) = ');
  READLN (SPEED2);
  WRITE ('HEADSTART OF FIRST CYCLIST (HOURS) = ');
  READLN (HEADSTART);

  (* COMPUTE DISTANCE INCREMENTS *)
  INCRMNT1 := SPEED1 * INTERVAL;
  INCRMNT2 := SPEED2 * INTERVAL;

  (* INITIALIZE DISTNCE1, DISTNCE2, AND TIME *)
  DISTNCE1 := SPEED1 * HEADSTART;
  DISTNCE2 := 0.0;
  TIME := 0.0;
  WRITELN;

  (* UPDATE TIME AND DISTANCES EACH INTERVAL *)
  WRITELN ('TIME' :6, 'DISTANCE1' :11, 'DISTANCE2' :11);
  WHILE DISTNCE1 > DISTNCE2 DO
    BEGIN
      WRITELN (TIME :6:2, DISTNCE1 :11:2, DISTNCE2:11:2);
      TIME := TIME + INTERVAL;
      DISTNCE1 := DISTNCE1 + INCRMNT1;
      DISTNCE2 := DISTNCE2 + INCRMNT2
    END (* WHILE *)
END.
```

FIRST CYCLIST SPEED (MPH) = <u>10.0</u>
SECOND CYCLIST SPEED (MPH) = <u>12.0</u>
HEADSTART OF FIRST CYCLIST (HOURS) = <u>0.5</u>

TIME	DISTANCE1	DISTANCE2
0.00	5.00	0.00
0.50	10.00	6.00
1.00	15.00	12.00
1.50	20.00	18.00
2.00	25.00	24.00

Fig. 3.4 Cycle race program and sample output.

Program Style

Printing a table

The statement

```
WRITELN ('TIME' :6, 'DISTANCE1' :11, 'DISTANCE2' :11)
```

prints three strings across a line. The number following each colon specifies a field width; a string is printed *right justified* in its field. Consequently, each string is preceded by two blanks as its length is smaller than its field width (by two characters). The three strings serve as the heading for a table.

The statement

```
WRITELN (TIME :6:2, DISTNCE1 :11:2, DISTNCE2 :11:2)
```

is used in the loop to print a table consisting of three columns of numbers. The rightmost digit of each number printed will be aligned with the rightmost character of its respective column heading as their field widths are the same.

3.4.2 Using a Sentinel Value

In the examples so far, the loop repetition condition could be determined from a careful reading of the problem statement. For example, the condition

```
ODDS <= LAST
```

was used in Chapter 2 to control the repetition of a loop that summed all odd numbers less than or equal to LAST. Often, the problem statement will simply specify that all data items are to be processed, and it is up to the programmer to provide a means of ensuring that this is done.

One way to accomplish this is to insert a sentinel value at the end of the data collection. A sentinel value can be used to signal the program that all of the data items have been read into the computer memory and processed. A sentinel value is a number that would not normally occur as a data item for the program. When that value is read, it can be recognized by the program as an indication that all of the actual data items have been processed.

The concept of a sentinel value can be incorporated in the WHILE loop pattern as illustrated in the sample refinement described below.

Step 2   *Process all input data items*

    2.1   Read first data item

    2.2   WHILE current data item is not the sentinel value DO

            BEGIN

                2.3 Print current data item

                2.4 Process current data item

                2.5 Read the next data item

            END (* WHILE *)

The variable into which each data item is read acts as a loop control variable. It must be tested prior to each loop repetition (Step 2.2). It must be initialized using a read step (Step 2.1) prior to entering the loop, and its value must be updated during each execution of the loop body using a second read step (Step 2.5). This is normally the last step in the loop, and is executed after all other processing of the current value has been performed. We illustrate these and other points concerning the use of the sentinel value in the following problem.

Problem 3.4:   Write a program that reads a list of student names and prints the name that comes first alphabetically as well as the number of names read.

Discussion: In order to gain some insight into a solution of this problem, we should consider how to go about finding the alphabetically first name in a long list of names without the computer. Most likely we would read down the list of names, one at a time, and remember only the name that was alphabetically first so far. If at some point in the list, we encounter a new name that precedes the one we are remembering, then we would remember the new name instead.

An example of this process is shown next.

Names	Effect of each name
SALLY	"Since SALLY is the first name, we will consider it to be alphabetically first initially.
BILL	BILL precedes SALLY, so BILL is the alphabetically first name.
DEBBIE	DEBBIE follows BILL, so BILL is still the first name.
ALAN	ALAN precedes BILL, so ALAN is the alphabetically first name"

We can use this procedure as a model for constructing an algorithm for solving Problem 3.4 on the computer. We will instruct the computer to process a single name at a time and to save the "smallest" name it has processed so far in the variable SMALLNAME. The "smallest" name will be the one that is first alphabetically.

In order to terminate loop repetition, we will use the sentinel value 'DONE' which is not likely to be a name in our list. The use of a sentinel value is desirable since we do not know beforehand how many names are to be processed.

In addition, since we wish to keep track of the number of names processed, we must introduce an output variable, COUNT, for this purpose. COUNT must be increased by one after each name is processed.

The data table and level one algorithm follow.

Data Table for Problem 3.4

Constants

SENTINEL = 'DONE', sentinel value

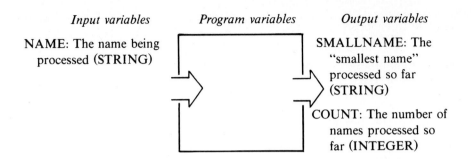

Input variables   *Program variables*   *Output variables*

NAME: The name being
processed (STRING)

SMALLNAME: The
"smallest name"
processed so far
(STRING)

COUNT: The number of
names processed so
far (INTEGER)

Level One Algorithm

1. Count the names and find the alphabetically first name (SMALL-
   NAME).
2. Print SMALLNAME and COUNT.

In refining Step 1, we must pick meaningful initial values for
SMALLNAME and COUNT. Since COUNT represents the number of names
processed so far, its initial value should be zero. The initial value of
SMALLNAME will be the first name in the list.

The algorithm is refined below. The PASCAL program is given in Fig. 3.5
along with a sample run.

Level Two Refinements

Step 1   *Count the names and find the alphabetically first name.*

1.1 Initialize COUNT to zero
1.2 Read the first name into NAME
1.3 Initialize SMALLNAME to NAME
1.4 WHILE NAME is not equal to SENTINEL DO
       BEGIN
              1.5 Store the smaller of NAME and SMALLNAME in
                   SMALLNAME
              1.6 Increase COUNT by one
              1.7 Read the next name into NAME
       END

Level Three Refinements

Step 1.5
       1.5.1 IF NAME is less than SMALLNAME THEN
                   SMALLNAME : = NAME

```
PROGRAM NAMESCAN;
(* FINDS THE ALPHABETICALLY FIRST NAME IN A LIST *)
```

(continued)

```
CONST
  SENTINEL = 'DONE';

VAR
  NAME, SMALLNAME : STRING;
  COUNT : INTEGER;

BEGIN
  (* COUNT THE NAMES AND FIND THE SMALLEST ONE *)
  COUNT := 0;
  WRITE ('ENTER A NAME OR "DONE" :');
  READLN (NAME);
  SMALLNAME := NAME;
  WHILE NAME <> SENTINEL DO
    BEGIN
      IF NAME < SMALLNAME THEN
        SMALLNAME := NAME;
      COUNT := COUNT + 1;
      WRITE ('ENTER A NAME OR "DONE": ');
      READLN (NAME)
    END; (* WHILE *)

  (* PRINT SMALLNAME AND COUNT *)
  WRITELN;
  WRITELN (COUNT, ' NAMES WERE PROCESSED');
  WRITELN ('THE ALPHABETICALLY FIRST NAME IS', SMALLNAME)
END.

ENTER A NAME OR "DONE": JOE
ENTER A NAME OR "DONE": SALLY
ENTER A NAME OR "DONE": ANN
ENTER A NAME OR "DONE": BILL
ENTER A NAME OR "DONE": DONE

4 NAMES WERE PROCESSED
THE ALPHABETICALLY FIRST NAME IS ANN
```

Fig. 3.5   Alphabetically first name program and sample run.

Program Style

Nested statements

In Fig. 3.5, there is an example of an IF statement *nested* or wholly contained within a WHILE statement. This type of statement nesting is quite common in PASCAL. We will have more to say about nested statements later.

Exercise 3.7: What would happen in the execution of the program in Fig. 3.5 if we accidentally omitted all data except the sentinel value?

Exercise 3.8: Modify Problem 3.4 so that each student's exam score and name are read. Print out the student with the highest score on the exam and that score.

Exercise 3.9: Modify the data table, algorithm and program for Problem 3.4, assuming the number of names to be processed is available before program execution. Compare COUNT to this value in the loop control step and eliminate the sentinel value completely.

Exercise 3.10: Modify the algorithm and data table so that the alphabetically first and last names are found and printed.

Exercise 3.11: On January 1, the water supply tank for the town of Death Valley contained 10,000 gallons of water. The town used 183 gallons of water a week and it expected no rain in the near future. Write a loop to compute and print the amount of water remaining in the tank at the end of each week. Your loop should terminate when there is insufficient water to last a week.

3.4.3   Counting Loops

The variable COUNT in Fig. 3.5 represents the number of data items processed so far and is called a *counter.* If we know the number of data items to be processed beforehand, a counter may be used to control loop repetition. Assuming that the number of names to be processed is stored in the variable named NUMNAMES, Step 1 of the algorithm for Problem 3.4 could be refined as follows.

Revised Level Two Refinements

Step 1   *Find the alphabetically first name.*

     1.1   Read the first name into NAME
     1.2   Initialize SMALLNAME to NAME
     1.3   Initialize COUNT to one
     1.4   WHILE COUNT is less than or equal to NUMNAMES DO
          BEGIN
                 1.5   Read the next name into NAME
                 1.6   Store the smaller of NAME and SMALLNAME in
                      SMALLNAME
                 1.7   Increase COUNT by one
     END (* WHILE *)

In this case, COUNT is used as the loop control variable, not NAME. COUNT is initialized to one in Step 1.3, tested at Step 1.4, and updated at Step 1.7.

The only problem remaining is when and how to initialize NUMNAMES. Obviously, NUMNAMES must be initialized before the loop is reached. One solution would be to make NUMNAMES a program constant; however, this would require modification of the program each time it was run for a different class size.

A better solution would be to make NUMNAMES an input variable. Since the value of NUMNAMES must be defined before any names are read, the data value representing NUMNAMES should be the very first data item read.

Exercise 3.12:   Write the data table and program for Problem 3.4 as modified above.

Exercise 3.13:   Write an algorithm and program to compute the average of N integers where N is provided as a data item.

3.5   THE FOR STATEMENT

3.5.1   Comparison of FOR and WHILE Statements

Since counting loops are quite common, PASCAL provides a *FOR statement* that simplifies the implementation of counting loops. The FOR statement is illustrated next.

Example 3.3:   The program in Fig. 3.6 uses the FOR statement to implement a loop that computes the sum of the first ten integers. The FOR statement

```
    FOR NEXT := 1 TO NUMBERITEMS DO
      SUM := SUM + NEXT;
```

specifies that the variable NEXT takes on all integer values from 1 to NUMBERITEMS (10); these values are added together in the FOR loop body.

The implementation of the loop using the WHILE statement is shown on the right of Fig. 3.6. In comparing these two versions, we see that the three loop control steps

1. initialize NEXT — NEXT := 1
2. test NEXT — WHILE NEXT <= NUMBERITEMS DO
3. update NEXT — NEXT := NEXT + 1

are summarized in the single line beginning with FOR. This line may be read as "for values of NEXT from 1 to NUMBERITEMS inclusive–do the following". The FOR statement enables us to implement counting loops more efficiently.

```
PROGRAM ADDTEN;
(* ADDS THE FIRST TEN INTEGERS *)

CONST
  NUMBERITEMS = 10;

VAR
  SUM, NEXT : INTEGER;

BEGIN
  SUM := 0;

  FOR NEXT := 1 TO NUMBERITEMS DO      NEXT := 1;
    SUM := SUM + NEXT;                 WHILE NEXT <= NUMBERITEMS DO
                                        BEGIN
                                          SUM := SUM + NEXT;
                                          NEXT := NEXT + 1
                                        END; (* WHILE *)

  WRITELN ('SUM = ', SUM)
END.
```

Fig. 3.6   FOR loop to add ten numbers and the equivalent WHILE loop.

Since a separate statement is not needed to update the loop control variable
NEXT, the FOR loop body contains only one statement. Hence, a BEGIN-END
pair is not required as in the WHILE loop implementation. The FOR statement
is summarized in the next display.

As indicated in the next display, the loop control variable may be any standard type, except REAL or STRING. In fact, any data type whose values may
be *enumerated,* or listed, is allowed (called *scalar data types*).

FOR Statement

> FOR *lcv* := *initial* TO *final* DO
>   *loop body*

Interpretation: The *loop body* is executed for each value of the loop control
variable, *lcv*, between *initial* and *final* inclusive. *Initial* and *final* may be constants, variables or expressions; however, *lcv, initial* and *final* must all be the
same type. Any scalar type (defined above) is permitted including INTEGER,
CHAR, and BOOLEAN.
Note 1: The value of *lcv* may not be modified in the *loop body.*
Note 2: The value of *final* is computed once, just before loop execution. Any
subsequent change in the variables that make up the final expression will not
affect the number of times the loop is executed.
Note 3: Upon exit from the FOR loop, the value of *lcv* is considered
undefined.
Note 4: If *initial* is greater than *final,* the loop body will not be executed at all.
Note 5: The alternate form

> FOR *lcv* := *initial* DOWNTO *final* DO

may be used to implement a loop that counts down from a larger *initial* value
to a smaller *final* value. An example would be

> FOR I := 5 DOWNTO −5 DO

In this case the loop body will not be executed at all if *initial* is less than *final.*

Example 3.4: The FOR loop below prints the characters from A to Z across a
line

```
FOR NEXTCHAR := 'A' TO 'Z' DO
   WRITE (NEXTCHAR);
```

The loop control variable, NEXTCHAR, must be of type CHAR. We shall see
why the character value 'A' is considered less than 'Z' in the next chapter.

It is also permissable to start the loop control variable at an initial value
that is greater than its final value. In this case, the word DOWNTO must be
used in the FOR statement instead of TO.

Example 3.5: The loop in Fig. 3.7 prints a table showing the conversion from
degrees Celsius to degrees Fahrenheit for temperatures starting at 5°C and de-
creasing to −5°C. A sample run is also shown.

```
PROGRAM DEGREES;
(* CELSIUS TO FAHRENHEIT CONVERSION *)

CONST
  MAXCELSIUS = 5;
  MINCELSIUS = -MAXCELSIUS;

VAR
  CELSIUS : INTEGER;
  FAHRENHEIT : REAL;

BEGIN
  WRITELN ('CELSIUS    FAHRENHEIT');
  FOR CELSIUS := MAXCELSIUS DOWNTO MINCELSIUS DO
    BEGIN
      FAHRENHEIT := 1.8 * CELSIUS + 32.0;
      WRITELN (CELSIUS :4, FAHRENHEIT :12:1)
    END
END.

CELSIUS    FAHRENHEIT
   5          41.0
   4          39.2
   3          37.4
   2          35.6
   1          33.8
   0          32.0
  -1          30.2
  -2          28.4
  -3          26.6
  -4          24.8
  -5          23.0
```

Fig. 3.7   Celsius to Fahrenheit program and output.

Exercise 3.14:   Redo the loops in the solutions to Exercises 3.12 and 3.13 using the FOR statement.

3.5.2   The Interest Rate Problem

The following problem also illustrates the use of the FOR loop.

Problem 3.5:   The banks in your area all advertise different interest rates for various kinds of long-term savings certificates. Usually the advertisements state the minimum investment period for the certificate (4 years, 6 years, etc.), and the yearly interest rate. We will write a program which, given an investment period in years, a yearly interest rate in percent, and an amount of deposit in dollars and cents, will compute and print the yearly interest amount and the value of the certificate at the end of each year of the investment period.

Discussion: An initial data table for this problem and level one algorithm are shown below.

Data Table for Problem 3.5

Input variables	Program variables	Output variables

PERIOD: Investment period in years (IN-TEGER)

RATE: Yearly interest rate (REAL)

DEPOSIT: Initial deposit (REAL)

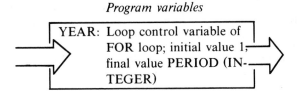

DECRATE: Decimal value of RATE (REAL)

INTEREST: Interest amount computed at the end of each year (REAL)

VALUE: Certificate value at the end of each year (REAL)

Level One Algorithm

1. Read DEPOSIT, PERIOD and RATE
2. For each year of the investment period, compute and print interest earned and certificate value.

From the level one algorithm, it is clear that a repetition of a short sequence of steps is needed in the refinement of Step 2. The repetition can easily be controlled by using a counter, YEAR, that takes on successive integral values from 1 (first year) through PERIOD (last year). The new data table entry and refinement of Step 2 follow.

Additional Data Table Entry for Problem 3.5

Program variables

YEAR: Loop control variable of FOR loop; initial value 1; final value PERIOD (IN-TEGER)

Level Two Refinements

Step 2   *Compute INTEREST and VALUE after each year*

    2.1   Initialize VALUE to DEPOSIT
    2.2   FOR YEAR := 1 TO PERIOD DO
          BEGIN
               Compute INTEREST earned for the current year
               Compute VALUE at end of year
               Print YEAR, INTEREST and VALUE
          END (* FOR *)

The program is given in Fig. 3.8, along with sample output for Period = 10 years, RATE = 12.25 percent and DEPOSIT = $3000.

```
PROGRAM CERTIFICATE;
(* BANK CERTIFICATE PROGRAM *)

VAR
  DEPOSIT, VALUE, INTEREST : REAL;
  RATE, DECRATE : REAL;
  PERIOD, YEAR : INTEGER;

BEGIN
  (* READ DEPOSIT, PERIOD, RATE *)
  WRITE ('AMOUNT = $');
  READLN (DEPOSIT);
  WRITE ('PERIOD (IN YEARS) = ');
  READLN (PERIOD);
  WRITE ('RATE (IN PERCENT) = ');
  READLN (RATE);
  DECRATE := RATE / 100.0;

  (* INITIALIZE VALUE TO INITIAL DEPOSIT *)
  VALUE := DEPOSIT;
  WRITELN ('INITIAL CERTIFICATE VALUE = $', VALUE : 10:2);
  WRITELN;

  (* COMPUTE INTEREST AND VALUE AFTER EACH YEAR *)
  WRITELN ('YEAR      INTEREST      VALUE');
  FOR YEAR := 1 TO PERIOD DO
    BEGIN
      INTEREST := VALUE * DECRATE;
      VALUE := VALUE + INTEREST;
      WRITELN (YEAR :3, INTEREST :13:2, VALUE :11:2)
    END (* FOR *)
END.
```

```
AMOUNT = $3000.00
PERIOD (IN YEARS) = 10
RATE (IN PERCENT) = 12.25
INITIAL CERTIFICATE VALUE = $    3000.00
```

YEAR	INTEREST	VALUE
1	367.50	3367.50
2	412.52	3780.02
3	463.05	4243.07
4	519.78	4762.85
5	583.45	5346.30
6	654.92	6001.22
7	735.15	6736.37
8	825.20	7561.57
9	926.29	8487.86
10	1039.76	9527.63

Fig. 3.8 Bank certificate program and sample run.

Exercise 3.15: Modify the temperature conversion program (Fig. 3.7) so that it will convert Fahrenheit temperatures to Celsius. Print out a table of conversions for temperatures ranging from 100°F down to 80°F.

Exercise 3.16: The factorial of a number, N, is defined to be the product of N and all positive integers less than N. It is denoted by the symbol N!.

$$N! = N \times (N-1) \times (N-2) \times \ldots 2 \times 1$$
$$e.g., 6! = 6 \times 5 \times 4 \times 3 \times 2 \times 1 = 720$$

Write a program that reads a number N and computes and prints its factorial.

3.6 THE WIDGET INVENTORY CONTROL PROBLEM

We will now turn our attention to the solution of a problem that illustrates the use of many of the control statements introduced in the chapter.

Problem 3.6: The Widget Manufacturing Company needs a program to help with the control of the manufacturing and shipping of widgets. Specifically, the program is to process orders for shipments of new widgets and check that there is sufficient inventory to fill the orders. If an order can't be filled due to insufficient stock, the program should print the message "NOT FILLED" next to the shipment request; otherwise, the message "FILLED" should be printed.

A sentinel value of zero will be used to indicate that all orders have been processed. The program should also print out the final value of the inventory, the number of widgets shipped, and the number of additional widgets that must be manufactured to fill all outstanding orders.

Discussion: The initial inventory value (STARTINV) must be read prior to processing any order. This value should also be stored as the initial value of the variable representing the current inventory (CURINV). Each order for widgets will be read into the variable ORDER and processed completely before the next order is read. The data table and level one algorithm follow.

Data Table for Problem 3.6

Constants

SENTINEL =0, sentinel value

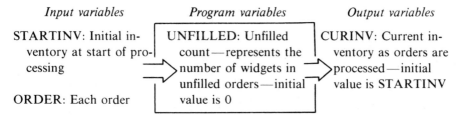

Input variables	*Program variables*	*Output variables*
STARTINV: Initial inventory at start of processing	UNFILLED: Unfilled count—represents the number of widgets in unfilled orders—initial value is 0	CURINV: Current inventory as orders are processed—initial value is STARTINV
ORDER: Each order		

ADDWIDGETS: Additional widgets required
to fill outstanding
orders

SHIPPED: Number of
widgets shipped

Level One Algorithm

1. Read initial inventory (STARTINV).
2. Initialize current inventory (CURINV) to STARTINV and unfilled count (UNFILLED) to zero.
3. Process all widget orders.
4. Print final inventory.
5. Compute and print widgets shipped (SHIPPED).
6. Compute and print new widgets needed (ADDWIDGETS).

We will focus our attention on Step 3 above first. The level two refinement below is based on the fact that a sentinel value will be used to control loop repetition.

Level Two Refinements

Step 3   *Process all widget orders*

    3.1   Read first order
    3.2   WHILE ORDER $<>$ SENTINEL DO
        BEGIN
                3.3 Process current order
                3.4 Read next order
        END

To refine Step 3.3, we must specify how each order will be processed. Each order should be compared to the current widget inventory (CURINV). If the order amount is less than the inventory, it will be filled and the inventory reduced. If an order is too large to be completely filled, the number of widgets needed for unfilled orders (UNFILLED) will be increased by the amount of this order, and the inventory is not changed.

Level Three Refinements

Step 3.3

    3.3.1   IF ORDER $<=$ CURINV THEN
        BEGIN
            Print that order is filled
            Reduce current inventory, CURINV, by ORDER
        END
        ELSE

(*continued on page 82*)

```
PROGRAM INVENTORY;
(* WIDGET INVENTORY CONTROL PROBLEM *)

CONST
  SENTINEL = 0;

VAR
  STARTINV, CURINV, ORDER,
  ADDWIDGETS, UNFILLED, SHIPPED : INTEGER;

BEGIN
  (* READ INITIAL INVENTORY *)
  WRITE ('INITIAL INVENTORY = ');
  READLN (STARTINV);

  (* INITIALIZE CURRENT INVENTORY AND UNFILLED COUNT *)
  CURINV := STARTINV;
  UNFILLED := 0;

  (* PROCESS ALL WIDGET ORDERS *)
  WRITELN ('ENTER WIDGET ORDERS, 0 TO STOP');
  READLN (ORDER);
  WHILE ORDER <> SENTINEL DO
    BEGIN
      (* DECIDE IF ORDER CAN BE FILLED *)
      IF ORDER <= CURINV THEN
        BEGIN
          WRITELN (ORDER :4, ' FILLED.');
          CURINV := CURINV - ORDER
        END
      ELSE
        BEGIN
          WRITELN (ORDER :4, ' NOT FILLED.');
          UNFILLED := UNFILLED + ORDER
        END; (* IF *)
      READLN (ORDER)
    END; (* WHILE *)

  (* PRINT FINAL INVENTORY *)
  WRITELN;
  WRITELN ('FINAL INVENTORY = ', CURINV);

  (* COMPUTE AND PRINT WIDGETS SHIPPED *)
  SHIPPED := STARTINV - CURINV;
  WRITELN ('WIDGETS SHIPPED = ', SHIPPED);

  (* COMPUTE AND PRINT NEW WIDGETS NEEDED *)
  IF UNFILLED > 0 THEN
    BEGIN
      ADDWIDGETS := UNFILLED - CURINV;
      WRITELN ('NEW WIDGETS NEEDED = ', ADDWIDGETS)
    END (* IF *)
END.
```

Fig. 3.9a   Widget inventory program.

BEGIN
Print that order is not filled
Increase unfilled count, UNFILLED, by ORDER
END

Besides printing each order as it is processed, the program output will show the final value of the widget inventory, the number of widgets shipped (SHIPPED), and the total number of widgets required to fill the outstanding orders (ADDWIDGETS). The number of widgets shipped is equal to the initial inventory minus the final inventory. The value of ADDWIDGETS may be computed by subtracting the final inventory from the accumulated sum of unfilled orders (UNFILLED). However, if there are no unfilled orders, then no additional widgets are required. The refinement of Steps 5 and 6 follows.

Additional Level Two Refinements

Step 5   *Compute and print widgets shipped*

5.1 SHIPPED := STARTINV − CURINV
5.2 Print SHIPPED

Step 6   *Compute and print new widgets needed*

6.1 IF UNFILLED > 0 THEN
         BEGIN
            ADDWIDGETS := UNFILLED − CURINV
            Print ADDWIDGETS
         END

We now have sufficient algorithm detail to write the program for the widget inventory problem as shown in Fig. 3.9a. A sample run is shown in Fig. 3.9b.

```
INITIAL INVENTORY = 100
ENTER WIDGET ORDERS, 0 TO STOP
30
   30 FILLED
40
   40 FILLED
50
   50 NOT FILLED
25
   25 FILLED
10
   10 NOT FILLED
3
    3 FILLED
0

FINAL INVENTORY = 2
WIDGETS SHIPPED = 98
NEW WIDGETS NEEDED = 58
```

Fig. 3.9b Sample run of widget program.

Program Style

Correlating algorithms with programs

A program is a group of statements that perform a specific task. Within a program, there are usually a number of subtasks to be carried out. For example, the body of a loop describes a particular subtask; the True Statement of a decision step also describes a subtask.

It is important to be able to identify the individual subtasks within a program and to associate each group of statements with a particular subtask to be performed by the program. The identification of these subtasks can be of considerable help in understanding a program, in correlating the program with the algorithm, and in finding and correcting logical errors that might exist. We believe that applying consistent rules of indentation and use of comments, as demonstrated in this chapter, will help in the identification of logically meaningful groups of statements within your program.

The algorithm is represented in an informal language that is like PASCAL but does not follow any strict syntactical rules. The algorithm is somewhat segmented in that each step is refined individually. These refinements are then implemented in PASCAL and combined to form the program body.

The approach we have taken in numbering algorithm steps should aid you in correlating algorithms with programs. For example, in comparing the algorithm with the program for the widget inventory control problem, you will notice that the number of each algorithm step is indicative of its relative position in the program. That is, the implementation of Step 1 precedes the implementation of Step 2. Similarly, the implementation of Step 3.2 (the WHILE loop) precedes the implementation of Step 4. This correspondence, of course, will be reflected in all of the algorithms and programs shown in the text.

With indentation and carefully chosen comments summarizing the effect of each control structure or group of statements, the program should read from top to bottom as a linear sequence of level one subtasks.

In Chapter 5, we will introduce an additional feature of PASCAL (the procedure) that will enable us to separate the detailed implementation of a complicated subtask from the level one outline of a program (main program). This will make the main program and its parts even easier to write, read and modify.

Exercise 3.17: Is it possible for an order for widgets to be filled even if the one before it was not? Hand-trace the algorithm for an initial inventory of 75 and orders for 20, 50, 100, 3, 15 and 12 widgets. Note that a trace with these data takes you down all decision paths that must be checked in order to gain reasonable assurance that the algorithm works.

3.7   DEBUGGING AND TESTING PROGRAMS

3.7.1   Introduction

It is very rare that a program runs correctly the first time execution is attempted. Often, one spends a considerable amount of time in removing errors or "bugs" from programs.

The process of removing errors or "bugs" from a program is called debugging. You will find that a substantial portion of your programming time is used for debugging. The debugging time can be reduced if you follow the algorithm and program development steps illustrated in the text without taking any shortcuts.

This approach requires a careful analysis of the problem description, the identification of the input and output data for the problem in a data table, and the careful development of the algorithm for the problem solution. The algorithm development should proceed on a step-by-step basis, beginning with an outline of the algorithm in the form of a level one list of subtasks. Additional algorithm detail (refinements) should be provided as needed, until enough detail has been added so that writing the program is virtually a mechanical process. The data table should be updated during the refinement process, so that all variables introduced in the algorithm are listed and clearly defined in the table.

Once the algorithm and data table are complete, a systematic hand simulation (or trace) of the algorithm, using one or two representative sets of data, can help eliminate many bugs before they show up during the execution of your program. When the hand trace is complete, the program may be written, using the data table and the algorithm refinements.

3.7.2   Syntax Errors

There are two general categories of errors that you may encounter when running programs:

- syntax errors
- run-time errors

Syntax errors are caused by statements that do not follow the precise rules of formation (*syntax rules*) of PASCAL. These errors are detected by the compiler during the translation of a PASCAL program. The compiler will identify lines containing most syntax errors by printing an *error diagnostic*, or message, following the statement in error. You should carefully compare the statement in error with those rules of PASCAL that could apply in order to correct your errors.

Syntax errors often result from mistakes in typing or punctuation. An example of such an error would be mistyping a reserved word. Other similar errors would be missing or extra commas, omission of a semicolon, inconsistent spelling of variable names, or substitution of = for := and vice-versa.

Unfortunately, the diagnostic message printed when the compiler detects a syntax error is often vague or confusing. Sometimes careful interpretation and clever detective work are needed to correlate the message with the actual error. A further complication is that an error in one program statement is likely to "confuse" the compiler and cause it to detect errors in subsequent program statements that are actually correct. For example, if the declaration of a variable is not recognized due to an error, all subsequent references to that variable will generate an "undefined variable" diagnostic message. For this reason, it is usually best to concentrate on the first few diagnostics generated by the compiler. Correcting these early mistakes will often drastically reduce the number of diagnostic messages printed in the next program run. After all syntax errors have been eliminated, the program will then execute, although it may still contain "bugs."

3.7.3   Syntax Diagrams

In order to prevent and correct syntax errors, you must have a precise understanding of the syntax rules of PASCAL. The displays provided in the text are one technique for specifying the syntactic form of each new statement. A more formal approach is the use of *syntax diagrams*, or *railroad diagrams.*

Each diagram shown in Fig. 3.10 specifies the syntactic form of a control statement introduced in this chapter. The circled elements in the diagram are re-

Compound Statement

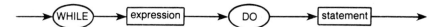

IF Statement

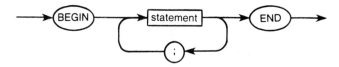

WHILE Statement

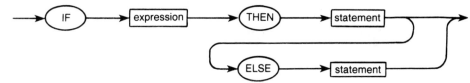

FOR Statement

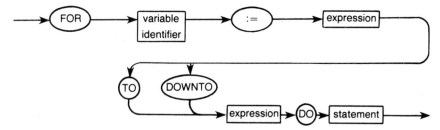

Fig. 3.10   Syntax diagrams for control statements.

served words and special symbols of the PASCAL language; the elements in boxes are other syntactic forms. There is a separate diagram for each syntactic form (i.e. there would also be syntax diagrams for the syntactic forms expression, statement and identifier).

Each syntax diagram should be traced in the direction indicated by the arrows (from left to right). This is quite easy for the syntax diagram for a WHILE statement. The syntax diagram for an IF statement shows that the ELSE clause may or may not be present.

Many paths may be traced through the syntax diagram for a compound statement as it contains a closed cycle or loop. This diagram indicates that a compound statement is always *delimited* (surrounded) by the words BEGIN and END. The number of statements is unspecified; however, a semicolon must be used to separate each statement from the next.

Rather than provide syntax diagrams throughout the text, we shall collect them in Appendix 4. If a program statement has a syntax error that you cannot readily identify or you are unsure as to the exact syntax to use, you should refer to the relevant syntax diagram for help. Ignore those paths containing syntactic forms that you have not yet encountered.

Exercise 3.18: Verify that each control statement in Fig. 3.9a is syntactically correct using the syntax diagrams.

3.7.4 Run-time or Execution Errors

Run-time errors are normally the result of programmer carelessness. They are not severe enough to prevent the compiler from translating the program; however, they will prevent the program from executing through to normal completion. Depending on the severity of the error, program execution may be terminated.

A common run-time error is caused by referencing a variable before its value has been defined. For example, the assignment statement

```
SUM := SUM + ITEM
```

cannot be executed in a meaningful manner unless the values of SUM and ITEM have been previously defined. Consequently, if you forget to initialize a variable used for counting or accumulation of results, a run-time error may occur.

Run-time errors are sometimes caused by mistakes that have been made in the logical organization of the steps in your program. Many errors in logic can be avoided if a careful, reasoned approach is taken to problem solving and program development. Logic errors that do occur can often be more easily diagnosed if some care and discipline have been applied in the design and coding of the program.

If a run-time error is detected, the compiler will print an error diagnostic and terminate execution of your program. It will also indicate the location of the statement that failed; however, it may take some clever detective work to figure out the exact cause of the error. Some common error diagnostics are "bad input format" (reading a character into a real or integer variable), "stack overflow" (using more memory space than is available), "integer overflow" (attempting to assign an integer value that is too large), and "floating point error" or "divide by zero."

As an example, if the formula for converting degrees Celsius to Fahrenheit were incorrectly written as

```
FAHRENHEIT := 1.8 / CELSIUS + 32.0;
```

the program in Fig. 3.7 would generate the following output

```
        CELSIUS    FAHRENHEIT
           5          32.4
           4          32.5
           3          32.6
           2          32.9
           1          33.8

        FLOATING POINT ERROR
        S# 1, P# 1, I# 67
        TYPE <SPACE> TO CONTINUE
```

Figure 3.11   Erroneous temperature conversion table.

The above output indicates that there was a "floating point error" during execution of the loop body when the value of the loop control variable (CELSIUS) was zero. This error resulted from dividing 1.8 by CELSIUS instead of multiplying. (Division by zero is illegal.)

Sometimes, it is not obvious which statement is incorrect. It would then be necessary to get a special program listing by inserting the statement

```
(*$L CONSOLE: *)
```

before the **PROGRAM** statement and recompiling the program. The above statement is not a comment but a special *compiler directive* that instructs the compiler to display an augmented listing of the program during compilation. The listing that would be generated is shown in Fig. 3.12.

```
1  1   1:D     1  (*$L CONSOLE: *)
2  1   1:D     1  PROGRAM DEGREES;
3  1   1:D     3  (* CELSIUS TO FAHRENHEIT CONVERSION *)
4  1   1:D     3
5  1   1:D     3  CONST
6  1   1:D     3     MAXCELSIUS = 5;
```

(continued)

```
  7  1   1:D     3     MINCELSIUS = -MAXCELSIUS;
  8  1   1:D     3
  9  1   1:D     3  VAR
 10  1   1:D     3     CELSIUS : INTEGER;
 11  1   1:D     4     FAHRENHEIT : REAL;
 12  1   1:D     6
 13  1   1:0     0  BEGIN
 14  1   1:1     0     WRITELN ('CELSIUS  FAHRENHEIT');
 15  1   1:1    41     FOR CELSIUS := MAXCELSIUS DOWNTO
                          MINCELSIUS DO
.16  1   1:2    55        BEGIN
 17  1   1:3    55           FAHRENHEIT := 1.8 / CELSIUS + 32.0;
 18  1   1:3    77           WRITELN (CELSIUS :4, FAHRENHEIT:12:1)
 19  1   1:2   108        END
 20  1   1:0   108  END.
```

Fig. 3.12   Augmented program listing.

The first column indicates the line number of each statement and the second column is the segment number (always 1 for us). The third column shows the procedure number (1 for now) and the level of statement nesting (**D** stands for the declaration part). The last column shows the *code offset* (number of memory bytes) of each statement. The next to last line in Fig. 3.11 specified that the error occurred at byte 67 of segment #1, procedure #1. The assignment statement begins at byte 55 and ends at byte 76. (A byte is the amount of memory required to store a single character.)

Even if your program executes through to completion, it may still contain errors. To verify that your program is indeed producing the correct results, it is useful to include extra print statements during the initial program development to display intermediate results. These results should be compared against hand calculations for one or more representative sets of data in order to verify that they are correct. The extra print statements can be removed prior to making your final program runs.

If your program executes but doesn't produce the desired results, there may be an error in logic. If there was not enough output information printed in your first run, it is often worthwhile to make an extra debugging run in which all pertinent variable values are printed at different steps in the execution of your program.

The print statements used for debugging should be added with some care and thought. Since your program is organized as a linear sequence of steps, it is desirable to print the values of variables that are changed in each step before and after execution of that step. You should carefully simulate the execution of each step to verify that the values printed are correct.

For decision and loop steps, it is a good idea to print the values of variables involved in the conditional test. These values should be printed just before execution of the test. For example, if the conditional test has the form

$$COUNT <= LAST$$

then you might insert the statement

```
WRITELN ('COUNT = ', COUNT, 'LAST = ', LAST);
```

just before the test. If a loop is used to accumulate a result, it is useful to print the accumulated value just after loop exit.

Often the first debugging run will do no more than tell you what step is in error. At this point you should concentrate on that step and insert additional print statements to trace its execution. Be careful when inserting extra print statements in a loop as a new set of values will be printed with each repetition of the loop. This may waste considerable time.

It is also worthwhile becoming familiar with the debugging tools provided by your PASCAL system. We will discuss some of these such as range and subscript testing later.

Once you have located an error, go back to your algorithm, modify the steps that you believe are in error and then completely retrace the modified algorithm. This last step is extremely important and one that is often overlooked. Each algorithm change may have important side effects that are difficult to anticipate. Making what seems to be an obvious correction in one step of the algorithm may introduce new errors into other algorithm steps. The only way to establish that there are no side effects is to retrace the revised algorithm.

Once the revised algorithm has been carefully checked out, write the new program statements that are needed, and correct and rerun your program. There is always a temptation to save time and make your changes directly in the program without first going back to the algorithm. If you resist this temptation, you will be better off in the long run.

3.7.5   Testing the Program

Once all errors have been removed and the program has executed to normal completion for at least one set of test data, the program should be tested as thoroughly as possible. In section 2.6.1, we discussed tracing an algorithm and suggested that enough sets of test data be provided to ensure that all paths through the algorithm are traced.

In a similar way, the final program should be tested with a variety of data. For example, to test the widget inventory program (Fig. 3.9a), one data set should be provided that contains orders that are not filled as well as orders that are filled. As suggested in Exercise 3.17, this data set should be prepared so that some orders are filled, even though earlier orders were not. A second data set should also be provided that only contains orders that are filled. (Why?)

3.7.6   Handling the Exceptions

As you get more experienced in programming, you will begin to write programs that not only handle all "normal" situations, but also the unexpected as well. For example, what would the widget inventory program do if the initial inventory value or any widget order happened to be negative? As currently implemented, all negative orders would automatically be filled. A better solution would be to ignore a negative order and print an "error message" indicating that an invalid order was received.

You are right if you are thinking that no reasonable person would request a negative order; however, users of programs often do not know what is reasonable and what is not. This is particularly likely to be true if the program user is different from the program designer. Consequently, experienced programmers practice "defensive programming" so that their programs will behave in a reasonable way even when the data are unreasonable.

Wherever possible, your programs should test for the occurrence of unusual data values and print an error message when they occur. Very often, these strange values will eventually result in a run-time error. Whether this happens or not, your program should print an error message to warn the user of a potential problem and its source.

3.8 COMMON PROGRAMMING ERRORS

There are many opportunities for error when using control statements. Be especially careful with the placement of semicolons in IF statements. A semicolon should not be used just before or after THEN or ELSE.

Remember to use a BEGIN-END pair around each compound statement. A missing BEGIN or END may be detected as a syntax error. However, if both the BEGIN and END are missing, your program will be translated but will not execute as intended. The WHILE statement below may execute forever (or until the program time limit is exceeded) unless a BEGIN-END pair is inserted around the indented statements. (Why?). As it stands now, the loop body consists of the WRITE statement only.

```
READLN (NEXT);
WHILE NEXT <> SENTINEL DO
   WRITE (NEXT);
   SUM := SUM + NEXT;
   READLN (NEXT)
```

It is always essential to verify that either your input data or some computation will eventually cause a loop-repetition condition to become false. This is especially important when the condition involves a test for equality or inequality. In Problem 3.4, the loop-repetition condition (NAME < > SENTINEL) will become false only if the sentinel value ("DONE") is read in. Otherwise, the loop will never terminate.

Be very careful when using tests for equality or inequality to control loop repetition. A loop to process all transactions while a bank balance is positive could be written as

```
WHILE BALANCE <> 0.0 DO
   loop body;
```

If the bank balance is never exactly zero, but instead goes from a positive amount to a negative amount, the above loop would never terminate. It would be safer to use

```
WHILE BALANCE > 0.0 DO
      loop body;
```

As we shall see in the next chapter, there is sometimes a small numerical error in computations involving type real data. This is another reason to avoid tests for exact equality or inequality with real data.

A common error in using FOR loops involves the specification of too many or too few loop repetitions. You should check carefully that the initial and final value parameters are specified correctly and that they are properly defined prior to loop entry. Remember, these parameters and the loop control variable must be the same type (not real). The loop control variable cannot be altered in the loop body.

3.9 SUMMARY

In this chapter, we took a closer look at the IF and WHILE statements and introduced the FOR statement. A number of examples were provided illustrating the use of these statements. A summary of these statements appears in Table 3.2.

We have carefully followed the methodology for problem solving described in chapter two. We identified the variables needed for solution of the problem in a data table; we represented the algorithm as a level one list of subtasks; we refined all nontrivial subtasks of the algorithm; and, subsequently, implemented the algorithm refinements in PASCAL. We have used comments and indentation in the PASCAL program to clarify the purpose of each section of code and enhance the readability of the final program.

If you follow this approach, you are likely to reduce significantly the amount of time spent debugging and testing your programs. It will also be much easier for you, or your instructor, to read and understand your program.

Statement	Effect
IF statement (single alternative)	

```
IF Y > X THEN                    If the condition Y > X is
   BEGIN                         true, the values of Y and
      TEMP := X;                 X are exchanged; otherwise,
      X := Y;                    they remain the same.
      Y := TEMP
   END (* IF *)
```

IF statement (double alternative)

```
IF GROSS > MINIMUM THEN          If the condition GROSS >
   BEGIN                         MINIMUM is true, the value of
      NET := GROSS - TAX;        TAX is deducted from GROSS to
      WRITE ('TAX DEDUCTED.')    compute NET, and a message is
   END                          printed; otherwise, NET is
ELSE                            the same as GROSS.
   NET := GROSS
```

(continued)

Statement	Effect
WHILE statement	

```
WHILE ODDS <= LAST DO
   BEGIN
      SUM := SUM + ODDS;
      COUNTER := COUNTER + 1;
      ODDS := ODDS + 2
   END (* WHILE *)
```

As long as the condition
ODDS <= LAST is true, the
values of SUM, ODDS and COUNTER
are increased as indicated in
the loop body. When the
condition becomes false, program execution resumes with
the first statement following
the loop body.

FOR statement

```
FOR NEXT := 1 TO NUMBERITEMS DO
   BEGIN
      WRITE (NEXT);
      SUM := SUM + NEXT
   END (* FOR *)
```

Print all integers between
one and NUMBERITEMS, in-
clusive, and accumulate them
in SUM.

Table 3.2   Summary of IF, WHILE and FOR Statements

PROGRAMMING PROBLEMS

A data table and refined algorithm should be provided for each problem.

3.7   Write a program to read in a list of integer data items and find and print the index of the first occurrence of the number 12. Your program should print an index value of 0 if the number is not found. (The index is the sequence number of the data item 12. For example, if the 8th data item read in is 12, then the index value 8 should be printed.)

3.8   Write a program to read in a collection of exam scores ranging in value from 1 to 100. Your program should count and print the number of outstanding scores (90–100), the number of satisfactory scores (60–89), and the number of unsatisfactory scores (1–59). Test your program on the following data:

63	75	72
72	78	67
80	63	75
90	89	43
59	99	82
12	100	

In addition, print each exam score and its category.

3.9   *Expanded payroll problem.* Write a program to process weekly employee time cards for all employees of an organization. Each employee will have three data items indicating an identification number, the hourly wage rate and the number of hours worked during a given week. Each employee is to be paid time-and-a-half for all hours worked over 40. A tax amount of 3.625 percent of gross salary will be deducted. The program output should show the employee's number and net pay.

3.10 Suppose you own a beer distributorship that sells Piels (ID number 1), Coors (ID number 2), Bud (ID number 3) and Iron City (ID number 4) by the case. Write a program to (a) read in the case inventory for each brand for the start of the week; (b) process all weekly sales and purchase records for each brand; and (c) print out the final inventory. Each case transaction will consist of two data items. The first item will be the brand identification number (an integer). The second will be the amount purchased (a positive integer value) or the amount sold (a negative integer value). The weekly inventory for each brand (for the start of the week) will also consist of two data items—the identification and initial inventory—for that brand. For now, you may assume that you always have sufficient foresight to prevent depletion of your inventory for any brand. (*Hint:* Your data entry should begin with eight values representing the case inventory. These should be followed by the transaction values.)

3.11 Write a program to read in an integer N and compute SLOW = Σi = 1 + 2 + 3 + 4 + ... + N (the sum of all integers from 1 to N, inclusive). Then compute FAST = (N × (N + 1))/2 and compare FAST and SLOW. Your program should print both SLOW and FAST and indicate whether or not they are equal. (You will need a loop to compute SLOW). Which computation method is preferable?

3.12 Write a program to find the largest value in a collection of N numbers, where the value of N will be the first data item read into the program.

3.13 Write a program to process a collection of checking account transactions (deposits or withdrawals) for Mr. Shelley's account. Your program should begin by reading in the previous account balance and then process each transaction, computing the new balance. Your output should appear in three columns, with withdrawals on the left, deposits in the middle and the new balance (after each transaction) on the right. Test your program with the following data.

Old balance = 325.50
Transactions: 25.00, −79.25, −60.00, 16.75, −259.47
42.00, −5.50

3.14 Modify the data table, algorithm and program of Problem 3.13 to compute and print the following additional information: The number of withdrawals, the number of deposits, the number of transactions, the total sum of all withdrawals, the total sum of all deposits.

3.15 Following the processing of the transaction −259.47 in Problem 3.13 (or 3.14), the balance was negative, indicating that Mr. Shelley's account was overdrawn. Modify your data table, algorithm and program so that the resulting new program will test for withdrawal amounts that are not covered. Have your program completely skip processing each such withdrawal and, instead, print an error message to indicate an overdrawn account. The account balance should not be altered by withdrawals that are not covered. Your program should count the number of such withdrawals and print a total at the end of execution. (Note that, in Problem 3.13 or 3.14, Mr. Shelley's final balance was positive. This indicates that he made a deposit during the current time period to cover the $259.47 withdrawal. What could be done to prevent such a transaction from being considered as overdrawn as long as the final account balance for the current period is positive?)

3.16 Write a program to compute and print the fractional powers of two ($\frac{1}{2}$, $\frac{1}{4}$, $\frac{1}{8}$, $\frac{1}{16}$, ...) in decimal form. Your program should print two columns of information, as shown next:

Power	Fraction
1	0.5
2	0.25
3	0.125
4	0.0625

3.17 Modify the program for Problem 3.16 to accumlate and print the sum of the fractions computed *at each step*. Add a third column of output containing the accumulated sum as shown below.

Sum
0.5
0.75
0.875
0.9375

Explain the results in this column. Could this value ever reach 1?

3.18 The trustees of a small college are considering voting a pay raise for the 12 full-time faculty members. They want to grant a 5½ percent pay raise. However, before doing so, they want to know how much this will cost the college. Write a program that will provide this information. Test your program for the following salaries:

$12,500	$14,029.50
$16,000	$13,250
$15,500	$12,800
$20,000.50	$18,900
$13,780	$17,300
$14,120.25	$14,100

Have your program print the initial salary, raise and final salary for each faculty member as well as the total amounts for all faculty.

3.19 Modify your solution to 3.18 so that faculty earning $14,000 or less receive a raise of 4 percent; faculty earning $14,000–$16,500 receive a raise of 5½ percent; and faculty earning more than $16,500 receive a raise of 7 percent.

3.20 The assessor in the local township has estimated the value of all 14 properties in the township. Properties are assessed a flat tax rate of 125 mils per dollar of assessed value, and each property is assessed at only 28 percent of its estimated value. Write a program to compute the total amount of taxes that will be collected on the 14 properties in the township. (A mil is equal to 0.1 of a penny.) The estimated values of the properties are:

$50,000	$48,000
$45,500	$67,000
$37,600	$47,100
$65,000	$53,350
$28,000	$58,000
$52,250	$48,000
$56,500	$43,700

STANDARD, SCALAR, AND SUBRANGE DATA TYPES

4

4.1 INTRODUCTION

4.1.1 Introduction to Data Types and Expressions

While writing earlier programs you may have thought about, and perhaps even written, assignment statements containing constants, parentheses and more than one arithmetic operator. You may have wondered whether or not PASCAL could be used to instruct the computer to manipulate something other than numbers and, if so, how?

In this chapter, we will see that PASCAL can be used to manipulate character data, Boolean values (TRUE and FALSE), as well as numbers. We will learn how to form PASCAL assignment statements of greater complexity than those used so far to specify numeric data manipulations, and we will introduce some simple manipulations of character and Boolean data. We will also show how to define our own data types.

Several built-in functions of PASCAL will be introduced. We will illustrate their use with different types of data.

4.1.2 The Declaration Part of a Program

The standard data types (REAL, INTEGER, BOOLEAN, CHAR, STRING) were first introduced in Section 1.7. This chapter provides a formal discussion of these data types and an introduction to programmer-defined data types as well.

Before beginning the discussion, it is worthwhile to examine the syntax diagrams for the declaration part of a program provided at the top of Fig. 4.1. There are some syntactic forms and reserved words shown that we have not yet encountered. Any or all of these may be bypassed by following the vertical line on the left.

So far, we have used declaration statements beginning with the reserved words CONST and VAR. In this chapter, we shall see how to define new data types (following the reserved word TYPE). The declaration of procedures and functions will be covered in the next chapter.

If we examine the syntax diagram for constant definitions (also in Fig. 4.1) we see that each constant definition consists of two syntactic forms, identifier and constant, connected by an equal sign (=); each constant definition is followed by a semicolon. The syntax diagram for constant can be used to verify that the declarations below are valid.

```
CONST
  MAX = 100;
  MIN = -MAX;
  SPEEDOFLIGHT = 2.998E+6;
  NAME = 'ALICE';
```

MAX is used in the definition of MIN (value, −100). This is valid since the constant identifier MAX is defined first. The constant SPEEDOFLIGHT is associated with a real value expressed in scientific notation (2,998,000). The *string value* 'ALICE' is associated with the constant identifier NAME.

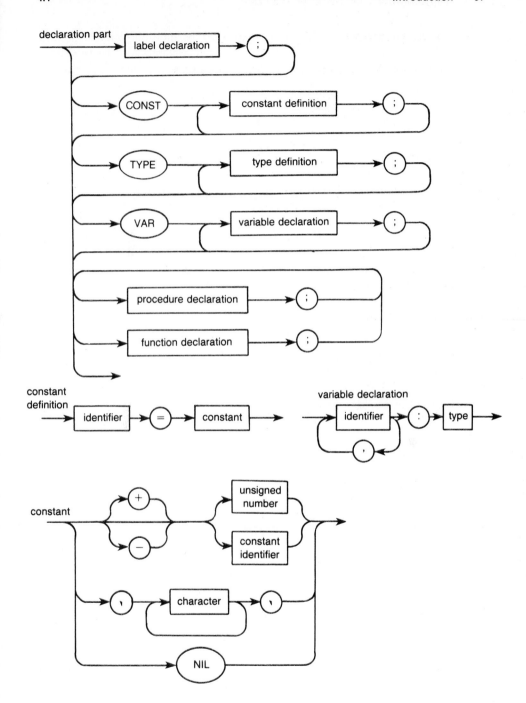

Fig. 4.1 Syntax charts for declaration part, constant definition, and variable declaration.

The syntax diagram specifies that there may be multiple variable declarations in a program following the word VAR. Each declaration consists of a list of identifiers followed by a colon, a data type and a semicolon. An example would be

```
VAR
    X, Y : REAL;
    COUNT, SUM : INTEGER;
    NEXT : CHAR;
```

4.2 NUMERIC DATA TYPES—REAL AND INTEGER

4.2.1 Review of Numeric Data Types

We have seen many examples involving the manipulation of real and integer type data in our programming so far. These data types are used in PASCAL for the storage and manipulation of numeric information.

These two data types were discussed in Section 1.7. We have used the data type INTEGER when counting and to represent data such as exam scores or widget orders which were known to be whole numbers. In most other instances, we used the data type REAL.

A real number in PASCAL is written as a string of digits containing a decimal point. There must be at least one digit before and after the decimal point.

Real data may also be represented using PASCAL scientific notation. A real data item written in scientific notation consists of a sign followed by a real number, followed by the letter E, another sign and an integer ($+$ signs may be omitted). (Examples: $-0.325E + 06$, $1.1E + 5$, $13764.25E - 10$).

In addition to the capability of storing fractions, real variables can be used to represent a considerably larger range of numbers than can integers. For example, on Apple computers, positive numbers from 10^{-38} (a very small fraction) to 10^{+38} may be stored in real variables; whereas the range of positive integers extends from 1 to 32767. The predefined constant MAXINT is equal to the largest integer that can be represented in each particular PASCAL implementation.

Operations involving integer variables are always exact, whereas there is often a small numerical error when real variables are manipulated. Also, on many computers, operations involving integer variables are considerably faster than operations involving real variables.

We have been careful to avoid mixing these two data types in expressions. Given the variable declarations

```
VAR
    COUNT : INTEGER;
    HOURS, RATE : REAL;
```

the expression

```
COUNT + 1
```

involves integer operands and computes an integer value; the expression

HOURS * RATE

involves real operands and computes a real value.

One reason for not mixing these types is the fact that many computers cannot directly manipulate real and integer data together.

Example 4.1:   If COUNT is an integer variable, the expression

COUNT + 2 . 5

is a mixed-type expression involving one integer operand (COUNT) and one real operand (2.5). In translating this expression, the PASCAL compiler must first generate an instruction to convert the integer operand to its equivalent real value before the indicated operation (+) can be performed. The result of an operation involving integer and real data is always a real value.

One additional reason for not mixing integer and real data is that PASCAL does not allow real values to be assigned to integer variables as the fractional part cannot be represented and would be lost. Hence, the assignment statements

COUNT : = 3 . 5 ;
COUNT : = COUNT + 1 . 0

would be illegal if COUNT is an integer variable. Since a whole number can always be considered to have a fractional part of zero, PASCAL allows integer values to be assigned to real variables; hence, the statement

HOURS : = COUNT + 10

would be legal.

Example 4.2:   The assignment statement

COUNT : = COUNT / 2

is illegal because the division operator, /, always computes a real value even when both its operands are integers. Hence, an expression being assigned to an integer variable must not contain any real data or the division operator.

4.2.2   Generalizing the Assignment Statement

In the first three chapters of the text, we used simple assignment statements containing expressions with, at most, one arithmetic operator (+ , − , *, /). Obviously, the PASCAL language would have a very limited mathematical capability if only expressions with a single operator were allowed. In fact, it is possible to represent almost any mathematical formula in PASCAL using expressions with multiple operators and parentheses. Parentheses are used to group terms in a PASCAL expression in the same way that they are used in algebra.

Example 4.3:   The following are all legal PASCAL expressions.

```
1.  7.5
2.  X + 7.5
3.  1.8 * C + 32
4.  A * (B + (C / D))
5.  (A - C) * (B - D)
6.  A - C * B - D
```

Since expressions 1 through 4 have real values, they may only be assigned to a real variable. Expressions 5 and 6 may be assigned to an integer variable only if A, B, C, and D are all integer variables. What is the difference between expressions 5 and 6?

Example 4.4:   In this example, the assignment statement

$$X := W / (Y + Z)$$

is evaluated assuming the real variable values shown below. (X is initially undefined.)

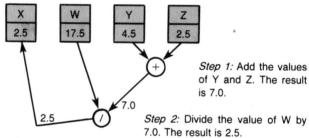

Step 1: Add the values of Y and Z. The result is 7.0.

Step 2: Divide the value of W by 7.0. The result is 2.5.

Step 3: Store the value of the expression in X.

Exercise 4.1:   Assuming X = 2.5, A = 4.0, B = 3.5, C = −3.0, D = 1.0, evaluate each of the expressions in Example 4.3.

4.2.3 Operators DIV and MOD

In addition to the arithmetic operators described in Table 1.1 (+, −, *, /), there are two operators, DIV and MOD, that may be used with integer operands only. The integer division operator, DIV, and modular division operator, MOD, are described in the next display.

Operators DIV and MOD

$$operand_1 \; DIV \; operand_2$$
$$operand_1 \; MOD \; operand_2$$

Interpretation: The operator DIV yields the integral part of the result of *operand₁* divided by *operand₂*; the operator MOD yields the remainder of this division. Both *operand₁* and *operand₂* must be integer constants, variables or expressions with integer values.

The expression 7 DIV 2 evaluates to the integral part of the result of 7 divided by 2 (value is 3). The expression 7 MOD 2 evaluates to the remainder of this division expressed as an integer (value is 1). This is because 7 divided by 2 is equal to 3 with a remainder of 1 as shown below:

$$
\begin{array}{r}
3 \quad \text{R1} \\
2 \overline{) \ 7} \\
\underline{6} \\
1
\end{array}
$$

Verify for yourself that N MOD 2 is equal to one if N is odd and zero (no remainder) if N is even.

The operators DIV and MOD may be used with integer operands only. Remember, an expression has an integer value if it involves only integer variables or constants and does not contain the real division operator, /.

Example 4.5: Several examples of the MOD and DIV operators are shown below. Verify that they are correct by performing the division.

expression	value
2 MOD 7	2
2 DIV 7	0
12 MOD 3	0
12 DIV 3	4
12 DIV 9	1
12 MOD 9	3

Example 4.6: Given the declarations

```
CONST
  PI = 3.14159;
  MAXI = 1000;
VAR
  X, Y : REAL;
  A, B, I : INTEGER;
```

the following statements are legal. They are evaluated assuming A is 3, B is 4 and Y is −1.0.

```
I := A MOD B              (I becomes 3)
I := (MAXI - 990) DIV A   (I becomes 3)
X := A / Y                (X becomes −3.0)
X := PI * Y               (X becomes −3.14159)
X := A DIV B              (X becomes 0.0)
X := A / B                (X becomes 0.75)
I := (MAXI - 990) MOD A   (I becomes 1)
```

The following statements are illegal; the reason each statement is illegal is written in parentheses following the statement.

I := A MOD Y	(Real operand Y for **MOD** operator)
I := PI * A	(Real value assigned to integer variable I)
X := PI·DIV Y	(Real operands for **DIV** operator)
I := A / B	(Real value assigned to integer variable I)
X := A MOD (A / B)	(Real operand (value of A / B) for MOD operator)

Exercise 4.2: Evaluate the following:

1) 22 DIV 7   7 DIV 22 22 MOD 7   7 MOD 22

Repeat this exercise for the pairs of integers:

2) 15, 16
3) 3, 23
4) 4, 16

Exercise 4.3: What values are assigned by the legal statements in Example 4.6, assuming A is 5, B is 2, and Y is 2.0?

4.2.4 Evaluating Arithmetic Expressions

In order to be certain that the PASCAL expressions we write produce the desired results, we must understand the way expressions are evaluated in PASCAL. For example, in the expression A + B * C, is the multiplication performed before the addition or vice versa? Is the expression X / Y * Z evaluated as (X / Y) * Z or X / (Y * Z)? We can formulate a set of *rules of evaluation* for PASCAL *expressions*. These rules, which are based upon the conventional rules of *operator precedence,* are summarized in Table 4.1.

(a) All parenthesized subexpressions must be evaluated first. Nested parenthesized subexpressions must be evaluated inside-out, with the innermost subexpression evaluated first.

(b) Operators in the same subexpression are evaluated in the following order:

  *, /, DIV, MOD first,
  +, −   last.

(c) Operators in the same subexpression and at the same precedence level (such as + and −) are evaluated left to right.

Table 4.1 Rules of Evaluation of Arithmetic Expressions

Example 4.7: Consider the expression

Z − (A + B DIV 2) + W * Y

containing integer variables only. The parenthesized *subexpression* (A + B DIV 2) is evaluated first [Rule (a)] beginning with B DIV 2 [RULE (b)]. Once the

value of **B DIV 2** is determined, it can be added to **A** to obtain the value of
(**A** + **B DIV 2**). Next the multiplication operation is performed [Rule (b)] and
the value for **W** * **Y** is determined. Then the value of (**A** + **B DIV 2**) is
subtracted from **Z** [Rule (c)], and, finally, this result is added to **W** * **Y**.

This sequence is illustrated in the diagram that follows. Each numbered circle shows the operator and the order in which it is evaluated. The lines connect
each operator with its operands.

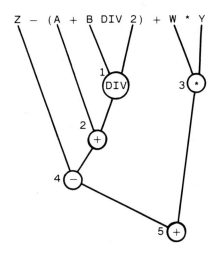

Example 4.8:   The formula for the area of a circle, $a = \pi r^2$, may be written in
PASCAL as

```
AREA := PI * RADIUS * RADIUS
```

where **PI** is the constant 3.14159. The evaluation of this formula is shown below.

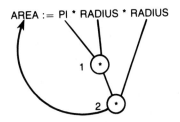

We shall see another way to specify **RADIUS** * **RADIUS** in the next section.

Example 4.9:   The formula for the average velocity, v, of a particle traveling on
a line between points p_1 and p_2 in time t_1 to t_2 is

$$v = \frac{p_2 - p_1}{t_2 - t_1}$$

This formula may be written and evaluated in PASCAL as shown below:

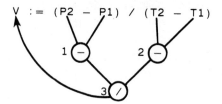

It should be obvious that inserting parentheses in an expression will affect the order of operator evaluation. If you are in doubt as to the order of evaluation that will be followed by the PASCAL compiler, you should use parentheses freely to specify clearly the intended order of evaluation.

Exercise 4.4:   Assume that you have the following variable declarations:

```
VAR
    COLOR, LIME, STRAW, YELLOW, RED, ORANGE : INTEGER;
    BLACK, WHITE, GREEN, BLUE, PURPLE, CRAYON : REAL;
```

Evaluate each of the statements below given the values: COLOR is 2, BLACK is 2.5, CRAYON is -1.3, STRAW is 1, RED is 3, PURPLE is 0.3E1.

```
a)  WHITE := COLOR * 2.5 / PURPLE
b)  GREEN := COLOR / PURPLE
c)  ORANGE := COLOR DIV RED
d)  BLUE := (COLOR + STRAW) / (CRAYON + 0.3)
e)  LIME := RED DIV COLOR + RED MOD COLOR
f)  PURPLE := STRAW / RED * COLOR
```

4.2.5   Writing Mathematical Formulas in PASCAL

There are two inherent difficulties in representing a mathematical formula in PASCAL; one concerns multiplication and the other concerns division. Multiplication can often be implied in a mathematical formula by writing the two items to be multiplied next to each other; e.g., a $=bc$. In PASCAL, however, the * operator must always be used to indicate multiplication as in:

$$A := B * C$$

The other difficulty arises in formulas involving division. We normally write these with the numerator and denominator on separate lines:

$$m = \frac{y - b}{x - a}$$

In PASCAL, all assignment statements must be written in a linear form; consequently, parentheses are often needed to separate the numerator from the denominator, and to indicate clearly the order of evaluation of the operators in the expression. The formula above would be written as

$$M := (Y - B) / (X - A)$$

Example 4.10: This example illustrates how several mathematical formulas can be written in PASCAL using expressions involving multiple operators and parentheses.

Mathematical formula	PASCAL expression
a. $b^2 - 4ac$	$B * B - 4 * A * C$
b. $a + b - c$	$A + B - C$
c. $\dfrac{a + b}{c + d}$	$(A + B) / (C + D)$
d. $\dfrac{1}{1 + X^2}$	$1 / (1 + X * X)$
e. $A \times - (B + C)$	$A * (- (B + C))$

The points just illustrated are summarized in the following list of *rules of formation* for PASCAL expressions.

1. Always specify multiplication explicitly by using the operator * where needed (see Example 4.10a).
2. Use parentheses when required to control the order of operator evaluation (see Examples 4.10c and d).
3. Never write two arithmetic operators in succession; they must be separated by an operand or parentheses (see Example 4.10e).

Exercise 4.5: Let A, B, C and X be the names of four variables of type real, and I, J and K the names of three type integer variables. Each of the statements below contains a violation of the rules of formation of arithmetic expressions. Rewrite each statement so that it is consistent with these rules.

a) X := 4.0 A * C   d) K := 3(I + J)
b) A := AC   e) X := A / BC
c) I := 2 * - J   f) I := J3

4.3 FUNCTIONS IN ARITHMETIC EXPRESSIONS

The *function* is a feature of PASCAL that is of considerable help in specifying numerical computations. Each function performs a different mathematical operation (square root, cosine, etc.) and computes a single value. Functions are referenced directly in an expression: the value computed by the function is then substituted for the function reference.

Example 4.11: SQRT is the name of a function that computes the square root of a non-negative value. In the statement

$$Y := 5.7 + SQRT(20.25)$$

the value computed by the function reference SQRT(20.25) is 4.5; the result of the evaluation of the addition operation is 10.2 (5.7 + 4.5), which is stored in the real variable Y.

PASCAL provides a number of standard mathematical functions, such as SQRT, that may be used by the programmer. The names and descriptions of these functions are given in Table 4.2. The function name is always followed by its *argument* enclosed in parentheses as shown in Example 4.11 (argument is 20.25). Any legal arithmetic expression may be used as an argument for these functions.

Name	Description of Computation	Argument	Result
ABS	The absolute value of the argument	real/integer	same as argument
EXP	The value of e (2.71828) raised to the power of the argument	real/integer	real
LN	The logarithm (to the base e) of the argument	real/integer	real
LOG	The logarithm (to the base 10) of the argument	real	real
PWROFTEN	The value of 10 raised to the power of the argument	integer	real
SQR	The square of the argument	real/integer	same as argument
SQRT	The positive square root of the argument	real/integer (positive)	real
ROUND	The closest integer value to the argument	real	integer
TRUNC	The integral part of the argument	real	integer
ATAN	The arc tangent of the argument	real/integer (radians)	real
COS	The cosine of the argument	real/integer (radians)	real
SIN	The sine of the argument	real/integer (radians)	real

Table 4.2 Mathematical Functions

Example 4.12:   The PASCAL functions SQR and SQRT may be used to compute the two roots of a quadratic equation in X of the form $AX^2 + BX + C = 0$. These roots are expressed in algebraic form as

$$r_1 = \frac{-B + \sqrt{B^2 - 4AC}}{2A}, \quad r_2 = \frac{-B - \sqrt{B^2 - 4AC}}{2A}$$

The PASCAL implementation would be

```
DISC := SQR(B) - 4 * A * C ;
IF DISC > 0 THEN
   BEGIN
      ROOT1 := (- B + SQRT(DISC)) / (2 * A);
      ROOT2 := (- B - SQRT(DISC)) / (2 * A)
   END (* IF *)
```

where the variable DISC is used to represent the *discriminant* $(B^2 - 4AC)$ of the equation. In this example, the argument of SQR is the variable B; the argument of SQRT is the variable DISC.

Except for ABS, SQR, ROUND and TRUNC, each of the functions listed in Table 4.2 *returns* (computes) a real value regardless of the argument type (real or integer). The type of the result computed by a reference to ABS or SQR is the same as the type of the argument.

The functions ROUND and TRUNC require arguments of type real and always return integer values. These functions determine the integral part of a real-valued expression; consequently the expressions

```
TRUNC(1.8 * X + 3.5)
ROUND(X * 2.5 / Y)
```

have integer values and may be assigned to an integer variable. TRUNC simply truncates, or removes, the fractional part of its argument; whereas, ROUND rounds its argument to the nearest whole number. (e.g. TRUNC(17.5) is 17 while ROUND(17.5) is 18; TRUNC(-3.8) is -3 while ROUND(-3.8) is -4)

Example 4.13:   The program in Fig. 4.2 illustrates the use of several arithmetic functions. The function references are inserted in the output list of the WRITELN statement. Since the argument of the SQRT function is ABS(X), the absolute value must be determined before the square root computation can be performed.

```
PROGRAM ARITHFUNC;
(* ILLUSTRATES ARITHMETIC FUNCTIONS *)

CONST
  SENTINEL = 0.0;

VAR
  X : REAL;

BEGIN
  WRITELN ('ENTER A REAL NUMBER OR 0.0 TO STOP');
  WRITELN;
  WRITELN ('X', 'TRUNC(X)' :16, 'ROUND(X)' :10,
           'ABS(X)' :10, 'SQR(X)' :10, 'SQRT(ABS(X))' :15);
  READLN (X);
  WHILE X <> SENTINEL DO
    BEGIN
      WRITELN (TRUNC(X) :17, ROUND(X) :10,
               ABS(X) :10:2, SQR(X) :10:2, SQRT(ABS(X)) :10:2);
      READLN (X)
    END (* WHILE *)
END.
```

```
ENTER A REAL NUMBER OR 0.0 TO STOP
```

X	TRUNC(X)	ROUND(X)	ABS(X)	SQR(X)	SQRT(ABS(X))
−7.8					
	−7	−8	7.80	60.84	2.79
49.0					
	49	49	49.00	2401.00	7.00
6.12					
	6	6	6.12	37.45	2.47
49.9					
	49	50	49.90	2490.01	7.06
−15.25					
	−15	−15	15.25	232.56	3.91
0.0					

Fig. 4.2 Arithmetic functions.

Example 4.14: The trigonometric functions SIN and COS are illustrated in the program in Fig. 4.3.

It is important to remember that the input argument to the trigonometric functions SIN, COS and ATAN must be expressed in radians. To convert from degrees, a measure familiar to most of us, we must use the fact that π radians equals 180 degrees. Using 3.14159 as an approximation of the value of π (accurate to five decimal places), we have

$$1 \text{ degree} = \pi/180 \text{ radians}$$
$$\theta \text{ degrees} = \theta \times \pi/180 \text{ radians}$$

as shown in the next program.

```
PROGRAM SINANDCOS;
(* AN ILLUSTRATION OF SIN AND COS FUNCTIONS *)


CONST
  PI = 3.14159;


VAR
  ANGLE : INTEGER;
  RADIANS : REAL;


BEGIN
  WRITELN,('ANGLE(IN DEGREES)', 'SIN(ANGLE)' :15,
           'COS(ANGLE)' :22);
  ANGLE := 0;
  WHILE ANGLE <= 180 DO
    BEGIN
      RADIANS := ANGLE * PI/180;
      WRITELN (ANGLE :9, SIN(RADIANS) :23, COS(RADIANS) :22);
      ANGLE := ANGLE + 15
    END (* WHILE *)
END.
```

ANGLE(IN DEGREES)	SIN(ANGLE)	COS(ANGLE)
0	0.00000	1.00000
15	2.58819E−1	9.65926E−1
30	5.00000E−1	8.66026E−1
45	7.07106E−1	7.07107E−1
60	8.66025E−1	5.00001E−1
75	9.65925E−1	2.58820E−1
90	1.00000	1.49012E−6
105	9.65926E−1	−2.58817E−1
120	8.66026E−1	−4.99998E−1
135	7.07108E−1	−7.07105E−1
150	5.00002E−1	−8.66024E−1
165	2.58822E−1	−9.65925E−1
180	2.98023E−6	−1.00000

Fig. 4.3 Trigonometric functions SIN and COS.

The WRITELN statement in the loop prints each angle followed by its sine and cosine. If you look closely at the output from the Example 4.14 program, you will note that neither the sine of 180 degrees nor the cosine of 90 degrees were computed to be identically zero. This is due to a loss of accuracy in the computations of these functions. Loss of accuracy is discussed in more detail in Section 4.9.

There is one additional function that may be used with an integer argument only. It is the function ODD that may be used to determine whether or not an integer variable or expression evaluates to an odd number. The function ODD is described in the next display.

Function ODD

ODD(*argument*)

Interpretation: The function ODD returns the value TRUE if its *argument* evaluates to an odd integer; otherwise, the value FALSE is returned.

The values TRUE and FALSE returned by function ODD are called *Boolean values*. The data type BOOLEAN is the subject of the next section.

Exercise 4.6: The numeric constant e is known as Euler's Number. It has had an established place in mathematics alongside the Archimedean number π for more than 200 years. The approximate value of e is 2.71828. Write a program that prints EXP(X) and LN(X) for integer values of X from 1 to 10.

Exercise 4.7: The formula for the velocity of a body dropped from rest is $v = gt$, where g is the acceleration due to gravity, and t is time (air resistance is ignored here). Write a loop to compute v at 10-second intervals (starting with $t = 0$) for a pickle dropped from a building that is 600 meters tall, with $g = 9.81$ meters/second. *Hint:* Use the formula $t = \sqrt{2s/g}$ to determine the time it takes for the pickle to hit the ground (s equals 600). Use this time to limit the number of repetitions of the loop that produces the table.

Exercise 4.8: Using the ROUND function, write a PASCAL statement to round any real value X to the nearest two decimal places. *Hint:* You will have to multiply by 100 before rounding.

4.4   BOOLEAN VARIABLES, EXPRESSIONS AND OPERATORS

4.4.1   Boolean Variables and Constants

Boolean expressions evaluate to the Boolean values TRUE or FALSE. We have used simple Boolean expressions, or conditions, to control loop repetition and to determine whether the True statement or False statement of an IF statement should be executed. Some examples of Boolean expressions used earlier are:

```
ORDER <= CURINV
ORDER <> SENTINEL
UNFILLED > 0
```

Boolean variables and constants can also be declared in PASCAL. A Boolean variable or constant can be set to either of the Boolean values, TRUE or FALSE. The statement

```
CONST
   DEBUG = TRUE;
```

specifies TRUE as the value of the Boolean constant DEBUG; the statement

```
VAR
    SWITCH, FLAG : BOOLEAN;
```

declares SWITCH and FLAG to be Boolean variables that may be assigned only the values TRUE and FALSE.

4.4.2 Boolean Operators

A Boolean variable or constant by itself is the simplest form of a Boolean expression (e.g., SWITCH). We have used the relational operators ($=$, $<$, $>$, etc.) with numeric data to form conditions or Boolean expressions (e.g. SALARY $<$ MINIMUM).

In addition, we can use the Boolean operators AND, OR and NOT to form more complicated Boolean expressions as shown below.

```
(SALARY < MINIMUM) OR (NUMDEPEND > 5)
(TEMP > 90) AND (HUMIDITY > .95)
ATHLETE AND (NOT FAILING)
```

The first Boolean expression could be used to determine which employees pay no income tax. It evaluates to TRUE if either condition in parentheses is TRUE. The second Boolean expression might be used to describe an unbearable summer day (high temperature and humidity). It evaluates to TRUE only when both conditions are TRUE. The third Boolean expression manipulates two Boolean variables (ATHLETE and FAILING). Any individual for whom this expression is TRUE is a candidate for intercollegiate sports.

The Boolean operators can be used with Boolean expressions only. They are described in the displays that follow.

Boolean Operator NOT

NOT *Boolean expression*

Interpretation: The NOT operator takes one operand which must be a *Boolean expression*. The value of the NOT operation is the *complement* (or negation) of its operand; i.e., NOT TRUE is FALSE and NOT FALSE is TRUE.

Boolean Operator AND

*Boolean expression*₁ AND *Boolean expression*₂

Interpretation: The AND operator takes two operands which must be Boolean expressions. The value of the AND operation is TRUE only if both operands are TRUE.

Boolean Operator OR

Boolean expression₁ OR *Boolean expression₂*

Interpretation: The OR operator takes two operands which must be Boolean expressions. The value of the OR operation is TRUE if either one or both operands are TRUE. The only case in which the value of the OR operation is FALSE is when both operands are FALSE.

When writing Boolean expressions, it is a good idea to enclose each Boolean subexpression in parentheses. In the absence of parentheses, the operator precedence shown in Table 4.3 is followed.

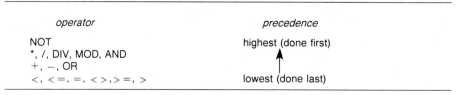

operator	precedence
NOT	highest (done first)
*, /, DIV, MOD, AND	
+, −, OR	
<, < =, =, < >,> =, >	lowest (done last)

Table 4.3 Operator Precedence Table

This table shows that the NOT operator has the highest precedence and that the relational operators have the lowest precedence. The arithmetic operators, along with AND and OR, fall in between. Since the relational operators have the lowest precedence, they may have to be used with parentheses to prevent syntax errors.

Example 4.15: The expression

$$X < Y + Z$$

involving the real variables X, Y and Z would be interpreted correctly as

$$X < (Y + Z)$$

since + has higher precedence than <. However, the expression

$$X < Y \text{ OR } Z < Y$$

would be erroneously interpreted as

$$X < (Y \text{ OR } Z) < Y$$

since OR has higher precedence than <. Obviously, (Y OR Z) is an illegal Boolean expression when Y and Z are real variables. Use parentheses as shown below to prevent a syntax error.

$$(X < Y) \text{ OR } (Z < Y)$$

Example 4.16:   The following are all legal Boolean expressions if X, Y and Z are type real, and FLAG is type Boolean. The value of each expression is shown in brackets assuming that X is 3.0, Y is 4.0, Z is 2.0 and FLAG is FALSE.

```
1.  (X > Z) AND (Y > Z)                          [TRUE]
2.  (X + Y / Z) <= 3.5                           [FALSE]
3.  (Z > X) OR (Z > Y)                           [FALSE]
4.  NOT FLAG                                      [TRUE]
5.  NOT FLAG OR ((Y + Z) >= (X - Z))             [TRUE]
6.  NOT (FLAG OR ((Y + Z) >= (X - Z)))           [FALSE]
7.  (X = 1.0) OR (X = 3.0)                        [TRUE]
8.  (0.0 < X) AND (X < 3.5)                       [TRUE]
9.  (X <= Y) AND (Y <= Z)                         [FALSE]
```

Example 3 is the PASCAL form of the relationship "Z greater than X or Y." It is often tempting to write this as

$$Z > X \text{ OR } Y$$

However, this is an illegal Boolean expression as the real variable Y cannot be an operand of the Boolean operator OR. Similarly, example 7 shows the correct way to express the relationship "X equal to 1.0 or 3.0" in PASCAL.

Example 8 is the PASCAL form of the relationship $0.0 < X < 3.5$, i.e., X lies between 0.0 and 3.5. Similarly, example 9 shows the PASCAL form of the relationship $X \leq Y \leq Z$.

We can also write assignment statements that assign a Boolean value to a Boolean variable. The statement

$$\text{SAME} := X = Y$$

assigns the value TRUE to the Boolean variable SAME when X and Y are equal; otherwise, the value of SAME is FALSE.

4.4.3   Program Flags

The prime numbers have been studied by mathematicians for many years. A *prime number* is an integer that has no divisors other than 1 and itself (e.g. 2, 3, 19, 37). In order to demonstrate that a number is not prime, we have to identify one or more divisors. In solving this problem, we introduce the use of a Boolean variable as a program flag.

Problem 4.1:   Find and print all exact divisors of an integer N other than 1 and N itself. If there are no divisors, print out the message "N is a prime number." The value of N will be provided as a data item to be read in by the program.

Discussion: The general approach we will take is to see whether we can find an integer, TRIALDIV, which divides N evenly (with no remainder). We shall test all integers between 2 and N − 1 as values of TRIALDIV.

The data table and algorithm follow. The data type of each variable is included in the data table.

Data Table for Problem 4.1

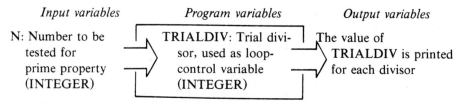

Input variables	Program variables	Output variables
N: Number to be tested for prime property (INTEGER)	TRIALDIV: Trial divisor, used as loop-control variable (INTEGER)	The value of TRIALDIV is printed for each divisor

Level One Algorithm

1. Read N.
2. Find and print all divisors of N between 2 and N − 1.
3. Print a message if N is prime.

In order to carry out Step 3, we need to know whether any divisors were found in Step 2. To accomplish this, we will introduce a Boolean variable, PRIME, whose value will indicate whether N is still considered prime (PRIME equal to TRUE) or is known to be not prime (PRIME equal to FALSE).

Program variables

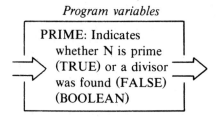

PRIME: Indicates whether N is prime (TRUE) or a divisor was found (FALSE) (BOOLEAN)

The variable PRIME is called a program flag. A program flag is a variable that is used to communicate to one program step the result of computations performed in another step. Initially, N will be considered prime, so PRIME is set to an initial value of TRUE. If a divisor is found in Step 2, PRIME should be reset to FALSE. The program will test PRIME at Step 3 to determine whether or not N is still considered a prime number. We will now complete the refinement of Steps 2 and 3.

Level Two Refinements

Step 2   *Find and print all divisors of N*

    2.1   Initialize PRIME to TRUE

 2.2 FOR TRIALDIV := 2 TO N − 1 DO
      2.3 Print TRIALDIV if it is a divisor of N and reset PRIME to
      FALSE

Step 3 *Print a message if N is prime*

 3.1 IF PRIME is TRUE THEN
     Print that N is prime

Step 2.3 must perform two separate operations if, and when, a divisor is
found. The refinement of Step 2.3 follows.

Level Three Refinements

Step 2.3

    2.3.1 IF TRIALDIV divides N THEN
         BEGIN
           Print TRIALDIV
           PRIME := FALSE
         END

As shown in Step 2 above, the algorithm checks all integers between 2 and
N − 1 inclusive as possible divisors of N. Since we know that there is no remainder when a divisor is exact, the Boolean expression

```
(N MOD TRIALDIV) = 0
```

may be used to test whether "TRIALDIV divides N" (Step 2.3.1).
    The program is given in Fig. 4.4 followed by two sample runs.

Program Style

Testing Program Flags

    Since PRIME is a Boolean variable, the simple Boolean expression

```
PRIME
```

may be used to test whether PRIME is TRUE instead of

```
PRIME = TRUE
```

which would have the same value.

```
PROGRAM PRIMENUMBER;
(* DETERMINES IF AN INTEGER IS A PRIME NUMBER *)

VAR
  N, TRIALDIV : INTEGER;
  PRIME : BOOLEAN;

BEGIN
  (* READ AN INTEGER *)
  WRITE ('ENTER AN INTEGER: '); READLN (N);

  (* FIND AND PRINT ALL DIVISORS OF N *)
  PRIME := TRUE;
  WRITELN ('LIST OF DIVISORS');
  FOR TRIALDIV := 2 TO N - 1 DO
    (* PRINT TRIALDIV IF IT DIVIDES N AND RESET PRIME *)
    IF (N MOD TRIALDIV) = 0 THEN
      BEGIN
        WRITELN (TRIALDIV :7);
        PRIME: = FALSE
      END; (* IF *)

  (* PRINT A MESSAGE IF N IS PRIME *)
  IF PRIME THEN
    WRITELN ('NO DIVISORS. ', N, ' IS PRIME'.)
END.

ENTER AN INTEGER: 100
LIST OF DIVISORS
      2
      4
      5
     10
     20
     25
     50

ENTER AN INTEGER: 29
LIST OF DIVISORS
NO DIVISORS. 29 IS PRIME
```

Fig. 4.4 Prime number program and sample runs.

Exercise 4.9: *For the more mathematically inclined.* The program shown in Fig. 4.4 tests all integer values between 2 and $N - 1$ inclusive to see if any of them divides N. This is, in fact, quite inefficient, for we need not test all of these values. Revise the algorithm shown in Fig. 4.4 to minimize the number of possible divisors of N that must be tested to determine whether or not N is prime. Make certain that your improved algorithm still works. (*Hints:* If 2 does not divide N, no other even number will divide N. If no integer value between 2 and $N/2$ divides N, then no integer value between $N/2 + 1$ and $N - 1$ will divide N. In fact, we can even specify a smaller maximum test value than $N/2$. What is it?)

4.5 STRING VARIABLES

4.5.1 Declaring String Variables

In UCSD PASCAL the data type STRING may be used for storing strings of characters. Up to 80 characters may be stored in a string variable. This limit may be changed by making an explicit declaration of type STRING[n] where n is an integer. The maximum length that can be declared is 255 characters. Although not required, explicit declaration should also be made if it is known beforehand that the string to be stored will contain fewer than 80 characters.

The declarations

```
VAR
    FIRST, LAST : STRING[15];
    ADDRESS : STRING[120];
    TITLE : STRING;
```

allocate storage for four string variables. Strings FIRST and LAST may each contain up to 15 characters, ADDRESS may contain up to 120 characters, and TITLE may contain up to 80 characters.

The symbols [and] may not be available on your keyboard. In this case, you will have to consult your PASCAL system manual to find the appropriate characters to use instead. On the Apple computer [is entered by pressing CTRL K simultaneously and] is entered by pressing SHIFT M. On the TRS-80, [is entered by pressing SHIFT ← simultaneously, and] is entered by pressing SHIFT →.

4.5.2 Storing String Data

FIRST and LAST (type STRING[15]) may each contain up to 15 characters. It is, of course, perfectly permissible to store fewer than 15 characters in FIRST or LAST; however, a *string overflow* error will result if you attempt to assign more than 15 characters. Only those characters actually stored in a string variable will be manipulated.

Example 4.17: The statements

```
FIRST := 'BILLY';
SECOND := 'JOEL';
WRITELN (FIRST, ' ', SECOND);
```

would cause the output line

```
BILLY JOEL
```

to be printed. If we later reassign FIRST and SECOND as

```
FIRST := 'B.';
SECOND := 'J.';
WRITELN (FIRST, SECOND);
```

the output line

```
B.J.
```

would be printed instead.

String data may also be read into string variables. When the statement

```
READLN (FIRST);
```

is executed, all characters typed before pressing the carriage return would normally be stored in FIRST. However, if more than 15 characters are typed, only the first 15 characters would be saved—any extra characters would be ignored. Unlike a string assignment, this would not cause an execution error.

4.5.3 Comparing String Data

The relational operators can be used to compare string data. As shown in Problem 3.4, if two strings of letters are compared, the result will depend on their lexicographic (dictionary) order.

Example 4.18:   The following Boolean expressions are all true.

```
'ACE'  <  'DEUCE'
'ACES'  >=  'ACE'
'CAT'  <  'DOG'
'SCAT'  <=  'SCATS'
'CAT'  <>  'CAT '
```

As shown above, strings of different lengths may be compared (e.g., 'ACE' < 'DEUCE'). As shown in the last line above, a blank character at the end of a string does make a difference. Obviously, the result of comparing two string variables will be based on the string data stored in those variables. We shall learn more about string comparison in the next section.

Exercise 4.10:   Under what circumstances would the Boolean expressions

```
FIRST  <  'FIRST'
FIRST  <  SECOND
```

be true?

4.6   CHARACTER VARIABLES AND FUNCTIONS

4.6.1   The Data Type CHAR

PASCAL provides a character data type that can be used for the storage and manipulation of the individual characters that comprise a person's name, address, etc. A character value consists of a single printable character (letter, digit, punctuation mark, etc.) enclosed in apostrophes. Character variables are declared using the reserved word CHAR in a declaration. A character value may be assigned to a character variable or associated with a constant identifier as shown below.

```
CONST
  STAR = '*';

VAR
  NEXTLETTER : CHAR;
```

```
BEGIN
    NEXTLETTER := 'A'
```

A character variable may be defined via a *character assignment statement* as shown above. Only a single character variable or value may appear on the right-hand side of a character assignment statement as there are no operators that manipulate character data. Character values may also be compared, read and printed.

Be careful not to confuse the data types CHAR and STRING[1]. These data types cannot be used interchangeably.

Example 4.19:   The program in Fig. 4.5 reads a sentence ending in a period and counts the number of blanks in the sentence. Each character typed after the prompting message is read into the variable NEXT and tested to see whether it is a blank. The statement

```
READ (NEXT)
```

reads one character at a time since NEXT is of type CHAR. In processing a READ (or READLN), the computer uses the declared type of a variable to determine whether a single character or an entire number or string should be entered. We shall discuss the differences between READ and READLN in Section 4.7.

```
PROGRAM BLANKCOUNT;
(* COUNTS THE NUMBER OF BLANKS IN A SENTENCE *)

CONST
    BLANK = ' ';
    PERIOD = '.';

VAR
    NEXT : CHAR;
    COUNT : INTEGER;

BEGIN
    (* PROCESS EACH CHARACTER UP TO THE PERIOD *)
    COUNT := 0;
    WRITELN ('TYPE A SENTENCE ENDING WITH A PERIOD');
    READ (NEXT);
    WHILE NEXT <> PERIOD DO
        BEGIN
            IF NEXT = BLANK THEN
                COUNT := COUNT + 1;
            READ (NEXT)
        END; (* WHILE *)

    WRITELN ('THE NUMBER OF BLANKS IS ', COUNT)
END.

TYPE A SENTENCE ENDING WITH A PERIOD
HERE IS ONE.
THE NUMBER OF BLANKS IS   2
```

Fig. 4.5 Counting blanks in a sentence.

Example 4.20:   The program in Fig. 4.6 reads a sentence ending in a period and prints each word on a separate line of output. Each character is read into the variable NEXT. If the character is a blank, then the current output line is terminated; otherwise, the character is printed on the current output line. All of the words shown at the bottom of Fig. 4.5 were provided in a single input line.

The statement

```
READ (KEYBOARD, NEXT)
```

differs from

```
READ (NEXT)
```

in that it reads a single character from the keyboard without echoing it on the screen; consequently, the program statement

```
WRITE (NEXT)
```

causes each non-blank character to be displayed for the first time.

```
PROGRAM WORDS;
(* PRINTS EACH WORD OF A SENTENCE *)
(* ON A SEPARATE LINE             *)

CONST
  BLANK = ' ';
  PERIOD = '.';

VAR
  NEXT : CHAR;

BEGIN
  (* CONTINUE UNTIL PERIOD IS READ *)
  READ (KEYBOARD, NEXT);
  WHILE NEXT <> PERIOD DO
    BEGIN
      (* ECHOPRINT CURRENT LETTER *)
      (* OR TERMINATE OUTPUT LINE *)
      IF NEXT <> BLANK THEN
        WRITE (NEXT)
      ELSE
        WRITELN;
      READ (KEYBOARD, NEXT)
    END (* WHILE *)
END.

THE
QUICK
BROWN
FOX
JUMPS
OVER
THE
LAZY
DOG
```

Fig. 4.6 Breaking a sentence into words.

Exercise 4.11:   Write a program that causes each character typed in to be duplicated. The string WHAT? would appear as WWHHAATT??

Exercise 4.12:   Modify the program in Fig. 4.5 to count the number of words in a sentence. The number of words is one more than the number of blanks if there is only one blank between words. Your program should ignore any extra blanks between words.

Exercise 4.13:   What would happen in Fig. 4.6 if more than one blank appeared between words of the sentence? Modify this program so that any extra blanks will be ignored.

Exercise 4.14:   Write a program that compresses or removes any blanks in a character string. All nonblank characters should be printed.

4.6.2   Character Manipulation Functions

In Fig. 4.5, the Boolean expressions

```
NEXT = BLANK
NEXT <> PERIOD
```

are used to determine whether two character variables have the same value or different values. Order comparisons can also be performed on character variables using the relational operators $<$, $<=$, $>$, $>=$. The order relations among characters are based on the internal numeric code or *ordinal number* associated with each character. A character is defined to be "less than" another character if its ordinal number is smaller. The ordinal numbers corresponding to the letters form an increasing sequence; hence, the order relation

$$'A' < 'B' < 'C' \ . \ . \ . \ < \ 'Z'$$

holds for the letters.

The characters '0' through '9' are not the same as the integers 0 through 9. However, their ordinal numbers form an increasing sequence; hence, the order relation

$$'0' < '1' < '2' < \ . \ . \ . \ < '9'$$

also holds.

The PASCAL function ORD returns the ordinal number of its character argument. For each character, this value is dependent upon the computer being used. However, on most computers, the value of ORD('B') is one more than the value of ORD('A') and one less than the value of ORD('C'). Similarly, the value of ORD('1') is one more than the value of ORD('0') and one less than the value of ORD('2'). (We shall assume that this is the case.)

The relationship between ORD('A') and ORD('0') determines whether the letter 'A' is considered less than the digit '0' or vice versa. The relative order of letters and digits is not specified in PASCAL and depends on the computer system. For the Apple computer, the digits precede the upper-case letters, and the upper-case letters precede the lower-case letters.

Example 4.21: Although the ordinal number corresponding to the character value '7' depends on the PASCAL system being used, the expression

$$ORD('7') - ORD('0')$$

evaluates to the integer seven on most computers (Why?).

Example 4.22: The program in Fig. 4.7 "encodes" a sentence by printing each letter followed by a numeric value. The letter A is replaced by 1, B by 2, etc. The assignment statement

$$CODE := ORD(NEXT) - ORD('A') + 1;$$

computes an integer value between 1 and 26 corresponding to each letter.

The Boolean expression

$$('A' <= NEXT) \text{ AND } (NEXT <= 'Z')$$

is true only when NEXT is a letter; therefore, any other characters that may be present are not encoded. The output shown is for the input sentence

THE QUICK BROWN FOX JUMPS OVER THE LAZY DOG.

The PASCAL function SUCC (successor) returns the character with the "next larger ordinal number." Hence, SUCC('A') is 'B' and SUCC('0') is '1'. By printing SUCC('Z'), we would find the character that directly follows the letters.

The PASCAL function PRED (predecessor) returns the character with the next smaller ordinal number. Hence, PRED('B') is 'A' and PRED('1') is '0'. The function SUCC is the *inverse* of PRED and PRED is the *inverse* of SUCC. This means that the value of SUCC(PRED('P')) or PRED(SUCC('P')) would be 'P'. We will continue our discussion of these functions in the section on scalar data types (Section 4.8.1).

```
PROGRAM ENCODE;
(* GENERATES A NUMERIC CODE FOR A SENTENCE *)

CONST
  BLANK = ' ';
  PERIOD = '.';
  STAR = '*';

VAR
  NEXT : CHAR;
  CODE : INTEGER;

BEGIN
  (* READ AND ENCODE EACH LETTER UP TO THE PERIOD *)
  READ (KEYBOARD, NEXT);
  WHILE NEXT <> PERIOD DO
    BEGIN
      IF NEXT = BLANK THEN
        WRITE (STAR :2)
      ELSE
        BEGIN
          (* COMPUTE CODE *)
          CODE := ORD(NEXT) - ORD('A') + 1;
```

(continued)

```
          WRITE (CODE :3)
        END; (* IF *)
      READ (KEYBOARD, NEXT)
    END; (* WHILE *)
  WRITELN (PERIOD)
END.
```

```
20 8 5 * 17 21 9 3 11 * 2 18 15 23 14 * 6 15 24 * 10 21 13 16
19 * 15 22 5 18 * 20 8 5 * 12 1 26 25 * 4 15 7.
```

Fig. 4.7   Encoding a string

    The function CHR determines the character corresponding to its integer argument. Hence, it is the *inverse* of the ORD function for the characters. A reference to CHR is undefined if its argument does not correspond to one of the ordinal numbers for the PASCAL character set. The function CHR is described in the next display.

The Function CHR

CHR(ordnum)

Interpretation: The value returned by CHR is the character with ordinal number corresponding to *ordnum,* where *ordnum* may be an integer constant or integer-valued expression.
Note: If there is no symbol that has *ordnum* as its ordinal number, the value of CHR is undefined.

Example 4.23: The *collating sequence* for a computer is a list of characters arranged in sequence according to ordinal number. The program in Fig. 4.8 will display part of the collating sequence for your computer. It prints 96 lines numbered 32 through 127. The statement

WRITELN (LINE, CHR(LINE) :2)

prints the number of each line followed by the character with that ordinal number. All the letters, digits and special symbols of PASCAL should be printed.

```
PROGRAM COLLATE;
(* PRINT COLLATING SEQUENCE *)

CONST
  MIN = 32;
  MAX = 127;
VAR
  NEXT : CHAR;
  LINE : INTEGER;

BEGIN
  (* PRINT EACH ORDINAL NUMBER AND CORRESPONDING CHARACTER *)
  FOR LINE := MIN TO MAX DO
    WRITELN (LINE, CHR(LINE) :2)
END.
```

Fig. 4.8   Printing the collating sequence.

Exercise 4.15: Modify the program in Example 4.22 to replace A by 26, B by 25, etc. instead. Also, provide two columns of output consisting of a character followed by its "code."

Exercise 4.16: Modify the program in Example 4.23 so that the collating sequence is printed as a string of characters and in reverse order.

4.7   MORE ON INPUT

4.7.1   Reading Numbers, Strings, and Characters

We have used the READ statement to enter individual characters and the READLN statement to enter string or numeric data. In this section, we shall present a more complete explanation of the data entry process in PASCAL.

When a READ or READLN statement is executed, the computer must read input data into memory. The number of characters actually read is determined by the type of the variable(s) receiving data. For example, if the variable is type CHAR, then only one character will be read.

Each data line that we type is terminated by pressing the carriage return (denoted by <CR>). The carriage return itself is considered a special character and is recognized by the PASCAL system. If the carriage return character is read when a variable of type CHAR is receiving data, the blank character will be stored in that variable. When the carriage return character is encountered while reading string data, this signals the computer that all characters in the string have been entered.

If the variable receiving data is type REAL or INTEGER, then the PAS-CAL system must read a numeric value. It does this by examining all input characters in sequence, ignoring any leading blanks and carriage returns, until the first non-blank character is encountered. If this character is neither a sign nor a digit, an error message is printed (illegal numeric character); otherwise, all characters following the first non-blank are processed until a character that cannot be part of the number (a blank, <CR>, letter, etc.) is encountered.

Example 4.24: If NUM1 and NUM2 are type REAL, the statement

                         READLN (NUM1 , NUM2)

would process the data lines below in the same way

                1.345 -6.78<CR>   │   1.345<CR>
                                    │ -6.78<CR>

It makes no difference whether the numeric data items are typed on one line or two; also, all leading blanks are ignored.

We have to be careful when mixing numeric data and character data on the same data line. Although we can't type anything after a string (Why not?), it is possible to type a string following a number or single character as shown next.

Example 4.25:   Given the declarations

```
VAR
    OPERATOR : CHAR;
    NUM1 : INTEGER;
    VAR1 : STRING;
```

The statement

```
READLN (NUM1, OPERATOR, VAR1)
```

would store the data line

```
1234*ACE<CR>
```

as shown below

The character * terminates the numeric data item (1234) and is stored in the variable OPERATOR (type CHAR).

     The statements

```
READLN (NUM1);
READLN (OPERATOR, VAR1);
```

would store the two data lines

```
1234<CR>
*ACE<CR>
```

in the same way. In this case, the first <CR> terminates the numeric data item, and the first character on the next line (*) is stored in OPERATOR.

4.7.2   READ and READLN

     There are two forms of the statement used for data entry in PASCAL, READ and READLN. Except for using the READ statement to enter individual characters, we have been using READLN for data entry. The reason for this will be discussed next.

     Whenever a READLN statement is executed, all characters typed on the current input line are processed; although extra characters at the end of the line will be "read" but not stored in memory. On the other hand, when a READ statement is executed, only those characters up to and including the last character stored in memory are processed. Any extra characters on the input line, including the carriage return character, may be processed by the next READ or READLN statement.

     The READLN statement can also be used without an input list. In this case, any characters on the current input line are effectively ignored as they are "read" but not stored in memory. Hence, the statements below behave identically.

```
        READLN (X,Y)    │    READ (X,Y);
                        │    READLN;
```

Example 4.26:   If the data lines

```
        135 ABC<CR>
        246<CR>
```

are read by the statements

```
        READLN (NUM1);
        READLN (NUM2)
```

then the first number (135) would be stored in NUM1. The remaining characters
on the first data line (through <CR>) would be ignored, and the next number
(246) would be stored in NUM2.

On the other hand, if the statements

```
        READ (NUM1);
        READ (NUM2)
```

are used to read the two data lines above, then the value of NUM1 will still be
stored correctly (135). However, an execution error (**IO ERROR: BAD INPUT
FORMAT**) will result when the PASCAL system encounters the letter A while
trying to read a numeric data item into NUM2. The statements

```
        READ (NUM1);
        READLN;
        READ (NUM2);
       ·READLN
```

will enter the data as desired.

If the statements

```
        READ (NUM1)
        READ (OPERATOR, VAR1);
```

were used in Example 4.25 to read the data lines

```
        1234<CR>
        *ACE<CR>
```

the result would be as shown below

The carriage return character at the end of the first line would be stored as a
blank (represented by □) in OPERATOR (type CHAR); the symbol * would become part of the string stored in VAR1.

Example 4.27:   If FIRST and SECOND are type STRING and the statements

```
READ (FIRST);
READ (SECOND);
```

are used to read a pair of strings typed on two data lines, the first string would
be stored in FIRST; however, the *null string* (a string of zero characters) would
be stored in SECOND. The reason for this is that the READ statement only
processes characters up to (but not including) the carriage return. The carriage
return character at the end of the first data line would also terminate the second
READ statement without any characters being read. The data lines would be entered correctly if READLN (FIRST) is used instead.

Exercise 4.17:   Explain what would happen if READLN were used instead of READ
in Fig. 4.5. How would the data have to be entered if READLN were used in Fig. 4.6?

4.7.3   The Function EOLN

When reading individual characters, it is often desirable to instruct the program to continue reading characters until it reaches the end of the current data
line. PASCAL provides the function EOLN for this purpose.

The EOLN function has an initial value of false. It will evaluate to true immediately after the character preceding the carriage return is read during execution of a READ statement only. It will be reset to false as soon as another character is read. The EOLN function always evaluates to false after a READLN
statement is executed.

The loop in Fig. 4.5 can be rewritten using the EOLN function as shown below. (The READ statement preceding the loop in Fig. 4.5 is not needed.)

```
(* PROCESS EACH CHARACTER ON THE INPUT LINE *)
WHILE NOT EOLN DO
   BEGIN
     READ (NEXT);
     IF NEXT = BLANK THEN
        COUNT :=   COUNT + 1
   END; (*WHILE*)
```

After each character is read and processed, the EOLN function is evaluated. If
the character just processed is part of the input sentence, the EOLN function
will evaluate to false (NOT EOLN is true) and the WHILE loop will be repeated. After the character preceding < CR > is processed, the EOLN function will
evaluate to true (NOT EOLN is false) and the WHILE loop will be exited.

The EOLN function is described in the next display.

EOLN Function

EOLN

Interpretation: The function EOLN returns a value of true if the character
preceding the carriage return was just read by a READ statement. It is reset
to false when the next READ or READLN statement begins execution.

Example 4.28:   The loop below

```
SUM := 0;
WHILE NOT EOLN DO
  BEGIN
    READ (NEXTNUM);
    SUM := SUM + NEXTNUM
  END; (* WHILE *)
WRITELN ('SUM = ', SUM)
```

will compute the sum of all numbers typed on a single data line. After each number on the line is read, it will be added to SUM and the EOLN function will be reevaluated. If the last number is followed by a carriage return, the EOLN function will evaluate to true and the loop will be exited. Note that loop exit will not occur if one or more blanks are typed before the carriage return is pressed.

Exercise 4.18:   Explain how you could use the loop in Example 4.28 to compute the sum of all numbers typed in regardless of whether they were all on the same line.

4.7.4   The Transcript Program

The next problem provides an illustration of reading numeric, string and character data.

Problem 4.2:   Write a program to generate student transcripts and compute the semester grade-point average for each student. The input data for this program will consist of each student's name, and the course identification, grade and credit hours for all courses taken during the semester.

Discussion: Before solving this problem, we must first determine how the data will be organized.

We shall assume that the data for each student begins with a header line containing the student's name, followed by all course data for that student. The data for each course will consist of a course identification string followed by the course grade and number of credits. A course identification string consisting of a slash (/) will terminate the course data for each student as shown in Fig. 4.9.

```
SALLY SMITH
CIS5
A   4
HIS120
B   3
GYM1
P   2
/
  .
  .
  .
```

Fig. 4.9 Sample data for transcript program.

To compute a student's semester grade-point average, GPA, we must divide the number of points earned, POINTS, by the number of credits taken, CRED-

ITS. The number of points earned for a course is determined by multiplying the credits for that course (CREDHOUR) by 4 for an A, 3 for a B, 2 for a C, 1 for a D, or 0 for an E. Any other grades will be ignored. The data table and algorithm follow.

Data Table for Problem 4.2

Constants

> ENDSTUDENT = '/', terminates each student's data
> SENTINEL = 'DONE', terminates all data

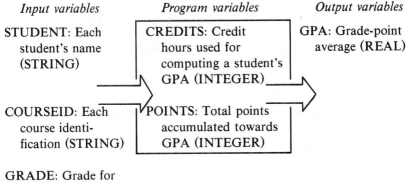

Input variables	*Program variables*	*Output variables*
STUDENT: Each student's name (STRING)	CREDITS: Credit hours used for computing a student's GPA (INTEGER)	GPA: Grade-point average (REAL)
COURSEID: Each course identification (STRING)	POINTS: Total points accumulated towards GPA (INTEGER)	

GRADE: Grade for each course (CHAR)

CREDHOUR: Credit hours for each course (INTEGER)

Level One Algorithm for Problem 4.2

1. For every student, compute and print the student's grade-point average.

Level Two Refinements

Step 1

1.1 Read the first student's name
1.2 WHILE more students DO
    BEGIN
        1.3 Process all course data and accumulate CREDITS and POINTS
        1.4 Compute and print semester grade-point average
        1.5 Read the next student's name
    END

The loop above will be executed for each student. It should terminate when the string "DONE" is read. The refinement of Step 1.3 will also contain a WHILE loop as shown next.

Level Three Refinements

Step 1.3

> 1.3.1 Initialize POINTS and CREDITS to zero
> 1.3.2 Read the first course identification into COURSEID
> 1.3.3 WHILE COURSEID < > ENDSTUDENT DO
> > BEGIN
> > > 1.3.4 Read GRADE and CREDHOUR
> > > 1.3.5 Add points earned for this course to POINTS and CREDHOUR to CREDITS
> > > 1.3.6 Read the next course identification into COURSEID
> > END

The program is shown in Fig. 4.10a. An IF statement is used to implement Step 1.3.5 assuming that only grades of A through E contribute to the student's grade-point average. The formula for points earned for a course

```
CREDHOUR * (ORD('A') - ORD(GRADE) + 4)
```

is based on the discussion in Section 4.6.2 and causes CREDHOUR to be multiplied by an integer from zero (for a grade of E) to four (for a grade of A). A sample run is provided in Fig. 4.10b.

```
PROGRAM TRANSCRIPT;
(* GENERATES STUDENT TRANSCRIPTS *)

CONST
  ENDSTUDENT = '/';
  SENTINEL = 'DONE';

VAR
  STUDENT, COURSEID : STRING;
  CREDHOUR, CREDITS : INTEGER;
  POINTS : INTEGER;
  GRADE : CHAR;
  GPA : REAL;

BEGIN
  (* READ THE FIRST STUDENT'S NAME *)
  WRITELN ('ENTER FIRST STUDENT NAME');
  READLN (STUDENT);

  (* PROCESS ALL COURSE DATA AND COMPUTE CREDITS AND POINTS *)
```
(continued)

```
WHILE STUDENT <> SENTINEL DO
  BEGIN
    CREDITS := 0;
    POINTS := 0;
    WRITE ('ENTER COURSE ID (OR /): ');
    READLN (COURSEID);
    WHILE COURSEID <> ENDSTUDENT DO
      BEGIN
        WRITE ('ENTER GRADE FOLLOWED BY CREDITS: ');
        READLN (GRADE, CREDHOUR);
        (* ADD POINTS EARNED FOR COURSE TO     *)
        (* POINTS AND CREDIT HOURS TO CREDITS *)
        IF (GRADE >= 'A') AND (GRADE <= 'E') THEN
          BEGIN
            POINTS := POINTS + CREDHOUR *
                     (ORD('A') - ORD(GRADE) + 4);
            CREDITS := CREDITS + CREDHOUR
          END;
        WRITE ('ENTER NEXT COURSE ID (OR /): ');
        READLN (COURSEID)
      END; (* WHILE *)

    (* COMPUTE AND PRINT SEMESTER GRADE POINT AVERAGE *)
    IF CREDITS <> 0 THEN
      GPA := POINTS / CREDITS
    ELSE
      GPA := 0.0;
    WRITELN ('GRADE POINT AVERAGE = ', GPA :4:2);
    WRITELN;

    (* READ THE NEXT STUDENT'S NAME *)
    WRITELN ('ENTER NEXT STUDENT NAME (OR DONE)');
    READLN (STUDENT)
  END (* WHILE *)
END.
```

Fig. 4.10a Transcript program.

```
ENTER FIRST STUDENT NAME
ELLIOT KOFFMAN
ENTER COURSE ID (OR /): CIS1
ENTER GRADE FOLLOWED BY CREDITS: A 3
ENTER NEXT COURSE ID (OR /): CIS2
ENTER GRADE FOLLOWED BY CREDITS: B 4
ENTER NEXT COURSE ID (OR /): /
GRADE POINT AVERAGE = 3.43

ENTER NEXT STUDENT NAME (OR DONE)
DONE
```

Fig. 4.10b Sample run of transcript program.

Program Style

Nested WHILE loops

There is a pair of nested WHILE loops in Fig. 4.10a. The inner loop is entered and executed through to completion during each repetition of the outer loop. The inner loop is used to process all course data for a given student. The body of this loop is executed once for every course record provided as input data.

Program Style

Use of sentinel values

One interesting feature of the transcript problem is that multiple sets of course data may be provided. Consequently, two sentinel values are needed. One to signal the end of each student's course data (the character /), and one to signal the end of all student data (the string "DONE").

4.8 SCALAR AND SUBRANGE DATA TYPES

4.8.1 Scalar Data Types

In all our programming so far, we have used the standard data types that are predefined in UCSD PASCAL (REAL, INTEGER, BOOLEAN, CHAR, STRING). We have been careful to use only the values associated with each of these types. For example, the values used with the standard type INTEGER are 0, 1, -1, 2, -2, etc. whereas the values used with the standard type BOOLEAN are TRUE and FALSE.

In many problems, we may wish to use other, more descriptive values. For example, if we are writing an inventory program for a beer distributor, then we might be interested in using values like BUD, COORS, SCHLITZ, etc. in our program. We could do this by defining a *scalar type* and listing the *scalar values* that may be used with a variable of that type. The declarations

```
TYPE
   BRAND = (BUD, COORS, SCHLITZ, MICHELOB);
VAR
   BEER : BRAND;
```

indicate that BRAND is a scalar type and that a variable of type BRAND (e.g. BEER) may be assigned any of the four values listed. The IF statement

```
IF BEER = COORS THEN
   WRITELN ('COORS PASSED THE TASTE TEST')
```

could be used to print a message when the scalar variable BEER contains the scalar value COORS.

The *type declarations* below define two scalar types, DAY and MONTH, that might be useful in a payroll program.

```
TYPE
    DAY = (SUNDAY, MONDAY, TUESDAY, WEDNESDAY, THURSDAY,
           FRIDAY, SATURDAY);
    MONTH = (JAN, FEB, MAR, APR, MAY, JUN, JUL, AUG, SEP,
             OCT, NOV, DEC);
```

Each declaration above specifies the name of a new data type and a list of scalar values for that type. The type declarations should be placed between any constant definitions (if present) and the variable declarations (See Fig. 4.1).

Having defined two new scalar types and associated scalar values, we can then declare variables of type DAY or MONTH.

```
VAR
    PAYDAY, FIRSTDAY, TODAY, TOMORROW : DAY;
    YEAREND, CURMONTH : MONTH;
    SALARY, TOTALSAL : REAL;
```

There are no operators for programmer-defined scalar values. Hence, only a single scalar value or scalar variable of the same type may appear in an expression being assigned to a scalar variable as shown next.

```
        YEAREND := DEC;
        FIRSTDAY := MONDAY;
        PAYDAY := FRIDAY;
        TODAY := FIRSTDAY
```

The first three statements assign a scalar value to a scalar variable as shown. The value and the variable must correspond in type. The last statement would cause the value of the scalar variable FIRSTDAY (type DAY) to be copied into TODAY (also type DAY). The statements

```
        PAYDAY := 5;
        PAYDAY := JAN
```

would be illegal as neither 5 nor JAN are legal scalar values for type DAY.

The IF statement

```
IF (TODAY = PAYDAY) AND (CURMONTH = YEAREND) THEN
   WRITELN ('TOTAL SALARY FOR YEAR = ', TOTALSAL)
```

causes a message and value to be printed if both equality relations are true.

The IF statement

```
        IF TODAY = SATURDAY THEN
            TOMORROW := SUNDAY
        ELSE
            TOMORROW := SUCC(TODAY)
```

uses the successor function (SUCC) to define TOMORROW. The successor function returns the next value listed in the type declaration of DAY (e.g. If the value of TODAY is MONDAY, TOMORROW will be defined as TUESDAY). The successor of the last scalar value listed in the scalar type declaration is undefined; hence, it would be erroneous to evaluate SUCC(SATURDAY). The predecessor function finds the previous scalar value in the list, e.g., PRED(SATURDAY) evaluates to FRIDAY, PRED(JAN) is undefined.

The function ORD is used to find the ordinal number corresponding to a scalar value. The ordinal number indicates the relative position of the scalar value in the list of values specified in the type declaration. The first scalar value in each list has an ordinal number of 0. Hence, the values of ORD(SUNDAY) and ORD(JAN) are zero; the values of ORD(MONDAY) and ORD(FEB) are one, etc.

Just as for character values, the order relations for scalar values are determined by their corresponding ordinal numbers. Hence, the Boolean expressions

```
SUNDAY  <  TUESDAY
TUESDAY  >  PRED(TUESDAY)
```

would both be TRUE.

It is also possible to use scalar variables and values to control the execution of a FOR statement (see Section 3.5.1). The header statements

```
FOR TODAY  := SUNDAY TO THURSDAY DO
FOR TODAY  := THURSDAY DOWNTO SUNDAY DO
```

may be used to implement loops that will be executed for the scalar values SUNDAY (ordinal number 0) through THURSDAY (ordinal number 5) inclusive.

The standard data types INTEGER, BOOLEAN and CHAR are also considered to be scalar types. The reason for this is that all the possible values associated with each of these types may be *enumerated,* or listed, just as for programmer-defined scalar types. This is not the case for type REAL.

The functions ORD, PRED and SUCC may be used with all three standard scalar types. The displays that follow summarize what we have learned about scalar type declarations and the functions ORD, PRED and SUCC.

Scalar Type Declaration

scalar type = (*list of scalar values*)

Interpretation: A new data type named *scalar type* is defined. The only values that can be assigned to a variable of this type are specified in the *list of scalar values.*

Note: Scalar values must be identifiers (i.e., start with a letter followed by letters and digits only). Each scalar value can appear in only one scalar type declaration. The scalar type declarations must be preceded by the word TYPE.

As indicated in the above display, each scalar value can appear in only one scalar type declaration. This requirement is necessary so that the compiler can unambiguously associate a scalar value in the program body with a particular scalar type. Since each number is already associated with the standard type **REAL** or **INTEGER**, it would be erroneous to declare a number as a scalar value.

It would also be incorrect to use a string value (e.g. 'SUNDAY') as a scalar value. Only identifiers that are not yet defined may be scalar values.

The Function ORD

ORD(*argument*)

Interpretation: The value returned by ORD is the ordinal number of its *argument*. The *argument* must evaluate to a programmer-defined scalar value or any value corresponding to the types **BOOLEAN**, **CHAR**, or **INTEGER**.

The Function PRED

PRED(*argument*)

Interpretation: PRED returns the value whose ordinal number is one less than the ordinal number of its *argument*. The *argument* must evaluate to a programmer-defined scalar value or any value corresponding to the standard types **BOOLEAN**, **CHAR** or **INTEGER**.
Note; If the ordinal number of the *argument* is zero, the value of PRED is undefined.

The Function SUCC

SUCC(*argument*)

Interpretation: SUCC returns the value whose ordinal number is one more than the ordinal number of its *argument*. The *argument* must evaluate to a programmer-defined scalar value or any value corresponding to the standard types **BOOLEAN**, **CHAR** or **INTEGER**.
Note: If the *argument* has the largest ordinal number for its type, the value of SUCC is undefined.

Exercise 4.19:   Given that the relation FALSE < TRUE holds, evaluate the following:

```
a. ORD(TRUE)
b. PRED(TRUE)
c. SUCC(FALSE)
d. ORD(TRUE) - ORD(FALSE)
```

Exercise 4.20:   Evaluate the following:

```
a. ORD(FRIDAY) - ORD(SUNDAY)
b. ORD(JUN) - ORD(JAN)
c. ORD(DEC)
d. ORD(PRED(SATURDAY))
```

4.8.2   Reading and Printing Scalar Values

The use of scalar variables makes PASCAL programs easier to read and understand. It is not necessary to invent an arbitrary numeric code to quantify non-numerical values; the scalar values can be used directly in the program.

Unfortunately, PASCAL does not allow the direct reading or printing of scalar values. Hence, we must normally read or print the corresponding ordinal number instead of the scalar value. We will illustrate this process in Section 4.8.5.

4.8.3   Subrange Types

Often, in writing programs we know beforehand that certain variables will be limited in their range of values. For example, in processing employee records, we can be certain that all our employees are between the ages of 10 and 100. If we encounter an age outside this range, it is likely that a mistake has been made in our program or that our input data are erroneous. Presumably, this error will be noticed if we read the printout carefully; however, mistakes often slip by. It would be nice if we could easily instruct the computer to inform us when the integrity of our data becomes suspect.

The subrange feature of PASCAL enables the programmer to specify reasonable bounds on variable values. The declarations below

```
TYPE
   AGE = 10..100;
   LETTER = 'A'..'Z';
```

define a subrange of the integers named AGE and a subrange of the characters named LETTER. We can then declare variables of these subrange types

```
VAR
   WORKAGE : AGE;
   NEXTCHAR : LETTER;
```

During program execution, if the number stored in WORKAGE is less than 10 or greater than 100, program execution will terminate and a diagnostic message will be printed. Similarly, if the character stored in NEXTCHAR contains a digit or punctuation symbol (not a letter), program execution will terminate.

PASCAL also allows subranges of previously declared scalar types to be defined. Hence, the declarations

```
TYPE
   DAY = (SUNDAY, MONDAY, TUESDAY, WEDNESDAY, THURSDAY,
          FRIDAY, SATURDAY);
   SCHOOLDAY = MONDAY..FRIDAY;
```

define SCHOOLDAY as a subrange of the scalar type DAY. A variable of type SCHOOLDAY can assume any of the scalar values MONDAY through FRIDAY.

A scalar value may appear in only one scalar type declaration; however, the same scalar value may be found in more than one subrange. In declaring subranges, we must be certain that the ordinal number of the first value specified is less than the ordinal number of the last value in the subrange. Subranges may not be defined over the real numbers. The subrange type declaration is described in the next display.

Subrange Type Declaration

$$sub\text{-}type = minval \ldots maxval$$

Interpretation: A new data type named *sub-type* is defined. *Minval* is the smallest value that may be assigned to a variable of type *sub-type*; *maxval* is the largest value that may be assigned. *Minval* and *maxval* must be scalar values for the same scalar type (either standard or previously defined). ORD (*minval*) must be less than ORD (*maxval*).

Note: A subrange type declaration must be preceded by the word TYPE and any scalar type declaration defining *minval* and *maxval*.

Subranges provide a convenient means of detecting unusual occurrences in our programs. Since we don't want our programs to "cry wolf" too often, we should be certain that the subranges specified are adequate for any reasonable set of data.

4.8.4 Subrange Operators and Type Compatibility

A variable whose type is a subrange may be manipulated in the same way as any other operand of the same *base type*. For example, the variable WORKAGE (type AGE) declared in the last section may be used with any of the operators that manipulate type INTEGER data (its base type). However, before storing a new value in the variable WORKAGE, the compiler always checks to make sure that it is within the required range (ten to 100).

These concepts may be expressed more formally using the concepts of type and assignment compatibility. Two data types are considered *type compatible* if they are the same type, or one is a subrange of the other, or they are both subranges of the same type. An expression is considered *assignment compatible* with a variable if their types are compatible, or if the expression is type integer and the variable is type real. Also, if the variable type is a subrange, then the value of the expression must be within range. If a variable and an expression are assignment compatible, then the expression may be assigned to the variable without error.

Example 4.29: The assignment statement

```
WORKAGE := WORKAGE - 95
```

is syntactically correct although it will result in a run-time error if executed. The expression is not assignment compatible with a variable of type AGE.

4.8.5 Use of Scalar and Subrange Types

The next example illustrates the use of scalar and subrange types.

Example 4.30:   The payroll program in Fig. 4.11a processes data of the form

```
WILLIAM SMILEY
1234        4.65        20
   1     8.0
   2     7.5
   3     7.5
   4     6.0
   5     7.5
   6     4.0
```

The employee's name, identification number (1234) and hourly rate ($4.65) are read in and the salary for the current week (week 20) is computed. Each time card above contains the ordinal number of the day (read into DAYNUMBER) and the hours worked on that day. The employee is paid double for each hour worked on the weekend. The program finds and prints the number of weekday and weekend hours worked as well as the salary for the week.

  The statement beginning with the word CASE and ending with END (* CASE *) is called a CASE statement and is used to convert the ordinal number of the day worked (0 through 6) to its corresponding scalar value (SUNDAY through SATURDAY). Remember, the scalar value cannot be read directly. If the value of DAYNUMBER matches the number listed to the left of the colon, the assignment statement on that line is executed, thereby defining TODAY. (The CASE statement will be studied further in the next chapter.) The IF statement adds the hours worked (HOURS) to WEEKDAY or WEEKEND depending on the value of TODAY. The program output is shown in Fig. 4.11b.

Program Style

Automatic range checking for integers

  In Fig. 4.11a, the type of each variable used for storage of an integer value is declared as a subrange. This practice should be followed whenever possible as it provides automatic range checking on the values stored in these variables during program execution.

```
PROGRAM NEWPAYROLL;
(* COMPUTES SALARY PAYING DOUBLE TIME ON WEEKENDS *)

TYPE
   DAY = (SUNDAY, MONDAY, TUESDAY, WEDNESDAY,
          THURSDAY, FRIDAY, SATURDAY);
   DAYRANGE = 0..6;
   IDRANGE = 1111..9999;
   WEEKRANGE = 1..52;
```

(continued)

```
VAR
  HOURS, RATE, SALARY, WEEKEND, WEEKDAY : REAL;
  TODAY : DAY;
  DAYNUMBER : DAYRANGE;
  IDNUMBER : IDRANGE;
  WEEK : WEEKRANGE;
  NAME : STRING[40];

BEGIN
  (*READ IN WEEK, EMPLOYEE NAME, NUMBER, AND HOURLY RATE*)
  WRITE ('WEEK = '); READLN (WEEK);
  WRITE ('ENTER EMPLOYEE NAME: '); READLN (NAME);
  WRITE ('ENTER EMPLOYEE NUMBER: #'); READLN (IDNUMBER);
  WRITE ('HOURLY RATE = $'); READLN (RATE);

  (* PROCESS EACH TIME CARD AND COMPUTE HOURS WORKED *)
  WEEKEND := 0.0;
  WEEKDAY := 0.0;
  WRITELN;
  WRITELN ('ENTER NEGATIVE NUMBER TO STOP OR');
  WRITE ('HOURS WORKED: '); READLN (HOURS);
  WHILE HOURS >= 0.0 DO
    BEGIN
      WRITE ('ORDINAL DAY NUMBER: '); READLN (DAYNUMBER);
      (* CONVERT TO A DAY OF THE WEEK *)
      CASE DAYNUMBER OF
        0 : TODAY := SUNDAY;
        1 : TODAY := MONDAY;
        2 : TODAY := TUESDAY;
        3 : TODAY := WEDNESDAY;
        4 : TODAY := THURSDAY;
        5 : TODAY := FRIDAY;
        6 : TODAY := SATURDAY
      END; (* CASE *)

      (* ADD HOURS TO WEEKDAY OR WEEKEND *)
      IF (TODAY = SATURDAY) OR (TODAY = SUNDAY) THEN
        WEEKEND := WEEKEND + HOURS
      ELSE
        WEEKDAY := WEEKDAY + HOURS;

      WRITE ('HOURS WORKED: '); READLN (HOURS)
    END; (* WHILE *)

  (* COMPUTE AND PRINT HOURS WORKED AND SALARY *)
  WRITELN;
  WRITELN ('WEEKDAY HOURS = ', WEEKDAY :4:1,
           ' WEEKEND HOURS = ', WEEKEND :4:1);
  SALARY := (WEEKDAY * RATE) + (WEEKEND * 2 * RATE);
  WRITELN ('SALARY FOR WEEK ', WEEK :2,
           ' = $' SALARY :7:2)
END.
```

Fig. 4.11a Payroll program with overtime.

```
WEEK = 20
ENTER EMPLOYEE NAME: WILLIAM SMILEY
ENTER EMPLOYEE NUMBER: #1234
HOURLY RATE = $4.65

ENTER NEGATIVE NUMBER TO STOP OR
HOURS WORKED: 4
ORIDNAL DAY NUMBER: 0
HOURS WORKED: 8
ORDINAL DAY NUMBER: 1
HOURS WORKED: 6.5
ORDINAL DAY NUMBER: 2
HOURS WORKED: 8
ORDINAL DAY NUMBER: 3
HOURS WORKED: 6.5
ORDINAL DAY NUMBER: 4
HOURS WORKED: 7.5
ORDINAL DAY NUMBER: 5
HOURS WORKED: -1

WEEKDAY HOURS = 36.5 WEEKEND HOURS =  4.0
SALARY FOR WEEK 20 = $ 206.93
```

Fig. 4.11b   Sample output for payroll program.

4.9   NUMERICAL ERRORS*

All of the errors discussed in earlier chapters have been programmer errors. However, even if a program is correct, it still may compute the wrong answer, especially if extensive numerical computation is involved. The cause of error is the inherent inaccuracy in the internal representation of data having fractional parts (real values as opposed to integer values).

All information is represented in the memory of the computer as a number. For most computers, data are represented using the binary number system (base 2), rather than the decimal system (base 10). Thus, the representation of information in the memory of the computer is in terms of binary digits (0's and 1's), rather than decimal digits (0-9). However, as shown in the next example, many decimal numbers do not have precise binary equivalents and, therefore, can only be approximated in the binary number system. (Is it possible to represent the fraction 1/3 exactly in the decimal number system?)

Example 4.31:   This example lists several binary approximations of the number 0.1. The precise decimal equivalent of the binary approximation and the numerical error are also shown.

_____

*This section may be omitted.

Number of binary digits	Binary approximation	Decimal equivalent	Numerical error
4	.0001	0.0625	0.0375
5–7	.0001100	0.09375	0.00625
8	.00011001	0.09765625	0.00234375
9	.000110011	0.099609375	0.000390625

We can see from this example that, as the number of binary digits used to represent 0.1 is increased, the decimal equivalent of the binary number gets closer to 0.1. The number of binary digits that can be used to represent a real number in the memory of the computer is limited by the size of a memory cell. The larger the cell, the larger the number of binary digits and the greater the degree of accuracy that can be achieved.

Due to the error in representing the decimal number 0.1, the loop below

```
TRIAL := 0.0;
WHILE TRIAL <> 1.0 DO
    BEGIN
        .
        .
        .
    TRIAL := TRIAL + 0.1
    END (* WHILE *)
```

may not terminate on some computers. That is because the value accumulated in TRIAL may never be sufficiently close to 1.0 for the loop repetition test (TRIAL < > 1.0) to fail.

It would be better to use TRIAL < 1.0 as the condition for loop repetition in place of the inequality test above. Even though the loop might then execute 11 times on some computers instead of ten times (why?), at least it will always terminate. Wherever possible, you should use integers to control loop repetition rather than real values.

The effect of a small error can become magnified when a long sequence of computations is performed. For example, in determining the sine or cosine of an angle, many operations are performed by the computer on real numbers (see Example 4.14). The repeated execution of a relatively simple computation may also cause a magnification of *round-off error* as the inaccuracy in each individual computation is accumulated. Such magnification can sometimes be diminished through the use of special functions or a reordering of the computations. You should be aware that the problem of round-off error exists, and that it may cause the same PASCAL program to produce different results when run on computers having memory cells of different sizes.

4.10   COMMON PROGRAMMING ERRORS

4.10.1   Data Type Errors

In working with arithmetic expressions, especially complicated ones, a good deal of care is necessary. Some of the more common programming errors involving expressions and assignment statements are listed below, along with their remedies. The compiler diagnostics for these errors may be similar in wording to the short descriptions that are given here, or they may simply read "Unrecognizable Statement" or "Illegal Statement." In some cases, the error may not be detected, since it may result in a legal statement, although not the one intended.

1. *Mismatched or unbalanced parentheses.* The statement in error should be carefully scanned, and left and right parentheses matched in pairs, inside-out, until the mismatch becomes apparent. This error is often caused by a missing parenthesis at the end of an expression.
2. *Missing operator in an expression.* This error is usually caused by a missing multiplication operator, *. The expression in error must be scanned carefully, and the missing operator inserted in the appropriate position.
3. *Arithmetic underflow or overflow or division by zero attempted.* Another type of numerical error is caused by attempts to manipulate very large real numbers or numbers that are very close in value to zero. For example, dividing by a number that is almost zero may produce a number that is too large to be represented (*overflow*). You should check that the correct variable is being used as a divisor and that it has the proper value. Arithmetic *underflow* occurs when the magnitude of the result is too small to be represented.
4. *String overflow* is caused by assigning to a string variable a string value that has more characters than can be stored in that variable.

One type of programming error that cannot be detected by a compiler involves the writing of expressions that are syntactically correct, but do not accurately represent the computation called for in the problem statement. All expressions, especially long ones, must be carefully checked for accuracy. Often, this involves the decomposition of complicated expressions into simpler subexpressions producing intermediate results. The intermediate results should be printed and compared with hand calculations for a simple, but representative data sample.

In declaring scalar types, make sure that a scalar value does not appear in more than one scalar type declaration. However, the same scalar value may appear in more than one subrange declaration.

The use of subranges should help in the detection of erroneous computations. If the value computed is outside the subrange, an "out of range" error message will be printed.

Care should be taken to ensure that the standard functions are not given illegal arguments. The functions **PRED**, **SUCC** and **ORD** cannot be used with real arguments. The function CHR will only accept an integer as its argument. On some systems, taking the square root or logarithm of a negative argument will produce an error message. Attempts to compute the logarithm of 0 will produce an error message on most systems. Program execution will terminate immediately after the error message is printed.

An additional source of error is using data and operators of one data type with another. For example, only variables of type INTEGER or REAL may be used with the arithmetic operators; only INTEGER data may be used with the operators MOD and DIV. It is normally incorrect to assign or read a value of one data type into a variable of another type, however, integer values may be stored in real variables.

4.10.2   READLN and EOLN Errors

A common mistake in using the EOLN function to control WHILE loop repetition is to expect the WHILE loop to terminate immediately when the carriage return character is read. However, this is not the case: the remainder of the loop body is always executed and loop repetition cannot terminate until the loop control step is reached and the EOLN function is reevaluated.

When reading strings or individual characters, be wary of the effect of the carriage return character. Remember, the carriage return character will be stored as a blank in a variable of type CHAR. If the carriage return character is the first character encountered while reading data into a string variable, the null string will be stored in that variable. To avoid these difficulties use the READLN statement whenever possible as it processes all characters typed on a data line including the carriage return. You should only use the READ statement to read individual characters.

As we mentioned earlier, one must be extremely careful when mixing strings and numbers on the same data line. We recommend keeping the string data and numerical data separated.

4.11   SUMMARY

The specification of multi-operator arithmetic assignment statements and the use of additional data types have been discussed. The rules of formation and evaluation of arithmetic expressions were summarized. The operations of addition ($+$), subtraction ($-$), multiplication (*), division (/), integer division (DIV) and modulo division (MOD) may be combined according to these rules to form complicated arithmetic expressions.

We also discussed the use of arithmetic functions in expressions. These expressions may be used in assignment statements on the right-hand side of the assignment operator ($:=$), in the output list portion of a write statement, and as arguments in function references. The arithmetic operators may only be used with operands of type INTEGER or REAL

Three other standard data types were introduced, STRING, CHAR and BOOLEAN, as well as user-defined scalar types and subranges. The Boolean operators AND, OR and NOT were used to form more complex Boolean expressions.

The concept of an ordinal number was discussed and the functions PRED, SUCC and ORD were introduced for the manipulation of scalar data types. The function CHR, the inverse of ORD, was used to find the character corresponding to a given ordinal number. In addition, the character by character reading of a string of input characters was illustrated, along with some simple examples of character string manipulation. The functions that manipulate strings will be described in Chapter 6.

Table 4.4 summarizes the operators and functions that may be used with each data type discussed in this chapter. The last column of this table indicates whether data of this type may be read or written. (See also Appendix 2.)

Data type	Operators	Argument of functions	READ/WRITE capability
real	:=, +, −, *, / =,<,<=,>,>=, <>	ABS, EXP, LN, SQR, SQRT, ROUND, TRUNC, ATAN, SIN, COS, LOG	READ/WRITE
integer	:=, +, −, *, / MOD, DIV =,<,<=,>,>=,<>	PRED, SUCC, CHR ABS, EXP, LN, SQR, SQRT, ATAN, SIN, COS, ODD, ORD, PWROFTEN	READ/WRITE
Boolean	:= =,<,<=,>,>=,<> NOT, AND, OR	PRED, SUCC, ORD	No
String	:= =,<,<=,>,>=,<>		READ/WRITE
char	:= =,<,<=,>,>=,<>	PRED, SUCC, ORD	READ/WRITE
scalar	:= =, <,<=,>,>=,<>	PRED, SUCC, ORD	No
subrange*	:= =,<,<,=,>,>=,<>	PRED, SUCC, ORD	Depends on base type

* The operators and functions listed here are the minimum. A subrange may also be used with the operators and functions for its base type. READ/WRITE capability is provided for a subrange of the integers or type CHAR.

Table 4.4 Data Types and Allowable Operators

We also illustrated the reading and printing of character strings and numerical data. We showed how the system function EOLN can be used to control input loop repetition. We also introduced the READ statement and showed how it could be used to read individual characters. We saw that the form READ (KEY-BOARD, . . .) could be used to suppress echoing the characters typed as data.

PROGRAMMING PROBLEMS

4.3   Write a program to compute the sum $1+2+3+4+...+N$ for any positive integer N; use a loop to accumulate this sum (S1). Then compute the value S2 by the formula

$$S2 = \frac{(N+1)N}{2}$$

Have your program print both S1 and S2, compare them, and print a message indicating whether or not they are equal. Test your program for values of $N = 1, 7, 25$.

4.4   The Hoidy Toidy baby furniture company has ten employees, many of whom work overtime (more than 40 hours) each week. They want a payroll program that reads the weekly time records (containing employee name, hourly rate (r), and hours worked (h) for each employee) and computes the gross salary and net pay as follows:

$$g = \text{gross salary} = \begin{cases} \text{h x r (if h} <= 40) \\ 1.5 \text{ r(h} - 40) + 40\text{r (if h} > 40) \end{cases}$$

$$p = \text{net pay} = \begin{cases} g \text{ (if g} <= \$65) \\ g - (15 + 0.45g) \text{ (if g} > \$65) \end{cases}$$

The program should print a five-column table listing each employee's name, hourly rate, hours worked, gross salary, and net pay. The total amount of the payroll should be printed at the end. It can be computed by summing the gross salaries for all employees. Test your program on the following data:

name	rate	hours
IVORY HUNTER	3.50	35
TRACK STAR	4.50	40
SMOKEY BEAR	3.25	80
OSCAR GROUCH	6.80	10
THREE BEARS	1.50	16
POKEY PUPPY	2.65	25
FAT EDDIE	2.00	40
PUMPKIN PIE	2.65	35
SARA LEE	5.00	40
HUMAN ERASER	6.25	52

4.5   Write a program to read in a collection of integers and determine whether each is a prime number. Test your program with the four integers 7, 17, 35, 96.

4.6   Let n be a positive integer consisting of up to 10 digits, $d_{10}d_9 ... d_1$. Write a program to list in one column each of the digits in the number n. The rightmost digit d_1 should be listed at the top of the column. (*Hint:* If $n = 3704$, what is the value of *digit* as computed according to the following formula?)

$$\text{digit} = n \text{ MOD } 10$$

Test your program for values of n equal to 6, 3704, and 170498.

4.7 An integer N is divisible by 9 if the sum of its digits is divisible by 9. Use the algorithm developed for Problem 4.6 to determine whether or not the following numbers are divisible by 9.

$$N = 154368$$
$$N = 621594$$
$$N = 123456$$

4.8 Redo Problem 4.7 by reading each digit of the number to be tested into the character variable DIGIT. Form the sum of the numeric values of the digits. [*Hint:* The numeric value of DIGIT (type CHAR) is ORD(DIGIT) – ORD('0').]

4.9 Each month a bank customer deposits $50 in a savings account. The account earns 6.5 percent interest, calculated on a quarterly basis (one-fourth of 6.5 percent each quarter). Write a program to compute the total investment, total amount in the account, and the interest accrued, for each of 120 months of a 10-year period. You may assume that the rate is applied to all funds in the account at the end of a quarter regardless of when the deposits were made.

The table printed by your program should begin as follows:

MONTH	INVESTMENT	NEW AMOUNT	INTEREST	TOTAL SAVINGS
1	50.00	50.00	0.00	50.00
2	100.00	100.00	0.00	100.00
3	150.00	150.00	2.44	152.44
4	200.00	202.44	0.00	202.44
5	250.00	252.44	0.00	252.44
6	300.00	302.44	4.91	307.35
7	350.00	357.35	0.00	357.35

Print all values accurate to two decimal places. How would you modify your program if interest were computed on a daily basis?

4.10 Compute a table of values of $X/(1 + X^2)$ for values of $X = 1,2,3,...,50$. Your table of values should be accurate to four decimal places and should begin as follows

X	$X/(1 + X^2)$
1	.5000
2	.4000
3	.3000
4	.2353
5	.1923
.	.
.	.
.	.

4.11 The interest paid on a savings account is compounded daily. This means that if you start with STARTBAL dollars in the bank, then at the end of the first day you will have a balance of

$$\text{STARTBAL} \times (1 + \text{rate}/365)$$

dollars, where rate is the annual interest rate (0.06 if the annual rate is 6 percent). At the end of the second day, you will have

$$\text{STARTBAL} \times (1 + \text{rate}/365) \times (1 + \text{rate}/365)$$

dollars, and at the end of N days you will have

$$\text{STARTBAL} \times (1 + \text{rate}/365)^N$$

dollars. Write a program that will process a set of data records, each of which contains values for **STARTBAL**, rate, and N and compute the final account balance.

4.12 Write a data table, algorithm and computer program to solve the following problem:

Compute the monthly payment and the total payment for a bank loan, given:

1. the amount of the loan
2. the duration of the loan in months
3. the interest rate for the loan

Your program should read in one record at a time (each containing a loan value, months value, and rate value), perform the required computation and print the values of the loan, months, rate, and the monthly payment, and total payment.

Test your program with at least the following data (and more if you want)..

Loan	Months	Rate
16000	300	12.50
24000	360	13.50
30000	300	15.50
42000	360	14.50
22000	300	15.50
300000	240	15.25

Notes:
1. The formula for computing monthly payment is

$$\text{monthly} = \left[\frac{\text{rate}}{1200.} \times \left(1. + \frac{\text{rate}}{1200.}\right)^{\text{months}} \times \text{loan}\right] \Bigg/ \left[\left(1. + \frac{\text{rate}}{1200.}\right)^{\text{months}} - 1.\right]$$

2. The formula for computing the total payment is

$$\text{total} = \text{monthly} \times \text{months}$$

Also, you may find it helpful to introduce additional variables defined below in order to simplify the computation of the monthly payment. You can print the values of ratem and expm to see whether your program's computations are accurate.

$$\text{ratem} = \text{rate}/1200.$$
$$\text{expm} = (1. + \text{ratem})$$

(*Hint:* You will need a loop to multiply expm by itself months times.)

4.13 The rate of radioactive decay of an isotope is usually given in terms of the half-life, H (the time lapse required for the isotope to decay to one-half of its original mass).

For the strontium 90 isotope (one of the products of nuclear fission), the rate of decay is approximately .60/H. The half-life of the strontium 90 isotope is 28 years. Compute and print; in table form, the amount remaining after each year for up to 50 years from an initial point at which 50 grams are present. (*Hint:* For each year, the amount of isotope remaining can be computed using the formula

$$r = \text{amount} * C^{(\text{Year}/H)}$$

where amount is 50 grams (the initial amount), and C is the constant $e^{-0.693}$ ($e = 2.71828$).)

4.14   Write a program that will scan a sentence and replace all multiple occurrences of a blank with a single occurrence of a blank.

4.15   Read a group of words separated by a blank. Echo print each word followed by a count of the number of letters it contains.

4.16   Read in a pair of characters representing the beginning and end of a range of characters respectively. Then read a group of words separated by a blank and print out each word whose first letter falls in the specified range.

4.17   Write a program that translates a string of words to Pig Latin. (*Hint:* You should save the first letter of each word and then echo print all letters up to the next blank. When the blank is reached, print the first letter of the current word followed by 'AY'. The character following a blank should be saved as the first letter of the next word.

INTERMEDIATE
CONTROL
STRUCTURES

5

5.1   INTRODUCTION

One of the most fundamental ideas of computer programming and problem solving concerns the subdivision of large and complicated problems into smaller, simpler and more manageable subproblems. Once these smaller tasks have been identified, the solution to the original problem can be specified in terms of these tasks; and the algorithms and programs for the smaller tasks can be developed separately.

We have tried to emphasize this technique of programming in all earlier examples through the use of algorithm refinement. In this process, each major part of a problem was identified in a level one algorithm and then broken down further into smaller subproblems during successive stages of refinement. A number of special control structures were introduced that enabled us to implement the solution to each of these subproblems in terms of clearly defined groups of statements.

PASCAL has other features, functions and procedures that facilitate solving problems in terms of their more manageable parts. Through the use of functions and procedures, we can write programs in much the same way as we refine algorithms. That is, we list the sequence of tasks that must be performed at a particular level and then provide the implementation details for tasks requiring extensive refinement as separate functions or procedures. The application of these features in the *top-down* approach to programming will be illustrated in this chapter.

We will first discuss the implementation of decisions with several alternatives. A new control structure, the CASE statement, will be introduced for this purpose. The use of compound, or nested, IF statements will also be illustrated.

5.2   MULTIPLE-ALTERNATIVE DECISIONS

5.2.1   The CASE Statement

There are many decisions in which there are multiple (more than two) alternatives to consider. One example is the new payroll problem of Fig. 4.11 which differentiates between seven ordinal numbers representing days of the week. We found the CASE statement to be a convenient way to perform this categorization. The CASE statement is described in the next display.

CASE Statement

```
             CASE selector OF
                 label₁: statement₁;
                 label₂: statement₂;
                          ·
                          ·
                          ·
                 labelₙ: statementₙ
             END
```

Interpretation: The *selector* (an expression) is evaluated and compared to each of the case labels. Each label is a list of one or more possible values for the *selector*, separated by commas. Only one *statement*$_i$ will be executed; if the value of the *selector* is listed in *label*$_i$, then *statement*$_i$ is executed. Control is next passed to the first statement following the case END. Each *statement*$_i$ may be a single or compound PASCAL statement.
Note 1: If the value of the *selector* is not listed in any case label, no statement is executed and control is passed to the first statement following the case END.
Note 2: A *selector* value may appear in, at most, one case label.
Note 3: The type of each value must correspond to the type of the *selector* expression.
Note 4: Any scalar or subrange data type is permitted (including INTEGER, BOOLEAN and CHAR, but not REAL or STRING.)

As indicated in Note 1 of the CASE statement display, nothing is done if the selector value does not match a case label. If no action is to be performed for a particular case label, then this could be indicated by placing the ";" or END (for the last case) immediately after the ":".

Example 5.1: The CASE statement could also be used in the transcript program (see Fig. 4.10a) to differentiate between other categories of grades besides those that are incorporated in the grade-point average (A through E). If there is a pass-fail option, a grade of P (pass) should increase credits earned only (accumulated in PASSCREDITS); a grade of F (fail) is ignored. Similarly, grades of W (withdraw) and I (incomplete) are ignored. The CASE statement implementation of this multiple-alternative decision is shown in Fig. 5.1.

```
CASE GRADE OF
   'A', 'B', 'C', 'D', 'E' :
                 BEGIN
                     POINTS := POINTS + CREDHOUR * (ORD('A')
                                            - ORD(GRADE) + 4);
                     CREDITS := CREDITS + CREDHOUR
                 END;
     'P' : PASSCREDITS := PASSCREDITS + CREDHOUR;
     'F', 'I', 'W' :
END (* CASE *)
```

Fig. 5.1 Categorization of GRADE.

It is not necessary that the CASE labels 'F', 'I' and 'W' be listed as nothing is done when the selector GRADE matches these values. In standard PASCAL, if GRADE has a value not listed as a case label, execution will be terminated and an error diagnostic will be printed. Note that it is not possible to represent the case label list for the first case as 'A'..'E'.

5.2.2 Compound IF Statement

There are situations in which the CASE statement cannot effectively be used to distinguish between multiple alternatives: for example, it may not be possible to write a scalar-valued selector expression that applies to all alternatives, or it may be too difficult to list all possible values of a selector as case labels. When this happens, a compound IF statement may be used instead.

Fig. 5.2 is a flow diagram of a decision that distinguishes between three different alternatives. It is implemented below using a compound (or nested) IF statement.

```
IF condition₁ THEN
     statement₁
ELSE
     IF condition₂ THEN
         statement₂
     ELSE
         statement₃
```

The above statement indicates that if $condition_1$ is TRUE, then $statement_1$ is executed; otherwise, if $condition_2$ is TRUE, then $statement_2$ is executed. If both conditions are FALSE, then $statement_3$ is executed.

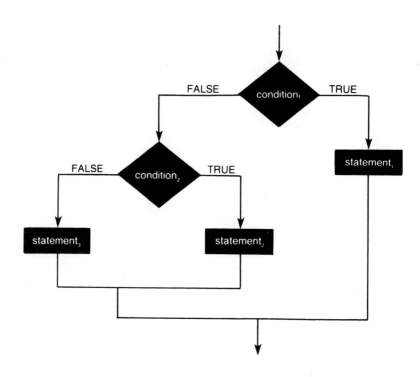

Fig. 5.2   Decision with three alternatives.

Compound IF statements can become quite complex. If there are more than three alternatives and indentation is not done consistently, it may be difficult for the programmer to determine to which IF a given ELSE clause belongs. (In PASCAL, this is the closest IF without an ELSE clause.) For this reason, we prefer to represent compound IF statements using the form below.

```
IF condition₁ THEN
    statement₁
ELSE IF condition₂ THEN
    statement₂
ELSE
    statement₃
```

Example 5.2: The compound IF statement below is used to differentiate between three different categories of exam scores (0–59, 60–89, 90–100).

```
IF SCORE >= 90 THEN
    WRITELN ('OUTSTANDING SCORE ', SCORE)
ELSE IF SCORE >= 60 THEN
    WRITELN ('SATISFACTORY SCORE ', SCORE)
ELSE
    WRITELN ('UNSATISFACTORY SCORE ', SCORE)
```

The compound IF statement may be extended to differentiate between n different categories $(n >= 3)$ as shown in the next display.

Compound IF Statement

```
IF condition₁ THEN
    statement₁
ELSE IF condition₂ THEN
    statement₂

        .
        .
        .

ELSE IF conditionₙ THEN
    statementₙ
ELSE
    statementₑ
```

Interpretation: *Condition*$_1$, *condition*$_2$, etc. are tested in sequence until a condition is reached that evaluates to TRUE. Only one *statement*$_i$ will be executed: if *condition*$_i$ is the first condition that is TRUE, then *statement*$_i$ is executed. If none of the conditions is TRUE, then *statement*$_E$ is executed. Regardless of which statement is executed, control is next passed to the first statement following *statement*$_E$. Each *statement*$_i$ (and *statement*$_E$) may be a single or compound PASCAL statement.

Note: The word ELSE and statement$_E$ may be omitted. In this case, none of the statements in the compound IF are executed when all conditions are FALSE.

Unlike the CASE statement, the compound IF is not a separate syntactic form in PASCAL. Rather, it simply provides a convenient means for organizing combinations, or nests, of IF statements. The CASE statement is the preferred method for implementing multiple-alternative decisions.

Program Style

Using statement$_E$ to verify data values

In Example 5.2, the ELSE alternative (statement$_E$) is executed by default for all exam scores of 59 or less. Although all exam scores are expected to be positive, it is normally a good idea to use statement$_E$ to print an error message in case the "impossible" happens and the value of SCORE is negative, or SCORE is greater than 100. As shown below, this can be done by tightening the first condition and adding an extra condition to verify that SCORE is positive.

```
IF (SCORE >= 90) AND (SCORE <= 100) THEN
    WRITELN ('OUTSTANDING SCORE ', SCORE)
ELSE IF SCORE >= 60 THEN
    WRITELN ('SATISFACTORY SCORE ', SCORE)
ELSE IF SCORE >= O THEN
    WRITELN ('UNSATISFACTORY SCORE ', SCORE)
ELSE
    WRITELN ('INVALID SCORE ', SCORE)
```

Exercise 5.1: Implement Example 5.2 using a CASE statement.

Exercise 5.2: Implement Example 5.1 using a compound IF statement.

Exercise 5.3: You are writing a program to print grade reports for students at the end of each semester. After computing and printing each student's grade point average (maximum 4) for the semester, you should use the grade point average to make the following decision:

  If the grade point average is 3.5 or above, print DEAN'S LIST;
  If the grade point average is above 1 and less than or equal to 1.99, print PROBA-
  TION WARNING;
  If the grade point average is less than or equal to 1, print YOU ARE ON PROBA-
  TION NEXT SEMESTER.

Write the PASCAL program segment using a compound IF statement.

5.2.3 Application of Multiple-alternative Decisions

The following problem illustrates the use of the CASE statement and the compound IF.

Problem 5.1: Write a program that determines whether a string of input characters is a real number, an integer, or non-numeric. The string should be printed followed by its category. Ignore any blanks that may be present.

Discussion: Each character should be examined and printed in sequence. If every character is a digit, then the string is an integer. If a single decimal point occurs, then the string is a real number. If more than one decimal point or any other character occurs, then the string is non-numeric. (We will ignore the possibility of a real number expressed in scientific notation.) Each number may begin with an optional + or − sign.

The data table is provided below followed by the level one algorithm with refinement of Step 1.

Data Table for Problem 5.1

| *Input variables* | *Program variables* | *Output variables* |

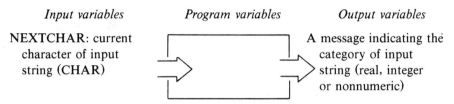

NEXTCHAR: current character of input string (CHAR)

A message indicating the category of input string (real, integer or nonnumeric)

Level One Algorithm

1. Read the first non-blank character and test for a sign.

2. Find the string category by reading each character and determining whether the string contains a single decimal point or any illegal characters. Ignore any blanks.

3. Print the string category.

Level Two Refinements

Step 1   *Read and test the first non-blank character*

   1.1   Read the first non-blank character into NEXTCHAR
   1.2   IF NEXTCHAR is a sign THEN
         Read NEXTCHAR

The refinement of Step 1.1 will use a WHILE loop to skip over any leading blanks as shown next.

Level Three Refinements

Step 1.1

   1.1.1   Read the first character into NEXTCHAR
   1.1.2   WHILE NEXTCHAR is a blank DO
         Read the next character into NEXTCHAR

In order to refine Steps 2 and 3, we will introduce a scalar variable CATE-
GORY with three scalar values (NODECIMAL, DECIMAL, NONNUMERIC).
The value of CATEGORY will be defined in Step 2 and tested in Step 3. The
additional data table entries and algorithm refinements are provided next.

Data types

CATTYPE = (NODECIMAL, DECIMAL, NONNUMERIC)

Program variables

CATEGORY : A scalar
variable representing
the category of the in-
put string (CATTYPE)

Additional Level Two Refinements

Step 2   *Find the string category*

2.1   Initialize CATEGORY to NODECIMAL
2.2   WHILE NOT EOLN DO
        BEGIN
              2.3 Reset CATEGORY to DECIMAL if NEXTCHAR is
                   the first decimal point; reset CATEGORY to NONNU-
                   MERIC if NEXTCHAR is not a digit or blank.
                   Read the next character into NEXTCHAR
        END

Step 3   *Print the string category*

3.1   CASE CATEGORY OF
        NODECIMAL : Print that the string is an integer
        DECIMAL : Print that the string is a real number
        NONNUMERIC : Print that the string is not a number
      END

A compound IF statement is used to refine Step 2.3 as shown next.

Additional Level Three Refinements

Step 2.3

2.3.1   IF NEXTCHAR is the first decimal point THEN
              BEGIN
                   CATEGORY := DECIMAL
                   Read NEXTCHAR
              END
              ELSE IF NEXTCHAR is a digit THEN

(*continued on page 158*)

```
PROGRAM STRINGTYPE;
(* STRING CATEGORY PROGRAM *)

TYPE
  CATTYPE = (NODECIMAL, DECIMAL, NONNUMERIC);

VAR
  NEXTCHAR : CHAR;
  CATEGORY : CATTYPE;

BEGIN
  (* READ AND TEST FIRST NON-BLANK CHARACTER *)
  WRITELN ('ENTER A STRING');
  READ (NEXTCHAR);
  WHILE NEXTCHAR = ' ' DO
    READ (NEXTCHAR);
  IF (NEXTCHAR = '+') OR (NEXTCHAR = '-') THEN
    READ (NEXTCHAR);

  (* FIND CATEGORY OF STRING *)
  CATEGORY := NODECIMAL;
  WHILE NOT EOLN DO
    BEGIN
      IF (NEXTCHAR = '.') AND (CATEGORY = NODECIMAL) THEN
        (* NEXTCHAR IS FIRST DECIMAL POINT *)
        BEGIN
          CATEGORY := DECIMAL;
          READ (NEXTCHAR)
        END
      ELSE IF (NEXTCHAR >= '0') AND (NEXTCHAR <= '9') THEN
        (* NEXTCHAR IS A DIGIT *)
        READ (NEXTCHAR)
      ELSE IF NEXTCHAR = ' ' THEN
        READ (NEXTCHAR)
      ELSE
        (* NEXTCHAR IS NOT A DIGIT OR BLANK *)
        BEGIN
          CATEGORY := NONNUMERIC;
          READ (NEXTCHAR)
        END (* IF *)
    END; (* WHILE *)

  (* PRINT CATEGORY OF STRING *)
  CASE CATEGORY OF
    NODECIMAL  : WRITELN ('IS AN INTEGER');
    DECIMAL    : WRITELN ('IS A REAL NUMBER');
    NONNUMERIC : WRITELN ('IS NON-NUMERIC')
  END (* CASE *)
END.

ENTER A STRING
123.456
IS A REAL NUMBER
```

Fig. 5.3 String category program.

```
                    Read NEXTCHAR
                ELSE IF NEXTCHAR is a blank THEN
                    Read NEXTCHAR
                ELSE
                    BEGIN
                        CATEGORY := NONNUMERIC
                        Read NEXTCHAR
                    END
```

The condition "NEXTCHAR is the first decimal point" in Step 2.3.1 may be refined as "NEXTCHAR is a decimal point and CATEGORY is NODECIMAL".

The program is shown in Fig. 5.3.

Program Style

Character comparisons

The program in Fig. 5.3 contains several examples of character comparisons and the use of the Boolean operators, AND and OR. The first Boolean expression is TRUE if NEXTCHAR is equal to ' + ' or ' − '. In the compound IF statement inside the loop (Step 2.3 of the algorithm), the first condition is true if NEXTCHAR contains a decimal point and a decimal point or nondigit has not yet occurred (value of CATEGORY is NODECIMAL).

The test for a digit is performed by determining whether NEXTCHAR is within the range '0' through '9'. This is valid since the ordinal numbers for the characters '0' through '9' form an increasing sequence. We shall learn a better way to perform this test in PASCAL by using the set data type in Chapter 7.

Exercise 5.4: Indicate how the program in Fig. 5.3 could be modified to recognize PASCAL scientific notation as a fourth category.

5.3 TOP-DOWN PROGRAMMING AND FUNCTIONS

5.3.1 Top-down Programming

Early in Chapter 2, we indicated that a desirable goal in problem solving was to break a complicated problem into independent subproblems and work on these subproblems separately. We have practiced this technique of problem decomposition throughout the text by drawing a level one algorithm outlining the subproblems to be solved as a list of steps. We have then separately refined each of these subproblems to fill in the details of an algorithm, subdividing each subproblem still further when necessary. This technique of specifying algorithms through stepwise refinement is often referred to as *top-down programming*.

Up to now, the logic or flow of control in the sample programs was relatively straightforward and easy to follow. Most programs consisted of short sequences of structures with little or no nesting. We now have the tools and the skill to write more complicated programs involving several levels of nesting. Such programs can become quite cumbersome and difficult to follow unless proper techniques are followed in their design and implementation.

Although we have used top-down programming in designing the algorithms in the text, we have not yet been able to carry this top-down process through to the implementation of our programs. What we would like to do is implement our programs in a stepwise manner as well. This will involve writing an initial program segment (the *main program*) that looks much like a level one algorithm. The program statements corresponding to the refinement of a subproblem will be written together as a separate program module called a *function or procedure.*

In order to write programs in this way, we must be able to designate sequences of statements that are to be treated as a separate module. In PASCAL, this is done through the *function or procedure declaration.* These declarations are placed in the declaration section of the main program right after the variable declarations (see Fig. 4.1). We shall see how to declare and use functions next.

5.3.2 Review of Built-in Functions

In Chapter 4 we described several built-in functions of PASCAL. They enable the programmer to easily incorporate some very common numerical computations into a program. Some of the functions that were described are SQRT (square root), ABS (absolute value), LN (logarithm), and the trigonometric functions SIN and COS.

Recall from Chapter 4 that a function is referenced (called) in an expression simply by specifying the name of the function, followed by its argument enclosed in parentheses. Whenever a call to a function is encountered in a program, control is transferred from the *calling program* to the function referenced. The function manipulates the argument, and when the function computation is complete, the result is returned and control is transferred back to the calling program at the point of the call. A function can be repeated many times with different arguments as illustrated next.

Example 5.3: The program segment below contains two *calls* to the built-in function SQRT.

```
            .
            .
            .
        X  := 24.0;
        Z  := 25.0;
        W  := SQRT(Z) + 6.5;
        Q  := SQRT(X + Z);
            .
            .
            .
```

In the first call, the argument Z has a value of 25.0; the result of the function execution, 5.0, is *returned* and added to 6.5. The value assigned to W is 11.5. In the second call, the argument is the expression X + Z. This expression must be evaluated before the function can be executed. Its value, 49.0, is passed to the function and the result, 7.0, is returned and assigned to Q. These calls are summarized below.

call to SQRT	function argument	argument value	function result	final effect of statement
first	Z	25.0	5.0	11.5 stored in W
second	X + Z	49.0	7.0	7.0 stored in Q

5.3.3 Defining New Functions

Often, the functions provided in PASCAL are not sufficient for the solution of a particular problem, and we may wish to write our own. In this section we will see how to write or *define* a new function.

Example 5.4: First we shall define a function that determines the sign of its real argument.

```
FUNCTION SIGN (X : REAL) : CHAR;

BEGIN
   IF X < O THEN
      SIGN := '-'
   ELSE
      SIGN := '+'
END; (* SIGN *)
```

The first statement in the function definition specifies the function name, SIGN. The *parameter list* (X : REAL) identifies the *formal parameter*, X, of the function and its type (REAL). The function type is specified following the parameter list (type CHAR). SIGN is a type CHAR function because it returns a character value as its result.

The formal parameter X is used in the function definition to represent the data to be manipulated. The body of the function (following BEGIN) consists of an IF statement that assigns a value ('−' or '+') to the function name, SIGN. This value is returned as the result of the function execution.

The assignment statements

```
SIGN := '-'
SIGN := '+'
```

are used to define the function result. One of these statements must be executed each time the function is called or the function result will be undefined. For the time being, this is the only way the function name will be manipulated in the function body.

We can call our function SIGN in the same way that the built-in functions are referenced.

Example 5.5: The statement

```
NEXT := SIGN (-3.8)
```

causes function SIGN to be executed. At the start of execution, the argument −3.8 is substituted for the formal parameter X. The result returned would be '−' which is stored in NEXT. The effect of this call to SIGN is illustrated below.

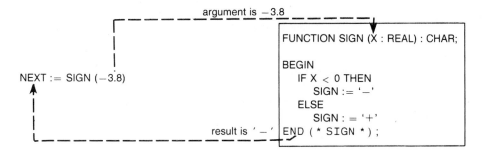

A function argument is also called an *actual parameter.* Function parameters provide a substitution mechanism that enables a function to be reused with different data. Changing the actual parameter would cause a different value to be substituted for the formal parameter and a different result to be returned.

The general form of a function definition is described in the next display. (We are assuming that all function parameters are value parameters. Value parameters will be defined in Section 5.4.2.)

Function Definition

FUNCTION *fname* (*formal parameter list*) : *result-type;*

local declaration section

BEGIN
   function body
END;

Interpretation: The function *fname* is defined. The formal parameters and their types are specified in the *formal parameter list.* The type of the function result is indicated by *result-type.*

Any identifiers that are declared in the *local declaration section* are defined only during the execution of the function.

The *function body* describes the data manipulation to be performed by the function. At least one statement of the form *fname* := *expression* must be included in the *function body.* This statement assigns a value to the function name; this value is returned as the function result upon completion of the *function body.*

Note 1: The result-type must be a standard data type or a previously defined scalar or subrange type.

Note 2: If there are no parameters, the formal parameter list and parentheses should be omitted.

The formal parameter list for a function has the syntactic form diagrammed below.

formal parameter list (function)

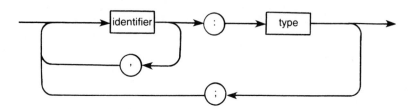

Each parameter type must be a standard or previously defined data type.

Some formal parameter lists, enclosed in parentheses, are shown next.

```
( X  :  REAL )
( X ,  Y  :  REAL )
( X ,  Y  :  REAL ;  M ,  N  :  INTEGER )
```

As illustrated, there may be multiple parameters in a formal parameter list. A comma is used to separate parameters of the same type; a semicolon is used to separate parameters of different types. The second list above describes X and Y as formal parameters of type REAL. In the next list, two additional formal parameters are specified: M and N—type INTEGER.

Example 5.6:   The function SAME in Fig. 5.4 is used to determine whether or not its three parameters have the same character value. The Boolean expression

```
( CH1  =  CH2 )  AND  ( CH2  =  CH3 )
```

evaluates to TRUE if CH1, CH2, and CH3 are equal; otherwise, it evaluates to FALSE. This value is assigned to SAME and returned as the function result.

```
FUNCTION SAME ( CH1 ,  CH2 ,  CH3  :  CHAR )  :  BOOLEAN ;

BEGIN
   SAME  : =  ( CH1  =  CH2 )  AND  ( CH2  =  CH3 )
END ;  ( * SAME * )
```

Fig. 5.4   Function SAME.

Example 5.7:   The function LARGEST defined in Fig. 5.5 finds the largest of its three integer arguments and is based on the algorithm in Problem 2.4.

The function LARGEST contains a declaration of the variable CURLARGE, which is used for storage of the larger of the first two function parameters. Since CURLARGE is declared in function LARGEST, it is considered a *local variable* that is only defined during the execution of the function body. A local variable does not retain its value from one execution of the function to the next; it is always undefined at the start of each new execution of the function.

```
FUNCTION LARGEST (FIRST, SECOND, THIRD : INTEGER) : INTEGER;
(* FINDS LARGEST OF ITS THREE ARGUMENTS *)

VAR
  CURLARGE : INTEGER;

BEGIN (* LARGEST *)
  IF FIRST > SECOND THEN
    CURLARGE := FIRST
  ELSE
    CURLARGE := SECOND;
  IF THIRD > CURLARGE THEN
    CURLARGE := THIRD;
  LARGEST := CURLARGE
END; (* LARGEST *)
```

Fig. 5.5 Function LARGEST.

5.3.4 Function Designators

To call a function, we must write a *function designator* in an expression. A function designator consists of the function name followed by the *actual parameter list* enclosed in parentheses (e.g., LARGEST (I, 10, M + N)). Commas are used as separators between actual parameters.

Fig. 5.6 provides an illustration of a *main program* that uses the function LARGEST to find the largest of five numbers, NUM1, NUM2, NUM3, NUM4 and NUM5. The function definition is inserted in the declaration part of the main program following the variable declarations.

In the main program body, the function LARGEST is called twice. After each execution of LARGEST, the largest of the three actual parameters is stored in a temporary variable (TEMP1 or TEMP2). The sequence of statement execution is outlined below. The main program steps are shown on the left; the function steps are shown on the right.

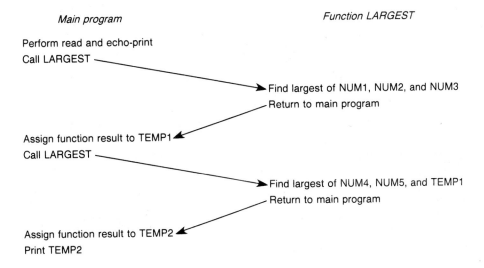

```
PROGRAM TESTLARGEST;
(* TESTS FUNCTION LARGEST *)

VAR
   NUM1, NUM2, NUM3, NUM4, NUM5 : INTEGER;
   TEMP1, TEMP2 : INTEGER;
```

```
FUNCTION LARGEST (FIRST, SECOND, THIRD : INTEGER) : INTEGER;
(* FINDS THE LARGEST OF ITS THREE ARGUMENTS *)

VAR
  CURLARGE : INTEGER;

BEGIN (* LARGEST *)
  IF FIRST > SECOND THEN
    CURLARGE := FIRST
  ELSE
    CURLARGE := SECOND;
  IF THIRD > CURLARGE THEN
    CURLARGE := THIRD;
  LARGEST := CURLARGE
END; (* LARGEST *)
```

```
BEGIN (* TESTLARGEST *)
  (* READ IN THE FIVE NUMBERS *)
  WRITELN ('ENTER FIVE INTEGERS');
  READLN (NUM1, NUM2, NUM3, NUM4, NUM5);

  (* FIND THE LARGEST NUMBER *)
  TEMP1 := LARGEST(NUM1, NUM2, NUM3);
  TEMP2 := LARGEST(NUM4, NUM5, TEMP1);

  (* PRINT THE LARGEST NUMBER *)
  WRITELN ('THE LARGEST NUMBER IS ', TEMP2)
END.

ENTER FIVE INTEGERS
  33 44 22 66 15
THE LARGEST NUMBER IS 66
```

Fig. 5.6 Using the function LARGEST.

Instead of the two assignment statements shown in Fig. 5.6, the single statement

```
TEMP2 := LARGEST(NUM4, NUM5, LARGEST(NUM1, NUM2, NUM3));
```

could also be used to find the largest number. This statement contains nested calls to the function LARGEST. The inner call is executed first, and its result is used as an actual parameter when the outer call is executed. The value returned by the outer call is stored in TEMP2.

The general form of a function designator is described in the next display.

Function Designator

fname(actual parameter list)

Interpretation: The function *fname* is executed. The first actual parameter is associated with the first formal parameter, the second actual parameter with the second formal parameter, etc.

Note: The actual parameters are separated by commas. Each actual parameter that is an expression is evaluated when *fname* is called. This value is assigned to the corresponding formal parameter. There should be the same number of actual and formal parameters; each actual parameter must be assignment compatible with its corresponding formal parameter. If there are no formal parameters, the *actual parameter list* and parentheses should be omitted.

Example 5.8: Fig. 5.7 shows a function that can be used to determine the number of days in any month of the twentieth century. The data types MONTH, YEARS and DAYS should be defined as follows.

```
TYPE
   MONTH = (JAN, FEB, MAR, APR, MAY, JUN, JUL, AUG, SEP, OCT,
            NOV, DEC);
   YEARS =  1900..1999;
   DAYS = 1..31;
```

An example of a function designator that calls the function **DAYSIN** would be

```
              DAYSIN (MAY, 1942)
```

Why would the function designator

```
              DAYSIN (1942, MAY)
```

be illegal?

```
FUNCTION DAYSIN (CURMONTH : MONTH; YEAR : YEARS) : DAYS;
(* DETERMINES THE NUMBER OF DAYS IN A GIVEN MONTH AND YEAR *)

BEGIN
  CASE CURMONTH OF
    APR, JUN, SEP, NOV : DAYSIN := 30;
    JAN, MAR, MAY, JUL, AUG, OCT, DEC : DAYSIN := 31;
    FEB : (* TEST FOR A LEAP YEAR *)
          IF YEAR MOD 4 = O THEN
            DAYSIN := 29
          ELSE
            DAYSIN := 28
  END (* CASE *)
END; (* DAYSIN *)
```

Fig. 5.7 Function DAYSIN.

Example 5.9:   The function DAYCONVERT shown in Fig. 5.8 could be used in the payroll program of Fig. 4.11a.

The function DAYCONVERT converts a numeric code to a scalar value of type DAY. The net effect would be a simpler main program since the subtask to convert to a scalar value is relegated to a separate function module.

The CASE statement would be replaced by the assignment statement

```
TODAY := DAYCONVERT(DAYNUMBER);
```

The function should be inserted in the declaration part of the program.

```
FUNCTION DAYCONVERT (DAYNUMBER : DAYRANGE) : DAY;
(* CONVERTS AN ORDINAL NUMBER TO A DAY *)

BEGIN
  CASE DAYNUMBER OF
    0 : DAYCONVERT := SUNDAY;
    1 : DAYCONVERT := MONDAY;
    2 : DAYCONVERT := TUESDAY;
    3 : DAYCONVERT := WEDNESDAY;
    4 : DAYCONVERT := THURSDAY;
    5 : DAYCONVERT := FRIDAY;
    6 : DAYCONVERT := SATURDAY
  END (* CASE *)
END; (* DAYCONVERT *)
```

Fig. 5.8   Function DAYCONVERT.

Exercise 5.5:   Write a function that computes the cube of any integer value.

Exercise 5.6:   Write a function that raises its first argument to the power indicated by its second argument.

Exercise 5.7:   Write a function that computes the tuition owed for a specified number of credit hours taken at your university.

5.4   PROCEDURES

5.4.1   Limitation of Functions

Functions are limited in that they can only be used to compute a single value. We will frequently need to write separate program modules that return more than one result. We may even desire to write modules that do not return any values, but instead perform some task such as printing the results of a prior computation. A *procedure* may be used for these purposes.

A procedure is very similar in form to a function. However, a procedure is not assigned a value and, therefore, has no type. Unlike a function, a procedure cannot be referenced in an expression; instead, a separate *procedure statement* is used to call it.

5.4.2   Definition and Use of Procedures

The definition of a procedure is similar to that of a function except the procedure header begins with the word PROCEDURE instead of FUNCTION.

There is no type declaration for the procedure following its parameter list, as there is no value associated with its execution. For this reason there is also no statement assigning a value to the procedure name inside the procedure body. A procedure returns results to the calling module by modifying certain of its actual parameters as illustrated next.

Example 5.10: Procedure BREAKDOWN in Fig. 5.9 finds the integral and fractional parts of a real number, represented by parameter X. The integral part is assigned to parameter WHOLE and the fractional part to parameter FRAC.

The three parameters of procedure BREAKDOWN are shown on separate lines. The reserved word VAR in the parameter list indicates that WHOLE and FRAC are *variable parameters.* A variable parameter is used by a procedure to return results to the calling program. The address of the corresponding actual parameter is passed to the procedure and the actual parameter (a variable) is manipulated by the procedure.

The parameter X is a *value parameter* since it is not preceded by the reserved word VAR. A value parameter is used only to pass data to the procedure. A local variable is initialized to the value of the corresponding actual parameter when the procedure is called. The local variable is manipulated by the procedure and any changes made to this local variable are not reflected in the corresponding actual parameter; i.e. its value is unchanged.

The main program body in Fig. 5.9 contains two *procedure statements* that call procedure BREAKDOWN. The procedure statement

```
BREAKDOWN (A, R1, I1);
```

is used to define the main program variables R1 and I1; its effect is described below assuming the data value 8.63 is first read into variable A.

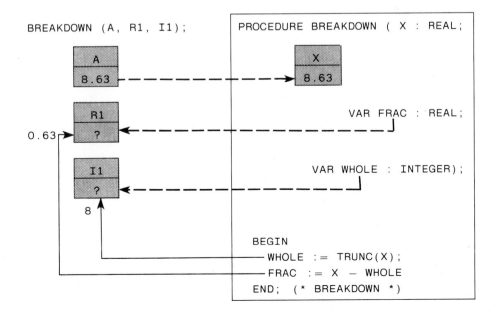

```
PROGRAM PROCTEST;
(* TESTS PROCEDURE BREAKDOWN *)

VAR
  A, B  : REAL;
  R1, R2 : REAL;
  I1, I2 : INTEGER;
```

```
PROCEDURE BREAKDOWN (X  : REAL;
                     VAR FRAC  : REAL;
                     VAR WHOLE  : INTEGER);
(* BREAKS A REAL NUMBER DOWN INTO ITS    *)
(* WHOLE AND FRACTIONAL PARTS            *)

BEGIN (* BREAKDOWN *)
  WHOLE := TRUNC(X);
  FRAC := X - WHOLE
END; (* BREAKDOWN *)
```

```
BEGIN (* PROCTEST *)
  WRITE ('ENTER TWO REAL NUMBERS: '); READLN (A, B);
  BREAKDOWN (A, R1, I1);
  BREAKDOWN (B, R2, I2);
  WRITELN;
  WRITELN (A :7:2, R1 :7:2, I1 :7);
  WRITELN (B :7:2, R2 :7:2, I2 :7)
END.
```

```
ENTER TWO REAL NUMBERS:  8.63  -15.25

   8.63     0.63      8
 -15.25    -0.25    -15
```

Fig. 5.9 Definition and call of procedure BREAKDOWN.

As indicated above, the value parameter X represents a local variable in the procedure (initial value is 8.63); the variable parameters FRAC and WHOLE represent the main program variables R1 and I1, respectively (initially undefined). Consequently, the assignment statement

$$WHOLE := TRUNC(X);$$

in BREAKDOWN assigns the value 8 to variable I1 and the assignment statement

$$FRAC := X - WHOLE$$

assigns the value 0.63 to variable R1. (TRUNC is described in Table 4.2).

The second procedure statement in the main program

$$BREAKDOWN (B, R2, I2);$$

would cause the integral part of variable B to be stored in variable I2 and the fractional part in variable R2 (all declared in the main program). Assuming the value -15.25 is read into B, the value of I2 would be -15 and the value of R2 would be -0.25.

Value parameters are one-way communication channels; they can be used to pass data into a procedure but cannot return results. Hence, if procedure **BREAKDOWN** contained the statement

$$X \; := \; SQRT(X) \; ;$$

then the value of the local variable represented by parameter X would be modified but not the corresponding actual parameter. For this reason, value parameters are said to *protect* their corresponding actual parameters from accidental modification by a function or procedure. All function parameters should normally be value parameters.

Variable parameters are two-way communication channels. Data can be passed into a procedure; any modifications to these data made by the procedure are returned to the calling program. Often, the value of a variable parameter is undefined before the procedure is called; however, its value should be defined by the execution of the procedure.

Since a variable parameter is used to return a procedure result, any corresponding actual parameter must be a variable of the same type. The address of this variable is passed to the procedure. On the other hand, the actual parameter corresponding to a value parameter may be an expression. The expression value is passed to the procedure. The expression must be assignment compatible with its corresponding formal parameter.

The declaration and call of a procedure are described in the displays that follow.

Procedure Declaration

PROCEDURE *pname* (*formal parameter list*);

local declaration section

BEGIN
  procedure body
END;

Interpretation: The procedure *pname* is defined. The formal parameters and their types are specified in the *formal parameter list.*

Any identifiers that are declared in the *local declaration section* are defined only during the execution of the procedure.

The *procedure body* describes the data manipulation to be performed by the procedure. The formal parameters represent the actual parameters in this data manipulation. Any changes to the variable parameters are returned to the calling module; any changes to the value parameters are local to the procedure.

Note: If there are no parameters, the *formal parameter list* and parentheses should be omitted.

Procedure Statement

pname (actual parameter list)

Interpretation: The procedure *pname* is executed. The first actual parameter is associated with the first formal parameter, the second actual parameter with the second formal parameter, etc. The value of the corresponding actual parameter at the time of call is assigned to each formal parameter that is a value parameter. Each actual parameter corresponding to a variable formal parameter must be a variable; this variable may be manipulated and defined by the procedure.

Note: The actual parameters are separated by commas. There should be the same number of actual and formal parameters; the type of each actual parameter and its corresponding formal parameter must satisfy Rule 2 in the next section. If there are no formal parameters, the *actual parameter list* and parentheses should be omitted.

Exercise 5.8: Explain why each of the procedure statements below is illegal given the declarations in the main program of Fig. 5.9.

  1. BREAKDOWN (B, I2, R2)   3. BREAKDOWN (X, FRAC, WHOLE)
  2. BREAKDOWN (B, R2)   4. BREAKDOWN (A, B, 37)

Do you think the statements below are legal? What would happen if they were executed?

  5. BREAKDOWN (B, B, I2)   6. BREAKDOWN (A, B, I1)

Exercise 5.9: Draw a diagram like the one shown in Example 5.10 to illustrate the effect of the second procedure statement in Fig. 5.9. Also illustrate the effect of the procedure statement

        BREAKDOWN (25.632, X, I1)

assuming that X is declared as a real variable in the main program as well as a parameter in **BREAKDOWN**. *Hint:* There is no relationship between these two declarations of identifier X; they represent different storage locations.

5.4.3 Correspondence between Actual and Formal Parameter Lists

A formal parameter list for a procedure is similar to that of a function except the reserved word **VAR** should be inserted before a group of variable parameters.

formal parameter list (procedure)

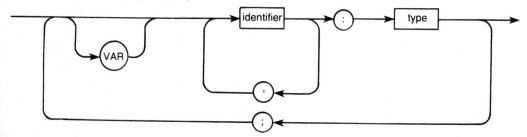

Some formal parameter lists, enclosed in parentheses, are shown next.

```
(CH3 : CHAR ; VAR X : REAL)
(VAR CH1, CH2 : CHAR ; CH3 : CHAR)
```

In both of these lists, CH3 (type CHAR) is a value parameter. In the first list, X is a variable parameter (type REAL); in the second list, CH1 and CH2 are variable parameters (type CHAR).

The formal parameter list, of course, determines the form of any actual parameter list that may be used in a call to a function or procedure. A formal parameter list always consists of a list of identifiers and their data types (also indicated by identifiers).

An actual parameter list is a list of expressions, variables or constants separated by commas. When a procedure statement is executed, a correspondence is established between each formal parameter and the actual parameter in the same relative position in the parameter list. The actual parameter list must satisfy the following rules for correspondence.

Rules for Parameter List Correspondence

1. There must be the same number of actual parameters as there are formal parameters in the procedure declaration.
2. For variable parameters, the data type of each actual parameter and its corresponding formal parameter must be the same. For value parameters, each actual parameter must be assignment compatible with its corresponding formal parameter.
3. An actual parameter corresponding to a variable formal parameter must be a variable.

Rule 3 indicates that only variables can be used as actual parameter corresponding to variable formal parameters. The reason for this is that procedures return results by modifying these variables during execution.

Example 5.11: The two formal parameter lists shown below are equivalent.

```
(VAR X, Y : REAL; M, N : INTEGER)
(VAR X : REAL; VAR Y : REAL; M : INTEGER; N : INTEGER)
```

The first two parameters in each list (X and Y) are variable parameters (type REAL), and the second two parameters are value parameters (type INTEGER). As shown, a comma may be used to separate parameters that are the same type in a list, and a semicolon is used to separate groups of parameters. The first list above is most compact and readable as parameters of the same type are listed together. In the last list, each parameter is specified individually. Any corresponding list of actual parameters must begin with two type REAL variables followed by two integer-valued expressions.

Example 5.12: The formal parameter list

```
(VAR A, B : REAL; C, D : INTEGER; VAR E : CHAR)
```

consists of three variable parameters (A, B and E) and two value parameters (C and D). If the main program contains the following declarations

```
VAR
    X, Y : REAL;
    M : INTEGER;
    NEXT : CHAR;
```

then any of the actual parameter lists below would be valid in a procedure statement:

```
(X, Y, M + 3, 10, NEXT)
(Y, X, M, M, NEXT)
(Y, X, 35, M DIV 10, NEXT)
```

The parameter correspondence specified by the first parameter list above is shown next. Each variable parameter is preceded by VAR.

actual parameter	formal parameter	data type
X	VAR A	REAL
Y	VAR B	REAL
M + 3	C	INTEGER
10	D	INTEGER
NEXT	VAR E	CHAR

For all the parameter lists above, the data type of each actual parameter is the same as its corresponding formal parameter (i.e., REAL, REAL, INTEGER, INTEGER, CHAR). As shown, it is perfectly legal to associate a constant (10) or an expression (M + 3) with a value parameter of the same type.

The actual parameter lists below would all be invalid for the reason specified:

(M, X, 30, 10, NEXT)	Type of M is not REAL
(X, Y, M, 10)	Parameter list is too short
(35.0, Y, M, 10, NEXT)	Real constant, 35.0, corresponds to variable parameter
(X, Y, M, M/10, NEXT)	Type of expression M/10 is REAL
(A, B, 30, 10, NEXT)	A and B are not variables in the main program.

Exercise 5.10: Indicate why each of the formal parameter lists below is invalid.

```
a) (VAR A, B : INTEGER, C : REAL)
b) (VAL M : INTEGER; VAR NEXT : CHAR)
c) (VAR ACCOUNT; TRANID : INTEGER)
d) (IDNUM : 111..999; VAR X : REAL)
```

Exercise 5.11: Given the procedure header

```
PROCEDURE MASSAGE (VAR A, B : REAL; X : SMALL);
```

and the declarations in the main program

```
TYPE
    SMALL = 1..10;

VAR
    X, Y, Z : REAL;
    M, N : SMALL;
```

indicate why each of the procedure statements below is illegal.

a) MASSAGE (X, Y, Z);
b) MASSAGE (X, Y, 8);
c) MASSAGE (M, Y, N);
d) MASSAGE (25.0, 15, X);
e) MASSAGE (X, Y, 15);
f) MASSAGE (X+Y, X-Y, Z);
g) MASSAGE (X, Y, M, 10);

5.5 APPLICATION OF TOP-DOWN DESIGN

In this section we shall use many of the features discussed in this chapter and illustrate the top-down approach in developing a *program system*. This approach will enable us to write each program module almost as soon as we specify its level one algorithm, rather than waiting until all algorithm steps are completely refined. The resulting program system will be much more readable as each major subtask will be implemented as a separate function or procedure module. The main program will consist, for the most part, of procedure statements and function designators that call these modules. A function will be used when only a single value is computed by the module. All data communication with each module will be through its parameter list.

Problem 5.2: Write a program to process the checks and deposit slips for a single checking account at the close of each month. The date, amount, and type of each transaction should be displayed along with information that summarizes the monthly transactions.

Discussion: Before developing the algorithm, we should first identify the input information that will be available and determine the desired form of the output. The input to our program will be in the form of a sequence of records of information. For each account to be processed, the data records are as follows:

  1. header record (containing four data items)
       depositor name
       account number
       starting balance
       month

2. one or more transaction records (each transaction record contains four
data items)

transaction type code
C for check
D for deposit
date of transaction (day of month)
account number
amount of transaction

A sample data collection is shown in Fig. 5.10 (top).

```
PETE  ROSE    1385   85.67  SEPTEMBER

      C     9   1385   79.15
      D    10   1380  200.00
      D    11   1385    3.57
      C    12   1385  125.67
      H    13   1385  100.00
```

```
DATE    CHECK   DEPOSIT   OTHER
  9     79.15
 10                       BAD ID NUMBER
 11              3.57
 12    125.67             PENALTY = $ 10.00
 13                       BAD TYPE CODE

STARTING BALANCE   = $ 85.67
FINAL BALANCE   = $ 0.09
```

Fig. 5.10 Input data (top) and desired output (bottom) for checking account problem (5.2).

For each depositor, the program should list all transactions in column form
followed by the summary statistics, as shown in Fig. 5.10 (bottom). This sample
run indicates that checks were written on the 9th and 12th of the month and a
deposit was made on the 11th. Furthermore, the check on September 12 was for
more money than the account balance; consequently, it was not paid and a $10
penalty was assessed. The transaction on September 10 contained an invalid account number; similarly, the transaction on September 13 contained a bad transaction type code (H). Except for printing the date and an error message, all such
transactions are ignored.

The data table for the main program and the level one algorithm are shown
next.

Data Table for Main Program (Problem 5.2)

Data types

IDRANGE = 1111..9999

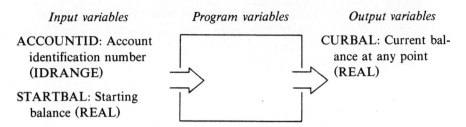

Input variables

ACCOUNTID: Account
  identification number
  (IDRANGE)

STARTBAL: Starting
  balance (REAL)

Program variables

Output variables

CURBAL: Current bal-
  ance at any point
  (REAL)

Procedures referenced in main program

> READHEADER: Reads and prints header record
> PROCESS: Processes all the transaction records

Level One Algorithm for Main Program

1. Read and print the account header record.
2. Process and print all transactions.
3. Print summary statistics including initial and final balances.

We have listed all variables that are manipulated by the main program in the data table. Other variables will be introduced where needed.

Step 3 of the level one algorithm requires no refinement; hence, it will be implemented directly in the main program. Rather than refine steps 1 and 2 at this point, we shall implement them as procedures READHEADER and PRO-CESS, described in the data table.

These procedures should be inserted where indicated by the comment

```
(*  INSERT PROCEDURES READHEADER AND PROCESS HERE  *)
```

in the declaration part of the main program (see Fig. 5.11a). It is possible to save each procedure as a separate disk file. In this case, the statements

```
(*$I UCSD3:READHEADER *)
(*$I UCSD3:PROCESS *)
```

direct the compiler to insert the named disk files in the main program. These statements must be placed between the variable declarations and any procedure and function definitions that may be present. A file being inserted in this manner must not contain another statement of this form.

(Comments beginning with the symbols (*$ may be used to set *option switches* in the compiler. The option described above is the *include file option*. We shall discuss other option switches in Chapter 8.)

In the procedure statement that calls each procedure, we should list as actu-al parameters all main program variables that are manipulated by the procedure. READHEADER is used to define ACCOUNTID and STARTBAL; PROCESS manipulates these values and defines CURBAL.

We will provide the actual parameter list for each procedure statement (or function designator) when we write the main program. In actual practice, it may be necessary to first define the procedure (or function) in order to determine what parameters are required and then write the corresponding actual parameter list.

```
PROGRAM CHECKACCOUNT;
(* PROCESS A CHECKING ACCOUNT *)

TYPE
  IDRANGE = 1111.. 9999;

VAR
  STARTBAL, CURBAL : REAL;
  ACCOUNTID : IDRANGE;

(* INSERT PROCEDURES READHEADER AND PROCESS HERE *)
(*$I UCSD3:READHEADER *)
(*$I UCSD3:PROCESS *)

BEGIN
  (* READ ACCOUNT HEADER AND MONTH *)
  READHEADER (ACCOUNTID, STARTBAL);

  (* PROCESS ALL TRANSACTIONS *)
  PROCESS (ACCOUNTID, STARTBAL, CURBAL);

  (* PRINT SUMMARY STATEMENT *)
  WRITELN;
  WRITELN ('STARTING BALANCE  = $', STARTBAL :8:2);
  WRITELN ('FINAL BALANCE = $', CURBAL :8:2)
END.
```

Fig. 5.11a   Main program for checking account problem (5.2).

The data table for **READHEADER** is shown below.

Data Table for Procedure READHEADER

Input parameters   *Output parameters*

   (none)   ACCOUNTID, STARTBAL

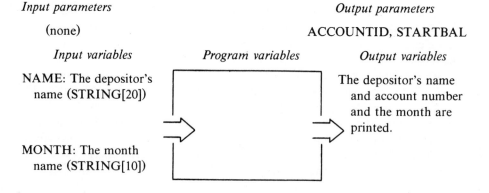

Input variables	*Program variables*	*Output variables*
NAME: The depositor's name (STRING[20])		The depositor's name and account number and the month are printed.
MONTH: The month name (STRING[10])		

The data table begins with the formal parameters for READHEADER. The program system will be easier to read and understand if each formal parameter is given the same name as its corresponding actual parameter whenever possible. A parameter is listed as an input parameter if its value is passed to the procedure; a parameter is listed as an output parameter if its value is defined by the procedure. Parameters listed as output parameters should be declared variable parameters as they are used to return results to the calling module; parameters listed as input parameters are normally value parameters.

When writing the procedure header, carefully compare it with the procedure statement to ensure that all parameters are listed and are in the correct order. This last step is extremely important. If two parameters are interchanged, or a parameter is missing or misspelled, the parameter list correspondence will be incorrect and the procedure will not execute as desired.

The remaining entries shown in the data table should be declared as local variables in READHEADER. The procedure is written in Fig. 5.11b.

```
PROCEDURE READHEADER (VAR ACCOUNTID : IDRANGE;
                      VAR STARTBAL : REAL);
(* READS ACCOUNT HEADER INFORMATION *)

VAR
  NAME : STRING[20];
  MONTH : STRING[10];

BEGIN
  (* READ NAME, ACCOUNT ID, STARTING BALANCE AND MONTH *)
  WRITE ('NAME: '); READLN (NAME);
  WRITE ('ACCOUNT #'); READLN (ACCOUNTID);
  WRITE ('STARTING BALANCE $'); READLN (STARTBAL);
  WRITE ('MONTH: '); READLN (MONTH)
END; (* READHEADER *)
```

Fig. 5.11b   Procedure READHEADER for checking account problem (5.2).

The procedure PROCESS must read and process all transaction records. Each transaction record contains four data items: the transaction type code (TRANCODE), the transaction date (TRANDATE), the transaction identification number (TRANID), and amount (TRANAMOUNT). PROCESS reads this data, echo prints the date, and updates the account balance or prints an error message. The data table and algorithm for procedure PROCESS follow.

Data Table for PROCESS

Input parameters	*Output parameters*
ACCOUNTID, STARTBAL	CURBAL

Constant

SENTINEL = '/', the sentinel transaction code

(continued)

Data types

> DAYSINMONTH = 1..31
> TRANTYPE = (CHECK, DEPOSIT, UNKNOWN)

Input variables	*Program variables*	*Output variables*
TRANDATE: Date of each transaction (DAYSINMONTH)		TRANDATE is echo-printed

TRANID: ID number for each transaction (IDRANGE)

TRANCODE: Type code for each transaction (CHAR)

TRANSACTION: Category of each transaction (TRANTYPE)

TRANAMOUNT: amount of each transaction (REAL)

Procedures referenced in PROCESS

> UPDATEONE: Updates the balance or prints an error message if the transaction is illegal.

Level One Algorithm for PROCESS

1. Print the table heading.
2. Process all transactions.

Level Two Refinements for PROCESS

Step 2   *Process all transactions*

> 2.1 Initialize CURBAL to STARTBAL
> 2.2 WHILE all transactions are not processed DO
> > BEGIN
> > > 2.3 Read each transaction record and print the date
> > > 2.4 Categorize the transaction as a check, deposit, or unknown
> > > 2.5 Update the balance (CURBAL) or print an error message if the transaction is illegal.
> > END

Step 2.4 simply converts from a character code (TRANCODE) to a scalar value of type TRANTYPE, which is stored in TRANSACTION. Character codes C and D are converted to scalar values CHECK and DEPOSIT, respectively. Any other character is converted to the scalar value UNKNOWN. (The sentinel code is /).

Step 2.5 of procedure PROCESS will be performed by a third procedure, UPDATEONE. Procedure UPDATEONE is called each time the loop in Step 2 is repeated.Procedure UPDATEONE must flag any illegal transactions (bad account ID or type code). All legal transactions should be processed by updating CURBAL and printing the transaction amount (TRANAMOUNT).

UPDATEONE may be declared in either of two places. It may be declared in the main program just before the definition of procedure PROCESS. Alternatively, it may be declared as a local procedure nested within PROCESS. Since UPDATEONE performs a subtask of PROCESS and is called only by PROCESS, we shall choose the latter option. Procedure PROCESS is provided in Fig. 5.11c. Procedure UPDATEONE should be inserted in the declaration section of procedure PROCESS when PROCESS is typed in. (Note that the include file option cannot be used to do this.)

```
PROCEDURE PROCESS (ACCOUNTID : IDRANGE;
                   STARTBAL : REAL;
                   VAR CURBAL : REAL);
(* PROCESSES ALL TRANSACTIONS *)

CONST
  SENTINEL = '/';

TYPE
  DAYSINMONTH = 1..31;
  TRANTYPE = (CHECK, DEPOSIT, UNKNOWN);

VAR
  TRANID : IDRANGE;
  TRANCODE : CHAR;
  TRANDATE : DAYSINMONTH;
  TRANAMOUNT : REAL;
  TRANSACTION : TRANTYPE;

(* INSERT PROCEDURE UPDATEONE HERE *)

BEGIN (* PROCESS *)
  (* PRINT USER INSTRUCTIONS AND TABLE HEADING *)
  WRITELN ('AFTER EACH PROMPT, ENTER TRANSACTION CODE (C/D)');
  WRITELN ('FOLLOWED BY DAY OF MONTH  <1..31>,');
  WRITELN ('ACCOUNT ID AND AMOUNT');
  WRITELN ('TYPE / TO STOP');
  WRITELN;
  WRITE ('C/D DAY #### $');
  WRITELN ('DATE' :8, 'CHECK' :10, 'DEPOSIT' :10, 'OTHER' :10);
```
                                                            (continued)

```
(* PROCESS ALL TRANSACTIONS *)
CURBAL := STARTBAL;
WRITE ('? ');
READ (TRANCODE);
WHILE TRANCODE  <> SENTINEL DO
  BEGIN
    (* READ REST OF TRANSACTION RECORD *)
    READLN (TRANDATE, TRANID, TRANAMOUNT);
    WRITE (TRANDATE :22);
    (* CATEGORIZE TRANSACTION *)
    IF TRANCODE  = 'C' THEN
      TRANSACTION := CHECK
    ELSE IF TRANCODE = 'D' THEN
      TRANSACTION := DEPOSIT
    ELSE
      TRANSACTION := UNKNOWN;
    (* UPDATE CURBAL *)
    UPDATEONE (ACCOUNTID, TRANID, TRANAMOUNT,
               TRANSACTION, CURBAL);
    WRITE ('? ');
    READ (TRANCODE)
  END (* WHILE *)
END; (* PROCESS *)
```

Fig. 5.11c Procedure PROCESS.

All the parameters passed to PROCESS should also be passed to UP-DATEONE except for STARTBAL, which is not needed. In addition, the values of TRANSMOUNT, TRANID, and TRANSACTION should be passed to UPDATEONE. The data table for UPDATEONE follows.

Data Table for Procedure UPDATEONE

Input parameters	Update parameters	Output parameters
ACCOUNTID, TRANID, TRANAMOUNT, TRANSACTION	CURBAL	(none)

Constant

PENALTY = 10.00, the amount of penalty for a bad check

CURBAL is listed as an *update parameter*. Each time UPDATEONE is called, the current value of CURBAL is passed from PROCESS; this value may be changed by UPDATEONE. The new value is returned to PROCESS (and eventually to the main program); hence, CURBAL should be declared as a variable parameter. The algorithm for UPDATEONE follows.

Level One Algorithm for UPDATEONE

1. Update CURBAL or print an error message if the transaction is illegal

Level Two Refinements

Step 1

    1.1 IF the ID numbers do not match **THEN**
          1.2 Print an error message
      ELSE
          1.3 Process each transaction with a valid ID

Level Three Refinements

Step 1.3

    1.3.1 **CASE TRANSACTION OF**
            DEPOSIT : Process deposit
            UNKNOWN : Print an error message
            CHECK : Process a check differentiating between a good
                        check and a bad check (overdraft)
        END

Procedure **UPDATEONE** is implemented in Fig. 5.11d. The output table generated by the program has the form shown in Fig. 5.10 (bottom).

```
PROCEDURE UPDATEONE (ACCOUNTID, TRANID : IDRANGE;
                            TRANAMOUNT : REAL;
                            TRANSACTION : TRANTYPE;
                            VAR CURBAL : REAL);
(* UPDATES CURBAL OR PRINTS AN ERROR MESSAGE *)

CONST
  PENALTY = 10.00;

BEGIN
  IF TRANID <> ACCOUNTID THEN
    (* INVALID TRANSACTION ID NUMBER *)
    WRITELN (' ' :25, 'BAD ID NUMBER')
  ELSE
    CASE TRANSACTION OF
      DEPOSIT : BEGIN (* PROCESS DEPOSIT *)
                  CURBAL := CURBAL + TRANAMOUNT;
                  WRITELN (' ' :10, TRANAMOUNT :10:2)
                END;
      UNKNOWN : WRITELN (' ' :25, 'BAD TYPE CODE');
      CHECK   : IF TRANAMOUNT <= CURBAL THEN
                  BEGIN (* PROCESS CHECK *)
                    CURBAL := CURBAL - TRANAMOUNT;
                    WRITELN (TRANAMOUNT :10:2)
                  END
```

(continued)

```
              ELSE
                BEGIN (* PROCESS BAD CHECK *)
                  CURBAL := CURBAL - PENALTY;
                  WRITELN (TRANAMOUNT :10:2, ' ' :15,
                          'PENALTY = $', PENALTY :6:2)
                END (* IF *)
        END (* CASE *)
END; (* UPDATEONE *)
```

Fig. 5.11d   Procedure UPDATEONE.

Program Style

Top down design

   The solution to the checking account problem illustrates a number of features of the top-down approach to problem solving and programming. We were able to implement the program in four compact sections of code or modules (the main program and three procedures). The top-down approach enabled us to implement each module in the program system relatively independently of the others. The modules were compact and simple enough that they could be written directly as a linear sequence of steps without extensive refinement. Each subtask requiring substantial refinement was relegated to a new procedure whose implementation was deferred until later.

   Variables for the program were also introduced in a stepwise fashion, in parallel with the algorithm development. All variables manipulated in the main program were introduced initially along with any variables that are manipulated in more than one algorithm step (ACCOUNTID is read in Step 1 of the main program and tested in Step 2). Additional local variables were defined in each procedure as needed. As illustrated, it is perfectly legal for one procedure to call another (PROCESS calls UPDATEONE), and for a procedure declaration to be nested (wholly contained) within another (UPDATEONE defined within PROCESS).

Program Style

Stubs

   An additional advantage of using procedures is that they enable the programmer to test certain sections of the program before all algorithm subtasks are implemented. For example, if procedures READHEADER and PROCESS are written but UPDATEONE is not, the two completed procedures can still be tested if a *stub* is inserted for UPDATEONE. A stub is a skeleton of the procedure consisting of the procedure header statement (including the parameter list) followed by a single WRITE statement in the procedure body. The WRITE statement should simply print a message indicating that the procedure was entered.

The absence of UPDATEONE will in no way affect the operation of READHEADER. Procedure PROCESS will also execute normally; however, the values returned to the main program will be different without UPDATEONE, as will the program output; each call to UPDATEONE will cause a message to be printed instead of a transaction amount. Nevertheless, by examining the program output, you can determine whether the main program and READHEADER and PROCESS appear to be operating correctly. We will have more to say about stubs in Section 8.7.

Exercise 5.12:   Rewrite Problem 5.1 using separate function or procedure modules to implement each of the three subtasks in the level one algorithm.

Exercise 5.13:   Modify the program system developed in this section so that counts of every type of transaction are maintained and printed in the summary statistics.

Exercise 5.14:   Modify the program system so that a number of different accounts can be processed in sequence. The records for each account will have the form shown in Fig. 5.10.

5.6   SCOPE OF AN IDENTIFIER

5.6.1   Local versus Global Identifiers

An identifier in PASCAL is the name of any variable, procedure, constant, scalar type or subrange. Not every identifier can be referenced in all the procedures of a program system. *The scope of an identifier* determines which procedures may reference a given identifier.

Scope of an Identifier

An identifier may be referenced only by the procedure in which it is declared and any other procedures nested within this procedure.

Fig. 5.12 outlines the nesting of procedures for Problem 5.2. A box is drawn around each procedure. The scope of each identifier declared in a procedure is indicated by the box around the procedure (called a *block*). The formal parameters of a procedure are included in its block.

PROGRAM CHECKACCOUNT

global identifiers
    IDRANGE, ACCOUNTID, STARTBAL, CURBAL

procedures

    PROCEDURE READHEADER

        formal parameters
            ACCOUNTID, STARTBAL

        local identifiers
            NAME, MONTH,

        BEGIN (* READHEADER *)
            . . . . .
        END; (* READHEADER *)

    PROCEDURE PROCESS

        formal parameters
            ACCOUNTID, STARTBAL, CURBAL

        local identifiers
            DAYSINMONTH, TRANTYPE, TRANDATE, TRANID,
            TRANCODE, TRANAMOUNT, TRANSACTION, SENTINEL

        procedures

            PROCEDURE UPDATEONE

                formal parameters
                    ACCOUNTID, TRANID, TRANAMOUNT
                    TRANSACTION, CURBAL

                local identifiers
                    PENALTY

                BEGIN (* UPDATEONE *)
                    . . . . .
                END; (* UPDATEONE *)

        BEGIN (* PROCESS *)
            . . . . .
        END; (* PROCESS *)

BEGIN (* CHECKACCOUNT *)
. . . . .
END.

Fig. 5.12   Nesting of procedures for problem 5.2.

Since all procedures are nested within the main program, any identifier declared in the main program may be referenced anywhere in the program system. For this reason, the identifiers declared in the main program are called *global identifiers*. (Examples of global identifiers are STARTBAL, CURBAL and ID-RANGE.) A global identifier used as the name of a variable is a *global variable*.

Identifiers that are declared in a procedure are local identifiers and may be referenced anywhere within that procedure. This means that a local identifier in procedure A may also be referenced in procedure B only if procedure B is declared (or nested) within procedure A. Such an identifier is considered nonlocal to procedure B. A global identifier is a special type of nonlocal identifier. These definitions are summarized in the next display. (Examples of nonlocal identifiers are TRANID and TRANCODE. They are declared as local identifiers in PROCESS, and hence are nonlocal to UPDATEONE which is declared in PROCESS.)

Global identifiers

Global identifiers are declared in the main program and may be referenced by the main program and any procedure in the program system.

Nonlocal identifiers

Nonlocal identifiers are identifiers that are declared outside the procedure in which they are referenced. The declaration of any procedure that references a nonlocal identifier must be nested within the procedure that declares the identifier.

Local identifiers

Local identifiers are identifiers that are declared within the procedure that references them.

It would be illegal for READHEADER (or the main program) to reference TRANID or TRANCODE. The reason is that procedure READHEADER is declared in the main program and is not nested within PROCESS where these identifiers are declared (see Fig. 5.12). The constant PENALTY (declared in UPDATEONE) may be referenced only by UPDATEONE as there are no other procedures declared in UPDATEONE.

It would be possible to make all variables global by declaring them all in the main program. In this case, each variable could be referenced in every procedure. However, we prefer to introduce new local variables as the need for them arises. This practice is consistent with the top-down approach to design: variables and program modules are defined in parallel as the problem solution (program system) develops. This practice also provides additional benefits of isolation and protection which will be discussed in Section 5.6.3.

Example 5.13: Since UPDATEONE is defined as a local procedure in PRO-CESS, it can reference all variables and parameters defined in PROCESS. Consequently, it would be possible to implement UPDATEONE as a *procedure without parameters* by using the header statement

PROCEDURE UPDATEONE;

in the procedure declaration. The procedure statement

UPDATEONE;

could then be used in PROCESS to call UPDATEONE. In both these statements, the parameter list and enclosing parentheses are not needed. Each identifier referenced in UPDATEONE would either be a local variable (PENALTY), a parameter of PROCESS (e.g., CURBAL), or a nonlocal identifier declared in PROCESS (e.g., TRANID). The reason this was not done will be discussed in Section 5.6.3.

Exercise 5.15: List the procedures that can reference each of the following identifiers:

```
a) ACCOUNTID
b) NAME
c) TRANDATE
d) PENALTY
e) READHEADER
f) PROCESS
```

Exercise 5.16: List all identifiers that can be referenced in procedure PROCESS.

5.6.2 Multiple Declarations of an Identifier

There is one additional issue concerning the scope of identifiers that should be addressed and that concerns the "ambiguity" arising from multiple declarations of an identifier. Although it is illegal to declare an identifier twice in the same procedure, or block, it is perfectly legal to declare an identifier in two different blocks. Thus, for example, we could declare a global variable named MONTH in the main program even though there is a declaration of MONTH in procedure READHEADER. These two variables named MONTH would be distinct, and any change in the value of one would not be reflected in the other (see Exercise 5.9).

Each reference to variable MONTH in procedure READHEADER would cause the local variable declared there to be manipulated. Each reference to variable MONTH anywhere else would cause the global variable MONTH to be manipulated. In general, a reference to any identifier is resolved by manipulating a local identifier if one with that name exists; otherwise, the non-local identifier with that name declared in the closest containing procedure of a nest will be manipulated.

Although all global variables in Problem 5.2 can be referenced in each procedure, they cannot all be accessed directly. The reason for this is that each global variable that is manipulated in a procedure is listed (declared) as a formal parameter in that procedure heading. Since this declaration is local to the procedure, it takes precedence over the original declaration in the main program. The global variables, therefore, are passed as parameters to each procedure.

The only global identifier that is not passed as a parameter is IDRANGE, which is the name of a subrange type. This global identifier is used in PROCESS to specify the type of local variable TRANID.

5.6.3 Nonlocal Variables and Side Effects

We mentioned earlier that global identifiers can be referenced by all procedures in a program system. Yet we have been careful not to do this and, instead, have passed global variables as parameters whenever they were needed.

There are two principal reasons for using parameters. The first is to provide the procedure (or function) with the flexibility to manipulate different data each time it is called. The programmer can easily modify the data that are communicated back and forth by changing the actual parameter list. This was done in Fig. 5.9 for procedure BREAKDOWN.

The second reason for using parameters is to protect the program system from harmful *side effects* that often occur when nonlocal or global variables are used for data communication instead of parameters (see Example 5.13). A change in the value of a nonlocal or global variable by a procedure is called a side effect.

The presence of side effects tends to obscure the program structure and makes it difficult to detect and correct errors. If procedures A and B reference the same global variable, then procedures A and B are "coupled together" through this variable. If procedure B executes first and erroneously modifies the value of this variable, procedure A may later appear to execute incorrectly when procedure B is really at fault. It is often very difficult to determine that the problem is caused by a side effect and to locate the offending procedure. On the other hand, if parameters are used exclusively for data transfer, then all data communication between procedures is clearly documented.

For the same reason, you should always declare an identifier used as a program variable in a procedure as a local identifier. Doing this isolates the variable from any other use of that identifier and protects the program system from side effects. For example, if identifier I is used as a FOR loop control variable in the main program and also in a procedure, harmful interaction could result unless identifier I is declared in both places. If identifier I is declared only in the main program, then each execution of the procedure could change the FOR loop variable in the main program (global variable I). (This is definitely not a good idea!) If identifier I is also declared in the procedure, then there are two separate, independent variables named "I" and only local variable I can be changed by the procedure.

If a procedure manipulates only its parameters and local variables, then it can be considered a "black box" with well defined input and output channels as indicated below.

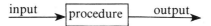

In order to verify that a procedure is executing correctly, we only have to examine the "output" of the procedure for a given "input". This can be done by echo printing all parameter values that are passed to the procedure immediately upon entry to the procedure. After completion of the procedure, the values returned should be printed in the calling module.

To accomplish this, a WRITE statement should be inserted as the first statement in the procedure body; this WRITE statement should print all formal parameters that are already defined (input and update parameters). A second WRITE statement should be inserted in the calling module following the procedure statement; this WRITE statement should print all actual parameters that are defined by the procedure (update and output parameters). By carefully comparing these two sets of values, you should be able to determine whether or not the procedure is operating correctly.

5.6.4   Forward References for Procedures

It would be illegal for the main program or READHEADER to call procedure UPDATEONE. As is the case for any identifier (including a procedure name), UPDATEONE may only be referenced by the procedure in which it is declared (PROCESS) and any procedure nested within PROCESS (UPDATEONE). The call of a procedure by itself is called *recursion*. Recursive calls will be discussed in Chapter 8.

The identifiers READHEADER and PROCESS are declared in the main program block and are global. In theory, this means that these procedures can call each other, as well as be called by the main program. In practice, only PROCESS can call READHEADER since the declaration of PROCESS follows procedure READHEADER. If we wish to call PROCESS from READHEADER as well, then we must insert a *forward reference* for PROCESS before defining READHEADER as shown next.

```
PROCEDURE PROCESS (ACCOUNTID...); FORWARD;

PROCEDURE READHEADER (VAR ACCOUNTID...);
         .  .  .  .  .
END;  (*READHEADER*)

PROCEDURE PROCESS;
         .  .  .  .  .
END;  (*PROCESS*)
```

The first statement above identifies PROCESS as a procedure that will be declared later. Note that the parameter list for PROCESS is included in the forward reference, not in the procedure declaration that follows.

5.7 COMMON PROGRAMMING ERRORS

5.7.1 CASE Statement Errors

In using a CASE statement, make sure that the CASE selector and labels are all the same scalar type. Remember that only lists of scalar values may be used as case labels and that no value may appear in more than one case label. Do not forget to insert the END (*CASE*); there is no matching BEGIN.

5.7.2 Compound IF Statement Errors

Care must be taken in listing the conditions to be used in a compound IF statement. If the conditions are not *mutually exclusive* (that is, if more than one of the conditions can be true at the same time), then the condition sequence must be carefully ordered to ensure the desired result.

5.7.3 Procedure and Function Errors

Make sure that all procedure and function declarations are placed between the variable declarations and the start of the main program (or containing procedure) body. Remember that procedure A may not reference an identifier declared in procedure B unless procedure A is wholly contained (nested) within procedure B. Any attempt to do so may result in an "undeclared identifier" diagnostic.

A procedure (or function) may not be called before it is declared unless a forward reference is inserted before the call. When writing functions, make sure that at least one statement assigning a value to the function name will be executed each time the function is called.

5.7.4 Parameter Errors

Unfortunately, there are many opportunities for errors when using parameters with procedures. The proper use of parameters is often a difficult concept for beginners to master. However, learning how to use parameters correctly will pay great dividends in all future programming.

When writing the formal parameter list, make sure that all identifiers used as parameter data types have been previously declared. Carefully compare each actual parameter list with its corresponding formal parameter list. The actual parameter list must have the same number of actual parameters as there are formal parameters.

The type of each actual parameter must be the same as its corresponding formal parameter (assignment compatibility is sufficient for value parameters). Expressions and constants can only correspond to value formal parameters; variables may correspond to variable or value formal parameters. Remember, only variable parameters communicate results back to the calling module.

Be wary of side effects. Declare all variables used in a procedure as local variables unless there is good reason not to. Use parameter lists for communicating with procedures. Carefully document with comments any exceptions to this policy.

5.8 SUMMARY

In this chapter, we discussed two approaches to implementing multiple-alternative decisions: the CASE statement and compound IF statement. The CASE statement is the preferred way of differentiating between a small group of scalar values. In other situations, the compound IF statement may be used.

We also illustrated the use of procedures and functions in PASCAL to implement programs in a modular fashion that is consistent with the top-down algorithm development process. Procedures, like functions, are also helpful in writing programs in which certain operations are performed more than once. These operations can be specified once as a procedure or function and then repeated as often as needed.

Functions are used to compute a single value only, whereas procedures may be used to determine any number of results. Functions return their result by assigning a value to the function name; a function is called through the use of a function designator in an expression. Procedures return their results by redefining variables in the calling module (actual parameters) that correspond to variable formal parameters in the procedure; a procedure is called through the use of a procedure statement.

A major portion of this chapter was concerned with the study of parameters and parameter lists. By using parameters, we can cause different data to be manipulated by a procedure (or function) each time we call it. The parameter list also provides a highly visible communication path between the calling program and the procedure. Communication through the parameter list reduces the likelihood of undesirable side effects. The net result is that the procedure is practically an independent program module that is reusable, highly portable and relatively easy to debug.

There are two types of parameters in PASCAL: value and variable parameters. A value parameter is used only for passing data into the procedure. The value of its corresponding actual parameter is stored locally and manipulated by the procedure; hence, the actual parameter value never changes.

Parameters that represent procedure results must be variable parameters. No local storage is allocated to a variable parameter; the data associated with its corresponding actual parameter (a variable) are manipulated when the procedure is executed.

We discussed the scope of identifiers in PASCAL and the fact that an identifier may be referenced by any procedure that is nested within the procedure declaring the identifier. This means that identifiers declared in the main program are global and may be referenced in any procedure. Variables declared in a procedure are local to that procedure and may be referenced only in that procedure and any other wholly contained (nested) procedure. In general, a reference to any variable is resolved by manipulating a local variable if one with that name exists; otherwise, the nonlocal variable with that name declared in the closest containing procedure of a nest will be manipulated.

PROGRAMMING PROBLEMS

5.3   Write a program that will read in a positive real number and determine and print the number of digits to the left of the decimal point. (*Hint:* Repeatedly divide the number by 10 until it becomes less than 1. Test the program with the following data:

4703.62	0.01
0.47	5764
10.12	40000

5.4   Write a program that uses procedures to find the range of values in a data collection (largest value − smallest value) and the mean value.

5.5   The function SIN(X) increases in value starting at X = 0 radians. Write a program to determine the value of X for which SIN(X) begins to decrease. (*Hint:* Calculate the value of SIN(X) beginning at X = 0 for intervals of .01 radians, and watch for a decrease.) Print a two-column table of X and SIN(X) as long as the increase continues. At the point of decrease, simply print X and stop.

5.6   The Norecall Auto Company keeps sales records for each employee. Each time an automobile is sold the following data are entered into the record:

   name of salesperson   make of car   date of sale   amount of sale

For example:

   LITTLE NELL   CADILLAC   6/6 $8532.67

Each month the company must collect the sales records for each employee, add up the number of sales and the sales amount, and compute the employee commission as follows

For sales up to $30,000,	five percent commission
For sales between $30,000–$50,000,	five percent commission on first $30,000
	eight percent commission on the rest
For sales over $50,000,	five percent of first $30,000
	eight percent of next $20,000
	fifteen percent of the rest

Write a program to perform these computations. For each employee, your program should print employee name, total sales count, total dollar amount of sales, and total commission. At the end, print grand totals of sales count, dollar amount, and commissions. Test your program on the following data.

LITTLE NELL	CADILLAC	6/6	$4500.00
LITTLE NELL	BUICK	6/7	$3200.00
LITTLE NELL	CADILLAC	6/9	$5200.00
LITTLE NELL	BUICK	6/12	$3900.00
LITTLE NELL	BUICK	6/12	$3700.00
LITTLE NELL	CADILLAC	6/18	$5100.00
LITTLE NELL	CADILLAC	6/24	$6000.00
BIG SIS	BUICK	6/8	$3800.00
BIG SIS	BUICK	6/20	$4100.00
BIG SIS	OLDS	6/30	$4900.00
MODERN MILLIE	CADILLAC	6/1	$6500.00
MODERN MILLIE	CADILLAC	6/3	$7300.00
MODERN MILLIE	CADILLAC	6/4	$5200.00
MODERN MILLIE	CADILLAC	6/8	$7800.00
MODERN MILLIE	BUICK	6/12	$3200.00
MODERN MILLIE	OLDS	6/14	$4200.00
MODERN MILLIE	CADILLAC	6/15	$5200.00
MODERN MILLIE	CADILLAC	6/18	$4700.00
MODERN MILLIE	BUICK	6/20	$5500.00
MODERN MILLIE	OLDS	6/22	$4900.00

Use a function to compute the commission.

5.7 Write a program to read in a collection of positive integers and print all divisors of each, except for 1 and the number itself. If the number has no divisors, print a message indicating that it is prime. Use a procedure to determine all of the divisors of each integer read. This procedure should set a flag, PRIME, to indicate whether or not an integer is prime. The main program should test the flag to decide whether or not to print the prime message (see Problem 4.1).

5.8 Do Problem 4.4 using a procedure to process each employee time card. Include computation and output steps for each employee in the procedure.

5.9 Write a program that will provide change for a dollar for any item purchased that costs less than one dollar. Print out each unit of change (quarters, dimes, nickels, or pennies) provided. Always dispense the biggest-denomination coin possible. For example, if there are 37 cents left in change, dispense a quarter, which leaves 12 cents in change, then dispense a dime, and then two pennies.

5.10 Write a program to read in a string of up to 10 characters representing a number in the form of a Roman numeral. Print the Roman numeral form and then convert to Arabic form (an integer). The character values for Roman numerals are

M	1000
D	500
C	100
L	50
X	10
V	5
I	1

Test your program on the following input.

LXXXVII	87
CCXIX	219
MCCCLIV	1354
MMDCLXXIII	2673
MCDLXXVI	?

5.11 The equation of the form

$$1. \quad mx + b = 0$$

(where m and b are real numbers) is called a linear equation in one unknown, x. If we are given the values of both m and b, then the value of x that satisfies this equation may be computed as

$$2. \quad x = -b/\dot{m}.$$

Write a program to read in N different sets of values for m and b and compute x. Test your program for the following five sets of values:

m	b
−12.0	3.0
0.0	18.5
100.0	40.0
0.0	0.0
−16.8	0.0

[*Hint:* There are three distinct possibilities concerning the values of x that satisfy the equation $mx + b = 0$.
1. As long as $m \neq 0$, the value of x that satisfies the original equation 1 is given by equation 2.
2. If both b and m are 0, then any real number that we choose satisfies $mx + b = 0$.
3. If $m = 0$ and $b \neq 0$, then no real number x satisfies this equation.]

5.12 Each year the legislature of a state rates the productivity of the faculty of each of the state-supported colleges and universities. The rating is based on reports submitted by each faculty member indicating the average number of hours worked per week during the school year. Each faculty member is ranked, and the university also receives an overall rank.

The faculty productivity rank is compared as follows:

1. faculty members averaging over 55 hours per week are considered "highly productive";
2. faculty members averaging between 35 and 55 hours a week, inclusive, are considered "satisfactory";
3. faculty members averaging fewer than 35 hours a week are considered "overpaid".

The productivity rating of each school is determined by first computing the faculty average for the school:

$$\text{Faculty average} = \frac{\Sigma \text{ hours worked per week for all faculty}}{\text{Number of faculty reporting}}$$

and then comparing the faculty average to the category ranges defined in (i), (ii), and (iii).

Write a program to rank the following faculty;

HERM	63
FLO	37
JAKE	20
MO	55
SOL	72
TONY	40
AL	12

Your program should print a three-column table giving the name, hours and productivity rank of each faculty member. It should also compute and print the school's overall productivity ranking.

5.13 Write a savings account transaction program that will process the following set of data

ADAM	1054.37	
W	25.00	
D	243.35	group 1
W	254.55	
Z		
EVE	2008.24	
W	15.55	group 2
Z		
MARY	128.24	
W	62.48	
D	13.42	group 3
W	84.60	
Z		
SAM	7.77	group 4
Z		
JOE	15.27	
W	16.12	
D	10.00	group 5
Z		
BETH	12900.00	
D	9270.00	group 6
Z		

The first record in each group (header) gives the name for an account and the starting balance in the account. All subsequent records show the amount of each withdrawal (W) or deposit (D) that was made for that account followed by a sentinel code (Z). Print out the final balance for each of the accounts processed. If a balance becomes negative, print an appropriate message and take whatever corrective steps you deem proper. If there are no transactions for an account, print a message so indicating.

5.14 *Variation on the mortgage interest problem — Problem 4.12.* Use FOR loops to write a program to print tables of the following form.

Home loan mortgage interest payment tables

Amount_____   Loan duration (Months)_____

Rate (Percent)	Monthly payment	Total payment
12.00		
12.25		
12.50		
12.75		
13.00		
13.25		
13.50		
.		
.		
.		
16.00		
16.25		
16.50		
16.75		
17.00		

Your program should produce tables for loans of 30, 40 and 50 thousand dollars, respectively. For each of these amounts, tables should be produced for loan durations of 240, 300 and 360 months. Thus, nine tables of the above form should be produced. Your program should contain three nested loops, some of which may be inside separate procedures, depending upon your solution. Be careful to remove all redundant computations from inside your loops, especially from inside the innermost loop.

5.15   *Quadratic-equation problem.* The equation of the form

$$(1) \quad ax^2 + bx + c = 0 \ (a, b, c \text{ real numbers, with } a \neq 0)$$

is called a quadratic equation in x. The real *roots* of this equation are those values of x for which

$$ax^2 + bx + c$$

evaluates to zero. Thus, if $a = 1$, $b = 2$, and $c = -15$, then the real roots of

$$x^2 + 2x - 15$$

are $+3$ and -5, since

$$(3)^2 + 2(3) - 15 = 9 + 6 - 15 = 0$$

and

$$(-5)^2 + 2(-5) - 15 = 25 - 10 - 15 = 0$$

Quadratic equations of the form (1) have either 2 real and different roots, 2 real and equal roots, or no real roots. The determination as to which of these three conditions holds for a given equation can be made by evaluating the discriminant d of the equation, where

$$d = b^2 - 4ac.$$

There are three distinct possibilities:
1.   If $d > 0$, then the equation has two real and unequal roots.
2.   If $d = 0$, the equation has two real and equal roots.
3.   If $d < 0$, the equation has no real roots.
Write a program to compute and print the real roots of quadratic equations having the following value of a, b, and c.

a	b	c
`1.0	2.0	−15.0
1.0	−1.25	−9.375
1.0	0.0	1.0
1.0	−80.0	−900.0
1.0	−6.0	9.0
0.0	0.0	0.0

If the equation has no real roots for a set of a, b and c, print an appropriate message and read the next set. *Hint:* If the equation has two real and equal roots, then the root values are given by the expression

$$\text{Root } 1 = \text{Root } 2 = -b/2a.$$

If the equation has two real and unequal roots, their values may be computed as

$$\text{Root } 1 = \frac{-b + \sqrt{d}}{2a}$$

$$\text{Root } 2 = \frac{-b - \sqrt{d}}{2a}$$

5.16 Write a program to solve the following problem:

Read in a collection of N data items, each containing one integer between 0 and 9, and count the number of consecutive pairs of each integer occurring in the data set. Your program should print the number of consecutive pairs of 0's, of 1's, 2's, . . ., and the number of consecutive pairs of 9's found in the data.

ARRAYS AND STRINGS

6

6.1   INTRODUCTION

In many applications, we are faced with the problem of storing and manipulating large quantities of data in memory. In our problems so far, we have been able to process relatively large amounts of data using only a few memory cells. This is because we have been able to process each individual data item and then reuse the memory cell in which that data item was stored.

For example, in Problem 3.6 we processed a set of widget orders. Each order was read into the same memory cell, named ORDER, and then completely processed. This order was then lost when the next order was read into memory. This approach allowed us to process a large number of orders without having to allocate a separate memory cell for each one. However, once an order was processed, it was impossible to reexamine it later.

There are many applications in which we may need to save data items for subsequent reprocessing. For example, we might wish to write a program that computes and prints the average of a set of exam scores and also the difference between each score and the average. In this case, all scores must be processed and the average computed before we can calculate the differences. We must, therefore, be able to examine the list of student exam scores twice, first to compute the average and then to compute the differences. Since we would rather not have to read in the exam scores twice, we will want to save all of the scores in separate memory cells during the first step, for reuse during the second step.

In processing each data item, it would be tedious to have to reference each memory cell by a different name. In this chapter, we will learn how to use another feature of PASCAL, called an *array,* for storing a collection of related data items. Use of the array will simplify the task of naming and referencing the individual items in the collection. By using an array, we will be able to enter an entire collection of data items using a single read statement inside a loop. Once the collection is stored in memory, we will be able to reference any of these items as often as we wish without ever having to reenter that item into memory.

We shall also discuss the manipulation of strings. Several UCSD PASCAL functions and procedures for string manipulation will be introduced. We will show how to use these functions to edit or rearrange textual data.

6.2   DECLARING ARRAYS

In all programming discussed so far in this text, each variable name used in a program has always been associated with a single memory cell regardless of its data type. An *array* is a collection of one or more adjacent memory cells, called *array elements,* that are associated with a single variable name. Whenever we want to tell the compiler to associate two or more memory cells with a single name, we must use an *array declaration* in which we state the name to be used and the number of elements to be associated with this name.

For example, the array declaration

```
VAR X : ARRAY[1..8] OF REAL
```

instructs the compiler to associate eight memory cells (array elements) with the name X. Each element of X may contain a single real value.

In order to process the data stored in an array, we must be able to reference each individual element. The array *subscript* is used to differentiate between elements of the same array. For example, if X is the array with eight elements declared above, then we may refer to the elements of the array X as shown in Fig. 6.1.

X[1]	X[2]	X[3]	X[4]	X[5]	X[6]	X[7]	X[8]
16	12	6	−2.5	−12	−24	−38	−54.6

| First element | Second element | Third element | | | | | Eighth element |

Fig. 6.1   The eight elements of the array X.

The *subscripted variable* X[1] can be used to reference the first element of the array X, X[2] the second element, and X[8] the eighth element. The integer enclosed in brackets is the array subscript.

Example 6.1:   Let X be the array shown in Fig. 6.1. Then the statement

```
SUM := SUM + X[4]
```

will cause the value −2.5 (the contents of the memory cell designated by X[4]) to be added to SUM.

The declaration of array X shown earlier uses a new data type called the *array type*. The array type is described in the next display.

Array Type Declaration

> *array type* = ARRAY[*subscript type*] OF *element type*

Interpretation: The identifier *array type* describes a collection of memory cells (array elements). The *subscript type* may be either of the standard types BOOLEAN or CHAR, any user-defined scalar type, or subrange. There is an array element corresponding to each scalar value in the *subscript type*. Normally, the *subscript type* is expressed as a subrange of the form MIN..MAX, where ORD(MIN) must be less than ORD(MAX).

The *element type* describes the type of each element in the collection or array. All elements of an array are the same type.

Note 1: The standard types REAL, INTEGER and STRING may not be used as a *subscript type;* however, any "reasonably sized" subrange of the integers may be a *subscript type*.

Note 2: The *element type* may be any standard or user-defined type.

The actual declaration of variables that are arrays may be done in two ways. The array type may be defined first and then its name used in the variable declaration, or the array type may be specified in the variable declaration. Both methods of declaring the array X of Fig. 6.1 are shown below.

```
TYPE
   SMALLARRAY = ARRAY[1..8] OF CHAR;

VAR
   X : SMALLARRAY;
```

or

```
VAR
   X : ARRAY[1..8] OF CHAR;
```

In the first approach, the array type **SMALLARRAY** is defined first. We recommend doing this, particularly if several different arrays are being declared that are of the same type. The second approach may also be used with scalar and subrange types (e.g. **VAR IDNUM** : 1111..9999;) ; although, we have not done so as yet.

Example 6.2:   A number of different array types are declared below. A sample of each array type is given in Fig. 6.2.

```
CONST
   MIN1 = 1;
   MIN2 = 7;
   MAX1 = 10;
   MAX2 = 20;

TYPE
   LETTERS = 'A'..'Z';
   SMALLCHAR = ARRAY [ MIN2..MAX1 ] OF CHAR;
   VALUES = ARRAY [ MIN1..MAX2 ] OF REAL;
   LETTERCOUNT = ARRAY [ LETTERS ] OF INTEGER;
   LETTERFOUND = ARRAY [ LETTERS ] OF BOOLEAN;
```

The first array type, SMALLCHAR, describes an array of characters. An array of this type has four elements with subscripts 7(MIN2), 8, 9, and 10(MAX1). Each element may contain a symbol from the PASCAL character set (CHAR). The second array type, VALUES, describes an array of real numbers. There are twenty elements in an array of this type (subscripts 1 through 20).

The last two array types, LETTERCOUNT and LETTERFOUND, describe arrays with 26 elements. The subscript type is the subrange LETTERS ('A'..'Z'); hence, there is an array element corresponding to each letter of the alphabet. Only integer values may be stored in the elements of an array of type LETTERCOUNT. Such an array could be used to count the number of times each letter occurred in a message. Each element in an array of type LETTERFOUND contains a Boolean value. An array of this type could be used to indicate which letters occurred in a message (corresponding element TRUE) and which did not (corresponding element FALSE).

VAR A : SMALLCHAR

A[7]	A[8]	A[9]	A[10]
+	;	Y	3

VAR B : VALUES

B[1]	B[2]	B[3]		B[19]	B[20]
5.5	−10.3	−19.7	. . .	24.52	13.0

VAR C : LETTERCOUNT

C['A']	C['B']	C['C']		C['Y']	C['Z']
5	6	0	. . .	1	0

VAR D : LETTERFOUND

D['A']	D['B']	D['C']		D['Y']	D['Z']
TRUE	TRUE	FALSE	. . .	TRUE	FALSE

Fig. 6.2 Four array types.

Exercise 6.1: Describe the following array types:

```
a)   ARRAY[1..20] OF CHAR
b)   ARRAY['0'..'9'] OF BOOLEAN
c)   ARRAY[-5..5] OF REAL
d)   ARRAY[BOOLEAN] OF INTEGER
```

6.3 ARRAY SUBSCRIPTS

In the preceding section, we introduced the array subscript as a means of differentiating among the individual elements of an array. We showed that an array element can be referenced by specifying the name of the array followed by a pair of brackets enclosing a subscript (e.g., X[4]).

In general, the subscript may be an expression; the type of the subscript expression must correspond to the declared subscript type. The compiler determines the particular array element referenced by evaluating the subscript expression.

Example 6.3: Let I be a memory cell containing the value 3, and let COUNTS be the array declared below and shown in Fig. 6.3.

```
        VAR COUNTS : ARRAY[1..10] OF INTEGER;
```

Then: `COUNTS[I]` refers to the 3rd element of the array `COUNTS`;
      `COUNTS[2*I]` refers to the 6th element of the array `COUNTS`;
      `COUNTS[5*I-6]` refers to the 9th element of the array `COUNTS`;
      `COUNTS[I+1]` refers to the 4th element of the array `COUNTS`.

As shown above, we will write arithmetic subscript expressions without blanks around the arithmetic operators.

If the type of the subscript expression does not correspond to the declared subscript type, an "incorrect type" error message will be printed during translation of the PASCAL program. If the value of the subscript expression is outside the subrange specified in the array declaration, there is no such array element and a "subscript value out of range" diagnostic will be printed during program execution.

It is important to understand the distinction between the array subscript, the value of the subscript (sometimes called an *index* to the array), and the contents of the array element. The subscript is enclosed in brackets following the array name. Its value is used to select one of the array elements for manipulation. The contents of that array element is either used as an operand or modified as a result of executing a PASCAL statement.

In Example 6.3, the subscript type and element type are the same (type INTEGER). The array element with subscript [I + 1] is the fourth element of the array when I is 3; the value of COUNTS [I + 1] is 14.

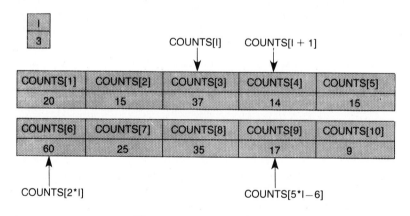

Fig. 6.3 Array COUNTS.

Example 6.4:   For the array COUNTS in Fig. 6.3, the statement

```
        COUNTS[8] := COUNTS[I+1]
```

copies the number in COUNTS[4] into COUNTS[8] when I is 3. The statement

```
        COUNTS[9] := COUNTS[I] + COUNTS[1]
```

stores the sum of the values of COUNTS[3] and COUNTS[1], or 57, in COUNTS[9]. On the other hand, the statement

```
COUNTS[10] := I + 1
```

simply stores the value of I + 1, or 4, in COUNTS[10]. The new array COUNTS is pictured next.

COUNTS[1]	COUNTS[2]	COUNTS[3]	COUNTS[4]	COUNTS[5]
20	15	37	14	15

COUNTS[6]	COUNTS[7]	COUNTS[8]	COUNTS[9]	COUNTS[10]
60	25	14	57	4

Example 6.5:   The declarations below describe an array named DOWNDAYS that has seven integer-valued elements.

```
TYPE
    DAY = (SUNDAY, MONDAY, TUESDAY, WEDNESDAY, THURSDAY,
           FRIDAY, SATURDAY);

VAR
    DOWNDAYS : ARRAY[DAY] OF INTEGER;
    TODAY : DAY
```

Since the subscript type is the scalar type DAY, only expressions that evaluate to one of the scalar values SUNDAY, MONDAY, etc. may be used as subscripts. Examples of legal subscripts for array DOWNDAYS would include FRIDAY, TODAY, PRED (TODAY), SUCC (TODAY) etc.

Exercise 6.2:   In Example 6.3, which elements in the array COUNTS are referenced if I is equal to 4 rather than 3?

Exercise 6.3:   Let I contain the integer 6 and let COUNTS be the array in Fig. 6.3. Which of the following references to elements of COUNTS are within range?

a) COUNTS[I]
b) COUNTS[3*I-20]
c) COUNTS[4+I]
d) COUNTS[I*3-12]

e) COUNTS[4*I-12]
f) COUNTS[I-2*I]
g) COUNTS[30]
h) COUNTS[I*I-1]

Exercise 6.4:   Given the array G as shown below

G[1]	G[2]	G[3]	G[4]	G[5]	G[6]	G[7]	G[8]	G[9]	G[10]
−11.2	12.0	−6.1	400.0	8.2	1.3	−.7	388.8	9.5	10.0

Array G

a)   What is the contents of G[2]?
b)   If I = 3, what is the contents of G[2*I−1]?
c)   What is the value of the condition G[I] <> 8.2 if I is equal to 3; if I is equal to 5?

d)   What will be the value of the variable FOUND after the statements below are executed?

```
FOUND := FALSE;
FOR I := 1 TO 10 DO
    IF G[I] = 388.8 THEN
        FOUND := TRUE
```

e)   What will the array G look like after the following statements are executed?

```
FOR I := 1 TO 5 DO
    G[I] := 2 * I;
FOR I := 6 TO 10 DO
    G[I] := 2 * G[I-5]
```

6.4   MANIPULATING ARRAY ELEMENTS

6.4.1   Sequential Access to Array Elements

In order to manipulate the individual elements of an array, the programmer must specify both the array name and its subscript. This is the case for array references in assignment statements, Boolean expressions, WRITE statements and READ statements.

Often, we desire to manipulate all the elements of an array in some uniform manner. For example, we may wish to set all element values to zero or print the value of every array element. In situations like this, we normally process the array elements in sequence, starting with the first subscript value and ending with the last subscript value. The FOR loop enables us to access easily all array elements in sequential order as shown in the next examples.

Example 6.6: The FOR loop below initializes all elements of the array COUNTS (see Fig. 6.3) to zero.

```
FOR I := 1 TO 10 DO
    COUNTS[I] := 0;
```

Example 6.7: The FOR loop in Fig. 6.4 stores the number of days in each month in the array DAYSINMONTH. It also stores the scalar value of each month (JAN, FEB, etc.) in the array MONTHVAL. The number of days in each month, starting with January and ending with December, should be provided as data to be read by the FOR loop. An execution error will result if any value read is outside the range 28 to 31.

The arrays DAYSINMONTH and MONTHVAL are shown below after execution of the FOR loop.

DAYSINMONTH

[JAN]	[FEB]	[MAR]	[APR]	[MAY]	[JUN]	[JUL]	[AUG]	[SEP]	[OCT]	[NOV]	[DEC]
31	28	31	30	31	30	31	31	30	31	30	31

MONTHVAL

[1]	[2]	[3]	[4]	[5]	[6]	[7]	[8]	[9]	[10]	[11]	[12]
JAN	FEB	MAR	APR	MAY	JUN	JUL	AUG	SEP	OCT	NOV	DEC

Once these data have been stored, it would be trivial to "convert" from a month number read as input data to a scalar value. The subscripted variable

MONTHVAL[I]

represents the scalar value associated with the Ith month (1 $<=$ I $<=$ 12). The subscripted variable

DAYSINMONTH[MONTHVAL[I]]

represents the number of days in the Ith month. (e.g. MONTHVAL[1] is JAN, DAYSINMONTH[MONTHVAL[1]] equals DAYSINMONTH[JAN] or 31).

```
TYPE
    MONTH = (JAN,FEB,MAR,APR,MAY,JUN,JUL,AUG,
             SEP,OCT,NOV,DEC);
    MONTHS = ARRAY[1..12] OF MONTH;
    MONTHDAYS = ARRAY[MONTH] OF 28..31;

VAR
    MONTHVAL : MONTHS;
    DAYSINMONTH : MONTHDAYS;
    NEXTMONTH : MONTH;

BEGIN
    (* INITIALIZE ARRAYS *)
    FOR NEXTMONTH := JAN TO DEC DO
      BEGIN
        READ (DAYSINMONTH[NEXTMONTH]);
        MONTHVAL[ORD(NEXTMONTH)+1] := NEXTMONTH
      END; (* FOR *)
```

Fig. 6.4 Accessing arrays with a FOR loop.

A summary of things to remember when using a FOR loop to provide sequential access to an array is given in the next display.

Sequential Access to Array Elements with FOR Loop

1. The FOR loop control variable should also be used as the subscript of the array being referenced; hence, the type of the loop control variable must be compatible with the subscript type.

2. The initial and final value parameters for the FOR loop control variable must match the declared subscript range.

Exercise 6.5:

a)   Declare and initialize an array that contains each letter of the alphabet in consecutive elements. Use the subrange 1..26 as the subscript type.

b)   Declare and initialize an array S of size 10 in which the value of each element is
the same as its subscript; i.e.,

$$S[1] = 1, S[2] = 2,...,S[10] = 10.$$

c)   Declare and initialize an array T of size 10 for which

$$T[1] = 10, T[2] = 9,...,T[10] = 1.$$

d)   Declare and initialize an array U of size 10 in which the value of each element
is the square of its subscript; i.e.,

$$U[1] = 1, U[2] = 4,...,U[10] = 100.$$

Exercise 6.6:   In Example 6.7, what is the relationship between each subscript for
MONTHVAL and the ordinal number of its corresponding month?

Exercise 6.7:   Declare an array PRIME consisting of ten elements. Write a loop for entering the first ten prime numbers into the array PRIME. Also, echo print the index and
the contents of each element of the array PRIME in the tabular form shown below.

N	PRIME[N]
1	1
2	2
3	3
4	5
.	.
.	.
.	.
10	23

6.4.2   Random Access to an Array

In many problems, we do not know beforehand which array elements will be
accessed or in what order. The order is *random* and is determined by input data
that may change from one execution of the program to another. In the example
below, the elements of the array CODE are first initialized in sequential order;
then, arbitrary elements of this array are selected for printing in random order.

Example 6.8:   The program in Fig. 6.5 generates cryptograms. A cryptogram is
a coded message formed by substituting a code character for each letter of an
original message. The substitution is performed uniformly throughout the original
message, i.e., all A's might be replaced by S, all B's by P, etc. All punctuation
(including blanks between words) remains unchanged.

The data table for Example 6.8 is shown next. In a data table, the subscript
type for an array will be enclosed in brackets following the array name; the element type will be given in parentheses following the description of the array. If
the array type has been given a name in a separate type declaration, then that
name will be specified in parentheses after the description of the array.

Data Table for Example 6.8

Data types

LETTER = 'A'..'Z'

Input variables	*Program variables*	*Output variables*

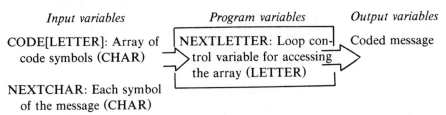

CODE[LETTER]: Array of   NEXTLETTER: Loop con-   Coded message
code symbols (CHAR)   trol variable for accessing
                          the array (LETTER)

NEXTCHAR: Each symbol
of the message (CHAR)

The FOR loop reads the code symbol for each letter into the array CODE. Afterwards, as each letter in the message is read (but not echoed) its corresponding code symbol is extracted from the array CODE and printed. Any character that is not a letter is printed. The Boolean expression

```
('A' <= NEXTCHAR) AND (NEXTCHAR <= 'Z')
```

is true only when NEXTCHAR is a letter.

The sample below shows the output that would be generated using a simple "next letter" code (substitute B for A, C for B,..., A for Z). After reading the first input line, the value of CODE['A'] would be 'B', the value of CODE['B'] would be 'C', etc. The cryptogram shown corresponds to the message

```
JACK BE NIMBLE, JACK BE QUICK!
```

```
ENTER CODE FOR EACH LETTER BELOW
ABCDEFGHIJKLMNOPQRSTUVWXYZ
BCDEFGHIJKLMNOPQRSTUVWXYZA

ENTER MESSAGE

KBDL CF OJNCMF, KBDL CF RVJDL!
```

The following problem also illustrates sequential and random access to the elements of an array.

Problem 6.1: Write a program that determines the number of occurrences of each letter of the alphabet in a segment of text.

Discussion: In order to solve this problem, we will store the number of occurrences of each letter in the array OCCURRENCE. If a letter is read from the text, the corresponding element of OCCURRENCE will be increased by one; all other characters will be ignored. The array OCCURRENCE must be initialized to all zeros. The data table and algorithm for the main program follow.

```
PROGRAM CRYPTOGRAM;

TYPE
  LETTER = 'A'..'Z';

VAR
  NEXTCHAR : CHAR;
  NEXTLETTER : LETTER;
  CODE : ARRAY[LETTER] OF CHAR;

BEGIN
  (* ENTER CODE FOR EACH LETTER *)
  WRITELN ('ENTER CODE FOR EACH LETTER BELOW');
  WRITELN ('ABCDEFGHIJKLMNOPQRSTUVWXYZ');
  FOR NEXTLETTER := 'A' TO 'Z' DO
    READ (CODE[NEXTLETTER]);
  WRITELN;

  (* ENCODE ALL SYMBOLS OF MESSAGE *)
  WRITELN ('ENTER MESSAGE');
  WHILE NOT EOLN DO
    BEGIN
      READ (KEYBOARD, NEXTCHAR);
      (* REPLACE EACH LETTER WITH CODE SYMBOL *)
      IF ('A' <= NEXTCHAR) AND (NEXTCHAR <= 'Z') THEN
        WRITE (CODE[NEXTCHAR])
      ELSE
        WRITE (NEXTCHAR)
    END (* WHILE *)
END.
```

Fig. 6.5 Cryptogram generator.

Data Table for Main Program

Data types

LETTER = 'A'..'Z'
COUNTERS = ARRAY [LETTER] OF INTEGER

Input variables	*Program variables*	*Output variables*
(none)	NEXTLETTER: Loop control variable (LETTER)	OCCURRENCE: Number of occurrences of each letter of the alphabet (COUNTERS)

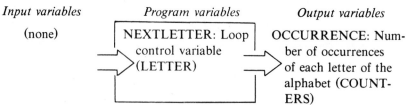

Procedures referenced

PROCESLINE: Reads and processes each line of text

Level One Algorithm

1. Initialize OCCURRENCE to all zeros.
2. Read and process each line of text.
3. Print the array OCCURRENCE.

Steps 1 and 3 are performed in the main program, shown in Fig. 6.6a. In the first FOR loop, the variable NEXTLETTER is used as the loop control variable and also as the array subscript. The array elements are accessed in sequence from 'A' to 'Z' and set to zero. The last FOR loop (Step 3) prints each letter from 'A' to 'Z', followed by the number of times it occurred.

```
PROGRAM TEXTPROCESS;
(* COUNTS NUMBER OF OCCURRENCES OF EACH LETTER*)

TYPE
   LETTER = 'A'..'Z';
   COUNTERS = ARRAY[LETTER] OF INTEGER;

VAR
   OCCURRENCE : COUNTERS;
   NEXTLETTER : LETTER;

(* INSERT PROCESLINE HERE *)
(*$I UCSD3:PROCESLINE *)

BEGIN
   (* INITIALIZE ARRAY OCCURRENCE TO ZEROS *)
   FOR NEXTLETTER := 'A' TO 'Z' DO
      OCCURRENCE[NEXTLETTER] := 0;

   (* READ AND PROCESS EACH LINE OF TEXT *)
   PROCESLINE (OCCURRENCE);

   (* PRINT FINAL RESULTS *)
   WRITELN;
   WRITELN ('LETTER  NUMBER OF OCCURRENCES');
   FOR NEXTLETTER := 'A' TO 'Z' DO
      WRITELN (NEXTLETTER :4, OCCURRENCE[NEXTLETTER] :8)
END.
```

Fig. 6.6a Counting occurrences of letters.

The procedure PROCESLINE reads and echo-prints the text, line-by-line. If a letter is read, the local variable NEXTCHAR selects the corresponding element of OCCURRENCE for update (addition of one).

The data table for PROCESLINE follows. The procedure is written in Fig. 6.6b; a sample run of the complete program is shown in Fig. 6.6c.

Data Table for PROCESLINE

Input parameters	Update parameters	Output parameters
(none)	OCCURRENCE	(none)
Input variables	*Program variables*	*Output variables*
NEXTCHAR: Each character in a line of text (CHAR)	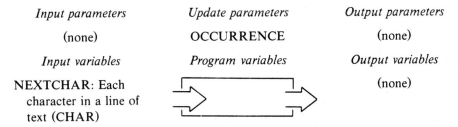	(none)

```
PROCEDURE PROCESLINE (VAR OCCURRENCE : COUNTERS);
(* READS AND PROCESSES EACH LINE OF TEXT *)

VAR
  NEXTCHAR : CHAR;

BEGIN
  WHILE NOT EOF DO
    BEGIN
      (* READ AND PRINT EACH LINE *)
      WHILE NOT EOLN DO
        BEGIN
          READ (NEXTCHAR);
          (* INCREASE OCCURRENCE COUNT FOR EACH LETTER *)
          IF ('A' <= NEXTCHAR) AND (NEXTCHAR <= 'Z') THEN
            OCCURRENCE[NEXTCHAR] := OCCURRENCE[NEXTCHAR]+1
        END; (* WHILE *)
      READLN
    END (* WHILE *)
END; (* PROCESLINE *)
```

Fig. 6.6b   Procedure PROCESLINE.

THIS PROGRAM WILL COUNT THE NUMBER OF OCCURRENCES
OF EACH LETTER OF THE ALPHABET IN THIS SENTENCE.

LETTER	NUMBER OF OCCURRENCES
A	4
B	2
C	6
D	0
E	12
F	3
G	1
H	6
I	4
J	0
K	0
L	4
M	2
N	6
O	6
P	2
Q	0
R	6
S	4
T	9
U	3
V	0
W	1
X	0
Y	0
Z	0

Fig. 6.6c   Sample run of Letter Counting Program.

The array OCCURRENCE is passed as an update parameter to procedure PROCESLINE. It is initialized to all zeros in the main program and redefined as PROCESLINE executes. We shall discuss the use of arrays as parameters in the next section.

In Fig. 6.6b, the EOF (end of file) function is used to control loop repetition. This function is initially false (NOT EOF is true); it may be set to true by pressing the <ETX> key (CTRL + C on the APPLE, CTRL/↓ + C on the TRS-80) after the last line is entered. We shall discuss this function further in Chapter 9.

The READLN statement at the bottom of Fig. 6.6b. is executed when the end of each input line is reached (EOLN is true). It resets the EOLN function to false so that the next data line may be read.

6.5 MANIPULATING ENTIRE ARRAYS

6.5.1 Type Equivalence of Arrays

Arrays may be passed as procedure (or function) parameters as shown in Fig. 6.6b. As with any parameters, the type of an array used as an actual parameter must be the same as its corresponding formal parameter.

Two arrays must have the same structure (same element and subscript types) in order to be considered the same type. Given the declarations

```
TYPE
    SMALLARRAY = ARRAY[1..10] OF REAL;

VAR
    U : SMALLARRAY;
    V, W : ARRAY[1..10] OF REAL;
    X : ARRAY[1..10] OF REAL;
    Y : ARRAY[0..9] OF REAL;
```

we might expect arrays U, V, W and X to be considered the same type as they all have ten real elements with subscripts one through ten. Array Y has ten real elements too, but its subscript type is different.

UCSD PASCAL would consider arrays U, V, W and X to be the same type. However, some compilers consider two arrays to be the same type only if one of the statements below is true.

   1. The arrays are declared to be the same named array type (e.g. SMALLARRAY).

or 2. The arrays are declared in the same variable declaration statement (e.g. V, W).

Given this more restrictive definition, only arrays V and W above would be considered the same type.

When dealing with multiple arrays of the same structure, it is always best to declare a named array type (e.g. SMALLARRAY) and then use this name in declaring each array as shown next.

```
TYPE
   SMALLARRAY = ARRAY[1..10] OF REAL;

VAR
   U : SMALLARRAY;
   V, W : SMALLARRAY;
   X : SMALLARRAY;
   Y : ARRAY[0..9] OF REAL;
```

Regardless of the PASCAL compiler used, the arrays U, V, W and X declared above would all be considered the same type. (This approach should be followed for all data structures being declared, not just arrays. Other data structures will be introduced in later chapters.)

If an array of type SMALLARRAY is a formal parameter, then the type identifier SMALLARRAY must appear in the parameter list (e.g. (VAR Z : SMALLARRAY)). The parameter list

```
   (VAR Z : ARRAY[1..10] OF REAL)
```

would be illegal since only identifiers may be used to specify parameter types.

6.5.2 Arrays as Parameters

In this section, we shall illustrate the use of arrays as parameters and describe the difference between arrays used as variable and value parameters.

Example 6.9: The procedure ADDARRAY, shown in Fig. 6.7, adds corresponding elements of two arrays and stores the result in a third array as illustrated below. All three arrays must be type ARRAYOFNUMBERS.

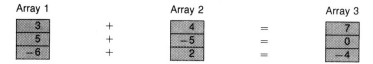

In Fig. 6.7, parameters A and B represent the two arrays that are added together. They, along with SIZE (number of array elements), are value parameters since they provide input data only. Parameter SUMS is a variable parameter as the array corresponding to parameter SUMS is defined (assigned values) by the procedure.

In the documentation provided (comment statements), A, B and SIZE are described as input parameters since they provide input data to the procedure. Their corresponding actual parameters must be defined (assigned values) before the procedure is called.

Parameter SUMS is described as an output parameter since it communicates results back to the calling program. The actual array corresponding to SUMS may or may not be defined prior to the procedure call. Any values stored in the corresponding actual array will be modified as the procedure executes.

The number of times the FOR loop is executed is determined by the parameter SIZE. Each execution of the loop forms the sum of the next pair of array elements.

```
PROCEDURE ADDARRAY (A, B : ARRAYOFNUMBERS;
                    SIZE : INTEGER;
                    VAR SUMS : ARRAYOFNUMBERS);
(* ADD ARRAY A TO ARRAY B - STORE SUM IN ARRAY SUMS *)
(* INPUT PARAMETERS                                 *)
(*    A, B - ARRAYS TO BE SUMMED                    *)
(*    SIZE - NR. OF ELEMENTS IN EACH ARRAY          *)
(* OUTPUT PARAMETERS                                *)
(*    SUMS - SUMS[I] IS THE SUM OF A[I] AND B[I]    *)

VAR
  I : INTEGER;

BEGIN
  FOR I := 1 TO SIZE DO
    SUMS[I] := A[I] + B[I]
END; (* ADDARRAY *)
```

Fig. 6.7 Procedure ADDARRAY.

Given the declarations

```
CONST
  N = 10;

TYPE
  ARRAYOFNUMBERS = ARRAY[1..N] OF INTEGER;

VAR
  W, X, Y, Z : ARRAYOFNUMBERS;
```

the procedure statement

```
ADDARRAY (W, X, N, Y)
```

forms the element-by-element sum of arrays W and X in array Y. The procedure statement

```
ADDARRAY (W, X, 5, Z)
```

forms the element-by-element sum of the first five elements only of arrays W and X in array Z; the remaining elements of array Z would not be changed.

When an array is used as a variable parameter, all elements of the corresponding actual array may be accessed directly by the procedure and assigned new values. When an array is used as a value parameter, a local copy of the array is made when the procedure is entered, and the procedure manipulates the local array. Initially, the local array has the same element values as its corresponding actual array; however, any changes made to the local array by the procedure are not reflected in the actual array.

The correspondence established by the call statement

```
ADDARRAY (W, X, N, Y)
```

is illustrated in Fig. 6.8; the arrows indicate the direction of information flow.

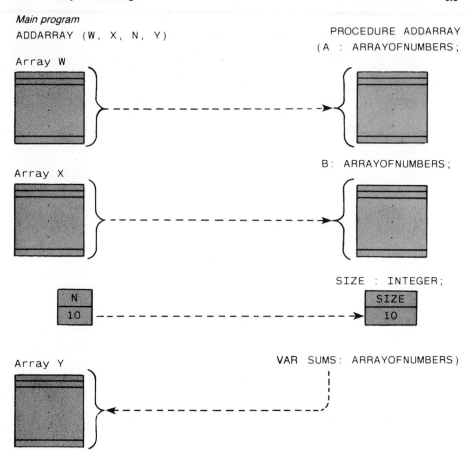

Fig. 6.8 Correspondence of array parameters.

Program Style

Efficiency of variable parameters versus protection of value parameters

Parameters A and B in Fig. 6.7 are declared as value parameters since they are used only for data entry into the procedure.

As shown in Fig. 6.8, the compiler must establish local copies of both of these arrays each time the procedure is executed. This uses valuable computer time and memory space.

For this reason, experienced programmers sometimes declare arrays used only for input purposes as variable parameters. When large arrays are involved, this can result in a considerable saving of time and memory space. However, the tradeoff is that the corresponding actual parameter is no longer protected from accidental modification by the procedure. Any changes made by the procedure (either by accident or design) will now be reflected in the actual array. This is not the case for arrays passed as value parameters.

Exercise 6.8:   Write a main program that reads two arrays of data, X and Y, and uses procedure ADDARRAY to compute two times X plus Y.

6.5.3   Individual Array Elements as Parameters

A single array element is represented by a subscripted variable (array name followed by its subscript). A subscripted variable may be used as an actual parameter in a procedure statement. As with any other variable, the type of the subscripted variable (array element type) and its corresponding formal parameter must be the same. (Assignment compatibility is sufficient for value parameters.)

Example 6.10:   Given the declarations in Example 6.9, the procedure statement

```
ADDARRAY (W, X, W[1], Y)
```

is perfectly legal; the subscripted variable W[1] corresponds to the parameter SIZE (both type INTEGER). However, an error will result during execution of procedure ADDARRAY if the value of W[1] is greater than ten (Why?).

Exercise 6.9:   Given the procedure header

```
PROCEDURE MASSAGE (A, B : REAL; X : SMALLARRAY);
```

and the declarations in the main program

```
TYPE
    SMALLARRAY = ARRAY[1..10] OF INTEGER;

VAR
    X, Y, Z : REAL;
    M, N : SMALLARRAY;
```

indicate which of the call statements below are illegal and why.

```
a) MASSAGE (X, Y, Z)
b) MASSAGE (X, Y, M)
c) MASSAGE (X, Y, M[1..5])
d) MASSAGE (Y, Z, X)
e) MASSAGE (M[2], Y, N)
f) MASSAGE (X[2], Y, N)
g) MASSAGE (25.0, 1.5, M)
h) MASSAGE (X, Y, M[10])
i) MASSAGE (M[1], M[2], N)
j) MASSAGE (X+Y, X-Y, M)
k) MASSAGE (X, Y, M, 10)
```

6.5.4   Copying and Comparing Arrays

In general, each element of an array must be manipulated individually. However, we saw earlier that an entire array may be passed as a parameter. It is also possible to copy one array to another array of the same type using a single assignment statement. If V and W are the same array type, then either statement below would copy the array V to the array W.

```
W := V                    │        FOR I := 1 TO 10 DO
                          │          W[I] := V[I]
```

Each element of array V would be copied into the corresponding element of array W.

This is the only way in which an entire array of data can be manipulated in an assignment statement. It would be illegal to perform arithmetic operations involving an array of data except by manipulating each array element individually in a FOR loop.

In UCSD (but not standard) PASCAL, it is also possible to compare two arrays of the same type using the relational operators $=$ or $< >$. Consequently, the Boolean expression $W = V$ would be true only if all corresponding elements of arrays W and V have the same value (i.e. $W[1] = V[1]$, $W[2] = V[2]$,...). The Boolean expression $W < > V$ would be true if at least one pair of corresponding elements has different values.

6.6   PARTIALLY FILLED ARRAYS

6.6.1   Reading Data into Part of an Array

In many problems, we may want to manipulate only a portion of an array, with the exact number of elements involved determined during each execution of the program. In this case, we should allocate enough array elements to accommodate the largest possible set of data items.

If we don't know beforehand how many data items are to be processed, a WHILE loop should be used for data entry. Normally the data entry process should continue as long as a sentinel value has not been read. To prevent reading more data values than there are array elements, it is a good idea to count the number of data values stored in the array; the data entry loop should be exited if the array becomes completely filled.

In procedure READPART of Fig. 6.9, the parameter COUNT is used as a subscript to the array M and determines which array element receives the next data item (stored in TEMP). COUNT is initialized to zero and increased by one before each value is read. COUNT also represents the number of data items read so far. The loop terminates when either the sentinel is read or the array is completely filled (COUNT equal to MAX). The final value of COUNT represents the number of array elements that contain input data.

It is important to realize that only a portion of the array represented by M is filled with data when the final value of COUNT is less than MAX. This means that the rest of the array is undefined; therefore, attempts to manipulate array elements with subscripts greater than COUNT will result in an error.

Exercise 6.10:   Write a procedure to fill part of an array assuming that the number of array elements to be filled (NUMITEMS) is provided as the very first data item. Be sure to test that NUMITEMS is in range before entering the array data. Print an error message and redefine NUMITEMS if it is not.

```
PROCEDURE READPART (VAR M : SMALLARRAY;
                         MAX : INTEGER;
                         SENTINEL : INTEGER;
                         VAR COUNT : INTEGER);
(* READS PART OF AN ARRAY M WITH MAX ELEMENTS          *)
(* DETERMINES THE NUMBER OF ARRAY ELEMENTS FILLED - COUNT *)

VAR
  TEMP : INTEGER;

BEGIN
  WRITELN ('ENTER EACH ARRAY ITEM');
  WRITELN ('OR ', SENTINEL, ' WHEN DONE');
  COUNT := 0;
  READ (TEMP);
  (* STORE EACH DATA ITEM IN M *)
  WHILE (TEMP <> SENTINEL) AND (COUNT < MAX) DO
    BEGIN
      COUNT := COUNT + 1;
      M[COUNT] := TEMP;
      READ (TEMP)
    END (* WHILE *)
END; (* READPART *)
```

Fig. 6.9 Procedure to read part of an array.

6.6.2 The Bowling Problem

The next problem uses an array PINCOUNT that may or may not be completely filled, and an array SCORE that is always filled.

Problem 6.2: Write a program that will compute a person's tenpin bowling score for one game, given the number of pins knocked down per ball. Print the score for each frame, as well as the cumulative score at the end of each frame.

Discussion: A bowling game consists of 10 *frames*. In tenpin bowling, a maximum of two balls may be rolled in each of the first nine frames, and two or three balls may be rolled in frame ten. Each frame is scored according to the following rules:

1. If the first ball rolled in a frame knocks down all 10 pins (called a *strike*), then the score for the frame is equal to 10 plus the total score on the next two balls rolled. Since all ten pins are down, no other balls are rolled in the current frame.
2. If the two balls rolled in the frame together knock down all 10 pins (called a *spare*), then the score for the frame is equal to 10 plus the score on the next ball rolled.
3. If the two balls rolled knock down fewer than 10 pins (no mark), then the frame score is equal to the number of pins knocked down.

The number of pins knocked down by each ball will be read into an array called PINCOUNT. Depending on the number of strikes bowled, PINCOUNT may contain anywhere from eleven to twenty-one entries. (Why?) Each entry will be an integer between zero and ten. The array SCORE (ten elements) will be used to save the score for each frame.

The data table and level one algorithm are shown below.

Data Table for Bowling Problem

Constants

MAXBALL = 21, maximum number of balls bowled

Data types

BALLRANGE = 1..MAXBALL
PINS = 0..10
SCORERANGE = 0..30
PINARRAY = ARRAY [BALLRANGE] OF PINS
SCOREARRAY = ARRAY [1..10] OF SCORERANGE

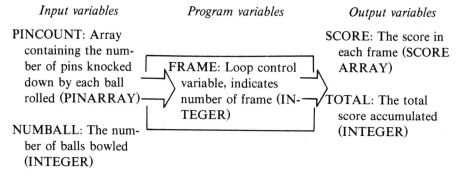

Input variables	*Program variables*	*Output variables*
PINCOUNT: Array containing the number of pins knocked down by each ball rolled (PINARRAY)	FRAME: Loop control variable, indicates number of frame (INTEGER)	SCORE: The score in each frame (SCORE ARRAY)
NUMBALL: The number of balls bowled (INTEGER)		TOTAL: The total score accumulated (INTEGER)

Procedures referenced

READPIN: Reads array PINCOUNT and defines NUMBALL.
FRAMESCORE: Computes score for every frame.

Level One Algorithm

1. Read pin count for each ball bowled and define NUMBALL.
2. Compute score for every frame.
3. Accumulate and print the running total by frame.

Step 3 is implemented in the main program shown in Fig. 6.10a. Procedure READPIN should be modeled after procedure READPART and is left as an exercise.

Procedure FRAMESCORE must add together the elements of array PINCOUNT that constitute the score for each frame (Step 2 above). The variable FIRSTBALL will serve as an index to the array PINCOUNT. As such, it will be used to select particular elements of PINCOUNT—the elements whose

```
PROGRAM BOWLING;
(* COMPUTE BOWLING SCORE *)

CONST
  MAXBALL = 21;

TYPE
  PINS = 0..10;
  SCORERANGE = 0..30;
  BALLRANGE = 1..MAXBALL;
  PINARRAY = ARRAY[BALLRANGE] OF PINS;
  SCOREARRAY = ARRAY[1..10] OF SCORERANGE;

VAR
  PINCOUNT : PINARRAY;
  SCORE : SCOREARRAY;
  NUMBALL, TOTAL, FRAME : INTEGER;

  (* INSERT PROCEDURES READPIN AND FRAMESCORE HERE *)
  (*$I UCSD3:READPIN *)
  (*$I UCSD3:FRAMESCORE *)

BEGIN
  (* READ PIN COUNT FOR EACH BALL AND DEFINE NUMBALL *)
  READPIN (PINCOUNT, MAXBALL, NUMBALL);

  (* COMPUTE SCORE FOR EVERY FRAME *)
  FRAMESCORE (PINCOUNT, NUMBALL, SCORE);

  (* ACCUMULATE TOTAL AND PRINT RESULT BY FRAME *)
  TOTAL := 0;
  WRITELN ('FRAME', 'SCORE' :9, 'TOTAL SCORE' :18);
  FOR FRAME := 1 TO 10 DO
    BEGIN
      TOTAL := TOTAL + SCORE[FRAME];
      WRITELN (FRAME :5, SCORE[FRAME] :9, TOTAL :15)
    END (*FOR*)
END.
```

Fig. 6.10a   Main program for bowling problem.

values represent the number of pins knocked down by the first ball rolled in each frame. FIRSTBALL should be increased by 1 each time a strike is bowled; otherwise, FIRSTBALL should be increased by 2. (Why?)

A sample of the array PINCOUNT is given below.

PINCOUNT[1]	PINCOUNT[2]	PINCOUNT[3]	PINCOUNT[4]	PINCOUNT[5]
10	7	3	5	3

. . .

This array shows that 10 pins were knocked down by the first ball, seven by the second, etc. The processing of this array is shown in Table 6.1.

Frame	FIRSTBALL	Frame score	Effect
1	1	10 + 7 + 3 = 20	STRIKE: Only one ball rolled in frame 1
2	2	7 + 3 + 5 = 15	SPARE: Two balls rolled in frame 2
3	4	5 + 3 = 8	NO MARK: Two balls rolled in frame 3
4	6	.	
		.	
		.	

Table 6.1 Processing Array PINCOUNT

Since PINCOUNT[1] is 10, a strike was bowled in the first frame. The frame score (20) is computed by adding together 10, PINCOUNT[2] and PINCOUNT[3]; FIRSTBALL is then set to 2. In the second frame, balls 2 and 3 are needed to knock down all 10 pins. Adding in the pins knocked down by the next ball, PINCOUNT[4], gives a frame score of 15; the index FIRSTBALL is then set to 4. Two balls are rolled in the third frame (balls 4 and 5). The frame score is 8, the value of FIRSTBALL is set to 6.

The data table and level one algorithm for FRAMESCORE follow.

Data Table for FRAMESCORE

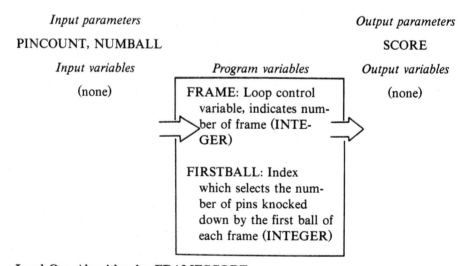

Input parameters	*Output parameters*
PINCOUNT, NUMBALL	SCORE

Input variables	*Program variables*	*Output variables*
(none)	FRAME: Loop control variable, indicates number of frame (INTEGER)	(none)
	FIRSTBALL: Index which selects the number of pins knocked down by the first ball of each frame (INTEGER)	

Level One Algorithm for FRAMESCORE

1. Initialize FIRSTBALL to 1.
2. Compute the score for each frame.

Level Two Refinements for FRAMESCORE

Step 2   *Compute the score for each frame*

   2.1 FOR FRAME := 1 TO 10 DO

2.2 IF FIRSTBALL is out of range THEN
        Print an error message
    ELSE
        Compute the score for the current frame and increase
        FIRSTBALL

Step 2.2 first tests whether FIRSTBALL is out of range. If not, it then processes the next elements of the array PINCOUNT (starting with PINCOUNT
[FIRSTBALL]) to determine the frame score. Step 2.2 is refined below.

Level Three Refinements for FRAMESCORE

Step 2.2

2.2.1 IF FIRSTBALL $>=$ NUMBALL THEN
           Print an error message
       ELSE IF a strike occurs THEN
           BEGIN
               Add together next three elements of PINCOUNT
               FIRSTBALL:= FIRSTBALL + 1
           END
       ELSE IF a spare occurs THEN
           BEGIN
               Add together next three elements of PINCOUNT
               FIRSTBALL:= FIRSTBALL + 2
           END
       ELSE
           BEGIN
               Add together next two elements of PINCOUNT
               FIRSTBALL:= FIRSTBALL + 2
           END

Procedure FRAMESCORE is shown in Fig. 6.10b. The subscript expressions FIRSTBALL and FIRSTBALL + 1 are used to reference the first and second balls rolled in the current frame, respectively. A strike occurs when
PINCOUNT[FIRSTBALL] is ten; a spare occurs when PINCOUNT
[FIRSTBALL] and PINCOUNT[FIRSTBALL + 1] together add up to ten. A
sample run of the bowling program is shown in Fig. 6.10c. (The execution of
procedure READPIN is not shown.)

Exercise 6.11: Write procedure READPIN. Be sure to define NUMBALL and print
an error message if too much data are provided.

Exercise 6.12: They do things a little differently in Massachusetts. The bowling pins
(called candlepins) are narrow at the top and bottom and wider in the middle. The balls
are about the size of a softball. The rules for a strike and spare are the same; however, the
bowler gets to roll a third ball in each frame if needed. Modify the bowling program to
score a candlepin game. (Any pins that fall on the lane are not cleared away in candlepins. This can help the bowler but should not affect your program.)

```
PROCEDURE FRAMESCORE (PINCOUNT : PINARRAY;
                      NUMBALL : BALLRANGE;
                      VAR SCORE : SCOREARRAY);
(* COMPUTES THE SCORE FOR EVERY FRAME *)

VAR
  FIRSTBALL, FRAME : INTEGER;

BEGIN
  FIRSTBALL := 1;
  FOR FRAME := 1 TO 10 DO
    (* COMPUTE SCORE FOR CURRENT FRAME & INCREASE
       FIRSTBALL *)
    IF FIRSTBALL >= NUMBALL THEN
      WRITELN (FIRSTBALL, 'IS OUT OF RANGE 1 TO', NUMBALL)
    ELSE IF PINCOUNT[FIRSTBALL] = 10 THEN
      BEGIN (* STRIKE *)
        SCORE[FRAME] := 10 + PINCOUNT[FIRSTBALL+1] +
                             PINCOUNT[FIRSTBALL+2];
        FIRSTBALL := FIRSTBALL + 1
      END (* STRIKE *)
    ELSE IF PINCOUNT[FIRSTBALL] +
            PINCOUNT[FIRSTBALL+1] = 10 THEN
      BEGIN (* SPARE *)
        SCORE[FRAME] := 10 + PINCOUNT[FIRSTBALL+2];
        FIRSTBALL := FIRSTBALL + 2
      END (* SPARE *)
    ELSE
      BEGIN (* NO MARK *)
        SCORE[FRAME] := PINCOUNT[FIRSTBALL] +
                        PINCOUNT[FIRSTBALL+1];
        FIRSTBALL := FIRSTBALL + 2
      END (*IF*)
END; (* FRAMESCORE *)
```

Fig. 6.10b Procedure FRAMESCORE.

FRAME	SCORE	TOTAL SCORE
1	17	17
2	9	26
3	13	39
4	3	42
5	9	51
6	20	71
7	16	87
8	6	93
9	7	100
10	16	116

Fig. 6.10c Sample run of bowling program.

6.7 ARRAYS OF STRINGS

6.7.1 Declaring String Arrays

The element type for an array can be any standard or user-defined type. Consequently, an array of strings can be declared and manipulated in PASCAL as shown below.

```
TYPE
   STUARRAY = ARRAY[1..100] OF STRING[20];

VAR
   STUDENT : STUARRAY;
```

The array STUDENT has 100 elements, each of which is a string of up to 20 characters.

We can reference any individual element (string) in the array STUDENT by specifying its subscript. The subscript value must be between one and 100. The Boolean expression STUDENT[1] < STUDENT[2] compares the strings in elements 1 and 2 of the array STUDENT.

6.7.2 Printing "Scalar" Values

Arrays with elements of type STRING are quite useful in many problems. One of the limitations in using programmer-defined scalar types is the fact that their values cannot be entered or displayed at a terminal. Through the use of arrays of strings, we can at least simplify the output problem.

Example 6.11: Each element of the array DAYNAME declared below

```
TYPE
   DAY = (SUNDAY, MONDAY, TUESDAY, WEDNESDAY, THURSDAY,
          FRIDAY, SATURDAY);
   DAYS = ARRAY [DAY] OF STRING[9];

VAR
   TODAY : DAY;
   DAYNAME : DAYS;
```

can store a string of up to nine characters. Since the subscript type is DAY, there are seven elements in DAYNAME with subscripts ranging from SUNDAY through SATURDAY. This array should be initialized so that each element contains the string corresponding to its subscript (e.g., DAYNAME[SUNDAY] := 'SUNDAY'). If this is done, the string denoting the scalar value of TODAY can be displayed using the statement

```
WRITELN (DAYNAME[TODAY])
```

Exercise 6.13:   Write a procedure that initializes the array DAYNAME described in Example 6.11.

Exercise 6.14:   Add an array MONTHNAME to Example 6.7. Rewrite the program segment in Fig. 6.4 as a procedure that reads the name of each month as well as the number of days in a month.

6.7.3   Application of Arrays

The next problem illustrates many of the techniques discussed in this chapter. It uses arrays for storage of string and numeric data.

Problem 6.3:   Write a program that reads a collection of student names and exam scores and assigns a letter grade to each student as follows. If the student's score is 10 or more points above class average, the grade is 'A'; if the student's score is ten or more points below class average, the grade is 'C'; otherwise, the grade is 'B'.

Discussion: It will be necessary to make two "passes" through the collection of exam scores. During the first pass, we will read each student's name and score and accumulate the total of all exam scores. This total score will then be used to compute the class average. During the second pass, we will compare each score to the class average and assign and print a letter grade along with the student's name and score. The data table and level one algorithm for the main program are shown below.

Data Table for Main Program

Constants

CLASSIZE = 120, the maximum number of students

Data types

STURANGE = 1..CLASSIZE
STUARRAY = ARRAY [STURANGE] OF STRING[10]
SCOREARRAY = ARRAY [STURANGE] OF INTEGER

Input variables	*Program variables*	*Output variables*
STUDENT: Array of student names (STUARRAY)	SUM: Accumulated sum of exam scores (INTEGER)	AVERAGE: Average score on the exam (REAL)
SCORE: Array of exam scores (SCOREARRAY)		COUNT: Number of students taking exam (INTEGER)

Procedures referenced

> ENTERSCORE: Reads each student's name and score. Computes SUM and COUNT
> CATEGORIZE: Finds and prints grade category for each student

Level One Algorithm

1. Read each student's name and score. Compute SUM and COUNT.
2. Compute and print AVERAGE.
3. Find and print grade category for each student.

Steps 1 and 3 will be implemented as procedures ENTERSCORE and CATEGORIZE, respectively. The main program is given in Fig. 6.11a.

In writing procedure ENTERSCORE, we must make allowance for the fact that not all class sizes are the same. Hence, we must count the number of students taking the exam as well as accumulate the sum of all scores. The data table for ENTERSCORE is shown after the main program.

```
PROGRAM EXAMS;
(* ASSIGN LETTER GRADES BASED ON CLASS AVERAGE *)

CONST
  CLASSIZE = 120;

TYPE
  STURANGE = 1..CLASSIZE;
  STUARRAY = ARRAY[STURANGE] OF STRING[10];
  SCOREARRAY = ARRAY[STURANGE] OF INTEGER;

VAR
  STUDENT : STUARRAY;
  SCORE : SCOREARRAY;
  SUM, COUNT : INTEGER;
  AVERAGE : REAL;

(* INSERT PROCEDURES ENTERSCORE AND CATEGORIZE HERE *)
(*$I UCSD3:ENTERSCORE *)
(*$I UCSD3:CATEGORIZE *)

BEGIN
  (* READ EACH STUDENT'S NAME AND SCORE -
     COMPUTE SUM AND COUNT *)
  ENTERSCORE (STUDENT, SCORE, CLASSIZE, SUM, COUNT);

  (* COMPUTE AND PRINT CLASS AVERAGE *)
  AVERAGE := SUM / COUNT;
  WRITELN ('AVERAGE SCORE = ', AVERAGE :6:1);

  (* FIND AND PRINT GRADE CATEGORY FOR EACH STUDENT *)
  CATEGORIZE (STUDENT, SCORE, AVERAGE, COUNT)
END.
```

Fig. 6.11a Main program for exam problem.

Data Table for ENTERSCORE

Input parameters		*Output parameters*
CLASSIZE		STUDENT, SCORE, SUM, COUNT

Input variables	*Program variables*	*Output variables*
NAME: Each student's name (STRING[10])		(none)

Procedure ENTERSCORE is shown in Fig. 6.11b. It is based on procedure READPART (See Fig. 6.9).

Procedure CATEGORIZE is implemented in a straightforward manner as a multiple-alternative decision inside a FOR loop. This procedure is shown in Fig. 6.11c. A sample output table generated by the program is shown in Fig. 6.11d.

```
PROCEDURE ENTERSCORE (VAR STUDENT : STUARRAY;
                      VAR SCORE : SCOREARRAY;
                      CLASSIZE : INTEGER;
                      VAR SUM, COUNT : INTEGER);
(*READ NAME AND SCORE - FIND SCORE TOTAL AND STUDENT COUNT*)

CONST
  SENTINEL = 'DONE';

VAR
  NAME : STRING[10];

BEGIN
  (* INITIALIZE SUM OF SCORES AND COUNT OF STUDENTS *)
  SUM := 0;
  COUNT := 0;

  (* READ EACH STUDENT'S NAME AND SCORE *)
  (* ADD ONE TO COUNT AND SUM TO SCORE *)
  WRITELN ('ENTER "DONE" OR');
  WRITE ('STUDENT NAME: '); READLN (NAME);
  WHILE (NAME <> SENTINEL) AND (COUNT < CLASSIZE) DO
    BEGIN
      COUNT := COUNT + 1;
      STUDENT[COUNT] := NAME;
      (*READ EACH SCORE AND ADD TO SUM * )
      WRITE ('SCORE: '); READLN (SCORE[COUNT]);
      SUM := SUM + SCORE[COUNT];
      WRITE ('STUDENT NAME: '); READLN (NAME)
    END (* WHILE *)
END; (* ENTERSCORE *)
```

Fig. 6.11b   Procedure ENTERSCORE.

Exercise 6.14:   Provide a data table and level one algorithm for CATEGORIZE.

Exercise 6.15: It may be desirable to use an array of counters to keep track of the number of grades in each category where COUNT['A'] would represent the count of A's, COUNT['B'] the count of B's, etc. Show what modifications would be required to Fig. 6.11.

Exercise 6.16: In determining a reasonable grade distribution, it would be useful to compute the standard deviation, DEV, of the class exam scores, as well as the average, AVE. Modify the grade program to compute the standard deviation. Use the value of AVE + DEV as the lower limit for a grade of A, and the value of AVE − DEV as the lower limit for a grade of B. Hint: To compute DEV, use the formula

$$DEV = \sqrt{\frac{\Sigma S^2}{C} - AVE^2}$$

where ΣS^2 is the sum of the squares of each score and C is the count of scores. For example, given the scores 63, 47, 82

$$\Sigma S^2 = 63^2 + 47^2 + 82^2 = 3969 + 2209 + 6724 = 12902.$$
$$\frac{\Sigma S^2}{C} = 4300.67$$

Then: $AVE = \dfrac{\Sigma S}{C} = \dfrac{63 + 47 + 82}{C} = \dfrac{192}{3} = 64,$

so $DEV = \sqrt{4300.67 - 64^2} = \sqrt{204.67} \approx 14.31$

```
PROCEDURE CATEGORIZE (STUDENT : STUARRAY;
                      SCORE : SCOREARRAY;
                      AVERAGE : REAL;
                      COUNT : INTEGER);
(* FIND AND PRINT GRADE FOR EACH STUDENT *)

VAR
  I : INTEGER;
  GRADE : CHAR;

BEGIN
  (* WRITE HEADING *)
  WRITELN;
  WRITELN ('STUDENT', 'SCORE' :13, 'GRADE' :10);

  (* ASSIGN LETTER GRADE TO EACH STUDENT *)
  FOR I := 1 TO COUNT DO
    BEGIN
      IF SCORE[I] > ROUND(AVERAGE + 10) THEN
        GRADE := 'A'
      ELSE IF SCORE[I] < ROUND(AVERAGE - 10) THEN
        GRADE := 'C'
      ELSE
        GRADE := 'B';
      WRITELN(STUDENT[I] :10, SCORE[I] :10, GRADE:8)
    END (* FOR *)
END; (* CATEGORIZE *)
```

Fig. 6.11c Procedure CATEGORIZE.

```
AVERAGE SCORE  =   80.0
```

STUDENT	SCORE	GRADE
JONES	75	B
SMITH	90	B
JACKSON	65	C
PETERS	70	B
WALSH	95	A
COHEN	85	B

Fig. 6.11d Sample output table for exam processing program (Problem 6.3).

6.8 MANIPULATING CHARACTER STRINGS

6.8.1 String Variables and Character Arrays

Many computer applications are concerned with the manipulation of character strings or textual data rather than numerical data. For example, computerized typesetters are used extensively in the publishing of books and newspapers; telephone directories and annual reports are updated on a regular basis using computer-based word processors; computers are used in the analysis of great works of literature.

Although there is little facility for manipulating character strings in standard PASCAL, UCSD PASCAL provides special functions and procedures for string manipulation. In this section, we will describe these features and illustrate how they can be used to manipulate string variables.

A string variable may be considered an array of characters with special properties. If FOOD is a string variable containing the string value 'CRACK-ERS', then it is possible to reference elements FOOD[1] (character C) through FOOD[8] (character S). A comparison of string variables and arrays follows.

Comparison of string variables and arrays

- The length of a string variable is *dynamic* (changeable) and is determined by the data stored in it. This length cannot be less than zero, nor more than the declared length of the string variable. The size of an array is fixed.
- A string variable can be read or written by executing a single READ(LN) or WRITE(LN) statement; an array must be read (or written) element by element using a loop.
- String variables and string data of different lengths may be manipulated together. Only arrays of the same type may be manipulated together.

A special type of array, called a *packed character array*, may be used in standard PASCAL to facilitate the manipulation of character strings. When an array is "packed," the compiler may store more than one character in each computer memory cell. This means that less storage will normally be required for storing a string in a packed character array. Another important benefit is that PASCAL makes it easier for the programmer to manipulate character strings that are stored in packed character arrays.

If N is a constant, the declaration

```
VAR
  Y : PACKED ARRAY[1..N] OF CHAR;
```

allocates storage for a character string of length N. This string may be written using a single WRITE(LN) statement; however, each character must be read individually. A string value consisting of exactly N characters (length N) may be assigned to Y, and Y may be compared to string values of length N as well as other variables of the same type. Packed character arrays may be used in UCSD PASCAL as well; although, it is generally preferable to use string variables.

6.8.2 The Function LENGTH

As we have seen, the working length of a string variable is determined by the data stored in it. This length cannot exceed the declared maximum for that variable (see Section 4.5.1). A string with zero characters is called a *null string*.

UCSD PASCAL provides a function named LENGTH that determines the current length of a string. This function is illustrated in the next example.

Example 6.12:   The program shown in Fig. 6.12 prints four strings (enclosed in *'s) followed by the length of each string.

```
PROGRAM STRINGLENGTH;
(* USES THE LENGTH FUNCTION *)

CONST
  DELIMITER = '*';

VAR
  STR1, STR2 : STRING;

BEGIN
  STR1 := 'ACES';
  WRITELN (DELIMITER, STR1, DELIMITER, LENGTH(STR1) :2);
  STR2 := 'PAIR OF ACES';
  WRITELN (DELIMITER, STR2, DELIMITER, LENGTH(STR2) :3);
  STR1 := ' ';
  WRITELN (DELIMITER, STR1, DELIMITER, LENGTH(STR1) :2);
  STR2 := '';
  WRITELN (DELIMITER, STR2, DELIMITER, LENGTH(STR2) :2)
END.

*ACES* 4
*PAIR OF ACES* 12
* * 1
** 0
```

Fig. 6.12 Printing string lengths.

The last output line shows that the null string assigned to STR2 has a length of zero. Note that the data previously stored in STR2 are lost.

6.8.3 Substrings and the Copy Function

It is often necessary to manipulate *substrings*, or segments, of a larger character string. We can use special substring features to break a character string into sections or to reference part of a character string. For example, we might want to extract the day (25) from the string value 'JUNE 25, 1981'. The UCSD PASCAL function COPY returns a substring as its value.

Function COPY

COPY (source, index, size)

Interpretation: The function value is the substring of *source*, starting at position *index* and consisting of *size* characters. *Source* must be a string variable or value; *index* and *size* must be type INTEGER.

If the string variable FORLOOP contains the string value

```
'FOR TODAY := MONDAY TO FRIDAY DO'
```

and LOOPVAR, STARTVAL and ENDVAL are type STRING, the statements

```
LOOPVAR  := COPY(FORLOOP,  5,  5);
STARTVAL := COPY(FORLOOP, 14,  6);
ENDVAL   := COPY(FORLOOP, 24,  6)
```

would assign the strings 'TODAY' to LOOPVAR, 'MONDAY' to STARTVAL, and 'FRIDAY' to ENDVAL. The last statement above causes the six characters starting with FORLOOP[24] (character F) to be copied to ENDVAL. The characters in positions FORLOOP[24] through FORLOOP[29] (string 'FRIDAY') are assigned to the string variable ENDVAL. Note that the string variable FORLOOP is unaffected by the COPY operations.

As mentioned earlier, we can reference any individual character in the string variable FORLOOP by specifying its position as a subscript (e.g., FORLOOP[1] is the first character). Whether referencing a single character or copying a substring, we must be sure that no character referenced is outside the range (working length) of the string variable (e.g., FORLOOP[32] is the last character that may be referenced).

Example 6.13:   Given the string variable DATE

the assignment statements

```
MONTH := COPY(DATE, 1, 4);
DAY := COPY(DATE, 6, 2);
YEAR := COPY(DATE, 10, 4)
```

would result in the string assignments below:

Example 6.14: The program in Fig. 6.13 prints each word of a string (SEN-TENCE) on a separate line. It assumes that a single blank occurs between words.

The variable FIRST always points to the start of the current word and is initialized to one. During each execution of the FOR loop, the Boolean expression

```
SENTENCE[NEXT] = BLANK
```

tests to see whether the next character is a blank. If it is, all characters from SENTENCE[FIRST] through SENTENCE[NEXT−1] are copied to WORD by the statement

```
WORD := COPY(SENTENCE, FIRST, NEXT−FIRST);
```

The current word is printed and FIRST is reset to point to the first character following the blank.

After the last character in SENTENCE is tested, the FOR loop will be exited. The IF statement that follows will print the last word in the sentence if it was not yet printed. This is only necessary when the last character in SEN-TENCE is non-blank. Compare this program with the one shown in Fig. 4.6.

Exercise 6.17: Indicate how you could modify the program in Fig. 6.13 to convert a sentence to a primitive form of "Pig Latin" in which the first letter of each word is moved to the end of the word, followed by the letters AY. The string "THE QUICK BROWN FOX JUMPED" would become "HETAY UICKQAY ROWNBAY OXFAY UMPEDJAY".

Exercise 6.18: Write a program to read in a sentence (containing no punctuation and with one blank between words) and print the first letters of the words all together on one line. You may assume a maximum of ten words in the sentence.

Exercise 6.19: Modify Example 6.13 so that the restriction of a single blank between words is removed. Your program will have to skip over a group of consecutive blanks.

```
PROGRAM PRINTWORDS;
(* PRINTS EACH WORD ON A SEPARATE LINE *)

CONST
  STRINGLEN = 80;
  BLANK = ' ';

VAR
  SENTENCE : STRING[STRINGLEN];
  FIRST, NEXT, SENTLEN : 1..STRINGLEN;
  WORD : STRING[20];

BEGIN
  (* READ A SENTENCE *)
  WRITELN ('TYPE IN A SENTENCE');
  READLN (SENTENCE);

  (* PRINT EACH WORD ON A SEPARATE LINE *)
  SENTLEN := LENGTH(SENTENCE);
  FIRST := 1;
  FOR NEXT := 1 TO SENTLEN DO
    IF SENTENCE[NEXT] = BLANK  THEN
      BEGIN
        WORD := COPY(SENTENCE, FIRST, NEXT-FIRST);
        WRITELN (WORD);
        FIRST := NEXT + 1
      END; (* IF *)

  (* PRINT THE LAST WORD IF IT IS NOT YET PRINTED *)
  IF SENTENCE[SENTLEN] <> BLANK THEN
    BEGIN
      WORD := COPY(SENTENCE, FIRST, SENTLEN-FIRST+1);
      WRITELN (WORD)
    END (* IF *)
END.

TYPE IN A SENTENCE
THIS IS IT.

THIS
IS
IT.
```

Fig. 6.13 Printing the words of a sentence.

6.8.4 The POS Function

In this section, we will describe the UCSD PASCAL function that searches a string (the source string) for a substring (the pattern). For example, if the source string is 'WHAT NEXT?', we could use this function to determine whether or not the pattern 'AT' occurred anywhere in this string ('AT' is found at position 3). The string search function, POS, is described in the next display.

POS Function

POS *(pattern, source)*

Interpretation: The string *source* is examined from left to right to determine the location of the first occurrence of the string *pattern*. If *pattern* is found, the value returned is the position in *source* of the first character of *pattern;* otherwise, the value returned is zero.

The function designators

```
POS('AT', 'WHAT NEXT?')
POS('T', 'WHAT NEXT?')
POS('XT', 'WHAT NEXT?')
POS('!', 'WHAT NEXT?').
```

would return values 3, 4, 8 and 0, respectively.

6.8.5   Concatenation of Strings

Sometimes we desire to *concatenate*, or join together, two or more shorter strings to form a longer string. The function CONCAT is described in the display below.

Function CONCAT

CONCAT *(string$_1$, string$_2$, . . . ,string$_n$)*

Interpretation: The function result is the string formed by concatenating all the string parameters *string$_1$*, *string$_2$*, etc. Two or more strings may be concatenated.

For the string variables DAY, MONTH, YEAR as defined in Example 6.13, the function designator

```
CONCAT (DAY, MONTH, YEAR)
```

would return the value '25JUNE1981'. The function designator

```
CONCAT (MONTH, ' ', DAY, ', ', YEAR)
```

would reconstruct the original string 'JUNE 25, 1981'.

The program in Fig. 6.14 uses many of the features discussed so far to generate cryptograms. A cryptogram is a coded message formed by substituting a code character for each letter of an original message. The substitution is performed uniformly throughout the original message; i.e., all A's might be replaced by S, all B's by M, etc. We will assume that all punctuation remains unchanged.

```
PROGRAM CRYPTO;
(*GENERATES A CRYPTOGRAM FOR A MESSAGE*)

VAR
  ALPHABET, CODE : STRING[26];
  MESSAGE, CRYPTOGRAM : STRING;
  MESSCHAR, CODECHAR : STRING[1];
  I : 1..80; POSITION : 0..26;

BEGIN
  (*INITIALIZE ALPHABET AND CRYPTOGRAM AND READ
    THE CODE AND ORIGINAL MESSAGE*)
  ALPHABET := 'ABCDEFGHIJKLMNOPQRSTUVWXYZ';
  CRYPTOGRAM := '';
  WRITELN ('ENTER CODE FOR EACH LETTER BELOW');
  WRITELN (ALPHABET);
  READLN (CODE);
  WHILE LENGTH(CODE) <> 26 DO
    BEGIN
      WRITELN ('YOU NEED 26 CHARACTERS IN THE ',
               'CODE STRING - TRY AGAIN');
      READLN (CODE)
    END; (*WHILE*)
  WRITELN ('ENTER MESSAGE'); READLN (MESSAGE);

  (*SUBSTITUTE THE CODE SYMBOL FOR EACH LETTER*)
  FOR I := 1 TO LENGTH(MESSAGE) DO
    BEGIN
      (*FIND CURRENT LETTER IN ALPHABET*)
      MESSCHAR := COPY(MESSAGE, I, 1);
      POSITION := POS(MESSCHAR, ALPHABET);
      IF POSITION <> 0 THEN
        (*APPEND CODE SYMBOL*)
        BEGIN
          CODECHAR := COPY(CODE, POSITION, 1);
          CRYPTOGRAM := CONCAT(CRYPTOGRAM, CODECHAR)
        END
      ELSE
        (*APPEND ORIGINAL SYMBOL*)
        CRYPTOGRAM := CONCAT(CRYPTOGRAM, MESSCHAR)
    END; (*FOR*)
  (*PRINT FINAL CRYPTOGRAM*)
  WRITELN ('THE CRYPTOGRAM TO BE SOLVED IS');
  WRITELN (CRYPTOGRAM)
END.
```

Fig. 6.14 Cryptogram generator.

The program begins by initializing **ALPHABET** to the alphabet string and the solution, **CRYPTOGRAM**, to the null string. It then reads a 26 character string representing the code. The first character in the code string is the code for an A, the second character is the code for a B, etc. The program next reads the message to be coded and forms the cryptogram, **CRYPTOGRAM**.

The cryptogram is generated by searching for each character of MESSAGE in the alphabet string using the statements

```
MESSCHAR := COPY(MESSAGE, I, 1);
POSITION := POS(MESSCHAR, ALPHABET);
```

where **MESSCHAR** is the Ith character in **MESSAGE**. If MESSCHAR is found (POSITION $<>$ 0), then the code character corresponding to that letter is appended to CRYPTOGRAM

```
CODECHAR := COPY(CODE, POSITION, 1);
CRYPTOGRAM := CONCAT(CRYPTOGRAM, CODECHAR)
```

If MESSCHAR is not a letter, then MESSCHAR itself is appended instead.

```
CRYPTOGRAM := CONCAT(CRYPTOGRAM, MESSCHAR)
```

Note that the Ith character in MESSAGE cannot be referenced as MESSAGE[I] in this program. This is because MESSAGE[I] is considered type CHAR; whereas, the functions POS and CONCAT require arguments of type STRING.

Compare this program with the one in Fig. 6.5.

6.8.6 Text Editing Problem

Problem 6.4: There are many applications for which it is useful to have a computerized text-editing program. For example, if you are preparing a laboratory report (or a textbook), it would be convenient to edit or modify sections of the report (improve sentence and paragraph structure, change words, correct spelling mistakes, etc.) at a computer terminal and then have a fresh, clean copy of the text typed at the terminal without erasures or mistakes.

Discussion: A Text Editor System is a relatively sophisticated system of subprograms that can be used to instruct the computer to perform virtually any kind of text alteration. As an example, consider the following sentence prepared by an overzealous member of the Addison-Wesley advertising group.

```
'THE BOOK BY KAUFMAN ON SD PASCAL IS GRRREAT?'
```

To correct this sentence we would want to specify the following edit operations:

1. Insert UC at position 24
2. Replace KAU by KOF
3. Delete RR
4. Replace ? by !

The corrected sentence would read

```
'THE BOOK BY KOFFMAN ON UCSD PASCAL IS GREAT!'
```

The main program for our text editor will read an input string (SOURCE) and interpret the edit commands. Separate procedures will be used to perform the actual editing operations.

The data table and level one algorithm follow.

Data Table for Text Editor Problem

Constants

> SOURCELEN = 255, maximum length of the string SOURCE
> SENTINAL = 'Q', the sentinel command

Data types

> BIGSTRING = STRING[SOURCELEN]

Input variables	*Program variables*	*Output variables*
SOURCE: The string being edited (BIGSTRING)		SOURCE: The edited string (BIGSTRING)
COMMAND: The edit command (CHAR)		

Procedures referenced:

> EDITSTRING : Performs an edit operation on a string.

Level One Algorithm

1. Enter the string (SOURCE) to be edited.
2. Perform all edit operations

Level Two Refinements

Step 2   *Perform all edit operations*

> 2.1 Read first edit command
> 2.2 WHILE COMMAND $<>$ SENTINEL DO
>   BEGIN
>   2.3 Perform the edit operation specified by COMMAND
>   2.4 Print the string SOURCE
>   2.5 Read next edit COMMAND
>   END

Step 2.3 is performed by procedure EDITSTRING. The main program is shown in Fig. 6.15a; the data table and algorithm for EDITSTRING follow.

```
PROGRAM TEXTEDIT;
(* EDITS A STRING *)

CONST
  SOURCELEN = 255;
  SENTINEL = 'Q';

TYPE
  BIGSTRING = STRING[SOURCELEN];

VAR
  SOURCE : BIGSTRING;
  COMMAND : CHAR;

(* INSERT PROCEDURE EDITSTRING HERE *)
(*$I UCSD3:EDITSTRING *)

BEGIN
  (* READ THE STRING TO BE EDITED *)
  WRITELN ('EDIT WHAT STRING?');
  READLN (SOURCE);

  (* PERFORM EDIT OPERATIONS ON SOURCE *)
  WRITE ('D(ELETE), I(NSERT), R(EPLACE), Q(UIT)? ');
  READ (COMMAND);
  WRITELN;
  WHILE COMMAND <> SENTINEL DO
    BEGIN
      EDITSTRING (COMMAND, SOURCE);
      WRITELN (SOURCE);
      WRITE ('D(ELETE), I(NSERT), R(EPLACE), Q(UIT)? ');
      READ (COMMAND);
      WRITELN
    END (* WHILE *)
END.
```

Fig. 6.15a   Main program for text editor.

Data Table for Procedure EDITSTRING

Input parameters	Update parameters	
COMMAND	SOURCE	
Input variables	*Program variables*	*Output variables*

OLDSTR: A string to be
deleted (STRING)

NEWSTR: A string to be
inserted (STRING)

LOCATION: The position of
a string to be inserted
(1..SOURCELEN)

INDEX: The position of
a string to be deleted
(0..SOURCELEN)

Procedures referenced:

> DELETE: Deletes a substring
> INSERT: Inserts a string of characters

Level One Algorithm for EDITSTRING

1. Categorize COMMAND and perform the required edit operation.

Level Two Refinements

Step 1

```
    1.1  CASE COMMAND OF
         'D' : BEGIN
                 1.2 Read string to be deleted (OLDSTR)
                 1.3 IF OLDSTR is in SOURCE THEN
                         delete OLDSTR
                     ELSE
                         Print an error message
               END
         'I' : BEGIN
                 1.4 Read string to be inserted and its desired location
                 1.5 Perform insertion
               END
         'R' : BEGIN
                 1.6 Read strings to be replaced and inserted
                 1.7 Perform replacement
               END (* CASE*)
```

UCSD PASCAL provides procedures to perform the insert and delete operations. If S is the string 'WHAT NEXT?', the procedure statement

```
                DELETE (S, 3, 2)
```

deletes the two character substring starting at position 3 ('AT'). The new value of S is 'WH NEXT?'. The procedure statement

```
                INSERT ('ERE', S, 3)
```

inserts the string 'ERE' at position 3 of string S. The final value of S is 'WHERE NEXT?'.

As illustrated above, we can easily perform a string replacement using DELETE and INSERT. The refinement of Step 1.7 is shown below; Procedure EDITSTRING is shown in Fig. 6.15b.

Level Three Refinements

Step 1.7

```
    1.7.1   IF OLDSTR is in SOURCE THEN
```

                    Delete OLDSTR and insert NEWSTR
             ELSE
                    Print an error message

```
PROCEDURE EDITSTRING (COMMAND : CHAR;
                         VAR SOURCE : BIGSTRING);
(* PERFORMS THE EDIT OPERATION SPECIFIED BY *)
(* COMMAND ON THE STRING SOURCE             *)

VAR
  OLDSTR, NEWSTR : STRING;
  INDEX : O..SOURCELEN;
  LOCATION : 1..SOURCELEN;

BEGIN
  CASE COMMAND OF
    'D' : BEGIN
            WRITE ('DELETE WHAT STRING? ');
            READLN (OLDSTR);
            INDEX := POS(OLDSTR, SOURCE);
            IF INDEX <> O THEN
              DELETE (SOURCE, INDEX, LENGTH(OLDSTR))
            ELSE
              WRITELN (OLDSTR, ' NOT FOUND.')
          END; (* 'D' *)
    'I' : BEGIN
            WRITE ('INSERT WHAT STRING? ');
            READLN (NEWSTR);
            WRITE ('POINT OF INSERTION? ')
            READLN (LOCATION);
            INSERT (NEWSTR, SOURCE, LOCATION)
          END; (* 'I' *)
    'R' : BEGIN
            WRITE ('REPLACE WHAT STRING? ');
            READLN (OLDSTR);
            INDEX := POS(OLDSTR, SOURCE);
            IF INDEX <> O THEN
              BEGIN
                DELETE (SOURCE, INDEX, LENGTH(OLDSTR));
                WRITE ('TO BE REPLACED BY? ');
                READLN (NEWSTR);
                INSERT (NEWSTR, SOURCE, INDEX)
              END
            ELSE
              WRITELN (OLDSTR, ' NOT FOUND.')
          END (* 'R' *)
  END (* CASE *)
END; (* EDITSTRING *)
```

Fig. 6.15b Procedure EDITSTRING.

Procedures **DELETE** and **INSERT** are described in the next displays.

Procedure DELETE

DELETE *(source, index, size)*

Interpretation: The next *size* characters are removed from string *source* starting with the character at position *index*. Parameter *source* must be a string and *index* and *size* should be type INTEGER.

Procedure INSERT

INSERT *(news, source, index)*

Interpretation: The string *news* is inserted before the character currently in position *index* of *source*. Parameters *news* and *source* must be strings and *index* should be type INTEGER.

Exercise 6.20:   Assume that DELETE and INSERT are not available. Implement these procedures using functions COPY and CONCAT.

Exercise 6.21:   What do you think would happen if a string insertion causes the string SOURCE to become larger than SOURCELEN characters? Modify EDITSTRING so that the edit commands I and R are not carried out in this case.

6.9 COMMON PROGRAMMING ERRORS

The most common error in using arrays is a subscript range error. This occurs when the subscript value is outside the subrange specified for that array type. Subscript range errors are not syntax errors; they will not be detected until program execution begins. They are most often caused by an incorrect subscript expression or by a loop parameter error or nonterminating loop. Before considerable time is spent in debugging, all suspect subscript calculations should be carefully checked for out-of-range errors. This can most easily be done by inserting diagnostic output statements in your program in order to print subscript values that might be out of range.

If an out-of-range subscript occurs inside a loop, you should make sure that the loop is terminating properly. If the loop control variable is not being updated as expected, then the loop may be repeated more often than required. This could happen, for example, if the update step came after the loop END statement or if the loop BEGIN and END were erroneously omitted.

You should also double check the subscript values at the loop boundaries. If these values are in range, it is likely that all other subscript references in the loop will be in range as well.

As with all PASCAL data types, make sure that there are no type inconsistencies. The subscript type and element type used in all array references must correspond to the types specified in the array declaration.

Similarly, the types of two arrays used in an array copy or comparison statement or as corresponding parameters must be the same. Remember to use only identifiers to specify the types of all array parameters.

When using string procedures and functions, be careful about the order of parameters. Do not use a type CHAR parameter where a string is required.

6.10 SUMMARY

In this chapter we introduced a special data structure called an array, which is a convenient facility for naming and referencing a collection of like items. We discussed how to inform the compiler that an array of elements is to be allocated, and we described how to reference an individual array element by placing a subscript in brackets, following the array name.

The FOR loop was shown to be a convenient structure for referencing each array element in sequence. We have used this structure to initialize arrays, read and print arrays, and to control the manipulation of individual array elements.

We also described the manipulation of character strings and arrays of strings. Several new functions and procedures were introduced for this purpose.

The arrays discussed in this chapter are often called *linear arrays* or *lists*. These arrays are "one dimensional," in that a single subscript is used to identify each array element uniquely. In Chapter 10 we shall examine a more complex data structure—an array of arrays, or a multi-dimensional array.

PROGRAMMING PROBLEMS

6.5 Let A be an array consisting of 20 elements. Write a program to read a collection of up to 20 data items into A, and then find and print the subscript of the largest item in A and that item.

6.6 The Department of Traffic Accidents each year receives accident count reports from a number of cities and towns across the country. To summarize these reports, the Department provides a frequency-distribution printout that gives the number of cities reporting accident counts in the following ranges: 0–99, 100–199, 200–299, 300–399, 400–499, 500 or above. The Department needs a computer program to read the number of accidents for each reporting city or town and to add one to the count for the appropriate accident range. After all the data have been processed, the resulting frequency counts are to be printed.

6.7 Write a program which, given the *taxable income* for a single taxpayer, will compute the income tax for that person. Use Schedule X shown in Fig. 6.16. Assume that "line 47," referenced in this schedule, contains the taxable income.

Example: If the individual's taxable income is $8192, your program should use the tax amount and percent shown in column 3 of line 7 (arrow). The tax in this case is

$$\$1590 + .25(8192. - 8000) = \$1638.$$

For each individual processed, print taxable earnings and the total tax. *Hint:* Set up three arrays, one for the base tax (column 3), one for the tax percent (column 3), and the third for the excess base (column 4). Your program must then compute the correct index to these arrays, given the taxable income.

Tax Rate Schedules

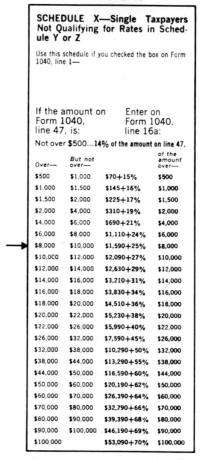

SCHEDULE X—Single Taxpayers Not Qualifying for Rates in Schedule Y or Z

Use this schedule if you checked the box on Form 1040, line 1—

If the amount on Form 1040, line 47, is:

Enter on Form 1040, line 16a:

Not over $500...14% of the amount on line 47.

Over—	But not over—		of the amount over—
$500	$1,000	$70+15%	$500
$1,000	$1,500	$145+16%	$1,000
$1,500	$2,000	$225+17%	$1,500
$2,000	$4,000	$310+19%	$2,000
$4,000	$6,000	$690+21%	$4,000
$6,000	$8,000	$1,110+24%	$6,000
$8,000	$10,000	$1,590+25%	$8,000
$10,0C0	$12,000	$2,090+27%	$10,000
$12,000	$14,000	$2,630+29%	$12,000
$14,000	$16,000	$3,210+31%	$14,000
$16,000	$18,000	$3,830+34%	$16,000
$18,000	$20,000	$4,510+36%	$18,000
$20,000	$22,000	$5,230+38%	$20,000
$22,000	$26,000	$5,990+40%	$22,000
$26,000	$32,000	$7,590+45%	$26,000
$32,000	$38,000	$10,290+50%	$32,000
$38,000	$44,000	$13,290+55%	$38,000
$44,000	$50,000	$16,590+60%	$44,000
$50,000	$60,000	$20,190+62%	$50,000
$60,000	$70,000	$26,390+64%	$60,000
$70,000	$80,000	$32,790+66%	$70,000
$80,000	$90,000	$39,390+68%	$80,000
$90,000	$100,000	$46,190+69%	$90,000
$100,000		$53,090+70%	$100,000

Fig. 6.16 Schedule X (from IRS Form 1040).

6.8 Assume for the moment that your computer has the very limited capability of being able to read and print only single decimal digits at a time; and to add together two integers consisting of one decimal digit each. Write a program to read in two ten-digit integers, add these numbers together, and print the result. Test your program on the following numbers.

$$X = 1487625$$
$$Y = 12783$$

$$X = 60705202$$
$$Y = 30760832$$

$$X = 1234567890$$
$$Y = 9876543210$$

Hints: Store the numbers X and Y in two character arrays X, Y, of size 10, one decimal digit per element. If the number is less than 10 digits in length, enter enough *leading zeros* (to the left of the number) to make the number 10 digits long.

X

1	2	3	4	5	6	7	8	9	10
0	0	0	1	4	8	7	6	2	5

Y

1	2	3	4	5	6	7	8	9	10
0	0	0	0	0	1	2	7	8	3

You will need a loop to add together the digits in corresponding array elements. You must start with the element with subscript value 10 and work toward the left. Do not forget to handle the carry, if there is one!

Use a variable, C, to indicate if a carry occurred in adding together X(1) and Y(1). C is set to '1' if a carry occurs here; otherwise, C will be '0'.

6.9 Write a data table, algorithm, and a program for the following problem. You are given a collection of scores for the last exam in your computer course. You are to compute the average of these scores, and then assign grades to each student according to the following rule.

If a student's score is within 10 points (above or below) of the average, assign the student a grade of SATISFACTORY. If the score is more than 10 points higher than the average, assign the student a grade of OUTSTANDING. If the score is more than 10 points below the average, assign the student a grade of UNSATISFACTORY. Test your program on the following data:

RICHARD LUGAR	55
FRANK RIZZO	71
DONALD SCHAEFFER	84
KEVIN WHITE	93
JAMES RIEHLE	74
ABE BEAME	70
TOM BRADLEY	84
WALTER WASHINGTON	68
RICHARD DALEY	64
RICHARD HATCHER	82

Hint: The output from your program should consist of a labelled three-column list containing the name, exam score, and grade of each student.

6.10 Write a program to read N data items into each of two arrays X and Y of size 20. Compare each of the elements of X to the corresponding element of Y. In the corresponding element of a third array Z, store:

$$+1 \quad \text{if X is larger than Y}$$
$$0 \quad \text{if X is equal to Y}$$
$$-1 \quad \text{if X is less than Y}$$

Then print a three-column table displaying the contents of the arrays X, Y, and Z, followed by a count of the number of elements of X that exceed Y, and a count of the number of elements of X that are less than Y. Make up your own test data with N less than 20.

6.11 The results of a true-false exam given to a Computer Science class has been coded for input to a program. The information available for each student consists of a student identification number and the students' answers to 10 true-false questions. The available data are as follows:

Student identification	Answers (1 = true; 0 = false)									
0080	0	1	1	0	1	0	1	1	0	1
0340	0	1	0	1	0	1	1	1	0	0
0341	0	1	1	0	1	1	1	1	1	1
0401	1	1	0	0	1	0	0	1	1	1
0462	1	1	0	1	1	1	0	0	1	0
0463	1	1	1	1	1	1	1	1	1	1
0464	0	1	0	0	1	0	0	1	0	1
0512	1	0	1	0	1	0	1	0	1	0
0618	1	1	1	0	0	1	1	0	1	0
0619	0	0	0	0	0	0	0	0	0	0
0687	1	0	1	1	0	1	1	0	1	0
0700	0	1	0	0	1	1	0	0	0	1
0712	0	1	0	1	0	1	0	1	0	1
0837	1	0	1	0	1	1	0	1	0	1

The correct answers are   0 1 0 0 1 0 0 1 0 1

Write a program to read the data records, one at a time, and compute and store the number of correct answers for each student in one array, and store the student ID number in the corresponding element of another array. Determine the best score, BEST. Then print a three-column table displaying the ID number, score and grade for each student. The grade should be determined as follows: If the score is equal to BEST or BEST-1, give an A; if it is BEST-2 or BEST-3, give a C. Otherwise, given an F.

6.12 Write a program to read N data items into two arrays X and Y of size 20. Store the product of corresponding elements of X and Y in a third array Z, also of size 20. Print a three-column table displaying the arrays X, Y and Z. Then compute and print the square root of the sum of the items in Z. Make up your own data, with N less than 20.

6.13 The results of a survey of the households in your township have been made available. Each record contains data for one household, including a four-digit integer identification number, the annual income for the household, and the number of members of the household. Write a program to read the survey results into three arrays and perform the following analyses:

i)   Count the number of households included in the survey and print a three-column table displaying the data read in. (You may assume that no more than 25 households were surveyed.)

ii) Calculate the average household income, and list the identification number and income of each household that exceeds the average.

iii) Determine the percentage of households having incomes below the poverty level. The poverty level income may be computed using the formula
$$p = \$3750.00 + \$750.00 * (m - 2)$$
where m is the number of members of each household.

Test your program on the following data.

Identification number	Annual income	Household members
1041	$12,180	4
1062	13,240	3
1327	19,800	2
1483	22,458	8
1900	17,000	2
2112	18,125	7
2345	15,623	2
3210	3,200	6
3600	6,500	5
3601	11,970	2
4725	8,900	3
6217	10,000	2
9280	6,200	1

6.14 Let VALUE be the value of a long-term savings certificate available at your local bank, let TERM be the term of the certificate (in years), and let RATE be the yearly interest rate. Write a program which, given VALUE, TERM and RATE, will compute and print the interest amount (rounded to two decimal places), and the accumulated certificate value for each of the years of the term. Your program should print out VALUE, TERM and RATE, and a three-column table containing the year (1, 2, 3, . . .), the interest for that year, and the accumulated value. Test your program for VALUE = $5000, TERM = 10 years, and RATE = 12 percent.

6.15 It can be shown that a number is prime if there is no smaller prime number that divides it. Consequently, in order to determine whether N is prime, it is sufficient to check only the prime numbers less than N as possible divisors (see Problem 4.2). Use this information to write a program that stores the first one hundred prime numbers in an array. Have your program print the array after it is done.

6.16 Write an interactive program that plays the game of HANGMAN. Read the word to be guessed into the string variable WORD. The player must guess the letters belonging to WORD. The program should terminate when either all letters have been guessed correctly (player wins) or a specified number of incorrect guesses have been made (computer wins). *Hint:* Use a string variable SOLUTION to keep track of the solution so far. Initialize SOLUTION to a string of *'s. Each time a letter in WORD is guessed, replace the corresponding '*' in SOLUTION with that letter.

6.17 Assume a set of sentences is to be processed. Each sentence consists of a sequence of words, separated by one or more blank spaces. Write a program that will read these sentences and count the number of words with one letter, two letters, etc., up to ten letters.

6.18 Write a program to read in a collection of character strings of arbitrary length. For each string read, your program should do the following:

 i)   print the length of the string:
 ii) count the number of occurrences of four letter words in each string:
 iii) replace each four letter word with a string of four asterisks and print the new string.

6.19 Write a program that removes all of the blanks from a character string and "compacts" all non-blank characters in the string. You should only have to scan the input string once from left to right.

RECORDS AND SETS

7

7.1 INTRODUCTION

In the previous chapter we introduced a data structure, the array, that is fundamental to programming and is included in almost every high-level programming language. In this section we will introduce two additional data structures that are available in PASCAL, but are not generally available in other languages. The availability of these data structures makes it much easier to organize and represent information in PASCAL. This is a major reason for the growing popularity of the PASCAL language.

The first new data structure to be discussed is the *record*. Like an array, a record is a collection of two or more related data items. However, unlike an array, the individual components of a record can contain data of different types. We can use a record to store a variety of kinds of information about a person, such as the person's name, marital status, age, date of birth, etc.

The second data type to be discussed is the set. A set is a collection of like objects called *set elements*. In this chapter, we shall learn how to perform the operations of set union, intersection, and difference in PASCAL and how to determine the elements that belong to a set.

7.2 DECLARING A RECORD

Before we can use a record in PASCAL, we first describe its general form in a type declaration. The declaration specifies the name of a record type and the name and type of each component or *field* of the record.

Example 7.1:   We wish to store the descriptive information shown in Fig. 7.1 for use in a computerized payroll program.

```
NAME: JOHN Q. PUBLIC
SOCIAL SECURITY NUMBER: 035-20-1111
NUMBER OF DEPENDENTS: 2
HOURLY SALARY: 3.98
```

Fig. 7.1 Employee data.

This description contains two character strings (NAME and SOCIAL SECURITY NUMBER), an integer value and a real value. We will define the structure of

```
TYPE
   EMPLOYEE = RECORD
      NAME : STRING[20];
      SOCSECURE : STRING[11];
      NUMDEPEND : INTEGER;
      RATE : REAL
   END; (* EMPLOYEE *)

VAR
   CLERK : EMPLOYEE;
```

Fig. 7.2 Declaration of record type EMPLOYEE and record variable CLERK.

this information as the record type EMPLOYEE (see Fig. 7.2).

The record variable CLERK will be the particular data element of type EM-PLOYEE described in Fig. 7.1. Since CLERK is a record variable of type EM-PLOYEE, the memory allocated for CLERK consists of storage space for two character strings (length 20 and length 11), an integer value and a real value.

The record variable CLERK is pictured below assuming the values shown in Fig. 7.1 have been stored in memory.

NAME	SOCSECURE	NUMDEPEND	RATE
JOHN Q. PUBLIC	035-20-1111	2	3.98

Fig. 7.3 Record variable CLERK.

As illustrated in the type declaration for EMPLOYEE, it is possible to spec-ify record fields corresponding to any standard or user-defined type. In addition, the type declaration of a field can be included within the record declaration. The record type declaration is described in the next display.

Record Type Declaration

$$rectype = \text{RECORD}$$
$$field_1 : type_1;$$
$$field_2 : type_2;$$

.

.

.

$$field_n : type_n$$
$$\text{END};$$

Interpretation: The identifier *rectype* is associated with the record structure be-ing described. The name of each field of *rectype* is specified ($field_i$) along with its data type ($type_i$).

Note: Type$_i$ may be any standard or user-defined data type including a struc-tured type such as an array or another record. If $type_i$ is a user-defined data type, it can either be defined before the record or as part of the record de-scription.

Exercise 7.1:   A catalogue listing for a textbook consists of the author's name, title, publisher and year of publication. Define a record type CATALOGUE for storage of this information.

Exercise 7.2:   Each part in an inventory is represented by its part number, a descriptive name, the quantity on hand and price. Define a record type PART.

7.3   MANIPULATING A RECORD—THE WITH STATEMENT

7.3.1   Referencing Individual Fields of a Record

In most instances, we manipulate each field of a record on an individual basis. In PASCAL, we are able to reference each record field using a *field selector* consisting of the record name followed by the field name. A period is used to separate the field name from the record name.

Example 7.2:   Fig. 7.3 gives an example of the record variable CLERK. This data could be stored in CLERK through the sequence of assignment statements:

```
CLERK.NAME := 'JOHN Q. PUBLIC';
CLERK.SOCSECURE := '035-20-1111';
CLERK.NUMDEPEND := 2;
CLERK.RATE := 3.98
```

Alternatively, if this information were provided as external data, then it could be read into CLERK as shown next.

```
READLN (CLERK.NAME);
READLN (CLERK.SOCSECURE);
READLN (CLERK.NUMDEPEND);
READLN (CLERK.RATE);
```

The above sequence assumes that the person's name is provided first, followed by the person's social security number. The last two values entered are the number of dependents and hourly wage rate.

Once data have been stored in a record, they can be manipulated in the same way as other data in memory. For example, the statements:

```
GROSS := 40.0 * CLERK.RATE;
TAXSALARY := GROSS - 14.40 * CLERK.NUMDEPEND
```

compute taxable salary (TAXSALARY) by deducting \$14.40 from gross salary (GROSS) for each dependent. The statement

```
WRITELN (CLERK.NAME)
```

prints the character string stored in the NAME field of CLERK.

Exercise 7.3:   Write the PASCAL statements required to print the values stored in CLERK in the form shown in Fig. 7.1.

7.3.2   The WITH Statement

It becomes quite tedious to write the complete field selector each time we wish to reference a field of a record. PASCAL enables us to abbreviate the field selector through the use of the WITH statement.

Example 7.3: The WITH statement in Fig. 7.4 reads data into the record variable CLERK.

```
WITH CLERK DO
   BEGIN
      READLN (NAME);
      READLN (SOCSECURE);
      READLN (NUMDEPEND, RATE)
   END (* WITH *)
```

Fig. 7.4 Use of WITH Statement.

As shown in Fig. 7.4, it is not necessary to specify both the record variable and field names inside the WITH statement. The record variable CLERK is identified in the WITH statement header; it is only necessary to specify the field name instead of the complete field selector (e.g., RATE instead of CLERK.RATE). The WITH statement is described in the next display.

WITH Statement

WITH *record-var* DO
statement body

Interpretation: The *statement body* is a single or compound statement. *Record-var* is the name of a record variable. Within the *statement body,* any field of *record-var* may be referenced by specifying its field name only.

Example 7.4: The program in Fig. 7.5 computes the distance from an arbitrary point on the X-Y plane to the origin (intersection of X axis and Y axis).

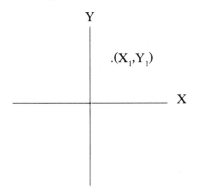

The values of the X and Y coordinates are entered as data and stored in the fields XCOORD and YCOORD of the record variable POINT1. The formula used to compute the distance from the origin to an arbitrary point (X_1, Y_1) is

$$distance = \quad X_1^2 + Y_1^2$$

Since the record variable POINT1 is specified in the WITH statement header, only the field names XCOORD and YCOORD are needed to reference the coordinates of the data point. Each coordinate is read separately since it is illegal to use a record variable by itself in a READ(LN) or WRITE(LN) statement (i.e., only individual fields of a record variable may be read or displayed at the terminal, not the entire record).

```
PROGRAM DISTORIGIN;
(* FINDS THE DISTANCE FROM A POINT TO THE ORIGIN *)

TYPE
  POINT = RECORD
    XCOORD : REAL;
    YCOORD : REAL
  END; (* POINT *)

VAR
  POINT1 : POINT;
  DISTANCE : REAL;

BEGIN
  WITH POINT1 DO
    BEGIN
      WRITE ('X = '); READLN (XCOORD);
      WRITE ('Y = '); READLN (YCOORD);
      DISTANCE := SQRT(SQR(XCOORD) + SQR(YCOORD));
      WRITELN ('DISTANCE TO ORIGIN = ', DISTANCE :10:2)
    END (* WITH *)
END.

X  = 3.00
Y  = 4.00
DISTANCE TO ORIGIN =      5.00
```

Fig. 7.5 Distance from point to origin.

7.3.3 Manipulating an Entire Record

In the problem below, we will see that it is possible to copy all the fields of one record variable to another record variable of the same type using a *record copy statement*. If CLERK and JANITOR are both record variables of type EMPLOYEE, the *record copy statement*

```
CLERK := JANITOR
```

copies all fields of JANITOR into the corresponding fields of CLERK.

It is also possible to pass a record variable as a parameter to a function or procedure. The actual parameter must be the same record type as its corresponding formal parameter.

The record copy statement is described in the next display.

Record Copy

$$recvar_1 := recvar_2$$

Interpretation: *Recvar*$_1$ and *recvar*$_2$ are the names of two record variables of the same type. The record copy statement copies all fields of *recvar*$_2$ to the corresponding fields of *recvar*$_1$.

Problem 7.1: Write a program to compute the perimeter of an arbitrary polygon.

Discussion: In order to solve this problem, we must be given the end points (corners) of the polygon as data. The length of each line segment (side) can be computed from its end points and added to the total length (PERIMETER). We shall assume that the coordinates of the end points are entered in order as we proceed clockwise around the polygon (1-2-3-4-5-1 in Fig. 7.6).

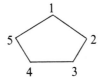

Fig. 7.6 End points of a polygon with 5 sides.

The record variable START will be used to remember the coordinates of the very first end point. When that coordinate is read for the second time, we will complete the processing of the polygon. The data table and level one algorithm are shown below; the main program is given in Fig. 7.7.

Data Table for Problem 7.1

Data types
```
POINT = RECORD
    XCOORD : REAL;
    YCOORD : REAL
END;
```

Input variables	*Program variables*	*Output variables*
START: First end point of polygon (POINT)		PERIMETER: Distance around polygon (REAL)

Functions referenced

     FINDPERIM: Computes perimeter by accumulating the sum of all segment lengths

Level One Algorithm

1. Read first end point into START.
2. Compute PERIMETER by accumulating the sum of all segment lengths.
3. Print PERIMETER.

```
PROGRAM POLYGON;
(* COMPUTES PERIMETER OF A POLYGON *)

TYPE
  POINT = RECORD
    XCOORD : REAL;
    YCOORD : REAL
  END; (* POINT *)

VAR
  START : POINT;
  PERIMETER : REAL;

(* INSERT FUNCTION FINDPERIM HERE *)
(*$I UCSD3:FINDPERIM *)

BEGIN
  (* READ FIRST ENDPOINT *)
  WRITE ('ENTER X, Y COORDINATES OF STARTING POINT: ');
  WITH START DO
    READLN (XCOORD, YCOORD);

  (* COMPUTE PERIMETER *)
  PERIMETER := FINDPERIM(START);

  (* PRINT THE FINAL RESULT *)
  WRITELN ('PERIMETER = ', PERIMETER :7:2)
END.
```

Fig. 7.7a Main program for polygon perimeter.

The function FINDPERIM is used to determine the perimeter of the polygon. We shall process one side at a time. It is only necessary to keep track of one pair of end points. We shall use two record variables, POINT1 and POINT2 (type POINT), to represent the line segment currently being processed.

The initial end point, START, will be POINT1 for the first line segment and POINT2 will be the next data value. For each line segment: the segment between POINT1 and POINT2 is processed, POINT2 for the current segment becomes POINT1 for the next segment, and a new POINT2 is read. The end point represented by START serves as POINT2 for the last line segment as well. The data table and algorithm for FINDPERIM are shown below.

Data Table for FINDPERIM

Input parameters

START: First end point
  of polygon (POINT)

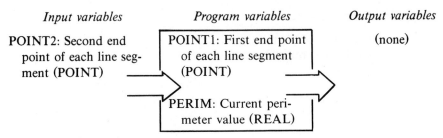

Input variables

POINT2: Second end point of each line segment (POINT)

Program variables

POINT1: First end point of each line segment (POINT)

PERIM: Current perimeter value (REAL)

Output variables

(none)

Functions referenced

COMPLENGTH: Computes the length of a side.

Level One Algorithm for FINDPERIM

1. Initialize the perimeter to zero and POINT1 and POINT2 to the coordinates of the first side.
2. Add the length of each side to the perimeter.

Level Two Refinements for FINDPERIM

Step 2   *Add the length of each side to the perimeter*

   2.1 WHILE more sides DO
       BEGIN
          2.2 Add length of current side to the perimeter
          2.3 Advance to the next side
       END

In order to determine if there are more sides, we must compare the second end point of the current side (POINT2) with START. If they are the same, we have reached the beginning of the polygon and should exit from the loop. The length of the last side must be added to the perimeter immediately after loop exit. The revised level two refinement of Step 2 follows.

Revised Level Two Refinements for FINDPERIM

Step 2   *Add the length of each side to the perimeter*

   2.1 WHILE POINT2 is not the starting point DO
       BEGIN
          2.2 Add length of current side to the perimeter
          2.3 Advance to the next side
       END
   2.4 Add length of last side to the perimeter

The implementation of function FINDPERIM is shown in Fig. 7.7b. There are a number of features illustrated in this program that are worth noting. The formal parameter START is a record (type POINT). Consequently, the corresponding actual parameter must be a record variable of type POINT; all fields of this record are passed to the function when it is called.

Within the loop, the statements

```
POINT1 := POINT2;
READLN (POINT2.XCOORD, POINT2.YCOORD)
```

are used to advance to the next side (Step 2.3). The first statement copies one record variable of type POINT to another. All fields of each record variable are copied without specifying the individual fields by name. Of course, record copy statements are legal only when both record variables are the same type.

The loop repetition test (Step 2.1) is implemented as

```
POINT2 <> START
```

As shown above, it is possible in UCSD (but not standard) PASCAL to compare two records using the relational operator = or < >. In Chapter 9, we shall learn how to read (write) a record from (to) a file of records. However, individual fields of a record must be manipulated separately in arithmetic expressions and when read or written at the terminal.

Record comparison is described in the display that follows.

Record Comparison

$$recvar_1 = recvar_2$$
$$\text{or } recvar_1 < > recvar_2$$

Interpretation: $recvar_1$ and $recvar_2$ are two record variables of the same type. These two records are considered identical (=) if all corresponding fields have the same value; otherwise they are not identical (< >).

The function COMPLENGTH computes the length of each line segment. The statement

```
PERIM := PERIM + COMPLENGTH(POINT1, POINT2);
```

calls the function COMPLENGTH and adds the function result to PERIM.

Program Style

Use of local variable to represent function result

The local variable, PERIM, is used to represent the current value of the perimeter. This additional variable is necessary as it would be incorrect to use the statement

```
FINDPERIM := FINDPERIM + COMPLENGTH(POINT1, POINT2);
```

to accumulate the perimeter value. The use of the function name FINDPERIM in the above expression would be considered an illegal recursive call to FINDPERIM since there is no parameter list. (Recursive calls will be studied in the next chapter.)

```
FUNCTION FINDPERIM (START : POINT) : REAL;
(* FINDS THE PERIMETER OF A POLYGON *)

VAR
  POINT1, POINT2 : POINT;
  PERIM : REAL;

(* INSERT FUNCTION COMPLENGTH HERE *)

BEGIN
  (* INITIALIZE PERIM, POINT1 and POINT2 *)
  PERIM := O;
  POINT1 := START;
  WRITELN ('ENTER STARTING POINT TO TERMINATE OR');
  WRITE ('NEXT POINT: ');
  READLN (POINT2.XCOORD, POINT2.YCOORD);

  (* ADD LENGTH OF EACH SIDE TO PERIM *)
  WHILE POINT2 <> START DO
    BEGIN
      (* ADD LENGTH OF CURRENT SIDE TO PERIM *)
      PERIM := PERIM + COMPLENGTH(POINT1, POINT2);
      (* ADVANCE TO NEXT SIDE *)
      POINT1 := POINT2;
      WRITE ('NEXT POINT: ');
      READLN (POINT2.XCOORD, POINT2.YCOORD)
    END; (* WHILE *)

  (* ADD LENGTH OF LAST SIDE TO PERIM AND DEFINE RESULT *)
  FINDPERIM := PERIM + COMPLENGTH(POINT1, START)
END; (* FINDPERIM *)
```

Fig. 7.7b Function FINDPERIM.

The function **COMPLENGTH** computes the length of the line segment from **POINT1** to **POINT2** using the formula

$$\text{SEGLENGTH} = \sqrt{(X_2 - X_1)^2 + (Y_2 - Y_1)^2}$$

where (X_1, Y_1) and (X_2, Y_2) represent the coordinates of the end points of the line segment (stored in **POINT1** and **POINT2**, respectively). The segment length is also printed. Function **COMPLENGTH** is shown in Fig. 7.7c.

```
FUNCTION COMPLENGTH (POINT1, POINT2 : POINT) : REAL;

VAR
  SEGLENGTH : REAL;

BEGIN
  (* COMPUTE LENGTH FROM POINT1 TO POINT2 *)
  SEGLENGTH := SQRT(SQR(POINT2.XCOORD - POINT1.XCOORD) +
                    SQR(POINT2.YCOORD - POINT1.YCOORD));

  (* PRINT SEGMENT LENGTH *)
  WRITELN ('SEGMENT LENGTH = ', SEGLENGTH :6:2);
  WRITELN;

  (* DEFINE FUNCTION VALUE *)
  COMPLENGTH := SEGLENGTH
END; (* COMPLENGTH *)
```

Fig. 7.7c Function COMPLENGTH.

A sample run of the polygon program is shown in Fig. 7.7d.

```
ENTER X, Y COORDINATES OF STARTING POINT: -1 -2
ENTER STARTING POINT TO TERMINATE OR
NEXT POINT: 3 -2
SEGMENT LENGTH =    4.00

NEXT POINT: -1 1
SEGMENT LENGTH =    5.00

NEXT POINT: -1 -2
SEGMENT LENGTH =    3.00

PERIMETER =    12.00
```

Fig. 7.7d Sample run of POLYGON program.

Exercise 7.4: Under what circumstances could the local variable SEGLENGTH be omitted from function COMPLENGTH?

7.4 ARRAYS OF RECORDS

PASCAL data structures are very general. It is possible to declare a record type with fields that are arrays or other records. Similarly, we can declare an array of records as will be shown next.

Example 7.5: In Section 6.7.3, we wrote a program to process a collection of student names and exam scores. The program assigned a letter grade to each student by first computing the class average and then comparing the student's score to the class average. It would seem reasonable to summarize the exam data for each student in a record as shown below.

```
TYPE
  EXAM = RECORD
    NAME : STRING[10];
    SCORE : INTEGER;
    GRADE : CHAR
  END; (* EXAM *)
```

An array named STUDENT could be used to store the exam data for the entire class.

```
      STURECORD = ARRAY[1..CLASSIZE] OF EXAM;

VAR
   STUDENT : STURECORD;
```

A sample of the first two elements of this array is shown below.

	NAME	SCORE	GRADE
STUDENT[1]	JONES, S.	98	A
STUDENT[2]	SMITH, P.	52	C

To reference any value stored in this array, it would be necessary to specify the array element subscript and field name (e.g., STUDENT[1].SCORE is 98).

The main program is rewritten in Fig. 7.8a using the new data structures. The major differences between the new main program and the old one (Fig. 6.11a) are in the declaration section. Instead of two separate arrays for each student name and exam score, we have combined these data, along with the student's letter grade, in a single array (STUDENT) with elements of record type EXAM. This is a much more natural representation.

The main program calls procedure ENTERSCORE (Fig. 7.8b) to read each student's name and score, count the number of students and accumulate the total of all scores. The average is then computed in the main program. Procedure CATEGORIZE (Fig. 7.8c) compares each student's score to this average, and assigns a letter grade to each student.

```
PROGRAM EXAMS;
(* ASSIGN LETTER GRADES BASED ON CLASS AVERAGE *)

CONST
  CLASSIZE = 120;

TYPE
  EXAM = RECORD
    NAME : STRING[10];
    SCORE : INTEGER;
    GRADE : CHAR
  END; (* EXAM *)
  STURECORD = ARRAY[1..CLASSIZE] OF EXAM;

VAR
  STUDENT : STURECORD;
  SUM, COUNT : INTEGER;
  AVERAGE : REAL;

(* INSERT PROCEDURES ENTERSCORE AND CATEGORIZE HERE *)
(*$I UCSD3:ENTERSCORE *)
(*$I UCSD3:CATEGORIZE *)
```

(continued)

```
BEGIN
  (* READ EACH STUDENT'S NAME AND SCORE -
     COMPUTE SUM AND COUNT *)
  ENTERSCORE (STUDENT, CLASSIZE, SUM, COUNT);

  (* COMPUTE AND PRINT CLASS AVERAGE *)
  AVERAGE := SUM / COUNT;
  WRITELN ('AVERAGE SCORE = ', AVERAGE :6:1);

  (* FIND AND PRINT GRADE CATEGORY FOR EACH STUDENT *)
  CATEGORIZE (STUDENT, AVERAGE, COUNT)
END.
```

Fig. 7.8a Student grade program with records.

```
PROCEDURE ENTERSCORE (VAR STUDENT : STURECORD;
                      CLASSIZE : INTEGER;
                      VAR SUM, COUNT : INTEGER);
(* READ NAME AND SCORE - FIND SCORE TOTAL AND STUDENT COUNT *)

CONST
  SENTINEL = 'DONE';

VAR
  TEMPNAME : STRING[10];

BEGIN
  (* INITIALIZE SUM OF SCORES AND COUNT OF STUDENTS *)
  SUM := 0;
  COUNT := 0;

  (* READ EACH STUDENT'S NAME AND SCORE *)
  (* ADD ONE TO COUNT AND SCORE TO SUM *)
  WRITELN ('ENTER "DONE" OR');
  WRITE ('STUDENT NAME: '); READLN (TEMPNAME);
  WHILE (TEMPNAME <> SENTINEL) AND (COUNT < CLASSIZE) DO
    BEGIN
      COUNT := COUNT + 1;
      WITH STUDENT[COUNT] DO
        BEGIN
          NAME := TEMPNAME;
          (* READ SCORE AND ADD TO SUM *)
          WRITE ('SCORE: '); READLN (SCORE);
          SUM := SUM + SCORE;
          WRITE ('STUDENT NAME: '); READLN (TEMPNAME)
        END (* WITH *)
    END (* WHILE *)
END; (* ENTERSCORE *)
```

Fig. 7.8b Procedure ENTERSCORE.

```
PROCEDURE CATEGORIZE (VAR STUDENT : STURECORD;
                          AVERAGE :REAL;
                          COUNT : INTEGER);
(* FIND AND PRINT GRADE CATEGORY FOR EACH STUDENT *)

VAR
   I : INTEGER;
   GRADE : CHAR;

BEGIN
   (* WRITE HEADING *)
   WRITELN;
   WRITELN ('STUDENT', 'SCORE' :13, 'GRADE' :10);

   (* FIND GRADE FOR EACH STUDENT *)
   FOR I := 1 TO COUNT DO
     WITH STUDENT[I] DO
       BEGIN
         IF SCORE > ROUND(AVERAGE + 10) THEN
           GRADE := 'A'
         ELSE IF SCORE < ROUND(AVERAGE - 10) THEN
           GRADE := 'C'
         ELSE
           GRADE := 'B';
         WRITELN (NAME :10, SCORE :10, GRADE :8)
       END (* WITH *)
END; (* CATEGORIZE *)
```

Fig. 7.8c Procedure CATEGORIZE.

Program Style

Using a WITH statement to reference array elements

The WITH statement inside the FOR loop in procedure CATEGORIZE (Fig. 7.8c) enables us to reference each memory cell in the array STUDENT by field name only. Since the record identifier used in the WITH statement is STUDENT[I], the field names SCORE and GRADE are abbreviated forms of the field selectors STUDENT [I].SCORE and STUDENT[I].GRADE, respectively.

Note that the position of the WITH statement header is extremely critical. Since we want to manipulate a different record (array element) each time the array index I is changed, the WITH statement must be nested inside the FOR loop:

```
FOR I := 1 TO COUNT DO
   WITH STUDENT[I] DO
```

After each repetition of the FOR loop, the index I is increased by one and the next record in the array STUDENT is selected. If the order were reversed

```
                    WITH STUDENT[I] DO
                      FOR I := 1 TO COUNT DO
```

then the record that is manipulated would be determined by the value of I when the WITH statement is first reached. (If I is undefined or out of range, an error will result.) Even though the index I is changed inside the WITH statement, the record (array element) manipulated would not change.

Procedure ENTERSCORE is shown in Fig. 7.8b. This procedure reads the name and exam score for each student. The field names SCORE and NAME are abbreviations for STUDENT[COUNT].SCORE and STUDENT [COUNT].NAME, respectively, since the record identifier STUDENT [COUNT] appears in the WITH statement header. The WITH statement must be nested inside the WHILE loop which uses COUNT as its loop control variable.

Exercise 7.5: Write a procedure to compute the standard deviation of the exam scores (see Exercise 6.16).

7.5 THE SET DATA TYPE

PASCAL is the first general purpose programming language to include the set data type. Those of you who grew up with the "new math" were probably introduced to sets at a very early stage in your study of mathematics. The set data type allows us to perform the common set operations of union, intersection and set difference in PASCAL programs. It also enables us to determine quite easily whether a particular data item is one of a special group of values using the set membership test.

In mathematics, a set is represented by a pair of curly braces containing a list of set elements. For example, if we restrict our attention to the integers between one and nine, the set of odd integers is represented as $\{1,3,5,7,9\}$; the set of even integers is represented as $\{2,4,6,8\}$. In PASCAL, square brackets are used instead of braces to denote sets.

Example 7.6: The statements below define a set type DIGIT and two set variables named ODD and EVEN. The set variables ODD and EVEN represent the sets described above.

```
                    TYPE
                      DIGIT = SET OF 1..9;

                    VAR
                      ODD, EVEN : DIGIT;

                    BEGIN
                      ODD := [1,3,5,7,9];
                      EVEN := [2,4,6,8]
```

Fig. 7.9 Defining the sets ODD and EVEN.

The set type declaration is described in the next display. Set operations will be discussed in the sections that follow.

Set Type Declaration

$$set\ type\ =\ \text{SET OF}\ base\ type$$

Interpretation: The identifier *set type* is defined over the values specified in *base type*. A variable declared to be of type *set type* is a set whose elements are chosen from the values in *base type*. The *base type* must be a scalar type. Hence, the reals may not be used; however, a subrange of the integers or characters may be a *base type*.

Note 1: Only scalar types may be specified as the *base type* of a set. Sets of records, arrays or strings are not permitted; however, a set type may be used as an array element type (array of sets) or a record field type.

7.6   SET OPERATIONS

7.6.1   Assignment, Empty Set and Universal Set

The initial elements of a set must always be specified using a set assignment statement before the set may be manipulated.

Example 7.7:   The statements below specify two sets defined over the base type MONTH.

```
TYPE
  MONTH = (JAN,FEB,MAR,APR,MAY,JUN,JUL,AUG,SEP,OCT,NOV,DEC);
  MONTHSET = SET OF MONTH;

VAR
  WINTER, SUMMER : MONTHSET;

BEGIN
  WINTER := [DEC,JAN,FEB];
  SUMMER := [JUN..AUG];
```

Each assignment statement consists of a set variable on the left and a set value on the right. A set value is indicated by a pair of brackets and a list of values from the base type of the set being defined. As shown in the assignment statement for SUMMER, a list of consecutive values may be denoted as a subrange.

It is also possible to have a set variable on the right of the assignment statement as well, provided both set variables have compatible base types. This would give both set variables the same value (a set).

Often, we wish to denote that, initially, a set is empty or has no elements. The empty set is indicated in PASCAL by a pair of brackets [].

```
                    SUMMER  := [ ]
```

A set variable must always be initialized before it can be used with any of the set operators. Very often, a set variable is initialized to the empty set or the universal set, the set consisting of all values of the base type. The universal set for a set of type MONTHSET would be denoted as [JAN..DEC].

Example 7.8:   The program segment below defines a set type LETTERSET with the characters 'A' through 'Z' as its base type. This means that the allowable elements for any set of this type are letters only. A set variable VOWEL (type LETTERSET) is initialized to the set of vowels, and a set variable LETTER is initialized to the universal set.

```
        TYPE
          LETTERSET = SET OF 'A'..'Z';

        VAR
          VOWEL, LETTER : LETTERSET

        BEGIN
          VOWEL  := ['A', 'E', 'I', 'O', 'U'];
          LETTER := ['A'..'Z'];
                     .
                     .
                     .
```

The general form of the set assignment statement is shown in the display below. As indicated, it is possible to write set expressions involving set manipulation operators. These operators are described in the next section.

Set Assignment

set-var := set-expression

Interpretation: The variable, *set-var*, is defined as the set whose elements are determined by the value of *set-expression*. The *set-expression* may be a set value (specified as [*list of elements*] or [*subrange*]), or another set variable. Alternatively, a *set-expression* may specify the manipulation of two or more sets using the PASCAL set operators. The base type of *set-var* and *set-expression* must be type compatible, and all the elements in *set-expression* must be included in the base type of set-var.

7.6.2   Set Union, Intersection and Difference

The set operators union, intersection and difference require two sets of the same type as operands. The union of two sets (set operator, +) is defined as the set of elements that are in either set or both sets.

```
    [1,3,4] + [1,2,4] is [1,2,3,4]
    [1,3] + [2,4] is [1,2,3,4]
    ['A','C','F'] + ['B','C','D','F'] is ['A','B','C','D','F']
```

The intersection of two sets (set operator, *) is defined as the set of all elements that are common to both sets:

```
[1,3,4] * [1,2,4] is [1,4]
[1,3] * [2,4] is []
['A','C','F'] * ['B','C','D','F'] is ['C','F']
```

The difference of set A and set B (set operator, −) is defined as the set of elements that are in set A but not in set B:

```
[1,3,4] - [1,2,4] is [3]
[1,3] - [2,4] is [1,3]
['A','C','F'] - ['B','C','D','F'] is ['A']
['B','C','D','F'] - ['A','C','F'] is ['B','D']
```

The operators $+$, $*$ and $-$ are treated as set operators when their operands are sets. These operators can be used to combine two sets to form a third set. If more than one set operator is used in an expression, the normal precedence rules for the operators $+$, $*$ and $-$ will be followed (see Table 4.1 in Section 4.2.4). When in doubt, it is best to use parentheses to specify the intended order of evaluation.

Often, we wish to insert a new element in an existing set. This is accomplished by forming the union of the existing set and a *unit set* consisting of the new element by itself:

$$[1,3,4,5] + [2] \text{ is } [1,2,3,4,5]$$

A common error is omitting the brackets around a unit set. The expression

$$[1,3,4,5] + 2$$

is illegal because one operand is a set and the other is an integer constant.

The set operators $+$, $*$, and $-$ are described next.

Set Operators

Intersection: $set_1 * set_2$
Union: $set_1 + set_2$
Difference: $set_1 - set_2$

Interpretation: Set_1 and set_2 are either set variables or set values (a list of elements enclosed in square brackets). The normal set theoretic definitions of set intersection, union and difference apply. The set operators return sets as values. Set_1 and set_2 should have compatible base types.

Example 7.9: Recall that a set type may be used as an array element type. The procedure in Fig. 7.10 defines an array of type DATEARRAY as described below.

```
TYPE
  DAY = (SUNDAY, MONDAY, TUESDAY, WEDNESDAY, THURSDAY,
           FRIDAY, SATURDAY);
  DATERANGE = 1..31;
  DATES = SET OF DATERANGE;
  DATEARRAY = ARRAY[DAY] OF DATES;
```

Each element of an array of type **DATEARRAY** is a set of integers (base type 1..31); the subscript type is the scalar type **DAY**.

The input parameters to the procedure specify the first day of the month (FIRSTDAY) and the number of days in the month (NUMDAYS).

The first FOR loop initializes each array element to the empty set. The second FOR loop uses the statement

```
DAYDATES[TODAY] := DAYDATES[TODAY] + [DATE];
```

to insert each value of DATE (from 1 to NUMDAYS) in the appropriate set (array element DAYDATES[TODAY]). The IF statement updates the array index TODAY which is initialized to FIRSTDAY.

When procedure execution is complete, the actual array element with subscript MONDAY, for example, will consist of the set of all dates in the month that fall on a Monday. If Sunday is the first day of the month and NUMDAYS is thirty or thirty-one, this will be the set [2, 9, 16, 23, 30].

```
PROCEDURE DATEASSIGN (VAR DAYDATES : DATEARRAY;
                          NUMDAYS : DATERANGE;
                          FIRSTDAY : DAY);
(* ASSIGNS DATES FOR ALL MONDAYS TO THE SET DAYDATES[MONDAY], *)
(* ETC. FIRSTDAY IS THE FIRST DAY OF THE MONTH                *)
(* NUMDAYS IS THE NUMBER OF DAYS IN THE MONTH                 *)

VAR
  TODAY : DAY;
  DATE : DATERANGE;

BEGIN
  (* INITIALIZE ALL ARRAY ELEMENTS TO THE EMPTY SET *)
  FOR TODAY := SUNDAY TO SATURDAY DO
    DAYDATES[TODAY] := [];

  (* INSERT EACH DATE IN THE ARRAY DAYDATES *)
  TODAY := FIRSTDAY;
  FOR DATE := 1 TO NUMDAYS DO
    BEGIN
      DAYDATES[TODAY] := DAYDATES[TODAY] + [DATE];
      (* UPDATE DAY OF THE WEEK *)
      IF TODAY = SATURDAY THEN
        TODAY := SUNDAY
      ELSE
        TODAY := SUCC(TODAY)
    END (* FOR *)
END; (* DATEASSIGN *)
```

Fig. 7.10 Procedure DATEASSIGN.

Exercise 7.6:   Correct the errors in the program below. It is supposed to form a set of odd numbers.

```
PROGRAM BUILDODD

VAR
   ODDNUMBERS = SET OF 1..25;

BEGIN
   I := 1;
   WHILE I <= 25 DO
      BEGIN
         ODDNUMBER := ODDNUMBERS + I;
         I := I + 2
      END (* WHILE *)
END.
```

Exercise 7.7:   If A and B are sets, then verify that (A*B) + (A−B) is A. Show that this is the case for the sample sets used in this section.

Exercise 7.8:   A is the set [1,3,5,7], B is the set [2,4,6], C is the set [1,2,3]. Evaluate the following:

a) A + (B − C)   d) C + (A − C)
b) A + (B * C)   e) C − (A − B)
c) A + B + C   f) (C − A) − B

7.6.3 Set Relational Operators

Sets may also be compared through the use of the relational operators =, <, >, etc. Both operands of a set relational operator must have the same base type. The operators = and < > are used to test whether or not two sets contain the same elements.

[1,3]   =   [1,3] is TRUE
[1,3]   < >   [1,3] is FALSE
[1,3]   < >   [2,4] is TRUE
[1,3]   =   [2,4] is FALSE
[1,3]   =   [3,1] is TRUE

As indicated by the last example above, the order in which the elements of a set are listed is not important ([1,3] and [3,1] denote the same set). However, we will normally list the elements of a set in ordinal sequence.

Other relational operators are used to determine subset and superset relationships. Set A is a *subset* of set B (A < = B) if every element of set A is also an element of set B.

[1,3]   < =   [1,2,3,4] is TRUE
[1,3]   < =   [1,3] is TRUE
[1,2,3,4]   < =   [1,3] is FALSE
[]   < =   [1,3] is TRUE

As indicated in the last example above, the empty set, [], is a subset of every set.

Set A is a *proper subset* of set B (A < B) if A is a subset of B and there is at least one element in B that is not in A.

$$[1,3] \quad < \quad [1,2,3,4] \text{ is TRUE}$$
$$[1,3] \quad < \quad [1,3] \text{ is FALSE}$$
$$[] \quad < \quad [1,3] \text{ is TRUE}$$

The relational operator > = is used to determine *superset* relations. Set A is a superset of set B (A > = B) if every element of B is also an element of A.

$$[1,2,3,4] \quad > = \quad [1,3] \text{ is TRUE}$$
$$[1,3] \quad > = \quad [1,2,3,4] \text{ is FALSE}$$
$$[1,3] \quad > = \quad [1,3] \text{ is TRUE}$$
$$[1,3] \quad > = \quad [] \text{ is TRUE}$$

Set A is a *proper superset* of set B (A > B) if A is a superset of B and there is at least one element of A that is not in B.

$$[1,2,3,4] \quad > \quad [1,3] \text{ is TRUE}$$
$$[1,3] \quad > \quad [1,3] \text{ is FALSE}$$
$$[1,3,4] \quad > \quad [1,2] \text{ is FALSE}$$
$$[1] \quad > \quad [] \text{ is TRUE}$$

In addition to the relational operators discussed above, there is a new operator, IN, which is used to determine whether or not a particular element is contained in a set (set membership test). The element being tested must be compatible with the base type of the set.

$$1 \quad \text{IN} \quad [1,2,3] \text{ is TRUE}$$
$$1 \quad \text{IN} \quad [2,4] \text{ is FALSE}$$
$$'A' \quad \text{IN} \quad ['A','C','F'] \text{ is TRUE}$$
$$'C' \quad \text{IN} \quad ['A','B','F'] \text{ is FALSE}$$

In Fig. 5.3, the test for a digit

```
(NEXTCHAR >= '0') AND (NEXTCHAR <= '9')
```

could be written more naturally as

```
NEXTCHAR IN ['0'..'9']
```

Similarly, the test for a letter in Fig. 6.6b could be written as

```
NEXTCHAR IN ['A'..'Z']
```

The set relational operators are summarized in the next display.

Set Relational Operators

Equality	:	set_1 $=$	set_2
Inequality	:	set_1 $<>$	set_2
Subset	:	set_1 $<=$	set_2
Proper Subset	:	set_1 $<$	set_2
Superset	:	set_1 $>=$	set_2
Proper Superset	:	set_1 $>$	set_2
Set Membership	:	set-el **IN**	set_1

Interpretation: Set_1 and set_2 are either set variables or set values. The value of a set relation (TRUE or FALSE) corresponds to the normal set-theoretic definitions of set equality, subset, superset, etc. The set membership operator, IN, evaluates to TRUE if set-el is a member of set_1.

Note 1: The base type of set_1 and set_2 must be compatible.

Note 2: The type of the element tested for set membership must be compatible with the base type of the indicated set.

Example 7.10: The procedure in Fig. 7.11 reads a hand of cards and stores each card in an array represented by the output parameter HAND. Each element of the array is a set whose members are the cards in a suit. The array HAND should be declared in the main program as shown next.

```
TYPE
   RANKSET = SET OF CHAR;
   SUIT = (CLUBS, DIAMONDS, HEARTS, SPADES);
   CARDS = ARRAY[SUIT] OF RANKSET;

VAR
   HAND : CARDS;
```

Each card is read as a pair of characters. The first character represents the rank of the card: the digits 2 through 9 stand for themselves; the picture cards are denoted by J, Q, and K (Jack, Queen, King); an Ace is denoted by A and a ten by the digit 1. The second character denotes the suit: C, D, H, or S.

After reading each card, the procedure checks to see that the rank and suit are legal by evaluating the Boolean expression

```
(RANK IN ['1'..'9','J','Q','K','A']) AND
(SUITCHAR IN ['C','D','H','S'])
```

If the above expression is true, the CASE statement is used to determine the value of CARDSUIT (a scalar value of type SUIT). If the card is not a duplicate, it is added to the appropriate element of HAND by the statement

```
HAND[CARDSUIT] := HAND[CARDSUIT] + [RANK];
```

Exercise 7.9: Indicate how you would change the procedure if two digits were used to represent a 10 (i.e. 10C would be the ten of Clubs).

```
PROCEDURE READHAND (VAR HAND : CARDS);
(* READS A COLLECTION OF CARDS AND  *)
(* STORES THEM IN ARRAY HAND        *)


CONST
  SENTINEL = '/';


VAR
  RANK, SUITCHAR : CHAR;
  CARDSUIT : SUIT;


BEGIN
  (* INITIALIZE EACH SUIT TO THE EMPTY SET *)
  FOR CARDSUIT := CLUBS TO SPADES DO
    HAND[CARDSUIT] := [];


  (* READ EACH CARD AND PLACE IT IN HAND *)
  WRITELN ('ENTER / TO STOP OR');
  WRITELN ('RANK (R) AND SUIT (S)');
  WRITELN ('RS'); READ (RANK);
  WHILE RANK <> SENTINEL DO
    BEGIN
      READ (SUITCHAR);
      WRITELN;
      IF (RANK IN ['1'..'9', 'J', 'Q', 'K', 'A']) AND
         (SUITCHAR IN ['C', 'D', 'H', 'S']) THEN
        BEGIN
          CASE SUITCHAR OF
            'C' : CARDSUIT := CLUBS;
            'D' : CARDSUIT := DIAMONDS;
            'H' : CARDSUIT := HEARTS;
            'S' : CARDSUIT := SPADES
          END; (* CASE *)


          (* TEST FOR DUPLICATE *)
          IF RANK IN HAND[CARDSUIT] THEN
            WRITELN (RANK, SUITCHAR, ' IS A DUPLICATE')
          ELSE
            HAND[CARDSUIT] := HAND[CARDSUIT] + [RANK]
        END
      ELSE
        WRITELN (RANK, SUITCHAR, ' IS ILLEGAL');
      WRITELN ('RS'); READ (RANK)
    END (* WHILE *)
END; (* READHAND *)
```

Fig. 7.11 Procedure to enter a hand of cards.

7.6.4 Printing a Set

The next example illustrates how to print the members of a set.

Example 7.11:   The program in Fig. 7.12 replaces each vowel in a line of text with a '$'. In addition, it prints an alphabetical list of all consonants in the line of text.

The set of consonants, CONSONANT, is defined as the difference of the universal set, LETTER, and the set of vowels, VOWEL. The set CONSOCCUR, used to keep track of the consonants occurring in the line of text, is initialized to the empty set. Each consonant that is read is inserted in CONSOCCUR by the statement

```
            CONSOCCUR := CONSOCCUR - [NEXT];
```

This statement forms the union of CONSOCCUR with the unit set consisting of the character stored in NEXT.

A set cannot appear in a WRITE statement. Hence, in order to print a set, it is necessary to print each element individually. This can be done by testing every value in the base type for set membership. If the test succeeds, that value should be printed.

The FOR loop in Fig. 7.12 contains an IF statement that tests each letter for membership in the set CONSOCCUR. That letter is printed only if the test succeeds. For the input line

```
      WHERE WERE YOU ALL ON SEPTEMBER 1, 1980?
```

the output generated by the program in Fig. 7.12 would be

```
      WH$R$ W$R$ Y$$ $LL $N S$PT$MB$R 1, 1980?

      THE CONSONANTS ARE:
      BHLMNPRSTWY
```

```
PROGRAM LETTERS;
(* REPLACE EACH VOWEL IN THE INPUT STRING WITH A $ *)
(* AND PRINT THE SET OF CONSONANTS                 *)

TYPE
  LETTERSET = SET OF 'A'..'Z';

VAR
  LETTER, VOWEL : LETTERSET;
  CONSONANT, CONSOCCUR : LETTERSET;
  NEXT : CHAR;

BEGIN
  (* INITIALIZE SETS *)
```

(*continued*)

```
CONSOCCUR := [ ];
VOWEL := [ 'A', 'E', 'I', 'O', 'U' ];
LETTER := [ 'A'..'Z' ];
CONSONANT := LETTER - VOWEL;

(* REPLACE EVERY VOWEL WITH A $ *)
WHILE NOT EOLN(KEYBOARD) DO
  BEGIN
    READ (KEYBOARD, NEXT);
    (* TEST FOR VOWEL OR CONSONANT *)
    IF NEXT IN VOWEL THEN
      WRITE ('$')
    ELSE IF NEXT IN CONSONANT THEN
      BEGIN
        (* INSERT NEXT IN CONSOCCUR *)
        CONSOCCUR := CONSOCCUR + [NEXT];
        WRITE (NEXT)
      END
    ELSE
      WRITE (NEXT)
  END; (* WHILE *)
WRITELN;
WRITELN;

(* PRINT OUT THE SET CONSOCCUR *)
WRITELN ('THE CONSONANTS ARE : ');
FOR NEXT := 'A' TO 'Z' DO
  IF NEXT IN CONSOCCUR THEN
    WRITE (NEXT);
WRITELN
END.
```

Fig. 7.12 Removing vowels and finding consonants.

Since the statement

```
READ (KEYBOARD, NEXT)
```

is used for data entry, the condition

```
NOT EOLN(KEYBOARD)
```

must be used to control loop repetition. This condition is true as long as the
< CR > key has not yet been pressed.

Another way of printing the members of the set CONSOCCUR is shown in
Fig. 7.13. Each letter (starting with 'B') is tested for set membership. Each element of CONSOCCUR is printed and then removed from CONSOCCUR using
the statement:

```
CONSOCCUR := CONSOCCUR - [NEXT]
```

The WHILE loop is repeated as long as there are still elements in CONS-
OCCUR (CONSOCCUR is not the empty set).

```
NEXT := 'B';
WHILE CONSOCCUR <> [] DO
  BEGIN
    IF NEXT IN CONSOCCUR THEN
      BEGIN
        WRITE(NEXT);
        CONSOCCUR := CONSOCCUR - [NEXT]
      END;
    NEXT := SUCC(NEXT)
  END (* WHILE *)
```

Fig. 7.13 Printing the set CONSOCCUR.

Exercise 7.10: Under what circumstances would the technique shown in Fig. 7.13 for printing a set be more efficient than the FOR loop used in Fig. 7.12? Why is NEXT initialized to 'B' rather than 'A'?

Exercise 7.11: Explain how you might write the program in Fig. 7.12 without sets.

7.6.5 Sets as Boolean Arrays

Since we can always use an array to represent a list of related data items, why bother to study sets and set operators in PASCAL? The main reason is that there are certain operations that can be performed more efficiently with sets than with arrays. For example, the set assignment statement

```
OPERATOR := OPERATOR - ['*']
```

can be used to delete the element '*' from the set OPERATOR. If OPERATOR were an array instead of a set, we would first have to locate the element with value '*' and then find some way to remove it. This would obviously be more difficult than writing a simple assignment statement.

The process of determining whether a particular value is an array and where it is located (its index) is called an *array search*. We shall illustrate how to search an array in Section 7.7. A very simple "search" can be performed on a set using the set membership operator. The value of the Boolean expression

```
'-' IN OPERATOR
```

indicates whether or not the element '−' is contained in the set OPERATOR. There is no index associated with the elements of a set.

An alternate approach would be to "simulate" a set using an array of Boolean values. As shown in Fig. 7.14, an array element containing the Boolean value TRUE would be a member of the simulated set ([1,3,4,5]); an array element containing the Boolean value FALSE would not. The array in Fig. 7.14 should be declared as

```
VAR
  S : ARRAY [0..9] OF BOOLEAN;
```

We could delete a simulated set element by simply resetting its corresponding array element value from TRUE to FALSE. Certainly, using the set data type makes these operations more convenient and natural.

S[0]	S[1]	S[2]	S[3]	S[4]	S[5]	S[6]	S[7]	S[8]	S[9]
FALSE	TRUE	FALSE	TRUE	TRUE	TRUE	FALSE	FALSE	FALSE	FALSE

Fig. 7.14   [1,3,4,5] represented as a Boolean array.

7.7   SEARCHING AN ARRAY OF RECORDS

A very common problem in working with arrays of data items is the need to *search* an array to determine whether a particular data item, called a *key*, is in the array. We might also want to know how many times the key is present and where in the array each copy of the key is located. An array search is analogous to determining whether a particular element is a member of a set. In the latter case, the answer can be easily determined using the set membership operator IN; searching an array requires a bit more effort.

The problem that follows will utilize the two new data structures introduced in this chapter and illustrate an array search.

Problem 7.2:   Write a program that could be used by a small bank (maximum of 20 checking accounts) to process the daily transactions (deposits and checks) against each account and maintain an up-to-date record of the balance for each account. At the end of the day, all account balances should be printed, followed by a list of accounts that were overdrawn at any time during the day. In addition, a list of all accounts that were active during the day and a list of inactive accounts should also be printed.

Discussion: Each account will be represented as a record consisting of the depositor's name, the balance at the start of the day and current balance. These records will be stored in the array ACCOUNT. The names and initial account balances will be provided as input data; the current balance for each account will initially be equal to the starting balance.

Once the initial account information has been entered, all transactions for the day will be processed one at a time. Each transaction record will specify the depositor name and transaction amount; a positive transaction amount indicates a deposit, and a negative amount indicates a check. Sets will be used for storage of the index numbers of all active and inactive accounts as well as any accounts that become overdrawn during the day. The data table and level one algorithm for the main program are shown below.

Data Table for Problem 7.2

Constants

> MAXDEPOSITOR = 20, the maximum number of depositors

Data types

> DEPOSITOR = RECORD
>   NAME : STRING[10];
>   STARTBAL : REAL;
>   CURRENTBAL : REAL
> END (* DEPOSITOR *)

> INDEX = 1..MAXDEPOSITOR

> BANKARRAY = ARRAY[INDEX] OF DEPOSITOR

> INDICES = SET OF INDEX

Input variables	*Program variables*	*Output variables*
ACCOUNT: Array of depositor records (BANKARRAY)	K: Loop control variable (INTEGER)	OVERDRAWN: Set of indices of overdrawn accounts (INDICES)
NUMDEPOSITOR: Actual number of depositors (INDEX)		ACTIVE: Set of indices of active accounts (INDICES)
		INACTIVE: Set of indices of inactive accounts (INDICES)

Procedures referenced

> ENTERDATA: Enters all initial account data.

> PROCESSTRAN: Processes all transactions and defines the sets ACTIVE, INACTIVE, and OVERDRAWN.

> DISPLAY: Prints the depositor names corresponding to a set of indices

Level One Algorithm

1. Enter all initial account data.
2. Process all transactions and define the sets ACTIVE, INACTIVE, and OVERDRAWN.
3. Print the depositor name and starting and ending balance for each account.
4. Print the depositor names corresponding to the sets of active accounts, inactive accounts, and overdrawn accounts.

As indicated in the data table, Steps 1, 2 and 4 are performed by procedures ENTERDATA, PROCESSTRAN, and DISPLAY, respectively. Step 3 is implemented as part of the main program, which is shown in Fig. 7.15a.

```
PROGRAM SAVINGS;

CONST
  MAXDEPOSITOR = 20;

TYPE
  DEPOSITOR = RECORD
    NAME : STRING[10];
    STARTBAL : REAL;
    CURRENTBAL : REAL
  END; (* DEPOSITOR *)
  INDEX = 1..MAXDEPOSITOR;
  BANKARRAY = ARRAY[INDEX] OF DEPOSITOR;
  INDICES = SET OF INDEX;
  TITLESTR = STRING[10];

VAR
  ACCOUNT : BANKARRAY;
  ACTIVE, INACTIVE, OVERDRAWN : INDICES;
  NUMDEPOSITOR : INDEX;
  K : INTEGER;

(* INSERT PROCEDURES ENTERDATA, PROCESSTRAN  *)
(* AND DISPLAY HERE                          *)
(*$I UCSD3:ENTERDATA    *)
(*$I UCSD3:PROCESSTRAN *)
(*$I UCSD3:DISPLAY      *)

BEGIN
  (* READ INITIAL ACCOUNT DATA *)
  ENTERDATA (ACCOUNT, NUMDEPOSITOR);

  (* PROCESS ALL TRANSACTIONS AND DEFINE     *)
  (* THE SETS ACTIVE, INACTIVE AND OVERDRAWN *)
  PROCESSTRAN (ACCOUNT, NUMDEPOSITOR, ACTIVE,
               INACTIVE, OVERDRAWN);

  (* PRINT NAME, STARTING AND ENDING BALANCE *)
  (* FOR EACH ACCOUNT                        *)
  WRITELN;
  WRITELN ('DEPOSITOR' :10, 'START BALANCE' :19,
           'END BALANCE' :17);
  FOR K := 1 TO NUMDEPOSITOR DO
    WITH ACCOUNT[K] DO
      WRITELN (NAME :10, STARTBAL :18:2, CURRENTBAL :16:2);

  (* PRINT THE SETS ACTIVE, INACTIVE AND OVERDRAWN *)
  DISPLAY (ACCOUNT, ACTIVE, 'ACTIVE', NUMDEPOSITOR);
  DISPLAY (ACCOUNT, INACTIVE, 'INACTIVE', NUMDEPOSITOR);
  DISPLAY (ACCOUNT, OVERDRAWN, 'OVERDRAWN', NUMDEPOSITOR)
END.
```

Fig. 7.15a Main program for savings account problem.

Procedure ENTERDATA (See Fig. 7.15b) reads all initial account data and initializes the current balance for each account to the starting balance. The actual number of depositors (NUMDEPOSITOR) should be read before any account data.

```
PROCEDURE ENTERDATA (VAR ACCOUNT : BANKARRAY;
                     VAR NUMDEPOSITOR : INDEX);
(* ENTER INITIAL ACCOUNT DATA *)

VAR
  J, TNUM : INTEGER;

BEGIN
  (* READ AND VALIDATE NUMDEPOSITOR *)
  WRITE ('NUMBER OF DEPOSITORS = '); READLN (TNUM);
  WHILE (TNUM < 1) OR (TNUM > MAXDEPOSITOR) DO
    BEGIN
      WRITELN (TNUM, ' IS OUT OF RANGE 1..', MAXDEPOSITOR);
      WRITE ('TRY AGAIN: '); READLN  (TNUM)
    END; (* WHILE *)
  NUMDEPOSITOR := TNUM;

  (* ENTER INITIAL ACCOUNT DATA AND  *)
  (* SET CURRENTBAL TO STARTBAL      *)
  WRITELN;
  WRITELN ('ENTER ACCOUNT DATA');
  FOR J := 1 TO NUMDEPOSITOR DO
    WITH ACCOUNT[J] DO
      BEGIN
        WRITE ('NAME: '); READLN (NAME);
        WRITE ('INITIAL BALANCE $'); READLN (STARTBAL);
        CURRENTBAL := STARTBAL
      END (* WITH *)
END; (* ENTERDATA *)
```

Fig. 7.15b　Procedure ENTERDATA.

Program Style

Graceful degradation of a program

Procedure ENTERDATA begins by reading the number of depositors into TNUM and verifying that this value is within the required range, 1..MAXDEPOSITOR. If so, TNUM is assigned to NUMDEPOSITOR; otherwise, an error message is printed. If an out-of-range value were assigned to NUMDEPOSITOR, the program would terminate immediately without providing any printed output. The approach taken here enables the program to continue execution and provides the user with useful diagnostic information.

Procedure PROCESSTRAN reads and processes each transaction. Since each transaction is completely processed before the next transaction is entered, only one record variable (TRAN) is needed to store the depositor name and transaction amount for the current transaction. The actual processing of each transaction is left to procedure UPDATE. The data table for PROCESSTRAN is provided next; the program is given in Fig. 7.15c.

Data Table for PROCESSTRAN

Constant

SENTINEL = 'DONE', sentinel value

Data types

TRANSACTION = RECORD
    TNAME : STRING[10];
    AMOUNT : REAL
END

Input parameters	*Update parameters*	*Output parameters*
NUMDEPOSITOR	ACCOUNT	ACTIVE, INACTIVE, OVERDRAWN

Input variables	*Program variables*	*Output variables*
TRAN: Each transaction (TRANSACTION)		(none)

Procedures referenced
    UPDATE: Updates appropriate record of ACCOUNT by
                TRAN.AMOUNT

Procedure PROCESSTRAN also defines the sets ACTIVE, INACTIVE, and OVERDRAWN. As shown in Fig. 7.15c, the sets ACTIVE and INACTIVE are initialized to the empty set before any transaction is processed. After all transactions are processed, set INACTIVE is defined as the difference of the set [1..NUMDEPOSITOR] and the set of active account indices (ACTIVE).

It is important to realize that the transactions do not follow any particular order and that there may be zero, one, or many transactions during the day for each depositor's account. In order to process the current transaction, each transaction amount (TRAN.AMOUNT) must be added to the current balance for the proper account. In other words, a particular record of the array ACCOUNT must be updated—namely, the record that contains the current balance for the depositor named in the transaction (TRAN.TNAME).

```
PROCEDURE PROCESSTRAN (VAR ACCOUNT : BANKARRAY;
                           NUMDEPOSITOR : INDEX;
                           VAR ACTIVE, INACTIVE, OVERDRAWN : INDICES);
(* PROCESSES ALL TRANSACTIONS AND DEFINES                      *)
(* THE SETS ACTIVE, INACTIVE AND OVERDRAWN                     *)

CONST
  SENTINEL = 'DONE';

TYPE
  TRANSACTION = RECORD
    TNAME : STRING[10];
    AMOUNT : REAL
  END; (* TRANSACTION *)

VAR
  TRAN : TRANSACTION;

(* INSERT PROCEDURE UPDATE HERE *)

BEGIN
  (* INITIALIZE THE SETS ACTIVE AND OVERDRAWN *)
  ACTIVE := [];
  OVERDRAWN := [];

  (* PROCESS ALL TRANSACTIONS *)
  WRITELN ('ENTER DATA FOR EACH TRANSACTION OR DONE');
  WITH TRAN DO
    BEGIN
      WRITE ('DEPOSITOR: '); READLN (TNAME);
      WHILE TNAME <> SENTINEL DO
        BEGIN
          (* READ TRANSACTION AMOUNT *)
          WRITE ('AMOUNT $'); READLN (AMOUNT);
          (* UPDATE ACCOUNT BALANCE *)
          UPDATE (ACCOUNT, TRAN, NUMDEPOSITOR,
                  ACTIVE, OVERDRAWN);
          WRITE ('DEPOSITOR: '); READLN (TNAME)
        END (* WHILE *)
    END; (* WITH *)

  (* DEFINE THE SET INACTIVE *)
  INACTIVE := [1..NUMDEPOSITOR] - ACTIVE
END; (* PROCESSTRAN *)
```

Fig. 7.15c Procedure PROCESSTRAN.

The value of TRAN.TNAME is the key that must be found in the array of ACCOUNT records. The elements of ACCOUNT are examined in sequence until the record whose NAME field matches the key is found. The CURRENTBAL field of this record should then be updated.

For example, consider the array ACCOUNT and the transaction shown below (record TRAN). Since TRAN.TNAME is 'KLEIN', the key is 'KLEIN' and the index of the record in ACCOUNT that matches the key is 3; hence ACCOUNT[3].CURRENTBAL should be updated.

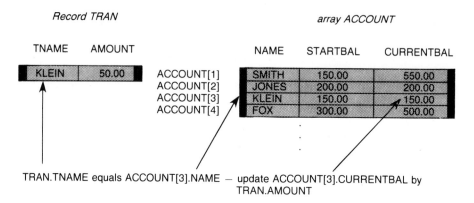

Record TRAN   *array ACCOUNT*

TRAN.TNAME equals ACCOUNT[3].NAME — update ACCOUNT[3].CURRENTBAL by TRAN.AMOUNT

The process of examining each record in ACCOUNT to find a key is called an *array search*. The steps to be performed when, and if, the search is successful are described in the level one algorithm for procedure UPDATE which follows.

Level One Algorithm for UPDATE

1. Search the array ACCOUNT for the key TRAN.TNAME
2. If the key is located, update the corresponding balance and add the account index to ACTIVE; otherwise, print a message indicating that TRAN.TNAME was not located.

A loop must be used to access each record of the array ACCOUNT (Step 1 above). The loop control variable, I, should start at one and increase by one after each loop repetition. Record I of array ACCOUNT will be the one examined. The search should continue as long as there are still records to check and the key has not yet been found.

In order to implement Step 2, a program flag, FOUND, can be used to indicate whether the search was successful. FOUND should be initialized to false and reset to true when the key is located. If FOUND is still false after all records in the array have been examined, then the key is invalid and an error message should be printed.

The program flag can also be used as part of the loop control in Step 1. Since each account name is assumed to be unique, the array search can be terminated as soon as FOUND becomes true. These points are summarized in the data table and algorithm refinements below.

Data Table for UPDATE

Input parameters	Update parameters
Input parameters	*Update parameters*
TRAN, NUMDEPOSI- TOR	ACCOUNT, ACTIVE, OVERDRAWN

Input variables	*Program variables*	*Output variables*
(none)	I: Loop control variable and array subscript (INTEGER) FOUND: Program flag —value of TRUE indicates key has been located, initially FALSE (BOOLEAN)	Prints a message if TRAN.TNAME is not found

Level Two Refinements for UPDATE

Step 1   *Search the array ACCOUNT for the key TRAN.TNAME*

1.1 Initialize FOUND to FALSE and I to 1
1.2 WHILE NOT FOUND AND there are more array elements DO
          IF the current element is TRAN.TNAME THEN
                  FOUND := TRUE
          ELSE
                  Advance to the next element

Step 2   *Update the balance for the depositor whose name is the key*

2.1 IF FOUND THEN
          BEGIN
              2.2 Update the balance for I'th depositor
              2.3 Add element I to the set ACTIVE
              2.4 IF the new balance is negative THEN
                      Add element I to the set OVERDRAWN
          END
          ELSE
          Print a message that TRAN.TNAME was not located

The program is given in Fig. 7.15d.

```
PROCEDURE UPDATE (VAR ACCOUNT : BANKARRAY;
                  TRAN : TRANSACTION;
                  NUMDEPOSITOR : INDEX; .
                  VAR ACTIVE, OVERDRAWN : INDICES);
(* UPDATES THE RECORD IN ARRAY ACCOUNT           *)
(* CORRESPONDING TO TRAN.TNAME                    *)

VAR
  I : INTEGER;
  FOUND : BOOLEAN;

BEGIN
  (* SEARCH THE ARRAY ACCOUNT FOR THE KEY TRAN.TNAME *)
  FOUND := FALSE;
  I := 1;
  WHILE NOT FOUND AND (I <= NUMDEPOSITOR) DO
    IF TRAN.TNAME = ACCOUNT[I].NAME THEN
      FOUND := TRUE
    ELSE
      I := I + 1;

  (* UPDATE THE BALANCE FOR THE DEPOSITOR TRAN.TNAME *)
  IF FOUND THEN
    WITH ACCOUNT[I] DO
      BEGIN
        CURRENTBAL := CURRENTBAL + TRAN.AMOUNT;
        ACTIVE := ACTIVE + [I];
        IF CURRENTBAL < 0.0 THEN
          OVERDRAWN := OVERDRAWN + [I]
      END (* WITH *)
  ELSE
    WRITELN (TRAN.TNAME, ' WAS NOT LOCATED. ',
             'TRANSACTION OF $', TRAN.AMOUNT :10:2,
             'IGNORED.')
END; (* UPDATE *)
```

Fig. 7.15d Procedure UPDATE.

The procedure **DISPLAY** is used to print the depositor names corresponding to each of the sets **ACTIVE**, **INACTIVE**, and **OVERDRAWN**. This procedure is called three times by the main program (See Fig. 7.15a); each time it prints a heading followed by a list of names unless its input set is empty. The procedure is shown in Fig. 7.15e. A sample output table is shown in Fig. 7.15f; the execution of procedure ENTERDATA is not shown.

Since OUTSET is a value parameter in DISPLAY, a local copy of the corresponding actual set is created each time DISPLAY is entered. Each set element is used to select a name from the depositor records (array ACCOUNT) which is then printed.

The array ACCOUNT is declared as a variable parameter (instead of a value parameter) even though it is used only for data input to DISPLAY. The reason is that it would be pointless and costly to create a local copy of this large array each time DISPLAY was called.

Exercise 7.12: Indicate how procedure UPDATE could be modified so that the index of an overdrawn account would be deleted from the set OVERDRAWN as soon as its corresponding balance becomes positive.

```
PROCEDURE DISPLAY (VAR ACCOUNT : BANKARRAY;
                       OUTSET : INDICES;
                       TITLE : TITLESTR;
                       NUMDEPOSITOR : INDEX);
(* PRINTS THE NAMES CORRESPONDING    *)
(* TO A SET OF INDICES               *)

VAR
   P : INTEGER;

BEGIN
   IF OUTSET <> [] THEN
     BEGIN
        WRITELN;
        WRITELN (TITLE, ' DEPOSITORS FOR TODAY');
        FOR P := 1 TO NUMDEPOSITOR DO
          IF P IN OUTSET THEN
             WRITE (ACCOUNT[P].NAME :12);
        WRITELN
     END (* IF *)
END; (* DISPLAY *)
```

Fig. 7.15e   Procedure DISPLAY.

```
DEPOSITOR: SMITH
TRANSACTION: -100.00

DEPOSITOR: JONES
TRANSACTION: -10.00

DEPOSITOR: ADAMS
TRANSACTION: 100.00

DEPOSITOR: JONES
TRANSACTION: -100.00

DEPOSITOR: WHITEMAN
TRANSACTION: 100.00
WHITEMAN WAS NOT LOCATED. TRANSACTION OF 100.00 IGNORED

DEPOSITOR: ADAMS
TRANSACTION: -150.00
```

(continued)

DEPOSITOR	START BALANCE	END BALANCE
JONES	100.00	-10.00
SMITH	200.00	100.00
ADAMS	300.00	250.00
BROWN	400.00	400.00
PETERS	500.00	500.00

```
ACTIVE    DEPOSITORS FOR TODAY
   JONES          SMITH          ADAMS

INACTIVE    DEPOSITORS FOR TODAY
   BROWN          PETERS

OVERDRAWN DEPOSITORS FOR TODAY
   JONES
```

Fig. 7.15f Sample run of savings account program.

7.8 COMMON PROGRAMMING ERRORS

7.8.1 Record Errors

When using records, the most common error is incorrectly specifying the record field to be manipulated. The full field selector (record variable and field name) must be used unless (1) the record reference is nested inside a **WITH** statement, or (2) the entire record is to be manipulated. So far we have discussed the latter option only for record copy and comparison statements and for records passed as parameters; When reading, or writing records at the terminal, each field must be processed separately.

If a record variable name is listed in a **WITH** statement header, then only the field name is required to reference fields of that record inside the **WITH** statement. The full field selector must still be used to reference fields of any other record variable.

If a variable represents an array of records, then the array subscript must be included in the field selector. If a **WITH** statement is being used, then the array name and subscript must be listed in the **WITH** statement header. If the subscript is updated in a loop, then the **WITH** statement must be nested inside the loop; otherwise, the array element (record) being manipulated will not change as the subscript value changes.

7.8.2 Set Errors

When using sets, remember that a set variable (like any variable) must always be initialized before it may be manipulated. It is easy to forget this when a set is initially empty ([]) or contains all values in its base type (the universal set).

The operands of the set manipulation operators (*, + and −) must be sets. Remember to enclose a single element in brackets (a unit set) when either adding it to an existing set or deleting it.

As with records, sets cannot be read or written at the terminal as a unit; each individual element of a set must be displayed separately. The set membership operator (IN) can be used to determine which base values are set elements and should be printed.

7.9 SUMMARY

In this chapter we studied two new data types, records and sets. Records were shown to be useful for organizing a collection of related data items of different types. Sets were used as an easy means of remembering certain data values in a collection. Unlike an array, there is no order (or index) associated with the elements of a set.

In processing records, we learned how to reference each individual component through the use of a field selector consisting of the record variable name and field name separated by a period. The WITH statement was introduced as a means of abbreviating the field selector. If a record variable name is specified in a WITH statement header, then the field name may be used by itself inside the WITH statement.

We also studied arrays of records as well as records that contained array fields. In both cases, we found that the subscript should be included as part of the field selector.

Each individual component of a record must be manipulated separately in a READLN or WRITELN statement or an arithmetic expression. However, it is permissable to assign one record variable to another record variable of the same type (record copy statement), to pass a record as a parameter to a procedure (or function), or to compare two records.

We saw that the set data type could be used for storage of a collection of values of the same type. The base type, specified in the declaration, indicates which values can belong to a set. Each set variable can contain zero (the empty set) or more elements from its base type. A set containing all the values in its base type is called the universal set.

PASCAL provides operators to perform the common set operations of intersection (*), union (+) and set difference (−), as well as relational operators to test for set equality and subset and superset relations. In addition, the set membership operator, IN, can be used to determine whether a given value is an element of a set. This operator is often used in printing the elements of a set. Each value in the base type must be tested to see if it is a member of the set. If a value is a member, then it is printed; otherwise, it is not.

The set membership operator makes it easy to "search" a set for a particular element. We also learned how to search an array to see if a desired value or key was present. An array search involves examining each element in sequence until either the key is found or all elements are examined without success. If the latter situation occurs, then the desired key is not present in the array.

We shall learn more about records in Chapter 9 where we will study hierarchical records (records of records) and files. In that chapter, we shall learn how to represent more highly structured data. We shall also see how to read (write) an entire record from (to) a file of records that is saved on disk.

PROGRAMMING PROBLEMS

7.3   An examination has been administered to a class of students, and the scores for
each student have been provided as data along with the student's name. Write a
program to do the following:
a) Determine and print the class average for the exam.
b) Find the median grade.
c) Scale each student's grade so that the class average will become 75. For example, if the actual class average is 63, add 12 to each student's grade.
d) Assign a letter grade to each student based on the scaled grade:
90–100 (A), 80–89 (B), 70–79 (C), 60–69 (D), 0–59 (F).
e) Print out each student's name in alphabetical order followed by the scaled grade
and the letter grade.
f) Count the number of grades in each letter grade category.

7.4   An array may be used to contain descriptions of people including name, height,
weight, sex, color of hair, color of eyes, religion. Write procedures that can be used
to read and store data into this array or print its contents.

7.5   Write a procedure that searches the array in Fig. 7.4 to find the "closest" description to a target description. The closest description is the one with the most fields
that are the same as the target (ignore the name field). Allow a reasonable range of
values for a height or weight match. Provide a second procedure that causes the descriptions of all people with a specified sex and religion to be printed.

7.6   A number expressed in scientific notation is represented by its mantissa (a fraction)
and its exponent. Write a procedure that reads two character strings representing
numbers in scientific notation and stores each number in a record with two fields.
Write a procedure that prints the contents of each record as a real value. Also write
a procedure that computes the sum, product, difference and quotient of the two
numbers. *Hint:* The string $-0.1234E20$ represents a number in scientific notation.
The fraction -0.1234 is the mantissa and the number 20 is the exponent.

7.7   Write a function that determines whether a character is a letter, digit, blank or special character.

7.8   Write a procedure that prints a set of letters in the form [A,B,D,G]. The square
brackets and commas should occur where shown.

7.9   Write a program that generates the Morse code equivalent of a sentence. The
Morse code for each letter should be stored in an array.

7.10 Read in a large body of text and develop a frequency count of the number of occurrences of each letter in the text. Use a set to represent the letters of the alphabet
(see Problem 6.1).

7.11 Write a function that converts a letter representing a chess piece to a scalar value
and print name. The letters are members of the set ['K', 'Q', 'R', 'B', 'N', 'P'] and
the corresponding scalar values would be (KING, QUEEN, ROOK, BISHOP,
KNIGHT, PAWN). Any character not in the set should be flagged as invalid.

7.12 A playing card can be represented by its rank 1 through 10, jack, queen, king or
ace and its suit (clubs, diamonds, hearts and spades). The data

10C   3D   JS   AC

could be used to represent the 10 of clubs, three of diamonds, jack of spades, and ace of clubs. Write a program that reads such data and prints a description of the cards. It should also flag any invalid descriptions and indicate whether or not a card has already occurred. *Hint:* See Example 7.10.

7.13   Assuming the program in Fig. 7.11 has read a bridge hand, evaluate the hand for bidding by counting the number of points. Use the following point count method:

rank	points
2..10	0
jack	1
queen	2
king	3
ace	4

Also, award one point for each suit that has only one card (not jack, queen, king or ace), and two points for each suit that is void (no cards of that suit).

REPEAT and GOTO Statements, Nested Structures, and Recursion

8

8.1 INTRODUCTION

In this chapter we shall complete the study of PASCAL control structures. A new loop, the REPEAT-UNTIL, will be introduced. We will also examine some examples of nested loops and discuss the use of the GOTO statement for exiting from a nest of loops and the EXIT statement for exiting from a procedure.

In Chapter 5, we introduced the procedure and showed how this feature could be used to help us construct nicely modularized programs that reflected the top-down, level-by-level refinement process that was used in the design of algorithms. We also indicated that procedures are helpful in writing programs in which it is necessary to perform certain operations (sequences of steps) more than once.

We will study a large program system containing several procedures and functions and introduce the program system chart as a means of documenting such a system. Finally, we shall see what happens when a procedure calls itself (recursion) and study an example of a recursive function and a recursive procedure.

8.2 REPEAT-UNTIL LOOP

The *REPEAT-UNTIL loop* is a conditional loop as is the WHILE loop. However, unlike the WHILE loop, the REPEAT-UNTIL loop is executed as long as its condition is FALSE, or until its condition evaluates to TRUE. (The WHILE loop is executed as long as its condition is TRUE.)

Example 8.1: In Fig. 8.1, a program segment that prints the powers of two between one and 1000 is implemented using both a WHILE statement (left) and REPEAT-UNTIL (right).

```
POWER := 1;                      POWER := 1;
WHILE POWER < 1000 DO            REPEAT
  BEGIN                            WRITE (POWER);
    WRITE (POWER);                 POWER := POWER * 2
    POWER := POWER * 2           UNTIL POWER >= 1000
END (*WHILE*)
```

Fig. 8.1 WHILE and REPEAT-UNTIL loops for printing powers of two.

Note that the keywords BEGIN and END are not needed in Fig. 8.1 to bracket the loop body in the REPEAT-UNTIL loop. (Why not?) The test used in the REPEAT statement (POWER >= 1000) is the complement of the test used in the WHILE statement (POWER < 1000). Recall that the complement of a condition is true when the original condition is false and vice versa. The REPEAT-UNTIL loop (REPEAT statement) is described in the next display.

REPEAT-UNTIL Loop (REPEAT Statement)

```
REPEAT
    loop-body
UNTIL condition
```

Interpretation: After each execution of the *loop body*, the *condition* is evaluated. If the *condition* is false, the *loop body* is executed again. If the *condition* evaluates to true, loop exit occurs and the next program statement is executed. *Note:* The *loop body* is always executed at least once.

One other important difference between the WHILE loop and the RE-PEAT-UNTIL loop involves the relative ordering of the conditional test and loop body execution. In the WHILE loop, the loop repetition test is performed before each execution of the loop body; the loop body is not executed at all if the initial test fails. In the REPEAT-UNTIL loop, the loop termination test is performed after each execution of the loop body; hence, the loop body is always executed at least once.

Example 8.2: The REPEAT statement below skips over any leading blanks that may precede a character data item. Compare this to the WHILE loop used for that purpose in Fig. 5.3.

```
REPEAT
    READ (NEXTCHAR)
UNTIL NEXTCHAR <> ' ';
```

Fig. 8.2 Skipping over leading blanks.

Example 8.3: Function FINDPERIM (See Fig. 7.7b.) is implemented in Fig. 8.2 using a REPEAT statement. The loop is repeated until the first end point (POINT1) of the line segment being processed is the same as the starting point (START). The last line segment is also processed inside the loop rather than by itself after loop exit as was done in Fig. 7.7b.

```
FUNCTION FINDPERIM (START : POINT) : REAL;
(* FINDS THE PERIMETER OF A POLYGON *)

VAR
   POINT1, POINT2 : POINT;
   PERIM : REAL;

(* INSERT FUNCTION COMPLENGTH HERE *)

BEGIN
   (* INITIALIZE PERIM AND POINT1 *)
   PERIM := 0;
   POINT1 := START;
```

(continued)

```
  (* ADD LENGTH OF EACH SIDE TO PERIM *)
  WRITELN ('ENTER STARTING POINT TO TERMINATE OR');
  REPEAT
    (* READ NEXT END POINT *)
    WRITE ('NEXT POINT: ');
    READLN (POINT2.XCOORD, POINT2.YCOORD);
    (* ADD LENGTH OF CURRENT SIDE TO PERIM *)
    PERIM := PERIM + COMPLENGTH(POINT1, POINT2);
    (* ADVANCE POINT1 UNTIL IT IS BACK TO START *)
    POINT1 := POINT2
  UNTIL POINT1 = START;

  (* DEFINE RESULT *)
  FINDPERIM := PERIM
END; (* FINDPERIM *)
```

Fig. 8.3 Function FINDPERIM with a REPEAT statement.

Example 8.4: Procedure UPDATE in Fig. 7.15d searches an array of records (array ACCOUNT) for a key (TRAN.TNAME). The search continues as long as there are elements remaining to be examined (I $<=$ NUMDEPOSITOR) and the key is not yet located (FOUND is FALSE). Another way of stating this is that the search should terminate either when there are no more array elements left (I $>$ NUMDEPOSITOR) or when the key is located (FOUND is TRUE). In Fig. 8.4, the search loop of UPDATE is implemented as a REPEAT-UNTIL loop with the above termination test.

In using REPEAT-UNTIL loops, it is important to remember that loop exit does not occur at the exact instant the loop termination test becomes TRUE. For example, even if FOUND is set to TRUE by the IF statement of Fig. 8.4, any remaining steps that might be specified in the loop body would still be carried out. Loop exit will not occur until after the loop termination condition is evaluated at the completion of the current execution of the loop body.

```
PROCEDURE UPDATE (VAR ACCOUNT : BANKARRAY;
                  TRAN : TRANSACTION;
                  NUMDEPOSITOR : INDEX;
                  VAR ACTIVE, OVERDRAWN : INDICES);
(* UPDATES THE RECORD IN ACCOUNT CORRESPONDING TO TRAN.TNAME *)
VAR
  I : INTEGER;
  FOUND : BOOLEAN;

BEGIN
  (* SEARCH THE ARRAY ACCOUNT FOR THE KEY TRAN.TNAME *)
  FOUND := FALSE;
  I := 1;
  REPEAT
    IF ACCOUNT[I].NAME = TRAN.TNAME THEN
      FOUND := TRUE
    ELSE
      I := I + 1
  UNTIL (I > NUMDEPOSITOR) OR FOUND;
```

(continued)

```
(* UPDATE THE BALANCE OF THE DEPOSITOR TRAN.NAME *)
IF FOUND THEN
  WITH ACCOUNT[I] DO
    BEGIN
      CURRENTBAL := CURRENTBAL + TRAN.AMOUNT;
      ACTIVE := ACTIVE + [I];
      IF CURRENTBAL < O THEN
        OVERDRAWN := OVERDRAWN + [I]
    END (* WITH *)
  ELSE
    WRITELN (TRAN.TNAME, 'WAS NOT LOCATED. ',
              'TRANSACTION OF ', TRAN.AMOUNT :10:2, 'IGNORED')
END; (* UPDATE *)
```

Fig. 8.4 Procedure UPDATE.

8.3 NESTED LOOPS

8.3.1 Introduction

Some program segments contain two or more nested loops. Nested loops are often quite difficult to write, read and debug. For this reason, we will examine some programs involving nested loops.

Example 8.5: Fig. 8.5 shows a sample run of a program with two nested FOR loops. This means that during each repetition of the outer loop, the inner loop must also be entered and executed until loop exit occurs. The number of times each loop is repeated depends upon its respective loop control parameters.

Each time the inner loop is reentered, its loop control variable (J) is reinitialized to one. The number of repetitions of the inner loop is determined by the value of the outer loop control variable. Each line labelled OUTER is printed by the outer loop in the nest; each line labelled INNER is printed by the inner loop.

```
PROGRAM NESTLOOP;

VAR
  I, J : INTEGER;

BEGIN
  WRITELN ('I' :15, 'J' :5);
  FOR I := 1 TO 3 DO
    BEGIN
      WRITELN ('OUTER' :5, I :10);
      FOR J := 1 TO I DO
        WRITELN ('INNER' :5, I :10, J :5)
    END (* FOR I *)
END.
```

```
               I    J
OUTER          1
INNER          1    1
```

(continued)

```
OUTER       2
INNER       2    1
INNER       2    2
OUTER       3
INNER       3    1
INNER       3    2
INNER       3    3
```

Fig. 8.5   Nested loops.

As illustrated, it is permissible to use the loop control variable of the outer loop as a parameter in the initialization, update or test of an inner loop control variable. However, the same variable should never be used as the loop control variable of both an outer FOR loop and an inner FOR loop in the same nest.

8.3.2   Printing a Bar Graph

Example 8.6:   The procedure in Fig. 8.6a plots the contents of the array represented by FREQUENCY in the form of a bar graph. The array corresponding to FREQUENCY must contain integer values. A sample array is shown below, followed by the data table for the program. The bar graph is drawn in Fig. 8.6b.

FREQUENCY[1]	FREQUENCY [2]	FREQUENCY [3]	FREQUENCY [4]	FREQUENCY [5]
8	32	24	16	3

Data Table for Example 8.6

Input parameters

FREQUENCY: Array to be plotted (SMALL-ARRAY)

N: Number of elements to be plotted (INTEGER)

Output parameters

(none)

Input variables

(none)

Program variables

ROW: Outer loop control variable, serves as index to FREQUENCY (INTEGER)

J: Inner loop control variable for printing each bar (INTEGER)

Output variables

A bar graph is drawn.

The length of each line in the bar graph indicates the number of occurrences, or frequency, of a particular class. For example, the second line shows that class two was the most popular with 32 occurrences.

```
PROCEDURE BARCHART (FREQUENCY : SMALLARRAY;
                          N : INTEGER);
(* DISPLAY ARRAY FREQUENCY AS A BAR GRAPH *)

VAR
  ROW, J : INTEGER;

BEGIN
  WRITELN ('CLASS', 'FREQUENCY PLOT' :24);
  FOR ROW := 1 TO N DO
    BEGIN
      (* START NEW BAR *)
      WRITE (ROW :3, 'I' :7);
      (* PRINT THE STARS FOR THE CURRENT ARRAY ELEMENT *)
      FOR J := 1 TO FREQUENCY[ROW] DO
        WRITE ('*');
      WRITELN
    END; (* FOR ROW *)
  WRITELN('           I----I----I----I----I----I----I----I')
END; (* BARCHART *)
```

Fig. 8.6a Procedure to print a bar graph.

```
CLASS                         FREQUENCY PLOT
  1         I********
  2         I*********************************
  3         I**********************
  4         I***************
  5         I***
            I----I----I----I----I----I----I----I
```

Fig. 8.6b Sample run of Fig. 8.6a.

The procedure in Fig. 8.6a contains a pair of nested FOR loops. The outer loop control variable, ROW, selects the element of FREQUENCY to be plotted. J is the loop control variable for the inner loop. Each execution of the inner loop causes another asterisk to be printed. The number of asterisks printed is determined by the value of FREQUENCY[ROW].

Exercise 8.1: Write out each line of the printout for the following program segment.

```
                    .
                    .
                    .
        FOR  I := 1 TO 2 DO
          BEGIN
            WRITELN ('OUTER', I);
            FOR  J := 1 TO 4 DO
              WRITELN ('INNER I', I, J);
            FOR  K := 4 DOWNTO 1 DO
              WRITELN ('INNER K', I, K)
          END (* FOR I *)
                    .
                    .
                    .
```

8.4 SORTING AN ARRAY

The problem that follows is an example of the use of nested loops in sorting, or rearranging in numerical order, the data stored in an array. Sorting programs are used in a variety of applications and the program developed here could easily be modified to sort alphanumeric data, such as last names, stored in an array of character strings. In this example, we will sort numeric data in ascending numerical order (smallest value first); however, it would be just as easy to sort the data in descending order (largest value first).

Problem 8.1:   Write a procedure to sort, in ascending order, an array of integer values.

Discussion: There are many different algorithms for sorting. We will use one of the simplest of these algorithms, the Bubble Sort. The Bubble Sort is so named because it has the property of "bubbling" the smallest items to the top of a list. The algorithm proceeds by comparing the values of adjacent elements in the array. If the value of the first of these elements is larger than the value of the second, these values are exchanged, and then the values of the next adjacent pair of elements are compared. This process starts with the pair of elements with indices 1 and 2 and continues through the pair of elements with indices $n-1$ and n, in an array containing n data items. Then this sequence of comparisons, called a *pass*, is repeated, starting with the first pair of elements again, until the entire array of elements is compared without an exchange being made. At this point, the array must be sorted.

As an example, we will trace through the sort of the integer array M as shown in Fig. 8.7. In this sequence of diagrams, diagram one shows the initial arrangement of the data in the array; the first pair of values are out of order and they are exchanged. The result is shown in diagram two. The new value of M [2], 60, is next compared to 83, the value of M [3]. In this case, no exchange is required and M [3] is next compared to M [4]. Since M [3] is greater than M [4], these values are exchanged as indicated in diagrams two and three. The last comparison in pass 1 is between M [4] (now 83) and M [5] (75); their values are exchanged as shown in diagrams three and four.

The sequence in Fig. 8.7 shows all exchanges that would be made during each pass through the adjacent pairs of array elements. After pass one, we see that the array is finally ordered except for the value 25 (see diagram four). Subsequent passes through the array will "bubble" this value up one array element at a time until the sort is complete. In each pass through M, the elements are compared in the following order: M [1] and M [2]; M [2] and M [3]; M [3] and M [4]; M [4] and M [5]. Note that even though the array is sorted at the end of pass 3, it will take one more pass through the array without any exchanges to complete the algorithm.

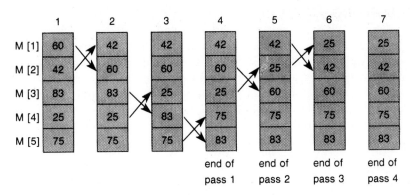

Fig. 8.7 Bubble Sort of array M.

Now that we have a general idea of how the algorithm works, we can write the data table and the level one algorithm for the Bubble Sort procedure.

Data Table for Problem 8.1

Input parameters	*Update parameters*	*Output parameters*
NUMITEMS: The number of array elements (INTEGER)	M: The array to be sorted (SMALLARRAY)	(none)

Level One Algorithm

1. REPEAT
    Rearrange all out-of-order pairs in array **M**
    UNTIL array **M** is sorted

The loop above should be repeated until array M is sorted, i.e. a pass is completed without any exchanges required. We shall use a Boolean variable, SORTED, to monitor whether or not any exchanges were made. The additional data table entry and refinement of Step one follow.

Additional Data Table Entries for Problem 8.1

Program variables

SORTED: Program flag— a value of TRUE at the completion of a pass indicates no exchanges were made and the array is sorted. A value of FALSE indicates at least one exchange was made (BOOLEAN).

Level Two Refinements

Step 1

    1.1 REPEAT
          1.2 Initialize SORTED to TRUE
          1.3 Exchange all out-of-order pairs in array M and set SORTED to
             FALSE if an exchange is made
    UNTIL SORTED

In order to examine all pairs of array elements, Step 1.3 should be implemented as a FOR loop. The loop control variable, I, will select the first array element of each pair being compared (I ranges from 1 to NUMITEMS−1); I + 1 is the subscript of the second element of each pair. As shown below, we will need an additional variable, TEMP, for temporary storage of one of the array element values being exchanged. The refinement of Step 1.3 follows; the SORT procedure is written in Fig. 8.8, assuming array M contains integer values.

Additional Data Table Entries for Procedure SORT

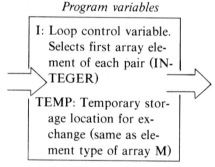

Program variables

I: Loop control variable. Selects first array element of each pair (INTEGER)

TEMP: Temporary storage location for exchange (same as element type of array M)

Level Three Refinements

Step 1.3

    1.3.1 FOR I := 1 to NUMITEMS−1 DO
          IF M [I] and M [I + 1] are out of order THEN
             BEGIN
                1.3.2 Exchange M [I] and M [I + 1]
                1.3.3 Set SORTED to FALSE
             END

Arranging a list of names in alphabetical order is a common problem in data processing. The procedure in Fig. 8.8 could be used to do this if array M contained character strings instead of numbers. The Boolean expression M [I]> M [I + 1] would compare adjacent character strings for alphabetical order. The type of parameter M would, of course, be different; the variable TEMP would be a string.

Program Style

Implementing algorithms with nested loops

Whenever nested loops are used, the inner loop is executed from start to finish for each repetition or *iteration* of an outer loop. In the Bubble Sort procedure, the inner loop will be executed for all values of I between 1 and NUMITEMS−1 for each execution of the outer loop.

This kind of repetition can be quite difficult to understand, much less to program. It is, therefore, often helpful to outline the logic of each loop separately, putting the loops together only at the final stage of implementation. This can be done simply by summarizing the activity of any loop nested within another (e.g., Step 1.3 in the level two refinement above), and then providing the details of execution of the inner loop in a separate place (the level three refinement of Step 1.3). The inner loop could also be implemented as a separate procedure if desired.

```
PROCEDURE SORT (VAR M : SMALLARRAY;
                   NUMITEMS : INTEGER);
(* BUBBLE SORT OF ARRAY M WITH NUMITEMS ELEMENTS *)

VAR
   SORTED : BOOLEAN;
   I, TEMP : INTEGER;

BEGIN
   (* PASS THROUGH ARRAY M UNTIL M IS SORTED *)
   REPEAT
     (* ASSUME M IS SORTED *)
     SORTED := TRUE;
     (* START NEW PASS *)
     FOR I := 1 TO NUMITEMS − 1 DO
       (* COMPARE EACH ADJACENT PAIR OF ELEMENTS *)
       IF M[I] > M[I+1] THEN
         BEGIN
           (* OUT OF ORDER − EXCHANGE AND RESET SORTED *)
           TEMP := M[I];
           M[I] := M[I+1];
           M[I+1] := TEMP;
           SORTED := FALSE
         END (* IF *)
     (* TEST SORTED AT COMPLETION OF PASS *)
   UNTIL SORTED
END; (* SORT *)
```

Fig. 8.8 Bubble Sort procedure.

Exercise 8.2: In Fig. 8.7, note that after pass k the kth largest value is in element M[N−k + 1]. Hence, it is only necessary to examine elements with indices less than N−k + 1 during the next pass. Modify the algorithm to take advantage of this.

Exercise 8.3: Modify the Bubble Sort procedure to sort the array M in descending order (largest number first). Trace the execution of your program on the initial array shown in Fig. 8.7.

Exercise 8.4: A more efficient version of the Bubble Sort algorithm advances the smaller of each pair of elements being exchanged as far up the array as it can go. For this version, the second exchange shown in Fig. 8.7 would not be completed until the value 25 was advanced to the first element of the array. At this point the array would be sorted. Write this version of the bubble sort. *Hint:* Replace the IF statement with a WHILE loop.

Exercise 8.5: A different technique for sorting an array with N elements consists of searching the entire array to find the smallest element and then exchanging it with the first element. Next, elements 2 through N are searched and the next smallest element is exchanged with the second array element. This process continues until only elements $N-1$ and N are left to examine. Implement the algorithm. *Hint:* Use a pair of nested FOR loops.

8.5   THE GOTO AND EXIT STATEMENTS

In the Bubble Sort procedure, we used the program flag SORTED to control repetition of the outer loop. If SORTED is set to FALSE in the inner loop, then the outer loop is repeated after completion of the inner loop; otherwise, the outer loop is exited after completion of the inner loop. In some problems, we desire to initiate the next repetition of the outer loop (without completing the inner loop) as soon as a particular event occurs in the inner loop. In other cases, we desire to exit immediately from an outer loop as soon as a particular event is detected in an inner loop. Both of these actions (initiate next loop repetition and loop exit) can be implemented using the GOTO statement.

The GOTO statement has the form

GOTO 27

The statement above causes an immediate transfer to the statement associated with label 27. Any integer from 1 to 9999 may be used as a label. A colon is used as a separator between a label and its associated statement as in

27 : *statement*

The declaration section for a procedure must declare all labels used in the procedure body. The label declaration statement precedes all other declarations in the procedure and has the form

LABEL
$label_1$, $label_2$,..., $label_n$;

Each label declared in a procedure must be associated with a single statement in the procedure body.

Example 8.7: In the procedure of Fig. 8.9, the next repetition of the outer loop is initiated by a transfer to label 20 if $condition_1$ is true; otherwise, if $condition_2$ is true, the outer loop is exited (transfer to label 30).

Note that label 20 followed by a colon is considered a statement even if no action is specified. This is the last statement in the outer loop. It would be incorrect to transfer to the FOR statement header in order to initiate the next loop repetition.

In order to use the GOTO statement, a compiler option switch must be set. The compiler directive (*$G + *) accomplishes this.

In general, it is much better to use a program flag or a conditional test in a WHILE or REPEAT statement to exit from a loop; however, the GOTO statement provides a convenient mechanism for terminating the repetition of a nest of loops from within the nest. In UCSD (but not standard) PASCAL, there is also an EXIT statement that can be used to exit from a block (program, procedure, or function). The use of the EXIT statement is illustrated next.

```
PROCEDURE LOOPS;
(*$G+*)

LABEL
   20, 30;

VAR
   I, J : INTEGER;
   . . . .

BEGIN
   . . . .

   FOR I := 1 TO 10 DO
      BEGIN
         FOR J := 1 TO 3 * I DO
            BEGIN
               . . . .

               IF condition1 THEN
                  (* NEXT OUTER *)
                  GOTO 20
               ELSE IF condition2 THEN
                  (* EXIT OUTER *)
                  GOTO 30;
               . . . .

            END; (* FOR J *)
         20 :
      END; (* FOR I *)
   30 : WRITELN ('LOOP REPETITION COMPLETE');
   . . . .

END; (* LOOPS *)
```

Fig. 8.9 Exiting a loop and starting the next iteration using a GOTO.

Example 8.8: Two actions are taken by procedure INNER in Fig. 8.10 if an error occurs. In the first situation (error$_1$ is true), the statement

EXIT(INNER)

is executed and procedure **INNER** is exited; however, execution of the main program continues with the next statement after the call to **INNER**. In the second situation (error$_2$ is true), the statement

EXIT(EXITTEST)

is executed causing program execution to be terminated. This latter action should be taken when an error is so severe that it makes no sense to continue with the rest of the program.

```
PROGRAM EXITTEST;
. . . .

PROCEDURE INNER;
. . . .

BEGIN (* INNER *)
   . . . .

   IF error1 THEN
      BEGIN
         WRITELN ('EXIT FROM INNER -- ERROR 1');
         EXIT (INNER)
      END
   ELSE IF error2 THEN
      BEGIN
         WRITELN ('TERMINATE EXITTEST -- ERROR 2');
         EXIT (EXITTEST)
      END; (* IF *)
   . . . .

END; (* INNER *)

BEGIN (* EXITTEST *)
   . . . .

   INNER;
   . . . .

END.
```

Fig. 8.10 Terminating a procedure or program using EXIT.

Program Style

GOTO and EXIT considered harmful

Overuse of the GOTO and EXIT statements is generally considered a poor programming practice as it leads to programs that are somewhat difficult to read and follow. Also, transferring from one section of code to another can result in important initialization statements being skipped.

    For similar reasons, it is generally unwise to use the EXIT statement. All blocks written so far contained a single exit point (the end of the block). The flow of control through blocks with multiple exits can be difficult to follow. Furthermore, if a function is exited prematurely, it is possible that its value will still be undefined. A legitimate use for the EXIT statement would be to abort a deeply nested chain of procedure calls upon encountering an error condition.

GOTO Statement

GOTO *label*

Interpretation: An immediate transfer to the statement associated with *label* occurs. The *label* must be associated with a single statement in the same block as the GOTO statement. Each label used in a block must be declared locally.

Label Declaration

LABEL
list of labels;

Interpretation: Each label in the *list of labels* must be an integer from 1 to 9999 and associated with exactly one statement in the body of the block that declares it. Commas are used to separate labels in the list. The label declaration precedes all other declarations.
Note: A label can only be declared once in a block.

EXIT Statement

EXIT *(block name)*

Interpretation: When the EXIT statement is executed, the block indicated by *block name* is exited immediately. *Block name* may be the name of the block containing the EXIT statement or of any other block in the chain of procedure and function calls.

Exercise 8.6: Rewrite Procedure UPDATE (Fig. 8.4) using a GOTO statement to exit from the search loop when the key is located. If the search loop is exited normally (key not found) the procedure should be exited (via an EXIT statement).

8.6   SOLVING A LARGER PROBLEM

8.6.1   Program System Charts

    As algorithms and programs become larger and more complicated and the number of modules used in a program begins to grow, it becomes increasingly important to maintain complete and concise documentation to illustrate the functional relationships and information flow among the modules. In this section we provide the solution to a simple statistics problem. In the process, we illustrate some conventions of programming style and documentation that we believe are helpful in describing the flow of information into and out of each module of a program.

Problem 8.2: Given a collection of N real numbers stored in an array, compute the range, mean (average), and median for this collection.

The initial data table and level one algorithm are shown below.

Data Table for Problem 8.2

Constants

MAXSIZE = 100, maximum number of array elements

Data types

REALARRAY = ARRAY [1..MAXSIZE] OF REAL

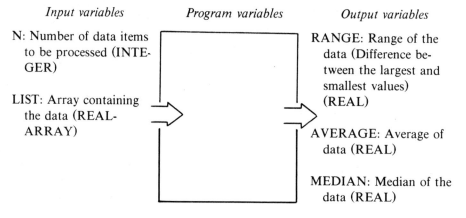

Input variables	*Program variables*	*Output variables*
N: Number of data items to be processed (INTE-GER)		RANGE: Range of the data (Difference between the largest and smallest values) (REAL)
LIST: Array containing the data (REAL-ARRAY)		AVERAGE: Average of data (REAL)
		MEDIAN: Median of the data (REAL)

Level One Algorithm for Problem 8.2

1. Enter N and the data for array LIST, verifying that N is between 1 and MAXSIZE.
2. Compute and print the range of values in LIST.
3. Compute and print the average.
4. Compute and print the median.

Each step in the algorithm represents a major task in the problem solution. Additional lower level subproblems may be identified within each of steps 2, 3 and 4. Each of these subtasks represents a refinement of a task shown at a higher level. We can represent the functional relationship among the main problem and all of the subproblems using a *program system chart* (Fig. 8.11).

The program system chart identifies the major subproblems of the original problem and illustrates the relationship among them. The solutions to the subproblems shown at one level in the chart can be specified in terms of the connected subproblems at the next lower level. For example, the program system chart indicates that the solution of the subproblem "compute median" may be specified in terms of the solution to the subproblems "sort data" and "compute middle value of sorted data." Similarly, in order to find the average, we must first solve the subproblem "compute sum."

Once the data table, level one algorithm and program system chart have been completed, we can begin to add data flow information to the program system chart and to work on the lower level refinements shown in the chart. In considering the refinements, it is necessary to decide which subtasks should be implemented as procedures or functions and which should be implemented as part of the solution of the task above it in the program system chart. In general, a subtask should be implemented using a function or procedure unless it occurs only once in the program system chart and is rather trivial. The subtasks "compute range" and "compute middle value" fall in this latter category.

The decision as to whether to write a procedure or a function depends upon the number of values to be returned. Functions are most convenient when a single value is to be computed. Such is the case in the tasks for computing the largest value, the smallest value, the average, and the median. The "enter N and data" task defines a simple variable N and an array of values; hence, it is written as a procedure (ENTERDATA). Similarly, the sort task rearranges an entire array of information (it does not compute a single value) and is, therefore, written as a procedure (SORT).

Fig. 8.12 shows a program system chart (updated from Fig. 8.11) that reflects the decisions just discussed. In addition, we have added a description of the information flow between the various program modules. For example, the array LIST and its size N are provided as input to function FINDMED. FINDMED passes LIST and N to SORT; the sorted array, LIST, is returned to FINDMED by sort.

At this point, we should add to the data table for the main program descriptions of the functions and procedures that are called.

Procedures referenced

ENTERDATA: Enters N and the data for array LIST, verifying that N is between one and MAXSIZE.

Functions referenced

LARGEST: Computes the largest of a collection of data items in an array.

(continued on page 308)

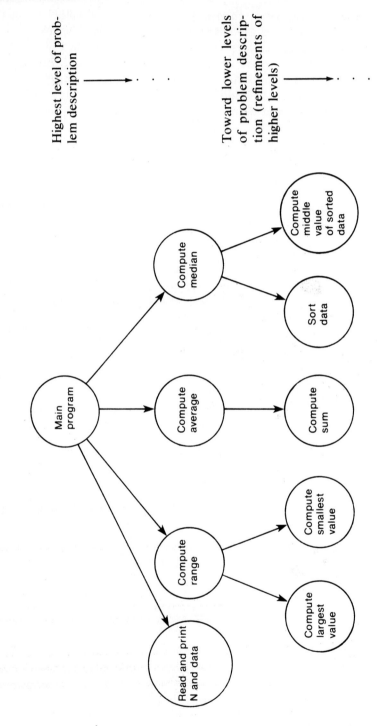

Highest level of problem description

Toward lower levels of problem description (refinements of higher levels)

Fig. 8.11 Program system chart for statistics problem (8.2).

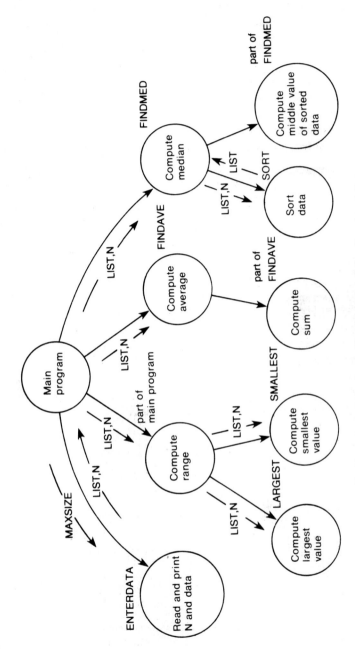

Fig. 8.12 Program system chart with data flow and function description for statistics problem (8.2).

SMALLEST: Computes the smallest of a collection of data items in an array.

FINDAVE: Computes the average of a collection of data items in an array.

FINDMED: Computes the median of a collection of data items in an array.

At this point, we are ready to write the main program (Fig. 8.13). We will treat SMALLEST, LARGEST, FINDMED and FINDAVE as functions with two parameters.

The main program represents the step-by-step implementation of the level one algorithm for the statistics problem. It is easy to follow as each major step stands out and is not obscured by the details required for implementation. Each

```
PROGRAM STATISTICS;
(* SIMPLE STATISTICS PROGRAM *)

CONST
  MAXSIZE = 100;

TYPE
  REALARRAY = ARRAY[1..MAXSIZE] OF REAL;

VAR
  LIST : REALARRAY;
  N : INTEGER;
  RANGE, AVERAGE, MEDIAN : REAL;

(* INSERT PROCEDURE ENTERDATA HERE *)
(* INSERT FUNCTIONS SMALLEST, LARGEST, FINDAVE, FINDMED HERE *)
(*$I UCSD3:ENTERDATA *)         (*$I UCSD3:SMALLEST *)
(*$I UCSD3:LARGEST *)          (*$I UCSD3:FINDAVE *)
(*$I UCSD3:FINDMED *)

BEGIN
  (* ENTER AND PRINT DATA VALUES *)
  ENTERDATA (LIST, MAXSIZE, N);

  (* FIND RANGE OF VALUES *)
  RANGE := LARGEST(LIST, N) - SMALLEST(LIST, N);
  WRITELN ('RANGE OF DATA = ', RANGE :10:2);

  (* FIND AVERAGE *)
  AVERAGE := FINDAVE(LIST,N);
  WRITELN ('AVERAGE VALUE = ', AVERAGE :10:2);

  (* FIND MEDIAN *)
  MEDIAN := FINDMED(LIST, N);
  WRITELN ('MEDIAN VALUE = ', MEDIAN :10:2)
END.
```

Fig. 8.13 Main program for simple statistics problem.

assignment statement calls one or more of the functions.

Data tables and algorithms for procedure ENTERDATA and the functions above may now be designed independently of the main program. The data tables and PASCAL implementations of SMALLEST, FINDAVE, ENTERDATA and SORT are straightforward and are left as exercises. (See Exercise 8.7.) The function LARGEST is shown in Fig. 8.14. We will continue to document functions and procedures as illustrated in Fig. 8.14.

```
FUNCTION LARGEST (LIST : REALARRAY;
                  N : INTEGER) : REAL;
(* FINDS LARGEST VALUE IN LIST                      *)
(*                                                   *)
(*          INPUT PARAMETERS                         *)
(*             LIST - ARRAY OF REAL VALUES           *)
(*             N - NUMBER OF ELEMENTS IN LIST        *)

VAR
  I : INTEGER;
  LARGE : REAL;

BEGIN
  (* INITIALIZE LARGE TO FIRST VALUE *)
  LARGE := LIST[1];

  (* EXAMINE REST OF ARRAY *)
  FOR I := 2 TO N DO
    (* REDEFINE LARGE IF CURRENT ELEMENT IS BIGGER *)
    IF LIST[I] > LARGE THEN
      LARGE := LIST[I];

  (* DEFINE LARGEST UPON COMPLETION OF LOOP *)
  LARGEST := LARGE
END; (* LARGEST *)
```

Fig. 8.14 Function LARGEST.

8.6.2 Finding the Median of a Collection of Data

We can complete the statistics problem by writing the function FINDMED.

Problem 8.3: Write a function FINDMED to determine the median of a collection of data items stored in an array.

Discussion: Figure 8.15 shows the portion of the program system chart (Fig. 8.12) that is relevant to the median function. The level one algorithm will simply reflect an ordering of the subproblems shown in the program system chart. The information involved in the solution of the problem at this level is shown in the program system chart and is described in the following data table.

Data Table for the Median Function (FINDMED)

Input parameters	*Update parameters*	*Output parameters*
N: The number of items in the array LIST (INTEGER)	LIST: The array containing the data to be processed	(none)

Procedure referenced

SORT: Sorts the data in LIST

Level One Algorithm

1. Sort the data in LIST.
2. Determine the middle value of the sorted data.

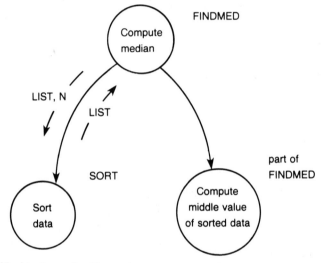

Fig. 8.15 Level one algorithm and program system chart for the median problem (8.3).

The next step in the solution of the median problem is to decide how to implement Steps 1 and 2 of the algorithm. Since sorting a collection of data is a somewhat complicated task, we will implement the sort by modifying procedure SORT described earlier (see Fig. 8.8). Once the data has been sorted, finding the median is rather easy, as shown in the refinement of Step 2 below. This algorithm is based upon the definition of the median as the middle value in an ordered list of data.

Level Two Refinement of FINDMED

Step 2   *Determine the middle value of the sorted data*

2.1   IF N is odd THEN
          2.2 Median is the middle item in the collection
       ELSE
          2.3 Median is the average of the two middle items in
                  the collection

We can now write the function FINDMED to find the median (see Fig. 8.16). One new variable was used in the definition of the function. This should be added to the data table as follows:

Program variables

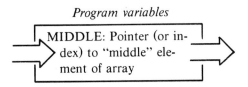

MIDDLE: Pointer (or index) to "middle" element of array

As shown in Fig. 8.16, it is perfectly permissible for a function to call a procedure. The definition of the module being called (SORT) should precede the definition of the calling module (FINDMED).

The array LIST is declared as a value parameter in FINDMED. A local copy of the corresponding actual array (also named LIST) will be made when FINDMED is first entered. This copy is passed as the first parameter to procedure SORT.

The first parameter in SORT must be declared a variable parameter as SORT rearranges the data in the array being sorted. The data associated with the parameter named LIST of FINDMED will be manipulated by SORT. Since LIST is a value parameter in FINDMED, these changes will be local to FINDMED and will not be reflected in the original array defined in the main program.

```
FUNCTION FINDMED (LIST : REALARRAY;
                  N : INTEGER) : REAL;
(* FINDS MEDIAN VALUE IN LIST                       *)
(*                                                  *)
(*      INPUT PARAMETERS                            *)
(*          LIST - ARRAY OF DATA                    *)
(*          N - NUMBER OF ELEMENTS IN LIST          *)

(* INSERT PROCEDURE SORT HERE *)

VAR
  MIDDLE : INTEGER

BEGIN
  (* SORT DATA IN LIST *)
  SORT (LIST, N);

  (* DETERMINE THE "MIDDLE" VALUE OF THE SORTED DATA *)
  MIDDLE := (N DIV 2) + 1;
  IF ODD(N) THEN
    FINDMED := LIST[MIDDLE]
  ELSE
    (* N IS EVEN - AVERAGE TWO MIDDLE VALUES *)
    FINDMED := (LIST[MIDDLE-1] + LIST[MIDDLE]) / 2
END; (* FINDMED *)
```

Fig. 8.16 Function FINDMED.

Exercise 8.7:   Write the procedures ENTERDATA and SORT.

Exercise 8.8:   Develop data tables and PASCAL forms for the functions SMALLEST and FINDAVE. Write these functions to complete the statistics problem.

Exercise 8.9:   In the program in Fig. 8.13, there is no reference to the computation of the sum or to the sorting of the data items (see the program system chart, Fig. 8.12). Why not?

Exercise 8.10:   If we examine the program system chart for the statistics problem (Fig. 8.12), we can see that the sort subtask does not enter the picture until the third level, where sorting is required to find the median of the data items. Yet the sort could have been quite helpful in the computation of the range. Since sorting is needed anyway, we might just as well have sorted the data first. Once this is done, the range can be computed as

$$RANGE := LIST[N] - LIST[1]$$

and the functions LARGEST and SMALLEST would no longer be needed. Rewrite the level one algorithm and the program system chart if the sort is done immediately after the reading of the data.

8.7   TESTING A PROGRAM SYSTEM

As the number of modules and statements in a program system grows, the possibility of error also increases. However, if each module is kept to a manageable size, then the possibility of error will increase much more slowly. Also, the limited use of global variables will minimize the likelihood of harmful side effects (see section 5.6.3).

Whenever possible, it is best to test each system module independently before putting the entire package together. This can be done by writing a short *driver program* consisting of necessary declarations, initialization of input parameters, and a call to the procedure being tested. The driver program should also print the results returned by the procedure being tested. A little time spent testing each procedure independently in this manner should significantly reduce the total time required to debug the entire program system. (Examples of driver programs would be the main programs for testing LARGEST and BREAKDOWN shown in Figs. 5.6 and 5.9).

If a procedure being tested calls another, it is often helpful to initially substitute a dummy procedure, or stub, for the second procedure (see section 5.5). The body of the stub should consist only of a WRITE statement indicating that the stub was entered. After the second level procedure is written and tested, it can be inserted in place of its stub.

After all the modules are tested independently, the entire program system should be debugged and tested. Some suggestions for preventing and detecting errors at this stage follow.

1. Accurate, written descriptions of all parameters and global variables of a procedure should be maintained. These descriptions should be included as comments in the procedure definition.

2. Leave a trace of execution by printing the name of each procedure as it is entered.
3. At least in the early debugging stage, the values of all input parameters and any global variables should be printed upon entry to a procedure.
4. Whenever possible, the values of input parameters and any global variables should be checked to see whether or not they fall within a meaningful range. For example, a parameter used to indicate the number of items in an array must always be positive and should not exceed the upper bound for the array. Meaningful diagnostics should be printed and appropriate action taken if the array range is violated.
5. It is often helpful while debugging to print the values of all output parameters and any global variables immediately after returning from a procedure.

8.8 RECURSION*

8.8.1 Introduction to Recursion

Recursion is a powerful tool that is sometimes useful in simplifying a problem solution. *Recursive definitions* are often encountered in the study of mathematics. For example, the set of natural numbers may be defined recursively as follows:

1. 1 is a natural number
2. The successor of a natural number is a natural number

where the successor of a number is obtained by adding one to that number.

The power of this recursive definition is its ability to define a set consisting of an infinite number of elements using only two statements. In a similar way, a recursive algorithm can specify an infinite number of computations using a few program statements and without looping.

Using recursion in problem solving often leads to a new problem which is similar to the original but smaller in scope. As an example, in the Towers of Hanoi problem shown below

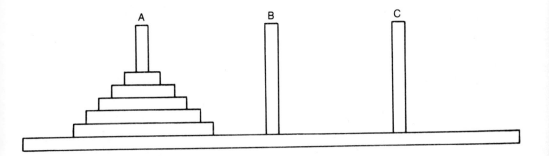

_____

*This section is optional and may be omitted.

the goal is to move N discs (N = 5) from peg A to peg C under the following constraints:

1. Only one disc may be moved at a time.
2. A larger disc can never be placed on a smaller disc.

A recursive solution would be:

1. Move the top N − 1 discs from peg A to peg B
2. Move the bottom disc from peg A to peg C
3. Move the top N − 1 discs from peg B to peg C

This approach has reduced the size of the problem from one involving N discs to two simpler problems involving only N − 1 discs, and a trivial problem involving only one disc. This reduction process can be applied repeatedly until the solution becomes transparent.

Recursion can be successfully applied to problems that have the following structure:

1. The solution is easy to specify for certain special conditions (called *stopping states*).
2. For any given situation or state, there are well-defined rules for proceeding to a new state that is either a stopping state or eventually leads to a stopping state (called *recursion steps*).

8.8.2   A Recursive Factorial Function

A simple example of a recursive solution is the computation of the factorial of a non-negative integer N (see Exercise 3.16). The stopping state is described first:

1. If N is zero, the factorial is one.

Next, the recursion step is described:

2. For N > 1, the solution is N times the factorial of (N − 1).

The recursion step has reduced the problem to finding the factorial of the next smaller number and multiplying that result by N. Obviously, N − 1 is closer to the stopping state (zero) than is N. Successive applications of the recursion step will eventually lead to the stopping state.

The PASCAL implementation of this recursive algorithm is shown in Fig. 8.17. The function FACTORIAL returns a value of one if its argument is zero. Otherwise, the value returned is determined by the value of the expression N * FACTORIAL (N − 1). Since FACTORIAL calls itself, it is considered a *recursive function*.

Each new call to FACTORIAL increases the level of recursion. The compiler saves the values of the function's parameter (N) and any local variables just before each new call. At the time of the call, the expression N − 1 is evaluated and assigned as the new value of the parameter N. Eventually, the parameter will be zero and a value of one is associated with the last call to FACTORIAL. As

```
FUNCTION FACTORIAL (N : INTEGER) : INTEGER;
(* RECURSIVE COMPUTATION OF N FACTORIAL *)

BEGIN
  (* TEST FOR STOPPING STATE *)
  IF N <= O THEN
    FACTORIAL := 1
  ELSE
    FACTORIAL := N * FACTORIAL(N-1)
END; (* FACTORIAL *)
```

Fig. 8.17 Function FACTORIAL.

the compiler returns from each level of recursion, it computes the value returned by multiplying the parameter value saved at this level by the result just returned from the previous level. Each return reduces the level of recursion by one. When the level of recursion is back to zero, the value returned represents the value of the initial function call.

The diagram in Fig. 8.18 illustrates this process for the statement

$$\text{NEWNUM} := \text{FACTORIAL}(6);$$

Level of
Recursion

0   FACTORIAL(6)

                       720

1   6 * FACTORIAL(5)

                          120

2   5 * FACTORIAL(4)

                            24

3   4 * FACTORIAL(3)

                              6

4   3 * FACTORIAL(2)

                              2

5   2 * FACTORIAL(1)

                              1

6   1 * FACTORIAL(0)

                              1

Fig. 8.18 Trace of execution of FACTORIAL(6).

There are seven levels of recursion (0 through 6) and six recursive calls to FAC-TORIAL plus the original call. The arrows pointing downward show the expression resulting from each application of the recursion step. After the last recursive call (FACTORIAL(0)), the function must return from each recursive call with a value. The value returned is computed by multiplying the result from the previous level and the value of the parameter N at the current level. These values are indicated alongside the arrows pointing upward. The value computed for FAC-TORIAL(6) and assigned to NEWNUM is 720.

8.8.3   Binary Search Algorithm

Now that we have a technique for sorting an array (Bubble Sort) we can write a search algorithm that is considerably more efficient than the one developed for Problem 7.2 (See Fig. 8.4). The *binary search algorithm* may be used to search an ordered array. It takes advantage of the fact that the array is ordered to eliminate half of the remaining array elements with each probe into the array. Consequently, if the array has 1000 elements, it will either locate the desired key or eliminate 500 elements with its first probe, and 250 elements with the next probe. It turns out that only ten probes will be needed to completely search an array with 1000 elements. (Why?)

Problem 8.4:   Write a procedure that performs a binary search of an ordered array.

Discussion: Since the array is ordered, all we have to do is compare the desired key with the middle element of the array. If their values are the same, then we are done. If the middle value is larger than the key, then we should search the lower half of the array next; otherwise, we should search the upper half of the array next (from MIDDLE + 1 to TOP).

The upper half of the array is eliminated by the first probe shown in the diagram below.

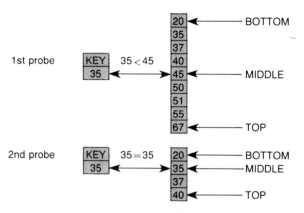

If BOTTOM and TOP define the portion of the array left to be searched, then

TOP should be reset to MIDDLE−1 as shown above. The key would be found on the second probe. The data table and recursive algorithm for the binary search follow.

Data Table for Binary Search

Input parameters

LIST: Array to be
searched

KEY: Desired value

BOTTOM: The first sub-
script in the search
array (INTEGER)

TOP: The last subscript
in the search array
(INTEGER)

Output parameters

INDEX: The index of
KEY if found; other-
wise, zero (INTEGER)

FOUND: Indicates
whether KEY was
found (TRUE) or not
(FALSE) (BOOL-
EAN)

Program variables

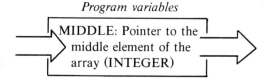

MIDDLE: Pointer to the
middle element of the
array (INTEGER)

Level One Algorithm for Binary Search

1. Define MIDDLE as the pointer to the middle element
2. Locate the KEY or reduce the search dimensions

Level Two Refinements

Step 1   *Define MIDDLE*

   1.1   MIDDLE := (BOTTOM + TOP) DIV 2

Step 2   *Locate the key or reduce the search dimensions*

   2.1   IF there are no elements left to search THEN
            2.2 Indicate failure and set INDEX to zero
         ELSE IF the middle element is the key THEN
            2.3 Indicate success and set INDEX to MIDDLE
         ELSE IF the middle element is greater than the key THEN
            2.4 Search the lower half of the array
         ELSE
            2.5 Search the upper half of the array

Steps 2.2 and 2.3 above are stopping states. In either stopping state, the

Boolean variable FOUND is set to indicate the result of the search (TRUE for success, FALSE for failure) and INDEX is set to the subscript of the key, or zero if the key is not located. These values are returned to the calling module.

In order to implement the recursion steps (2.4 and 2.5), new values must be passed to the input parameters BOTTOM (Step 2.5) or TOP (Step 2.4) by the statements that call the procedure recursively. These new values define the search limits for the next probe into the array. In the initial call to the recursive procedure, BOTTOM and TOP should be defined as the first and last elements of the array, respectively. The procedure BINARYSEARCH is shown in Fig. 8.19.

```
PROCEDURE BINARYSEARCH (VAR LIST : SMALLARRAY;
                        KEY : INTEGER;
                        BOTTOM, TOP : INTEGER;
                        VAR INDEX : INTEGER;
                        VAR FOUND : BOOLEAN);
(* PERFORMS A BINARY SEARCH OF AN ARRAY                          *)
(*                                                               *)
(* INPUT PARAMETERS                                              *)
(*      LIST - ORDERED ARRAY OF DATA                             *)
(*      KEY - VALUE TO BE LOCATED                                *)
(*      BOTTOM - INDEX TO FIRST ELEMENT IN THE ARRAY             *)
(*      TOP - INDEX TO LAST ELEMENT IN THE ARRAY                 *)
(* OUTPUT PARAMETERS                                             *)
(*      INDEX - LOCATION OF KEY OR ZERO IF NOT FOUND             *)
(*      FOUND - INDICATES SUCCESS(TRUE) OR FAILURE(FALSE)        *)

VAR
  MIDDLE : INTEGER;

BEGIN
  (* DEFINE MIDDLE *)
  MIDDLE := (BOTTOM + TOP) DIV 2;

  (* LOCATE KEY OR REDUCE SEARCH DIMENSIONS *)
  IF TOP < BOTTOM THEN
    BEGIN
      FOUND := FALSE;
      INDEX := 0
    END
  ELSE IF LIST[MIDDLE] = KEY THEN
    BEGIN
      FOUND := TRUE;
      INDEX := MIDDLE
    END
  ELSE IF LIST[MIDDLE] > KEY THEN
    BINARYSEARCH (LIST, KEY, BOTTOM, MIDDLE - 1, INDEX, FOUND)
  ELSE
    BINARYSEARCH (LIST, KEY, MIDDLE + 1, TOP, INDEX, FOUND)
END; (* BINARYSEARCH *)
```

Fig. 8.19 Procedure BINARYSEARCH.

The array LIST is declared as a variable parameter even though it is used as an input parameter. If LIST were a value parameter instead, then each recursive call would generate another local copy of the actual array. This would waste time and memory space needlessly.

Exercise 8.11:   Trace the search of the array LIST shown in this section for a key of 40. Specify the values of BOTTOM, MIDDLE, and TOP during each recursive call.

Exercise 8.12:   Implement the binary search algorithm without recursion. Use a loop that is repeated until the key is located or there are no more array elements left to search.

Exercise 8.13:   The Fibonacci Series is defined recursively as follows:

1. The first Fibonacci number is one.
2. The second Fibonacci number is one.
3. Any other Fibonacci number is equal to the sum of the preceding two Fibonacci numbers.

Write a recursive function that computes the Fibonacci number corresponding to its argument. Why is this an inefficient approach?

Exercise 8.14:   Assume each character string terminates in a dollar sign ($) and that the null string (length 0) starts with a $. Write a recursive function that finds the length of its character string argument. Do not use the function LENGTH.

8.9   COMMON PROGRAMMING ERRORS

8.9.1   REPEAT-UNTIL Errors

The main problem in using a REPEAT-UNTIL is too many loop repetitions. A REPEAT-UNTIL loop can execute forever if its conditional test remains false. This situation may be indicated by an array subscript that is out-of-bounds. Also, remember that the exit for the REPEAT-UNTIL loop cannot occur until the loop termination test is evaluated, after the completion of the loop body. Consequently, the loop body is always executed at least once.

8.9.2   GOTO Errors

Make sure that any label used in a block (or procedure) is declared in the declaration section of that block. A label may only be declared once in a block; however, there may be more than one GOTO statement that transfers to a given label. Make sure that every label used with a GOTO statement is associated with exactly one statement in the block; otherwise, you will have a "missing label" or "multiply defined" label error. It is illegal to transfer into a block (or procedure) from outside the block. Similarly, it is illegal to transfer out of a procedure using a GOTO. (The EXIT statement may be used to transfer out of a procedure.)

8.9.3   Nested Loop Errors

Make sure you trace all nested loops carefully and check all boundary values. If a loop control variable is used as an array subscript, verify that it is within range at the boundary values. Remember, it is illegal to modify the loop control variable value inside a FOR loop, or to use the same loop control variable for nested FOR statements.

8.9.4   Recursion Errors

Avoid using recursion in problems that can be more easily solved using iterative algorithms. When using recursive functions or procedures, make sure that you provide a stopping state and that the stopping state can always be reached. Otherwise, recursion will continue beyond the limits allowed by the system.

8.10   SUMMARY

Three new control statements were introduced in this chapter. The REPEAT statement is an effective means of specifying that a group of statements (a loop) is to be executed until a termination condition becomes true.

The GOTO statement can be used to exit from a nest of loops; the EXIT statement can be used to exit from a procedure. These statements should be used sparingly. Remember, every label used with a GOTO must be associated with exactly one statement in the block in which it is declared.

Nested loops and their operation were discussed. Every inner loop of a nest is entered and executed to completion each time an outer loop is repeated.

One technique for sorting an array, the Bubble Sort, was discussed along with the binary search algorithm which is a very efficient algorithm for searching a sorted array. The binary search algorithm was written as a recursive procedure, or as a procedure that calls itself. We introduced recursion and showed how it could be used to transform certain problems into similar problems of smaller size.

The design of a large program system was studied and the program system chart was presented as a means of documenting the flow of information and control in such a system. We also provided hints on testing and debugging the individual modules of a program system through the use of drivers and stubs.

PROGRAMMING PROBLEMS

8.5   Write a program system that reads a body of text and finds the frequency of occurrence of words of different lengths and also the frequency of occurrence of all letters in the text. Generate output plots (histograms) of both sets of results.

8.6   An array of records is used to keep track of the books in a library. Each record contains the following information:

1. Title
2. Author(s)
   a. Number of authors
   b. Names (one long string)

3. Publisher
   a. Name
   b. Date
   c. Location
4. Catalogue number (a string)

Write a program system that performs the following operations:

1. Lists all books published in a given year
2. Lists the books in order by catalogue number
3. Lists all books written by a given author.

Hint: You will have to sort the array to perform Step 2.

8.7 Assuming that several sets are represented as Boolean arrays with the same subscript type, write procedures that will perform all of the set operations described in Chapter 7. Test your program system.

8.8 Write the sort algorithm described in Exercise 8.5 as a recursive procedure. You will also need a function that finds the smallest element given the lower and upper bounds of an array.

8.9 Write a procedure that searches a subject string to see if a target substring is located in the string. Your procedure should begin its search at a specified location in the subject string and return a Boolean flag to indicate the search result. Also return the location of the first character of the first occurrence of the substring and the number of occurrences.

8.10 Write the recursive algorithm for the Towers of Hanoi problem described in Section 8.8.1. Your program should print the starting tower and ending tower each time a single disk is moved.

8.11 The greatest common divisor of two positive integers I and J is the largest integer N that divides both I and J with zero remainder. An algorithm for determining N was devised by the famous mathematician Euclid:

1. Let L be the larger of I and J and S the smaller.
2. Let R be the remainder of L divided by S (an integer value).
3. If R is nonzero, reset L to S and S to R and repeat steps 2 and 3.

Implement this algorithm as a function and write a main program to read in four positive integers and find the greatest common divisor, GCD, of all four numbers (the largest integer that divides them all). *Hint:* GCD(N1, N2, N3, N4) = GCD (GCD(N1,N2), GCD(N3,N4)).

8.12 Define a function FNQ that calculates the square root of a single argument without using SQRT. *Hint:* One simple scheme for computing the square root, the Newton-Raphson method, requires that you start with an initial guess of the correct answer and then repeatedly refine this guess, obtaining more accurate ones. The formula for finding a more accurate guess from the old one is

$$\text{new guess} = 1/2(\text{old guess} + \frac{N}{\text{old guess}})$$

where N is the argument whose square root is required. When a new guess is found, it replaces the old guess in the formula, and "another new guess" is computed. This process continues until

$$| \text{ new guess } - \text{ old guess } | \leq \text{ epsilon}$$

where epsilon is some suitably chosen small value(such as 0.0001). The brackets indicate that the absolute value of the difference between guesses is compared to epsilon.

Write a program to call FNQ and compare your result to the value computed by SQRT. Test your program for the values 3, 9, 50, 99 and 100. Use N/2 as an initial value of old guess.

8.13 The electric company charges its customers according to the following schedule:

8 cents a kilowatt-hour (kwh) for electricity used up to the first 300 kwh;
6 cents a kwh for the next 300 kwh (up to 600 kwh);
5 cents a kwh for the next 400 kwh (up to 1000 kwh);
3 cents a kwh for all electricity used over 1000 kwh.

Write a function to compute the total charge for each customer. Write a program to call this function using the following data:

Customer number	Kilowatt-hours used
123	725
205	115
464	600
596	327
601	915
613	1011
722	47

The calling program should print a three-column table listing the customer number, hours used and the charge for each customer. It should also compute and print the number of customers, total hours used and total charges.

8.14 Each week the employees of a local manufacturing company turn in time cards containing the following information:

i) an identification number (a five-digit integer),
ii) hourly pay rate (a real number),
iii) time worked Monday, Tuesday, Wednesday, Thursday and Friday (each a four-digit integer of the form HHMM, where HH is hours and MM is minutes).

For example, last week's time cards contained the following data:

Employee number	Hourly rate	Time worked (hours, minutes)				
		Monday	Tuesday	Wednesday	Thursday	Friday
16025	4.00	0800	0730	0800	0800	0420
19122	4.50	0615	0800	0800	0800	0800
21061	4.25	0805	0800	0735	0515	0735
45387	3.50	1015	1030	0800	0945	0800
50177	6.15	0800	0415	0800	0545	0600
61111	5.00	0930	0800	0800	1025	0905
88128	4.50	0800	0900	0800	0800	0700

Write a program system that will read the above data and compute for each employee the total hours worked (in hours and minutes), the total hours worked (to the nearest quarter-hour), and the gross salary. Your system should print the data shown above with the total hours (both figures) and gross pay for each employee. You should assume that overtime is paid at 1½ times the normal hourly rate, and that it is computed on a weekly basis (only on the total hours in excess of 40), rather than on a daily basis. Your program system should contain the following modules:

a) A function for computing the sum (in hours and minutes) of two four-digit integers of the form HHMM (*Example:* 0745 + 0335 = 1120);
b) A function for converting hours and minutes (represented as a four-digit integer) into hours, rounded to the nearest quarter hour (*Example:* 1120 = 11.25);
c) A function for computing gross salary given total hours and hourly rate;
d) A function for rounding gross salary accurate to two decimal places.

Test your program using the data above.

8.15   *Internal Sort/Merge.* Let A and B be two arrays of size 10, and C an array of size 20. Write a program system to read two lists of data, one of size N1 and the other of size N2 (N1, N2 ≤ 10) into A and B respectively, sort A and B in ascending order, and then merge A and B into C maintaining the ascending order. The merge process is illustrated below for N1 = 5, N2 = 3. The numbered lines between arrays A and B indicate the order of comparison of the pairs of elements in A and B. The smaller of each pair of numbers is always merged into array C; the larger is then compared with the next entry in the other array (either A or B).

A(1)	A(2)	A(3)	A(4)	A(5)	A(6)	A(7)	A(8)	A(9)	A(10)
-10.5	-1.8	3.5	6.3	7.2	?	?	?	?	?

1 2 3 4 5 6

B(1)	B(2)	B(3)	B(4)	B(5)	...	B(10)
-2.5	3.1	5.7	?	?		?

C(1)	C(2)	C(3)	C(4)	C(5)	C(6)	C(7)	C(8)	C(9)	...	C(20)
-10.5	-2.5	-1.8	3.1	3.5	5.7	6.3	7.2	?		?

When one of the arrays A or B has been exhausted, do not forget to copy the remaining data from the other array into C.

8.16   The expression for computing C(n,r), the number of combinations of n items taken r at a time, is

$$C(n,r) = \frac{n!}{r!(n-r)!}$$

Assuming that we already have available a function for computing n! (see Fig. 8.17), write a function for computing C(n,r). Write a program that will call this function for n = 4, r = 1; n = 5, r = 3; n = 7, r = 7; and n = 6, r = 2.

8.17   *Statistical measurements with functions—a simple linear-curve fit problem.* Scientists and engineers frequently perform experiments designed to provide measurements of two variables X and Y. They often compute measures of central tendency (such as the mean) and measures of dispersion (such as the standard deviation) for these variables. They then attempt to decide whether or not there is any relationship between the variables, and, if so, to express this relationship in terms of an equation.

If there is a relationship between X and Y that is describable using a linear equation of the form

$$Y = aX + b.$$

the data collected is said to *fit a linear curve*.

For example, the ACE Computing Company recently made a study relating aptitude test scores to programming productivity of new personnel. The six pairs of scores shown below were obtained by testing 6 randomly selected applicants and later measuring their productivity.

Applicant	Aptitude score (Variable X)	Productivity (Variable Y)
1	$x_1 = 9$	$y_1 = 46$
2	$x_2 = 17$	$y_2 = 70$
3	$x_3 = 20$	$y_3 = 58$
4	$x_4 = 19$	$y_4 = 66$
5	$x_5 = 20$	$y_5 = 86$
6	$x_6 = 23$	$y_6 = 64$

ACE wants to find the equation of the line that they can use to predict the productivity of workers tested in the future. They are also interested in obtaining means and standard deviations for the variables X and Y. The required computations can be performed as follows:

1. Compute SUMX $= \Sigma X$ $= x_1 + x_2 \ldots + x_6$
   SUMY $= \Sigma Y$ $= y_1 + y_2 + \ldots + y_6$
   SUMXY $= \Sigma X \cdot Y$ $= x_1 y_1 + x_2 y_2 + \ldots + x_6 y_6$
   SUMXSQ $= \Sigma X^2$ $= x_1^2 + x_2^2 + \ldots + x_6^2$
   SUMYSQ $= \Sigma Y^2$ $= y_1^2 + y_2^2 + \ldots + y_6^2$
2. Compute MEANX $= $ SUMX/N   where $N = 6$
   MEANY $= $ SUMY/N
3. Compute STDDVX $= \sqrt{\text{SUMXSQ}/N - \text{MEANX}^2}$
   STDDVY $= \sqrt{\text{SUMYSQ}/N - \text{MEANY}^2}$
4. Compute a and b in $Y = aX + b$ using the equation

$$a = \frac{\text{SUMXY} - N \times \text{MEANX} \times \text{MEANY}}{\text{SUMXSQ} - N \times \text{MEANX}^2}$$
$$b = \text{MEANY} - a \times \text{MEANX}$$

Write functions to carry out the above computations. Test your program on the aptitude/productivity data just shown.

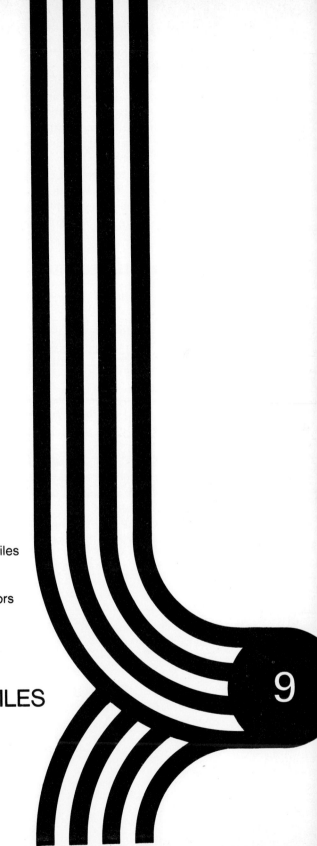

HIERARCHICAL RECORDS AND FILES

9.1   INTRODUCTION

In this chapter, we will reexamine records. We will study records with components that are also records (hierarchical records) and learn how to reference and manipulate their fields. In addition, we will introduce record variants. These are records whose form changes in a specified way to accommodate data with varying storage requirements.

The second major topic in this chapter is the study of files. Files are used to store large amounts of data. We shall learn how to create new files and modify existing files. In addition, we shall learn more about the system files INPUT, OUTPUT and KEYBOARD which are predefined as INTERACTIVE files.

9.2   HIERARCHICAL RECORDS

In Chapter 7, we studied the record type EMPLOYEE described below.

```
EMPLOYEE = RECORD
   NAME : STRING[10];
   SOCSECURE : STRING[11];
   NUMDEPEND : INTEGER;
   RATE : REAL
END; (*EMPLOYEE*)
```

Each field of this record is either a simple type or an array. It is also permissible in PASCAL to use the other structured data types, records and sets, as fields of a record.

As an example, we shall expand our description of an employee by adding new fields for storage of the employee's address and date of birth. The record type NEWEMPLOYEE is declared in Fig. 9.1, along with two additional record types, DATE and ADDRESS.

If PROGRAMMER is a record variable of type NEWEMPLOYEE, the hierarchical structure of PROGRAMMER is sketched below:

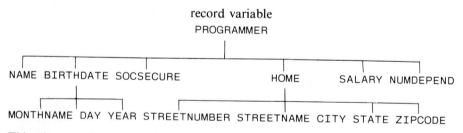

This diagram shows that PROGRAMMER is a record with six fields and that two of these fields (BIRTHDATE and HOME) are also records (*subrecords* of PROGRAMMER). The fields of each subrecord are indicated at the bottom of the diagram.

```
TYPE
  MONTH = (JAN,FEB,MAR,APR,MAY,JUN,JUL,AUG,SEP,OCT,NOV,DEC);
  MONTHS = ARRAY[1..12] OF MONTH;
  ADDRESS = RECORD
    STREETNUMBER : INTEGER;
    STREETNAME, CITY, STATE : STRING[10];
    ZIPCODE : INTEGER
  END; (* ADDRESS *)

  DATE = RECORD
    MONTHNAME : MONTH;
    DAY : 1..31;
    YEAR : 1900..1999
  END; (* DATE *)

  NEWEMPLOYEE = RECORD
    NAME : STRING[10];
    SOCSECURE : STRING[11];
    BIRTHDATE : DATE;
    HOME : ADDRESS;
    SALARY : REAL;
    NUMDEPEND : INTEGER
  END; (* NEWEMPLOYEE *)
```

Fig. 9.1   Record type NEWEMPLOYEE.

In order to reference a field in this diagram, we must trace a complete path to it from the top. For example, the field selector

PROGRAMMER.BIRTHDATE.YEAR

references the field **YEAR** of the subrecord **PROGRAMMER.BIRTHDATE**; the field selector

PROGRAMMER.YEAR

would be incomplete and undefined.

The record copy statement

PROGRAMMER.BIRTHDATE := DAYOFYEAR

is legal if **DAYOFYEAR** is a record variable of type **DATE**. This statement copies each field of **DAYOFYEAR** into the corresponding field of the subrecord **PROGRAMMER.BIRTHDATE**.

In many situations, the **WITH** statement can be used to shorten the field selector. The statement

```
WITH PROGRAMMER.BIRTHDATE DO
  WRITELN ('YEAR OF BIRTH = ', YEAR, ' DAY OF BIRTH = ', DAY)
```

prints two fields of the subrecord **PROGRAMMER.BIRTHDATE**. It is also permissible to use a list of identifiers in a **WITH** statement. The statement

```
WITH PROGRAMMER, BIRTHDATE, HOME DO
  WRITELN (NAME, ' LIVES IN ', CITY, ' AND WAS BORN IN ',
          YEAR)
```

prints the field **NAME**, one field of the subrecord **PROGRAMMER.HOME** and one field of the subrecord **PROGRAMMER.BIRTHDATE**. It is equivalent to the nested form below.

```
                    WITH PROGRAMMER DO
                      WITH BIRTHDATE DO
                        WITH HOME DO
                          WRITELN ( . . . . . )
```

The procedure in Fig. 9.2 reads all data for an employee. The array **MONTHVAL** is the array of scalar values defined in Example 6.7 (i.e. **MONTHVAL** [1] := **JAN**, etc.).

```
PROCEDURE READEMPLOYEE (VAR PERSON : NEWEMPLOYEE;
                            MONTHVAL : MONTHS);
(* READS DATA FOR A RECORD VARIABLE PERSON                   *)
(* OF TYPE NEWEMPLOYEE                                       *)
(*                                                           *)
(* INPUT PARAMETER                                           *)
(*      MONTHVAL - ARRAY OF MONTH NAMES                      *)
(* OUTPUT PARAMETER                                          *)
(*      PERSON - RECORD VARIABLE BEING DEFINED               *)

VAR
  MONTHNUM : INTEGER;

BEGIN
  WITH PERSON DO
    BEGIN
      (* READ NAME *)
      WRITE ('NAME: '); READLN (NAME);
      (* READ SOCIAL SECURITY *)
      WRITE ('SOCIAL SECURITY #'); READLN (SOCSECURE);

      (* READ DATE OF BIRTH *)
      WITH BIRTHDATE DO
        BEGIN
          WRITELN ('ENTER MONTH <1..12>, DAY <1..31> AND YEAR');
          READLN (MONTHNUM, DAY, YEAR);
          MONTHNAME := MONTHVAL[MONTHNUM]
        END; (* WITH *)

      (* READ ADDRESS *)
      WITH HOME DO
        BEGIN
          WRITELN ('ENTER STREET NUMBER AND NAME');
          READLN (STREETNUMBER, STREETNAME);
          WRITE ('CITY :'); READLN (CITY);
          WRITELN ('ENTER ZIPCODE AND STATE');
          READLN (ZIPCODE, STATE)
        END; (* WITH *)
```

(continued)

```
       (* READ SALARY AND NUMBER OF DEPENDENTS *)
       WRITELN ('ENTER SALARY AND NUMBER OF DEPENDENTS');
       READLN (SALARY, NUMDEPEND)
     END (* WITH *)
END; (* READEMPLOYEE *)
```

Fig. 9.2 Procedure READEMPLOYEE.

9.3 RECORD VARIANTS*

All record variables of type NEWEMPLOYEE have the same form and
structure. It is possible, however, to define record types that have some fields
that are the same for all variables of that type (*fixed part*) and some fields that
may be different (*variant part*).

For example, we might wish to include additional information about an employee based on the employee's marital status. For all married employees, we
might want to know the spouse's name and number of children living at home.
For all divorced employees, we might want to know the date of the divorce. For
all single employees, we might want to know whether or not the employee lives
alone. This new employee type, EXECUTIVE, is described in Fig. 9.3.

The fixed part of a record always precedes the variant part. The fixed part
of record type EXECUTIVE is defined as in Section 9.2. The variant part begins
with the phrase

CASE MS: MARITALSTAT OF

defining a special field MS, of type MARITALSTAT, that is called the *tag field*.
The value of the tag field (MARRIED, DIVORCED, or SINGLE) determines
the form of the remainder of the record. If the value of the tag field is MAR-
RIED, there are two additional fields, SPOUSENAME and CHILDHOME; oth-
erwise, there is only one additional field, DIVORCEDATE (type DATE) or
LIVESALONE (type BOOLEAN).

```
       TYPE
          MARITALSTAT = (MARRIED, DIVORCED, SINGLE);
          EXECUTIVE = RECORD
             (* FIXED PART *)
             NAME : STRING[10];
             SOCSECURE : STRING[11];
             BIRTHDATE : DATE;
             HOME : ADDRESS;
             SALARY : REAL;
             NUMDEPEND : INTEGER;
             (* VARIANT PART *)
             CASE MS : MARITALSTAT OF
                MARRIED :
                   (SPOUSENAME : STRING[10];
                    CHILDHOME : INTEGER);
                DIVORCED :
                   (DIVORCEDATE : DATE);
```

(continued)

---

*This section is optional and may be omitted.

```
                    SINGLE :
                      (LIVESALONE : BOOLEAN)
          END;    (* EXECUTIVE *)
```

Fig. 9.3   Record type EXECUTIVE.

An example of each type of record is shown below. Only the variant part is shown, starting with the tag field, since the fixed parts all have the same form.

employee 1 – MARRIED

fixed part	MS	SPOUSENAME	CHILDHOME
. . .	MARRIED	JANE	2

employee 2 – DIVORCED

fixed part	MS	DIVORCEDATE. MONTHNAME	DIVORCEDATE. DAY	DIVORCEDATE. YEAR
. . .	DIVORCED	MAY	20	1975

employee 3 – SINGLE

fixed part	MS	LIVESALONE
. . .	SINGLE	TRUE

For each variable of type EXECUTIVE, the compiler will allocate sufficient storage space to accommodate any of the record variants shown above. However, only one of the variants may be defined at any given time as determined by the tag field value. Hence, if BOSS is a record of type EXECUTIVE and the value of BOSS.MS is MARRIED, then only the variant fields BOSS.SPOUSENAME and BOSS.CHILDHOME may be referenced; all other variant fields are undefined.

The complete syntax for a record with fixed and variant parts is described in the next display.

Record Type with Variant Part

$$
\begin{array}{l}
record\text{-}id = \text{RECORD} \\
\quad\quad field_1 : type_1; \\
\quad\quad field_2 : type_2; \\
\\
\quad\quad\quad\quad\quad\quad\cdot \\
\quad\quad\quad\quad\quad\quad\cdot \\
\quad\quad\quad\quad\quad\quad\cdot \\
\quad\quad field_n : type_n; \\
\quad\quad \text{CASE } tag : tag\text{-}type \text{ OF} \\
\quad\quad\quad\quad label_1 : (field\ list_1); \\
\quad\quad\quad\quad label_2 : (field\ list_2); \\
\\
\quad\quad\quad\quad\quad\quad\cdot \\
\quad\quad\quad\quad\quad\quad\cdot \\
\quad\quad\quad\quad\quad\quad\cdot \\
\quad\quad\quad\quad label_k : (field\ list_k) \\
\quad\quad \text{END};
\end{array}
$$

fixed part

variant part

Interpretation: The field list for the fixed part is declared first. The variant part starts with the reserved word CASE. *Tag* represents the tag field of the record; the tag field name is separated by a colon from its type (*tag-type*) which must be a previously defined scalar or subrange.

The CASE labels (*label*$_1$, *label*$_2$,...,*label*$_k$) are lists of values of the tag field. *Field list*$_i$ describes the record fields associated with *label*$_i$. Each element of a field list specifies a field name and its type; the elements in the field list are separated by semicolons. The field list is enclosed in parentheses.

Note 1: All field names must be distinct. The same field name may not appear in the fixed and variant parts or in two field lists of the variant part.

Note 2: An empty field list (no variant part for that CASE label) is indicated by an empty pair of parentheses, ( ).

Note 3: It is possible for a field list to also have a variant part. If so, it must follow the fixed part, if any, of the field list.

Note 4: Only one END is needed.

Although all field names must be distinct, it is permissible for two fields to be declared as the same record type. This is the situation for fields BIRTH-DATE and DIVORCEDATE of record type EXECUTIVE (both type DATE). When the tag field value is DIVORCED, the field selectors BOSS.BIRTHDATE.MONTHNAME and BOSS.DIVORCEDATE.MONTHNAME may be used to reference the scalar values representing the month of birth and month of divorce, respectively.

A CASE statement is often used in processing the variant part of a record. By using the tag field as the CASE selector, we can ensure that only the currently defined variant is manipulated. The processing of a record variant is illustrated in the next two examples.

Example 9.1: Procedure READEXECUTIVE (see Fig. 9.4) may be used to read a record of type EXECUTIVE. The fixed part may be read by procedure READEMPLOYEE (see Fig. 9.3). The formal parameter list for READEM-PLOYEE should be the same as for READEXECUTIVE.

```
PROCEDURE READEXECUTIVE (VAR PERSON : EXECUTIVE;
                         MONTHVAL : MONTHS);
(* READS DATA FOR A RECORD VARIABLE PERSON             *)
(* OF TYPE EXECUTIVE                                   *)
(*                                                     *)
(* INPUT PARAMETER                                     *)
(*      MONTHVAL - ARRAY OF MONTH NAMES                *)
(* OUTPUT PARAMETER                                    *)
(*      PERSON - RECORD VARIABLE BEING DEFINED         *)

VAR
  MONTHNUM : INTEGER;
  MARITAL, LIVESTAT : CHAR;

(* INSERT READEMPLOYEE AND MARITALCONVERT HERE *)
```

(*continued*)

```
BEGIN
  (* READ FIXED PART *)
  READEMPLOYEE (PERSON, MONTHVAL);

  (* READ VARIANT PART *)
  WITH PERSON DO
    BEGIN
      (* DEFINE TAG FIELD *)
      WRITE ('MARITAL STATUS: ');  READ (MARITAL);
      WRITELN;
      MS := MARITALCONVERT(MARITAL);
      (* READ REST OF RECORD - FORM DEPENDENT ON MS *)
      CASE MS OF
        MARRIED :
          BEGIN
            WRITE ('SPOUSE: '); READLN (SPOUSÉNAME);
            WRITE ('NUMBER OF CHILDREN AT HOME: ');
            READLN (CHILDHOME)
          END;
        DIVORCED :
          WITH DIVORCEDATE DO
            BEGIN
              WRITELN ('ENTER MONTH <1..12>, DAY <1..31>');
              WRITELN ('AND YEAR OF DIVORCE');
              READLN (MONTHNUM, DAY, YEAR);
              MONTHNAME := MONTHVAL[MONTHNUM]
            END; (* WITH *)
        SINGLE :
          BEGIN
            WRITE ('LIVES ALONE ? (Y OR N)');
            READ (LIVESTAT);
            WRITELN;
            LIVESALONE := LIVESTAT = 'Y'
          END
      END (* CASE *)
    END (* WITH *)
END; (* READEXECUTIVE *)
```

Fig. 9.4 Procedure READEXECUTIVE.

A CASE statement is used to process the variant part of the record parameter PERSON. The value stored in the tag field, MS, determines which of the alternatives listed in the CASE statement is executed.

Note that the record field LIVESALONE is only defined when the value of MS is SINGLE. It is assigned the value of the Boolean expression LIVESTAT = 'Y' (i.e. if LIVESTAT equals 'Y' then LIVESALONE is true; otherwise, LIVESALONE is false.)

Example 9.2: The record type FIGURE can be used to represent a geometric object. It only has a variant part as described next.

```
TYPE
  FIGKIND = (RECTANGLE, SQUARE, CIRCLE);
  FIGURE = RECORD
    CASE FIG : FIGKIND OF
      RECTANGLE : (WIDTH, HEIGHT : REAL);
      SQUARE : (SIDE : REAL);
      CIRCLE : (RADIUS : REAL)
    END;
```

The program in Fig. 9.5a enters data describing a geometric figure and computes its perimeter and area. The first letter entered (R, S, or C) indicates the type of figure to be processed. This letter is converted by function FIGCONVERT to a scalar value of type FIGKIND (RECTANGLE, SQUARE, CIRCLE, EMPTY) where the scalar value EMPTY has been added to signal an illegal input character. A sample run is shown in Fig. 9.5b.

```
PROGRAM GEOMETRY;
(* COMPUTES PERIMETER AND AREA OF A FIGURE *)

CONST
  PI = 3.14159;

TYPE
  FIGKIND = (RECTANGLE, SQUARE, CIRCLE, EMPTY);
  FIGURE = RECORD
    CASE FIG : FIGKIND OF
      RECTANGLE : (WIDTH, HEIGHT : REAL);
      SQUARE : (SIDE : REAL);
      CIRCLE : (RADIUS : REAL);
      EMPTY : ()
    END; (* FIGURE *)

VAR
  OBJECT : FIGURE;
  FIGTYPE : CHAR;
  PERIMETER, AREA : REAL;

(* INSERT FUNCTION FIGCONVERT HERE *)

BEGIN
  WRITELN ('R(ECTANGLE, S(QUARE, OR C(IRCLE ? ');
  READ (FIGTYPE);
  WRITELN;
  WITH OBJECT DO
    BEGIN
      FIG := FIGCONVERT(FIGTYPE);
      CASE FIG OF
        RECTANGLE :
          BEGIN
            WRITE ('ENTER WIDTH AND HEIGHT: ');
```

(continued)

```
            READLN (WIDTH, HEIGHT);
            AREA := WIDTH * HEIGHT;
            PERIMETER := 2 * (WIDTH + HEIGHT);
            WRITELN ('AREA = ', AREA :7:2,
                    '        PERIMETER = ', PERIMETER :7:2)
          END;
        SQUARE :
          BEGIN
            WRITE ('LENGTH OF SIDE: '); READLN (SIDE);
            AREA := SQR(SIDE);
            PERIMETER := 4 * SIDE;
            WRITELN ('AREA = ', AREA :7:2,
                    '        PERIMETER = ', PERIMETER :7:2)
          END;
        CIRCLE :
          BEGIN
            WRITE ('RADIUS: '); READLN (RADIUS);
            AREA := PI * SQR(RADIUS);
            PERIMETER := 2 * PI * RADIUS;
            WRITELN ('AREA = ', AREA :7:2,
                    '        PERIMETER = ', PERIMETER :7:2)
          END;
        EMPTY : WRITELN ('FIGURE ', FIGTYPE, ' IS INVALID')
      END (* CASE *)
    END (* WITH *)
END.
```

Fig. 9.5a Program to compute areas and perimeters.

```
R(ECTANGLE, S(QUARE, OR C(IRCLE ? R
ENTER WIDTH AND HEIGHT : 5 6.5
AREA = 32.50        PERIMETER = 23.00
```

Fig. 9.5b A sample run of the program in Fig. 9.5a.

Exercise 9.1: Add the variant

```
        TRIANGLE : (SIDE1, SIDE2, ANGLE : REAL);
```

to FIGURE and modify the program in Fig. 9.5a to process triangles as well.

Exercise 9.2: Write the functions MARITALCONVERT (called in Fig. 9.4) and FIGCONVERT (called in Fig. 9.5a).

9.4   TEXT AND INTERACTIVE FILES

9.4.1   Introduction to Files

In all our programming so far, we have provided a separate group of external data items for each program. These data items "belonged" to that program and could not be used by another. Each data item was read from the keyboard as the program executed, and could not be read more than once. Furthermore, all output generated was printed on the screen and could not be processed at some later time.

It would be desirable to be able to save a file of data on disk just as we save a program file. This would enable us to reuse the data for a program as often as we wish without having to retype it. Similarly, the output generated by a program could be saved as a file and used later as input data for another program.

A file is physically located in secondary storage (disk) rather than the main computer memory (See Section 1.2.5). Consequently, files can be extremely large. Each file consists of a collection of *file components* of the same type. Normally, only one component of a file will be stored in main memory and processed at a given time.

9.4.2   Files of Characters

Before discussing user-defined file types, we shall discuss two file types that are predefined in UCSD PASCAL—TEXT and INTERACTIVE. Both TEXT and INTERACTIVE are file types whose individual components are elements of the PASCAL character set. You have been using two files of characters throughout this book without being aware of it. The system file INPUT (type INTERACTIVE) consists of all characters entered as data at the keyboard. The system file OUTPUT consists of all characters displayed on the screen.

Rather than enter data interactively during program execution, it is possible to create and save a file of characters in advance using the system editor. This data file can later be specified as the input file for a program and read during execution of that program.

Generally, any file of characters that we create and store on disk will be type TEXT. The system files INPUT, KEYBOARD, and OUTPUT are type INTERACTIVE since they are read or displayed interactively (as they are created). No permanent record of these files is retained on disk.

The terminal session shown in Fig. 9.6 creates and saves a data file named 'VOL1:MYFILE'. This file is stored on disk volume VOL1: and consists of a sequence of individual characters as shown below.

file 'VOL1:MYFILE'

I		A	M		A	N		I	N	P	U	T		F	I	L	E	.		R	E	A	D		M	E	!		EOF

The shaded boxes represent the end-of-line marks that are inserted in the file whenever a carriage return < CR > is pressed. The box marked EOF represents a special character used to denote the end of a file. The end-of-file mark is inserted when the < ETX > key is pressed.

```
>EDIT: A(DJST, C(PY, D(LETE, F(IND, I(NSRT, J(MP, R(PLACE,
       Q(UIT, X(CHNG, Z(AP
I
I AM AN INPUT FILE.<CR>
READ ME!<CR>
<ETX>
>EDIT: A(DJST, C(PY, D(LETE, F(IND, I(NSRT, J(MP, R(PLACE,
       Q(UIT, X(CHNG, Z(AP
Q
>QUIT:
     U(PDATE THE WORKFILE AND LEAVE
     E(XIT WITHOUT UPDATING
     R(ETURN TO THE EDITOR WITHOUT UPDATING
     W(RITE TO A FILE NAME AND RETURN
W
WRITE TO WHAT FILE? VOL1:MYFILE
```

Fig. 9.6 Creating a file of type text.

The program in Fig. 9.7 is used to read each character of file 'VOL1:MYFILE' and display it on the screen. The statement

```
          VAR
             INFILE : TEXT;
```

identifies INFILE as a file of type TEXT. The statement

```
          RESET (INFILE, 'VOL1:MYFILE');
```

associates INFILE with the actual file named 'VOL1:MYFILE' (or 'VOL1: MYFILE.TEXT') created earlier. The RESET statement *opens* the file for input by setting the file position pointer for file INFILE to the first character in the file. The *file position pointer* keeps track of the next character to be read in a file.

```
PROGRAM ECHOTEXT;
(* ECHO PRINTS A DATA FILE *)

VAR
  NEXTCH : CHAR;
  INFILE : TEXT;

BEGIN
  (* OPEN INFILE FOR INPUT *)
  RESET (INFILE, 'VOL1:MYFILE')

  (* ECHO EVERY CHARACTER *)
  WHILE NOT EOF(INFILE) DO
    BEGIN
      READ (INFILE, NEXTCH);
      WRITE (NEXTCH)
    END; (* WHILE *)

  (* TERMINATE PROCESSING OF INFILE *)
  CLOSE (INFILE)
END.
```

Fig. 9.7 Echo printing a data file of type TEXT.

Inside the loop, the statements

```
READ (INFILE, NEXTCH);
WRITE (NEXTCH)
```

read and echo print the character selected by the file position pointer for INFILE. Since the end-of-line mark is converted to a blank when stored in NEXTCH, it will print as a blank; the number of characters printed per line will depend only on the screen size.

The loop repetition test

```
NOT EOF(INFILE)
```

uses the built-in function EOF (end-of-file) to test whether all characters of file INFILE have been processed. The value of EOF(INFILE) is initialized to false and remains false as long as there are characters in file INFILE that have not yet been read. After all characters in file INFILE are echo printed, the WHILE loop will be exited and the statement

```
CLOSE (INFILE)
```

terminates the processing of file INFILE. Any file that is opened for input or output must be closed.

The program segment in Fig. 9.8 could be used to display each input line of file INFILE on a separate output line.

```
WHILE NOT EOF(INFILE) DO
  BEGIN
    WHILE NOT EOLN(INFILE) DO
      BEGIN
        READ (INFILE, NEXTCH);
        WRITE (NEXTCH);
      END; (* LINE *)
    READLN (INFILE);
    WRITELN
END; (* FILE *)
```

Fig. 9.8   Line-by-line echo print.

The inner loop will be exited whenever the character selected by the file position pointer is an end-of-line mark. The READLN statement advances the file position pointer for INFILE to the first character of the next input line. The WRITELN statement terminates the line being displayed at the terminal.

The effect of the first execution of the READLN statement is illustrated below.

Before READLN (INFILE)

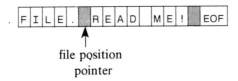

file position
pointer

After first READLN (INFILE)

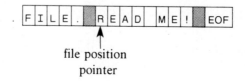

file position
pointer

The second execution of READLN advances the file position pointer to the end-of-file mark causing the loop repetition test NOT EOF(INFILE) to fail.

After second READLN (INFILE)

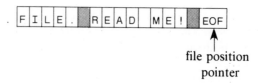

file position
pointer

In the program segment shown in Fig. 9.8, file INFILE is passed as the first parameter to the built-in functions EOF and EOLN and the system procedures READ and READLN. If this parameter is omitted, the system file INPUT is assumed to be the file being read or tested. (We have previously used the system file KEYBOARD as a parameter to indicate that data should be read from the keyboard, but not displayed.)

As an alternative to printing each character at the terminal, we can save some or all of these characters on an output file. The procedure shown in Fig. 9.9 creates an output file that consists of only the non-blank characters in the input file.

```
PROGRAM SQUEEZE;
(* CREATING A FILE OF NON-BLANK CHARACTERS *)

CONST
  BLANK = ' ';

VAR
  NEXTCH : CHAR;
  INFILE, OUTFILE : TEXT;

BEGIN
  (* OPEN INFILE FOR INPUT *)
  (* OPEN OUTFILE FOR OUTPUT *)
  RESET (INFILE, 'VOL1:MYFILE');
  REWRITE (OUTFILE, 'VOL1:COMPRESS');

  (* COPY NON-BLANK CHARACTERS TO OUTFILE *)
  WHILE NOT EOF(INFILE) DO
    BEGIN
      WHILE NOT EOLN(INFILE) DO
```

(*continued*)

```
        BEGIN
           READ (INFILE, NEXTCH);
           IF NEXTCH <> BLANK THEN
              WRITE (OUTFILE, NEXTCH)
        END; (* WHILE *)
      READLN (INFILE);
      WRITELN (OUTFILE)
    END; (* WHILE *)

  (* CLOSE ALL FILES *)
  CLOSE (INFILE);
  CLOSE (OUTFILE, LOCK)
END.
```

Fig. 9.9 Compressing a file.

The statement

```
        REWRITE (OUTFILE, 'VOL1:COMPRESS');
```

associates OUTFILE with the external file named 'COMPRESS' on volume VOL1: and initializes this file to a file of zero components. The string 'COM-PRESS' is temporarily inserted in the file directory of volume VOL1: by the PASCAL system and 'VOL1:COMPRESS' will be the name used to reference this file in the future if it is retained as a permanent file. The name OUTFILE is used throughout the program to refer to the file being created.

The statement

```
        IF NEXTCH <> BLANK THEN
           WRITE (OUTFILE, NEXTCH)
```

appends each non-blank character read to the end of the file being created.

The statement

```
        WRITELN (OUTFILE)
```

inserts an end-of-line mark in file OUTFILE. This statement is executed whenever an end-of-line mark is encountered in the input file. After the input file (INFILE) shown earlier is processed, file OUTFILE would be stored on disk as

file OUTFILE

The last statement in the program

```
        CLOSE (OUTFILE, LOCK)
```

instructs the PASCAL system to make OUTFILE a permanent file. The file string 'COMPRESS' is retained in the directory of disk VOL1. If the statement

```
        CLOSE (OUTFILE)
```

were used instead, the file string 'COMPRESS' would be removed from the disk directory and all would be lost.

File OUTFILE can be associated with the line printer on your system (if one is available) by using the statement

```
REWRITE (OUTFILE, 'PRINTER:');
```

to open the output file. The statement

```
WRITE (OUTFILE, NEXTCH)
```

will send NEXTCH to the line printer instead of storing it on disk. In general, any program writing to a text file can be modified in this way to use the line printer as an output device. The file variable associated with the line printer (OUTFILE above) should be specified as a parameter in each WRITE(LN) statement that directs output to the line printer. The CLOSE statement is not required here and should be omitted. (On some systems, the RESET statement must be used to open the file associated with the line printer.)

In the next sections, we shall learn how to process user-defined file types with records as components. We shall utilize many of the features already discussed and introduce the system procedures PUT and GET for the storage and retrieval of file records, respectively.

Exercise 9.3: What would happen if the READLN command were omitted from the program in Fig. 9.9?

Exercise 9.4: Modify the program in Fig. 7.15c to read data from an input file instead of the keyboard.

9.5 USER-DEFINED FILE TYPES

We can define file types with components that are any standard or user-defined data type. Generally, the components of a file are records. (We shall use these terms interchangeably.) Instead of using the system editor, a file of records must be created by execution of a PASCAL program. The data for that program could be entered interactively or read from a previously created file of type TEXT.

Example 9.3: The program in Fig. 9.10 creates a file that represents the inventory of a bookstore. Each component of this file, INVENTORY, is a record of type BOOK since INVENTORY is declared as type BOOKFILE (FILE OF BOOK). The information saved in each component consists of a four-digit stock number, the author and title, the price, and the quantity on hand.

Since a file is generally too large to be stored in its entirety in main memory, a *file buffer variable* is allocated in main memory for each file being processed by a program. The buffer variable contains storage space for the file component currently being processed and it acts as a "window" through which the file can be accessed.

The buffer variable for file INVENTORY is represented by INVENTORY↑.

```
PROGRAM BUILDINV;
(* CREATE INVENTORY FILE FROM DATA ENTERED AT TERMINAL *)

TYPE
  BOOK = RECORD
    STOCKNUM : 1111..10000;
    AUTHOR : STRING[20];
    TITLE : STRING[20];
    PRICE : REAL;
    QUANTITY : INTEGER
  END; (* BOOK *)
  BOOKFILE = FILE OF BOOK;

VAR
  INVENTORY : BOOKFILE;
  MORE : CHAR;

BEGIN
  (* OPEN FILE INVENTORY *)
  REWRITE (INVENTORY, 'VOL1:INVENTORY');

  (* READ ALL BOOK DATA AND CREATE INVENTORY FILE *)
  MORE := 'Y';
  WHILE MORE = 'Y' DO
    BEGIN
      (* ASSEMBLE DATA IN FILE BUFFER VARIABLE *)
      WITH INVENTORY↑ DO
        BEGIN
          WRITE ('STOCK #'); READLN (STOCKNUM);
          WRITE ('AUTHOR: '); READLN (AUTHOR);
          WRITE ('TITLE: '); READLN (TITLE);
          WRITE ('PRICE $'); READLN (PRICE);
          WRITE ('QUANTITY = '); READLN (QUANTITY)
        END; (* WITH *)
      PUT (INVENTORY);
      WRITE ('MORE RECORDS ? (Y OR N) '); READ (MORE);
      WRITELN
    END; (* WHILE *)

  (* CLOSE INVENTORY FILE *)
  WRITELN ('FILE INVENTORY CREATED');
  CLOSE (INVENTORY, LOCK)
END.
```

Fig. 9.10 Creating file INVENTORY.

On some systems, the carat symbol (∧) is used instead of the up arrow. (*Caution*: The up arrow character should be a different key than the one used to position the cursor upwards.)

The **REWRITE** statement opens file **INVENTORY** for output. The **WHILE** loop causes the individual data fields of each book to be read and written as a record (type **BOOK**) to file **OUTFILE**.

The statement

WITH INVENTORY↑ DO

specifies file buffer variable INVENTORY↑ as the record to be manipulated. Consequently, the input data are assembled in this file buffer variable. The statement

PUT (INVENTORY);

appends the data in this file buffer variable to the current end of file INVENTORY. The file buffer variable becomes undefined after each PUT operation.

After all records are processed, file INVENTORY is closed and retained as a permanent file. After a file has been closed, it is possible to reopen it for further processing.

Example 9.4: Procedure ECHOPRINT (see Fig. 9.11) reads all records of the file represented by parameter INVENTORY and prints the stock number, price, and quantity fields of each record. A record number is also printed indicating the relative position of each record in the file, starting with record number 0. The file's directory name is first read into variable FILENAME.

```
PROCEDURE ECHOPRINT (VAR INVENTORY : BOOKFILE);
(* ECHO PRINT A FILE *)

VAR
  FILENAME : STRING[15];
  RECNUM : INTEGER;

BEGIN
  (* OPEN INVENTORY FILE FOR INPUT *)
  WRITE ('FILE TO BE PRINTED: '); READLN (FILENAME);
  RESET (INVENTORY, FILENAME);

  (* ECHO ALL RECORDS *)
  RECNUM := 0;
  WHILE NOT EOF(INVENTORY) DO
    BEGIN
      WITH INVENTORY↑ DO
        WRITELN (RECNUM, STOCKNUM, PRICE, QUANTITY);
      GET (INVENTORY);
      RECNUM := RECNUM + 1
    END; (* WHILE *)

  (* CLOSE INVENTORY FILE *)
  WRITELN ('ALL RECORDS PRINTED');
  CLOSE (INVENTORY)
END; (* ECHOPRINT *)
```

Fig. 9.11 Procedure ECHOPRINT.

The GET operator is used in procedure ECHOPRINT to copy the file component selected by the file position pointer to the file buffer variable (INVENTO-

RY↑). After the copy is performed, the file position pointer is advanced as illustrated in Fig. 9.12. As shown, the file position pointer always points ahead to the next record to be accessed.

After RESET (INVENTORY)

INVENTORY↑   file INVENTORY

1112	1234	1689	
SAM . . .	BILL . . .	JOE . . .	
PASCAL . . .	HOW . . .	MY . . .	
8.25	6.95	7.80	
50	200	25	

file position
pointer

INVENTORY↑ buffer:

| 1112 |
| SAM . . . |
| PASCAL . . . |
| 8.25 |
| 50 |

After GET (INVENTORY)

INVENTORY↑   file INVENTORY

1112	1234	1689	
SAM . . .	BILL . . .	JOE . . .	
PASCAL . . .	HOW . . .	MY . . .	
8.25	6.95	7.80	
50	200	25	

file position
pointer

INVENTORY↑ buffer:

| 1234 |
| BILL . . . |
| HOW . . . |
| 6.95 |
| 200 |

Fig. 9.12 RESET and GET operations.

   Procedure ECHOPRINT begins by reading the name of the file to be processed into string variable FILENAME. The RESET operation repositions the file position pointer to the first file component and initializes the end-of-file function (EOF(INVENTORY)) to false. The PASCAL system performs an initial GET operation, copying the first file component (record number 0) to the file buffer variable and advancing the file position pointer to the second file component (record number 1).

   During each repetition of the WHILE loop, the current value of the three specified fields of the file buffer variable are printed, and the next file component is copied to the file buffer variable. After the last record is copied to the file buffer variable, the file position pointer is advanced beyond the end of the file. However, the value of EOF (INVENTORY) remains false until the next GET operation is attempted. Consequently, the WHILE loop will be executed one more time causing the last file component to be displayed.

   The file operators introduced so far are described in the displays that follow.

File Declaration

file-id = FILE OF *comp-type*

Interpretation: The file type *file-id* is declared with components of type *comp-type*.

REWRITE Procedure

REWRITE (*outfile, filestring*)

Interpretation: The REWRITE procedure opens file *outfile* for writing. File *outfile* is initialized to a file of zero components. The string *filestring* is inserted in the file directory. If *outfile* is made a permanent file, *filestring* will be retained in the directory as its name.

RESET Procedure

RESET (*infile, filestring*)

Interpretation: If *filestring* is located in the disk directory, then this file is opened for input as file *infile*; otherwise, an I/O execution error will occur. If there is no error, the EOF function for file *infile* is initialized to false and an initial GET operation is performed.

EOF Function

EOF (*infile*)

Interpretation: The function value is initialized to false when file *infile* is opened. The function value is changed to true when a GET operation is performed after the file position pointer has advanced beyond the last file record. For a file of characters (TEXT or INTERACTIVE) the function value is changed to true immediately after the last character is read.

GET Operator

GET (*infile*)

Interpretation: The data in the component of file *infile* selected by its file position pointer are transferred to the associated file buffer variable (*infile↑*) and the file position pointer is advanced to the next file component.

PUT Operator

PUT (*outfile*)

Interpretation: The buffer variable *outfile↑* is appended to file *outfile* and *outfile↑* becomes undefined.

> **CLOSE Procedure**
>
> > CLOSE (*file*)
> > CLOSE (*file*, LOCK)
> > CLOSE (*file*, PURGE)
>
> **Interpretation:** The first form should be used to close an existing file that has been opened for reading or to close a newly created file that is not to be retained. The parameter LOCK specifies that a new file is to be retained. The parameter PURGE specifies that an existing file is to be deleted.

The CLOSE statement is not part of standard PASCAL. In standard PASCAL, both RESET and REWRITE are used with a single parameter only; the parameter *filestring* is not used.

The PUT and GET operators may also be used with TEXT and INTERACTIVE files; although, it is generally more convenient to use READ and WRITE. The main difference between TEXT and INTERACTIVE files is that an initial GET operation is not performed when an INTERACTIVE file is opened; an initial GET is performed on all other file types opened for input.

Exercise 9.5:   Show the first three lines generated by procedure ECHOPRINT for the file in Fig. 9.12.

Exercise 9.6:   Write a program that reads a name and a list of three exam scores for each student in a class, and copies this information onto a sequential file called GRADES.

Exercise 9.7   Write a procedure that reads and echo prints the file GRADES.

9.6   FILE UPDATE AND MERGE

9.6.1   Adding Components to a File

It is very rare that a file is not changed in some way after it is created. For example, we may wish to add new items to our inventory file or perhaps modify some of the existing items. We shall discuss how to modify files in this section.

Example 9.5:   Our bookstore has received a new shipment of books and we would like to add the new titles to the end of the inventory file created by the program in Fig. 9.10. There are many ways to do this. One would be to use procedure ECHOPRINT to advance the file-position pointer just beyond the current last record. Additional data could then be read and appended to the end of the file using a WHILE loop similar to that shown in Fig. 9.10.

If there is no more room on the disk, then it would be necessary to create a new file on another disk that is a duplicate of the original inventory file. Additional data could then be appended to the new file. Procedure COPYFILE in Fig. 9.13 creates a new file (OUTFILE) that is a copy of an existing file (INFILE). The statements

```
              OUTFILE↑ := INFILE↑;
              PUT (OUTFILE);
              GET (INFILE)
```

are used to copy each record from the existing file to the new file. Note that we could also use system **FILER** to transfer (command T) the existing file to another disk; however, in this case the file position pointer would not be positioned at the end of the newly created file.

```
PROCEDURE COPYFILE (VAR INFILE, OUTFILE : BOOKFILE);
(* COPIES INFILE TO OUTFILE *)

VAR
  INNAME, OUTNAME : STRING[15];

BEGIN
  (* OPEN FILES *)
  WRITE ('TRANSFER WHAT FILE? '); READLN (INNAME);
  RESET (INFILE, INNAME);
  WRITE ('TRANSFER TO? '); READLN (OUTNAME);
  REWRITE (OUTFILE, OUTNAME);

  WHILE NOT EOF(INFILE) DO
    BEGIN
      OUTFILE↑ := INFILE↑;
      PUT (OUTFILE);
      GET (INFILE)
    END;

  (* CLOSE FILES *)
  CLOSE (INFILE);
  CLOSE (OUTFILE, LOCK)
END; (* COPYFILE *)
```

Fig. 9.13   Procedure COPYFILE.

In all of the file operations performed so far, each file was processed as a sequential file. The records of a sequential file must always be processed serially (in order) from beginning to end. We shall illustrate a different approach to file access in the next section.

9.6.2   Updating a Random Access File

Very often, we wish to read a file and modify one or more of its components based on new information. This process is called *updating* a file. In this section, we shall discuss how to update a file in UCSD PASCAL.

UCSD (but not standard) PASCAL allows us to access any arbitrary component of a file without first reading all components (records) that precede it. A file whose components may be accessed in an arbitrary order is called a *random access file*. Each record has a unique record number that indicates its relative position in the file (beginning with record 0). We must specify the number of the record that we wish to access; this number must be between 0 and $n-1$ if there are n records on the file.

Example 9.6: The program in Fig. 9.14 updates the bookstore inventory file based on today's sales of books. Each update transaction is entered at the terminal by specifying the number of the record (RECNUM) to be updated and the amount sold (SOLD). The program constant MAXRECNUM is the number of the last record on the file.

The inventory file must be opened for reading (and writing) using the RE-SET statement. If the value of RECNUM is within range, the first statement

```
SEEK (INVENTORY, RECNUM);
```

advances the file position pointer to record number RECNUM. The GET operation transfers this record to the file buffer variable and advances the file position pointer to the next record. The QUANTITY field of the file buffer variable is updated and the next SEEK returns the file position pointer to the record just read. The PUT operation replaces the old record with the data stored in the file buffer variable.

The SEEK procedure is described in the next display.

Procedure SEEK

SEEK (*iofile, recnum*)

Interpretation: The file position pointer is advanced to record number *recnum* of file *iofile*. Unpredictable results may occur if the value of *recnum* is negative or greater than $n-1$ for a file with n records. It is also unadvisable to perform two SEEK operations without an intervening GET or PUT.

```
PROGRAM BOOKUPDATE;
(* PERFORM A RANDOM ACCESS UPDATE *)

CONST
  MAXRECNUM = 100;

TYPE
  BOOK = RECORD
    STOCKNUM : 1111..10000;
    AUTHOR : STRING[20];
    TITLE : STRING[20];
    PRICE : REAL;
    QUANTITY: INTEGER
  END; (* BOOK *)
  BOOKFILE = FILE OF BOOK;

VAR
  INVENTORY : BOOKFILE;
  SOLD, RECNUM : INTEGER;
  INNAME : STRING[15];
```

```
BEGIN
  (* OPEN INVENTORY FILE FOR UPDATE *)
  WRITE ('INVENTORY FILE: '); READLN (INNAME);
  RESET (INVENTORY, INNAME);

  (* PROCESS ALL VALID UPDATE DATA *)
  WRITE ('ENTER RECORD # OR -1 : '); READLN (RECNUM);
  WHILE (RECNUM) >= O) AND (RECNUM <= MAXRECNUM) DO
    BEGIN
      SEEK (INVENTORY, RECNUM);
      GET (INVENTORY);
      WRITE ('QUANTITY SOLD = '); READLN (SOLD);
      INVENTORY↑.QUANTITY := INVENTORY↑.QUANTITY - SOLD;
      SEEK (INVENTORY, RECNUM);
      PUT (INVENTORY);
      WRITE ('ENTER RECORD # OR -1 : '); READLN (RECNUM)
    END; (* WHILE *)
  IF RECNUM = -1 THEN
    WRITELN ('UPDATE COMPLETE. ')
  ELSE
    WRITELN ('PROGRAM TERMINATED. RECORD # ', RECNUM,
             ' IS OUT OF RANGE O TO ', MAXRECNUM);

  (* CLOSE INVENTORY FILE *)
  CLOSE (INVENTORY)
END.
```

Fig. 9.14 Random access file update.

9.6.3 Sequential File Update

Random access files are not supported in standard PASCAL. If the majority of the records in a file are to be updated, then it will probably be more efficient to perform a sequential update; accessing all records in serial (rather than in random) order. In this case, the stock number of the record to be updated can be specified instead of its record number (relative position) which may not be known. However, a sequential update would require that all file records and all update transactions be arranged in order by stock number (or some other field).

Instead of selectively changing certain entries of an existing file, it will be necessary to create a brand new file whose components are similar or identical to the original. We must read each file component in sequence and determine whether or not it requires modification. If so, we change the affected fields of that component and copy it onto the new file. If no modification is required, the original file component is copied onto the new file. When we are all done, the new file will have the same number of components as the original file.

Problem 9.1: We wish to update the bookstore inventory file based on today's sales of books. Each update transaction specifies the stock number and amount of the item sold. We will assume that these entries are arranged in sequence according to stock number, as are the components of the file INVENTORY. The update operation should create a new inventory file.

Discussion: Each sales entry will be read into the record variable CURSALE. Each file component will be read from INVENTORY and copied to an output file (NEWINVENTORY) after any necessary updating.

Since the sales entries and file components are ordered by stock number, we can determine whether or not a file component needs updating by simply comparing its stock number to the current sales entry stock number (CURSALE. STOCK). If the file component's stock number is less than CURSALE.STOCK, then it should be copied directly to NEWINVENTORY (no sale of that book). If the file component's stock number matches CURSALE.STOCK, then the inventory amount should be reduced, the updated file component copied to NEWINVENTORY, and the next sales entry read. If a file component has a stock number greater than CURSALE.STOCK, this indicates that there was no prior file component that matched the current sales entry; consequently, CURSALE.STOCK is either out-of-order or invalid. In either case, an error message should be printed. After all sales entries are processed, any remaining file components should be copied directly to NEWINVENTORY.

The data table for Problem 9.1 is shown below followed by the level one algorithm.

Data Table for Problem 9.1

Constants

> SENTINEL = 10000, a sentinel stock number

Data types

> IDRANGE = 1111..SENTINEL
>
> BOOK = RECORD
>   STOCKNUM : IDRANGE;
>   AUTHOR : STRING[20];
>   TITLE : STRING[20];
>   PRICE : REAL;
>   QUANTITY : INTEGER
> END
>
> SALE = RECORD
>   STOCK : IDRANGE;
>   AMOUNT : INTEGER
> END
>
> BOOKFILE = FILE OF BOOK

Input variables	*Program variables*	*Output variables*
INVENTORY: Initial inventory file (BOOK-FILE)		NEWINVENTORY: Updated inventory file (BOOKFILE)

CURSALE: Stock number
and amount of each sale
(SALE)

Level One Algorithm

1. Prepare file INVENTORY for input and file NEWINVENTORY for output.
2. For each sales entry, write all file components with stock numbers smaller than CURSALE.STOCK directly to NEWINVENTORY; update the matching file component before writing it. Print an error message if the sales entry is not matched.
3. Copy any remaining components of file INVENTORY to file NEWINVENTORY.

The refinement of Step 2 will consist of a loop that reads each sales entry and calls procedure MATCHCOPY to copy all file components with smaller stock numbers and update the matching component if found (Step 2.3 below). An error message should be printed if MATCHCOPY is not able to locate the current sales entry stock number (CURSALE.STOCK). We shall use a program flag, FOUND, to indicate whether or not MATCHCOPY was successful. The additional data table entries and algorithm refinement follow.

Program variables

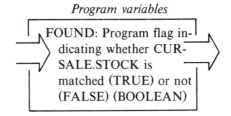

FOUND: Program flag indicating whether CURSALE.STOCK is matched (TRUE) or not (FALSE) (BOOLEAN)

Procedures referenced

MATCHCOPY: Writes all file components with stock numbers smaller than CURSALE.STOCK directly to NEWINVENTORY; updates the matching file component before writing it.

Level Two Refinements

Step 2   *For each sales entry, update the matching file component*

   2.1 WHILE more update transactions DO
      BEGIN
        2.2 Read the current sales entry
        2.3 Write all file components with smaller stock numbers directly to NEWINVENTORY; update the matching file component if present, and set FOUND
        2.4 IF NOT FOUND THEN
           Print an error message
      END

The file update process is illustrated in Table 9.1 for a collection of sales entries and a sample inventory file. Only the stock number and quantity are shown for each file component. The value of FOUND after each call to MATCHCOPY is shown to the right of the current sales entry for that call. Column 4 describes the effect of each sales entry, and column 5 shows the updated inventory file.

INVENTORY		Sales entry		FOUND	Effect of each sale	NEWINVENTORY	
1111	15	1111	5	TRUE	Update #1111	1111	10
		1234	15	FALSE	#1234 is invalid		
1345	15	1345	10	TRUE	Update #1345	1345	5
2222	20	4444	15	TRUE	Copy #2222 and #3333,	2222	20
3333	30				update #4444	3333	30
4444	15					4444	0
5556	30	10000			No more sales-copy	5556	30
6005	10				#5556 and #6005	6005	10
10000	0				and sentinel record	10000	0

Table 9.1 Sample File Update

To simplify Step 3 of the algorithm, we should reserve the largest stock number (10000) for a sentinel record and append this sentinel record to the end of file INVENTORY when it is first created. This record should also appear at the end of file NEWINVENTORY.

The main program is written in Fig. 9.15a. The sentinel stock number is entered to signal that all update transactions are read. After this, the last step in the main program (Step 3) is accomplished by the statements

```
CURSALE.AMOUNT := 0;
MATCHCOPY (CURSALE, INVENTORY, NEWINVENTORY, FOUND);
```

Since CURSALE.STOCK (value 10000) is larger than every file component stock number, any remaining file entries should be copied directly to NEWINVENTORY by procedure MATCHCOPY. The sentinel record will be updated and also copied.

```
PROGRAM UPDATEINVENTORY;
(* UPDATES INVENTORY FILE BASED ON CURRENT *)
(* SALES AND CREATES FILE NEWINVENTORY     *)

CONST
  SENTINEL = 10000;

TYPE
  IDRANGE = 1111..SENTINEL;
  BOOK = RECORD
    STOCKNUM : IDRANGE;
    AUTHOR : STRING[20];
    TITLE : STRING[20];
    PRICE : REAL;
    QUANTITY : INTEGER
  END; (* BOOK *)
```

(continued)

```
SALE = RECORD
  STOCK : IDRANGE;
  AMOUNT : INTEGER
END; (* SALE *)
BOOKFILE = FILE OF BOOK;

VAR
  INVENTORY, NEWINVENTORY : BOOKFILE;
  CURSALE : SALE;
  FOUND : BOOLEAN;

(* INSERT PROCEDURE MATCHCOPY HERE *)
(*$I UCSD5:MATCHCOPY                 *)

BEGIN
  (* PREPARE FILES INVENTORY AND NEWINVENTORY *)
  RESET (INVENTORY, 'VOL1:INVENTORY');
  REWRITE (NEWINVENTORY, 'VOL1:NEWINVEN');

  (* PROCESS ALL SALES *)
  WITH CURSALE DO
    BEGIN
      WRITELN ('ENTER 10000 OR A');
      WRITE ('STOCK # '); READLN (STOCK);
      WHILE STOCK <> SENTINEL DO
        BEGIN
          WRITE ('AMOUNT SOLD = '); READLN (AMOUNT);
          MATCHCOPY (CURSALE, INVENTORY, NEWINVENTORY,
                     FOUND);
          (* FLAG INVALID STOCK NUMBERS *)
          IF NOT FOUND THEN
            WRITELN ('INVALID STOCK NUMBER');
          WRITE ('STOCK #'); READLN (STOCK)
        END (* WHILE *)
    END; (* WITH *)

  (* COPY ALL REMAINING FILE COMPONENTS TO NEWINVENTORY *)
  CURSALE.AMOUNT := 0;
  MATCHCOPY (CURSALE, INVENTORY, NEWINVENTORY, FOUND);

  (* CLOSE FILES *)
  WRITELN ('UPDATE COMPLETE. ');
  CLOSE (INVENTORY);
  CLOSE (NEWINVENTORY, LOCK)
END.
```

Fig. 9.15a Main program for sequential file update.

The data table and algorithm for procedure MATCHCOPY are shown next.

Data Table for MATCHCOPY

Input parameters	*Update parameters*	*Output parameters*
INVENTORY, CUR-SALE	FOUND	NEWINVENTORY

Level One Algorithm for MATCHCOPY

1. Write all file components with stock numbers smaller than CURSALE. STOCK to NEWINVENTORY.

2. Update the next file component if it matches CURSALE.STOCK and signal success or failure.

    Steps 1 and 2 can be refined in a straightforward manner as shown next.

Level Two Refinements

Step 1   *Write all file components with smaller stock numbers*

    1.1   WHILE the file stock number is too small AND NOT EOF (INVEN-TORY) DO
          BEGIN
                Write the current file component to NEWINVENTORY
                Read the next file component from INVENTORY
          END

Step 2   *Update the next file component if it matches CURSALE.STOCK*

    2.1   IF the stock numbers match THEN
          BEGIN
                FOUND := TRUE
                Reduce the inventory amount by CURSALE.AMOUNT
                Write the updated file component to NEWINVENTORY
                Read the next file component from INVENTORY
          END
          ELSE
                FOUND := FALSE

    Procedure MATCHCOPY is shown in Fig. 9.15b.

Program Style

Passing a Boolean parameter as an error indicator

    The Boolean parameter FOUND is set by procedure MATCHCOPY just before returning to the main program. The main program tests the corresponding actual parameter (also named FOUND) to determine whether to print an error message or not.

    This technique of using a Boolean parameter to indicate the success or failure of a procedure is quite common in programming. It is a natural extension of the use of program flags to communicate results from one program step to another.

> **Program Style**
>
> *Effect of incorrect data values*
>
> In the program for Problem 9.1, there are a number of checks for bad input data. Procedure MATCHCOPY prints a warning message in the event an inventory quantity becomes negative. This could happen if the current sales amount is incorrect.
>
> It is also important to warn the user of an invalid or out-of-sequence stock number for the current sales entry (CURSALE.STOCK). If CURSALE. STOCK is incorrect and too small, FOUND will be set to false, MATCH-COPY will be exited without copying any file components, and an error message will be printed. However, if CURSALE.STOCK is incorrect and very large, a group of file components will be copied to NEWINVENTORY until a file component with a stock number greater than CURSALE.STOCK is reached. This may mean that subsequent valid sales entries will be incorrectly flagged as invalid because their matching file components have already been processed. It is not feasible to "back up" file INVENTORY and reexamine these earlier file components.
>
> If the current sales entries are in sequence by stock number, then only incorrect stock numbers will be flagged. In this case, all sales entries with valid numbers will be processed as desired.

```
PROCEDURE MATCHCOPY (CURSALE : SALE;
                     VAR INVENTORY, NEWINVENTORY : BOOKFILE;
                     VAR FOUND : BOOLEAN);
(* COPIES FILE COMPONENTS WITH STOCK NUMBERS SMALLER THAN   *)
(* CURSALE.STOCK FROM INVENTORY TO NEWINVENTORY. UPDATES    *)
(* THE FILE COMPONENT WITH MATCHING STOCKNUMBER IF PRESENT  *)
(* AND SETS FOUND TO INDICATE SEARCH RESULT                 *)
(*                                                          *)
(* INPUT PARAMETERS                                         *)
(*    CURSALE - CURRENT SALES ENTRY                         *)
(*    INVENTORY - ORIGINAL INVENTORY FILE                   *)
(* UPDATE PARAMETERS                                        *)
(*    FOUND - INDICATES WHETHER OR NOT CURSALE.STOCK IS     *)
(*               (OR WAS) MATCHED                           *)
(* OUTPUT PARAMETER                                         *)
(*    NEWINVENTORY - NEW INVENTORY FILE                     *)

VAR
  QTY : INTEGER;

BEGIN
  (* COPY ALL FILE COMPONENTS WITH STOCKNUMBER   *)
  (* SMALLER THAN CURSALE.STOCK TO NEWINVENTORY  *)
  WHILE (INVENTORY↑.STOCKNUM < CURSALE.STOCK) AND
        NOT EOF(INVENTORY) DO
    BEGIN
      NEWINVENTORY↑ := INVENTORY↑;
```

(continued)

```
      PUT (NEWINVENTORY);
      GET (INVENTORY)
    END; (* WHILE *)

  (* UPDATE THE NEXT FILE COMPONENT IF IT MATCHES    *)
  (* CURSALE.STOCK AND SIGNAL SUCCESS OR FAILURE     *)
  WITH INVENTORY↑ DO
    IF STOCKNUM = CURSALE.STOCK THEN
      BEGIN
        FOUND := TRUE;
        QTY := QUANTITY - CURSALE.AMOUNT;
        IF QTY >= O THEN
          QUANTITY := QTY
        ELSE
          WRITELN ('ERROR IN STOCK #', STOCKNUM,
                   'QUANTITY = ', QTY);
        NEWINVENTORY↑ := INVENTORY↑;
        PUT (NEWINVENTORY);
        GET (INVENTORY)
      END
    ELSE
      FOUND := FALSE
  END; (* MATCHCOPY *)
```

Fig. 9.15b Procedure MATCHCOPY.

Exercise 9.8: Trace the execution of the program in Fig. 9.15 for the following sales entries: 1111 10, 2222 20, 3333 30, 5555 10. First, try the inventory file: 1111 30, 1115 10, 2000 18, 2500 90. Next, add three more file components: 3333 50, 4444 10, 5555 10. Finally, add the file components: 6666 10, 7777 15. Indicate which file components are processed by each call to MATCHCOPY and the value assigned to FOUND. Also, indicate which sales entries are flagged as invalid.

Exercise 9.9: Write a procedure that adds a fourth exam score to each component of the file GRADES created in Exercise 9.6. Assume that each student's name and fourth exam score are entered as data.

9.5.4 The File Merge Problem

A common problem when working with files is to update one file (master file) by merging information from a second file (update file). This process is illustrated in the following problem.

Problem 9.2: The Junk Mail Company has recently received a new mailing list (file UPDATE) that it wishes to merge with its master file (file OLDMASTER). Each of these files is in alphabetical order by name. The company wishes to produce a new master file (NEWMASTER) that is also in alphabetical order. Each file component is a record of type CLIENT

```
      CLIENT = RECORD
        NAME : STRING[20];
        HOME : ADDRESS
      END (*CLIENT*)
```

where ADDRESS is the record type described earlier in Section 9.2.

```
ADDRESS = RECORD
  STREETNUMBER : INTEGER;
  STREETNAME, CITY, STATE : STRING[10];
  ZIPCODE : INTEGER
END (*ADDRESS*)
```

Discussion: We will find it helpful to have a sentinel record at the end of each of the files UPDATE and OLDMASTER. The sentinel is the same for both files; one copy should be written at the end of the NEWMASTER file as well. The sentinel record contains the name 'ZZZ', which alphabetically follows all normal entries.

The file usage is summarized in the data table shown below. The level one algorithm follows the data table.

Data Table for Merge Problem

Data types

> CLIENTFILE = FILE OF CLIENT

Input files	*Output files*
OLDMASTER: The original mailing list in alphabetical order by name (CLIENTFILE)	NEWMASTER: The final mailing list, formed by merging OLDMASTER and UPDATE (CLIENTFILE)
UPDATE: The additions to be made to OLDMASTER, also in alphabetical order by name (CLIENTFILE)	

Procedures referenced

> MERGECOPY: Merges files OLDMASTER and UPDATE to file NEW-MASTER

Level One Algorithm for Main Program

1. Prepare files OLDMASTER and UPDATE for input and file NEWMASTER for output.
2. Merge files OLDMASTER and UPDATE to file NEWMASTER

Step 2 is performed by procedure MERGECOPY. The main program is shown in Fig. 9.16a.

Since the input files are in alphabetical order, MERGECOPY should read the first components and copy the smaller (alphabetically) to NEWMASTER. Next, the second component of the file that contained the smallest component

```
PROGRAM MERGE;
(* MERGES FILES OLDMASTER AND UPDATE    *)
(* TO CREATE NEWMASTER                   *)

TYPE
  ADDRESS = RECORD
    STREETNUMBER : INTEGER;
    STREETNAME, CITY, STATE : STRING[10];
    ZIPCODE : INTEGER
  END; (* ADDRESS *)
  CLIENT = RECORD
    NAME := STRING[20];
    HOME : ADDRESS
  END; (* CLIENT *)
  CLIENTFILE = FILE OF CLIENT;

VAR
  OLDMASTER, UPDATE, NEWMASTER : CLIENTFILE;

(* INSERT PROCEDURE MERGECOPY HERE *)
(*$I UCSD5:MERGECOPY                    *)

BEGIN
  (* OPEN FILES *)
  RESET (OLDMASTER, 'USCD5:OLDMASTER');
  RESET (UPDATE, 'UCSD5:UPDATE');
  REWRITE (NEWMASTER, 'UCSD5:NEWMASTER');

  (* MERGE FILES OLDMASTER AND UPDATE TO NEWMASTER *)
  MERGECOPY (OLDMASTER, UPDATE, NEWMASTER);

  (* CLOSE FILES *)
  WRITELN ('MERGE COMPLETE ');
  CLOSE (NEWMASTER, LOCK);
  CLOSE (OLDMASTER);
  CLOSE (UPDATE)
END.
```

Fig. 9.16a   File merge program.

should be read and compared to the first component of the other input file. Again, the smaller component should be copied to NEWMASTER, and the next component on its input file should be read. This process should continue until the sentinel record on each input file is read.

The algorithm is illustrated in Table 9.2 for two sample files (shown on the left); only the NAME fields of each file are shown. The file buffer variables OLDMASTER↑ and UPDATE↑ contain the file components being compared at each point. The alphabetically smaller name in columns 3 and 4 is always copied to NEWMASTER as shown in column 5. The sentinel name ZZZ should be copied to the end of NEWMASTER as the last step.

OLDMASTER	UPDATE	OLDMASTER↑	UPDATE↑	NEWMASTER
ABE	BOB	ABE	BOB	ABE
DAN	CAT	DAN	BOB	BOB
MEG	EVE	DAN	CAT	CAT
SUE	ZZZ	DAN	EVE	DAN
ZZZ		MEG	EVE	EVE
		MEG	ZZZ	MEG
		SUE	ZZZ	SUE
		ZZZ	ZZZ	ZZZ

Table 9.2 Sample File Merge

The data table and algorithm for MERGECOPY follow.

Data Table for MERGECOPY

Input parameters	*Output parameters*
OLDMASTER, UPDATE	NEWMASTER

Level One Algorithm for MERGECOPY

1. Compare the names of the current clients. Copy the client with the alphabetically smaller name onto NEWMASTER. Read the next client from the file containing the client that was just copied. Continue to merge until the end of both files is reached.
2. Copy the sentinel record to NEWMASTER.

Level Two Refinements

Step 2

2.1   REPEAT
          IF OLDMASTER↑.NAME < UPDATE↑.NAME THEN
              2.2 Append OLDMASTER↑ to NEWMASTER and get the
                  next record of OLDMASTER
          ELSE IF OLDMASTER↑.NAME = UPDATE↑.NAME THEN
              2.3 Append UPDATE↑ to NEWMASTER and get the
                  next record of OLDMASTER and UPDATE
          ELSE
              2.4 Append UPDATE↑ to NEWMASTER and get the
                  next record of UPDATE
      UNTIL the end of both input files is reached

As shown in Step 2.3 the more recent address (contained in UPDATE↑) is copied to NEWMASTER when both file buffer variables contain the same client name. This will be the case when the sentinel record of each input file is read. After the sentinel record is copied to NEWMASTER both EOF function tests will evaluate to true and procedure MERGECOPY (see Fig. 9.16b) will be exited.

```
PROCEDURE MERGECOPY (VAR OLDMASTER, UPDATE,
                          NEWMASTER : CLIENTFILE);
(* MERGES OLDMASTER AND UPDATE TO FILE NEWMASTER     *)
(* MAINTAINING ALPHABETICAL ORDER                    *)
(*                                                   *)
(* INPUT PARAMETERS                                  *)
(*    OLDMASTER - ORIGINAL MASTER CLIENT FILE        *)
(*    UPDATE - FILE OF NEW CLIENTS                   *)
(* OUTPUT PARAMETERS                                 *)
(*    NEWMASTER - NEW MASTER CLIENT FILE             *)

BEGIN
  REPEAT
    IF OLDMASTER↑.NAME < UPDATE↑.NAME THEN
      BEGIN
        NEWMASTER↑ := OLDMASTER↑;
        PUT (NEWMASTER);
        GET (OLDMASTER)
      END
    ELSE IF OLDMASTER↑.NAME = UPDATE↑.NAME THEN
      BEGIN
        NEWMASTER↑ := UPDATE↑;
        PUT (NEWMASTER);
        GET (OLDMASTER);
        GET (UPDATE)
      END
    ELSE
      BEGIN
        NEWMASTER↑ := UPDATE↑;
        PUT (NEWMASTER);
        GET (UPDATE)
      END (* IF *)
    UNTIL EOF(OLDMASTER) AND EOF(UPDATE)
END; (* MERGECOPY *)
```

Fig. 9.16b   Procedure MERGECOPY.

Exercise 9.10:   Let FILEA and FILEB be two files containing the name and identification number of the students in two different programming classes. Assume that these files are arranged in ascending order by student number and that no student is in both classes. Write a program to read the information on FILEA and FILEB, and merge them onto a third file (FILEC) retaining the ascending order.

9.7   COMMON PROGRAMMING ERRORS

9.7.1   Record Errors

In working with hierarchical records, one must be extremely careful in specifying field selectors. Remember that a complete path to the field must be specified. For example, if we wished to reference the field of record variable PRO-GRAMMER that represents the year of birth, it would not be sufficient to write

PROGRAMMER.YEAR

Instead, the full field selector

PROGRAMMER.BIRTHDATE.YEAR

must be specified if YEAR is a field of the sub-record PROGRAMMER. BIRTHDATE.

If a record has both fixed and variant parts, be sure to define the fixed part first. Remember that the value of the tag field determines the form of the variant part. Consequently, only the fields corresponding to the current tag field value are defined and may be referenced. It would be illegal to attempt to reference a field associated with a different tag field value. Also, all field names for a given record must be distinct.

9.7.2 File Errors

When defining new files, remember that the file name must be listed in the program statement and its file type declared in the type declaration section. In using the READ or WRITE procedure with a text file, be sure to specify the file name as the first argument of the READ or WRITE procedure.

In using text files, be sure that the type of each variable in the input or output list is suitable. This includes variables of type CHAR, REAL, INTEGER, and STRING. Remember that READ(LN), WRITE(LN) and EOLN may only be used with text files. The GET and PUT operators must be used with other file types.

When processing random access files, the record number passed to the SEEK procedure must be between 0 and $n-1$ if there are n records.

9.8 SUMMARY

In this chapter, we revisited the record data type and studied hierarchical records as well as record variants. We learned how to reference the fields of a hierarchical record by including any relevant sub-record names in the field selector. We also used nested WITH statements to abbreviate the full field selector. A CASE statement whose case selector was the tag-field name was used to reference fields in the variant part of a record.

We studied two predefined files of characters, TEXT and INTERACTIVE.

We also learned how to create and manipulate files of records. Once created, a file can be reused by different PASCAL procedures or programs. We performed both a sequential and random update of an existing file and saw how to merge two files onto a third file.

PROGRAMMING PROBLEMS

9.3   Consider the inventory file shown in Table 9.1. In Problem 9.1, we assumed that the entries on this file were in sequence according to stock number, ordered from 1, 2, and so on. Write a program to read the stock entries for a dozen or so inventory items and build a sequential file containing these items. (You are not to make any assumptions concerning the ordering of the stock numbers of these items).

9.4   Write a program to read the sequential file created in Problem 9.3, sort the file in ascending order according to stock number and write the results on a new file. You may assume that the entire sequential file will fit in memory at once (Use an array large enough to accommodate the sequential file entries that you made in Problem 9.3).

9.5   Create a sequential file SALMEN containing the salaries of 10 men, and a second sequential file SALWOMEN containing the salaries of 10 women. For each employee on these files, there is an employee number (four digits), an employee name (a string) and an employee salary. Each file is arranged in ascending order by employee number. Write a program that will read each of these files and merge the contents onto a third file, SALARY, retaining the ascending order of employee numbers. For each employee written to the file SALARY, write an "M" (for male) or an "F" (for female) following the employee number.

9.6   Write a program to read and print the file SALARY and compute the average salary for all employees.

9.7   Assume you have a file of records each containing a person's last name, first name, birth date, and sex. Create a new file containing only first names and sex. Also, print out the complete name of every person whose last name begins with the letter A, C, F, or P through Z and was born in a month that begins with the letter J.

MULTIDIMENSIONAL ARRAYS

10

10.1   INTRODUCTION

We have been introduced to several simple data types: real, integer, string, Boolean, character, scalar and subrange types. In addition, we have used several data structures for identifying and referencing a collection of similar data items. One of these, the array, enables us to store a list of related data items in memory. All of these data items are referred to by the same name, and the array subscript is used to distinguish among the individual array elements.

In this chapter, the use of the array will be extended to facilitate the convenient organization of related data items into tables and lists of more than one dimension. For example, we will see how a two-dimensional array with three rows and three columns can be used to represent a tic-tac-toe board. This array has nine elements, each of which can be referenced by specifying the row subscript (1, 2, or 3) and column subscript (1, 2, or 3), as shown in Fig. 10.1. Similarly, we shall see that arrays of three or more dimensions can be used to represent collections of data items that can be conveniently described in terms of a multidimensional picture.

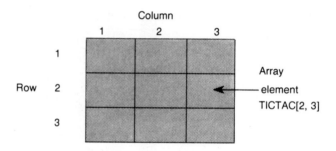

Fig. 10.1   Representation of a tic-tac-toe board as a two-dimensional array, TICTAC.

10.2   DECLARATION OF MULTIDIMENSIONAL ARRAYS

The declarations

```
VAR
    TICTAC : ARRAY[1..3] OF ARRAY[1..3] OF CHAR;
```

or

```
VAR
    TICTAC : ARRAY[1..3, 1..3] OF CHAR;
```

allocate memory space for an array TICTAC with nine elements.

The first declaration states that the element type for the array TICTAC (subscript type—1..3) is, in fact, an array itself (subscript type—1..3, element type—CHAR). The second form is a more convenient abbreviation that is also recognized by the compiler. It states that TICTAC is a two-dimensional array with row subscript 1..3 and column subscript 1..3. The general form of the multi-dimensional array declaration is described in the next display.

Array Type (Multidimensional)

> ARRAY[*subscript*$_1$] OF ARRAY[*subscript*$_2$] OF . . . ARRAY[*subscript*$_n$] OF
> *element-type*

or   ARRAY[*subscript*$_1$, *subscript*$_2$,..., *subscript*$_n$] OF *element-type*

Interpretation: *Subscript*$_i$ represents the subscript-type of dimension i of a multidimensional array. Any finite scalar type or subrange may be specified. The *element-type* may be any standard or previously defined data type.

The array TABLE declared below

```
VAR
    TABLE : ARRAY[1..7, 1..5, 1..6] OF REAL;
```

consists of three dimensions: The first subscript may take on values from 1 to 7; the second, from 1 to 5; and the third from 1 to 6. There are a total of $7 \times 5 \times 6$, or 210 elements in the array TABLE.

10.3   MANIPULATION OF MULTIDIMENSIONAL ARRAYS

10.3.1   Manipulation of Individual Array Elements

We would like to be able to identify and reference the individual elements of a multidimensional array. This is accomplished by using a subscripted reference to the array, as shown next.

Subscripted Array Reference (Multidimensional Arrays)

$$array\text{-}name \ [s_1, s_2,..., s_n]$$

Interpretation: Each of the s_i is a subscript expression corresponding to the subscript-type of dimension i. The value of each expression determines which element of *array-name* is manipulated.

In the case of a two-dimensional array, the first subscript of an array reference is considered the row subscript and the second subscript the column subscript. Consequently, the subscripted array reference

```
TICTAC[2,3]
```

selects the element in row 2, column 3 of the array **TICTAC** shown in Fig. 10.1. (This row/column convention is derived from the area of mathematics called *matrix algebra*. A *matrix* m is a two-dimensional arrangement of numbers. Each element in m is referred to by the symbol m_{ij}, where i is the number of its row and j is the number of its column.)

Example 10.1:   Consider the array TICTAC drawn below.

This array contains three blank elements (TICTAC [1,2], TICTAC [2,1], TICTAC [2,3]); three elements with value 'X' (TICTAC [1,1], TICTAC [3,1], TICTAC [3,2]); and three elements with value 'O' (TICTAC [1,3], TICTAC [2,2], TICTAC [3,3]).

Example 10.2:   A university offers 50 courses at each of five campuses. We can conveniently store the enrollments of these courses in the array ENROLL declared below.

```
TYPE
   CAMPUS = (MAIN, AMBLER, CENTER, DELAWARE, MONTCO);

VAR
   ENROLL : ARRAY[1..50, CAMPUS] OF INTEGER;
```

This array consists of 250 elements; ENROLL [I, CENTER] represents the number of students in course I at CENTER campus.

If we wish to have this enrollment information broken down further according to student class, we would need a three-dimensional array with 1000 elements:

```
TYPE
   CAMPUS = (MAIN, AMBLER, CENTER, DELAWARE, MONTCO);
   CLASS = (FRESHMAN, SOPHOMORE, JUNIOR, SENIOR);

VAR
   ENRANK : ARRAY[1..50, CAMPUS, CLASS] OF INTEGER;
   CAMP : CAMPUS;
```

The subscripted array reference ENRANK [I, MAIN, SENIOR] would represent the number of seniors taking course I at MAIN campus.

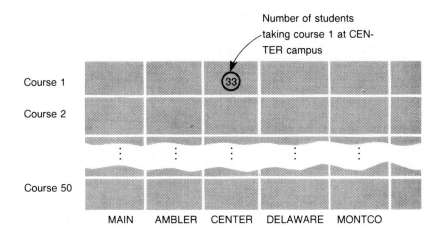

(a) Two-dimensional Array ENROLL

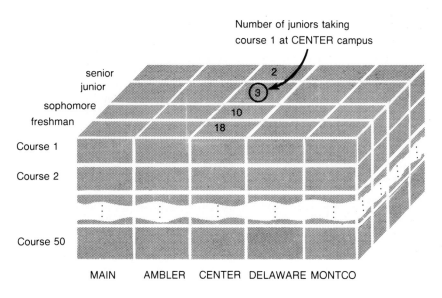

(b) Three-dimensional array ENRANK

Fig. 10.2 (a) Two-dimensional array ENROLL. (b) Three-dimensional array ENRANK.

In Fig. 10.2, the circled element, **ENROLL** [1, CENTER], has a value of 33. The numbers shown in the array **ENRANK** represent the number of students of each rank in course 1 on **CENTER** campus.

Example 10.3:   The program segment

```
CLASSUM := 0;
FOR RANK := FRESHMAN TO SENIOR DO
  CLASSUM := CLASSUM + ENRANK[1, CENTER, RANK];
```

computes the total number of students of all ranks in course 1 at CENTER campus.

The program segment

```
CLASSUM := 0;
FOR CAMP := MAIN TO MONTCO DO
  FOR RANK := FRESHMAN TO SENIOR DO
    CLASSUM := CLASSUM + ENRANK[1, CAMP, RANK];
```

computes the total number of students in course 1 (regardless of rank or campus).

Exercise 10.1:   Given the array ENRANK shown in Fig. 10.3, write program segments to perform the following operations:

- a) Find the number of juniors in all classes at all campuses. Students will be counted once for each course in which they are enrolled.
- b) Find the number of sophomores on all campuses who are enrolled in course 25.
- c) Compute and print the number of students at MAIN campus enrolled in each course and the total number of students at MAIN campus in all courses. Students will be counted once for each course in which they are enrolled.
- d) Compute and print the number of upper-class students in all courses at each campus, as well as the total number of upper-class students enrolled. (Upper-class students are juniors and seniors.) Again, students will be counted once for each course in which they are enrolled.

10.3.2 Relationship Between Loop Control Variables and Array Subscripts

Sequential referencing of array elements is frequently required when working with multidimensional arrays. This process often requires the use of nested loops (see Example 10.4) since more than one subscript must be incremented in order to process all or a portion of the array elements. It is very easy to become confused in this situation and interchange subscripts or nest the loops improperly. If you are in doubt as to whether or not your loops and subscripts are properly synchronized, you should include extra print statements to display the subscript and array element values.

Example 10.4:   The pair of nested loops in Fig. 10.3 prints the array TICTAC as a tic-tac-toe board as shown at the bottom of the figure.

```
WRITELN ('_____');
FOR ROW := 1 TO 3 DO
  BEGIN
    (* PRINT NEXT ROW *)
```

(continued)

```
                    FOR COLUMN := 1 TO 3 DO
                        WRITE (TICTAC[ROW, COLUMN] :2);
                    WRITELN;
                    WRITELN ('_____')
                END; (* FOR *)
```

```
            _____
             X   O
            _____
                 O
            _____
             X X O
            _____
```

Fig. 10.3 Printing a tic-tac-toe board.

The next problem provides another illustration of the use of loop control variables to control the order in which elements of a multidimensional array are processed.

Problem 10.1: Write a procedure that will be used after each move is made in a computerized tic-tac-toe game to see if the game is over. When the game is over, the procedure should indicate the winning player or the fact that the game ended in a draw.

Discussion: To see whether a player has won, procedure CHECKOVER must check each row, column, and diagonal on the board to determine if all three cells are occupied by the same player. A draw occurs when all cells on the board are occupied, but neither player has won. The status of the game will be indicated by an output parameter of type STATE. The main program would contain the type declarations below.

```
TYPE
    BOARD = ARRAY[1..3, 1..3] OF CHAR;
    STATE = (NOTOVER, XWINS, OWINS, DRAW);
```

The data table and level one algorithm for procedure CHECKOVER follow.

Data Table for CHECKOVER

Input parameters	*Output parameters*
TICTAC: An array which shows the current state of the tic-tac-toe board after each move (BOARD)	STATUS: Indicates the current status of the game (STATE)

Level One Algorithm for CHECKOVER

1. Assume the game is not over (STATUS := NOTOVER).
2. Search each row for a win. If a win exists, reset STATUS to XWINS or OWINS.
3. If the game is not over, search each column for a win. If a win exists, reset STATUS to XWINS or OWINS.
4. If the game is not over, test each diagonal for a win. If a win exists, reset STATUS to XWINS or OWINS.
5. If the game is not over, search for an empty cell. If no empty cell is located, reset STATUS to DRAW.

To implement Steps 2 and 3, we will use a separate WHILE loop that is repeated for each row or column as long as the game is not yet over (STATUS is still NOTOVER). The parameter STATUS will be set to XWINS or OWINS as soon as a win is found.

To determine whether a win exists, we will use a function CHECKWIN that will return a value of XWINS or OWINS if the three array elements in a particular row, column or diagonal are the same (and not blank) and will return NOTOVER otherwise. The input parameters for CHECKWIN will be the three elements of TICTAC that are to be compared. The additional data table entries and algorithm refinements are shown below.

Additional Data Table Entries (Problem 10.1)

Program variables

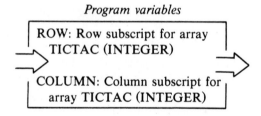

ROW: Row subscript for array TICTAC (INTEGER)

COLUMN: Column subscript for array TICTAC (INTEGER)

Function referenced

CHECKWIN: Tests a row, column, or diagonal; returns a value of XWINS or OWINS if all three elements are the same ('X' or 'O'); otherwise, returns a value of NOTOVER.

Level Two Refinements

Step 2   *Search each row for a win and reset STATUS*

2.1 ROW := 1
2.2 WHILE (STATUS = NOTOVER) AND (ROW <= 3) DO
         BEGIN
                 2.3 Check the current row for a win and reset STATUS
                 2.4 ROW := ROW + 1
         END

The refinements of Steps 3 and 4 are similar to Step 2 above. The refinement of Step 5 follows.

Step 5   *Set STATUS to DRAW if there is no empty cell*

5.1   IF STATUS = NOTOVER THEN
       BEGIN
             5.2 Assume the game is a draw.
             5.3 Search array TICTAC for an empty cell. If one is found,
                 the game is not over.
       END

STATUS will be set to DRAW in Step 5.2. We will use a nested pair of FOR loops to implement the search in Step 5.3. If an empty cell is located, STATUS will be reset to NOTOVER.

Procedure CHECKOVER is shown in Fig. 10.4a. FUNCTION CHECKWIN is shown in Fig. 10.4b.

```
PROCEDURE CHECKOVER (TICTAC : BOARD);
                        VAR STATUS : STATE);
(* CHECK IF TIC-TAC-TOE GAME IS OVER AND FIND WINNER     *)
(*                                                        *)
(* INPUT PARAMETERS                                       *)
(*      TICTAC - CURRENT GAME BOARD                       *)
(* OUTPUT PARAMETERS                                      *)
(*      STATUS - STATE OF THE GAME                        *)
VAR
  ROW, COLUMN : INTEGER;

(* INSERT FUNCTION CHECKWIN HERE *)

BEGIN
  (* ASSUME THE GAME IS NOT OVER *)
  STATUS := NOTOVER;

  (* SEARCH EACH ROW FOR A WIN AND SET STATUS *)
  ROW := 1;
  WHILE (STATUS = NOTOVER) AND (ROW <= 3) DO
    BEGIN
      STATUS := CHECKWIN(TICTAC[ROW, 1], TICTAC[ROW, 2],
                  TICTAC[ROW, 3]);
      ROW := ROW + 1
    END; (* WHILE *)

  (* SEARCH EACH COLUMN FOR A WIN AND SET STATUS *)
  COLUMN := 1;
  WHILE (STATUS = NOTOVER) AND (COLUMN <= 3) DO
    BEGIN
      STATUS := CHECKWIN(TICTAC[1, COLUMN], TICTAC[2, COLUMN],
                  TICTAC[3, COLUMN]);
      COLUMN := COLUMN + 1
    END; (* WHILE *)
```

(continued)

```
(* CHECK EACH DIAGONAL FOR A WIN AND RESET STATUS *)
IF STATUS = NOTOVER THEN
  STATUS := CHECKWIN(TICTAC[1, 1], TICTAC[2, 2], TICTAC[3, 3]);
IF STATUS = NOTOVER THEN
  STATUS := CHECKWIN(TICTAC[1, 3], TICTAC[2, 2], TICTAC[3, 1]);

(* SET STATUS TO DRAW IF THERE IS NO EMPTY CELL *)
IF STATUS = NOTOVER THEN
  BEGIN
    (* ASSUME THE GAME IS A DRAW - SEARCH FOR AN EMPTY CELL *)
    STATUS := DRAW;
    FOR ROW := 1 TO 3 DO
      FOR COLUMN := 1 TO 3 DO
        IF TICTAC[ROW, COLUMN] = ' ' THEN
          STATUS := NOTOVER
  END (* IF *)
END; (* CHECKOVER *)
```

Fig. 10.4a Procedure CHECKOVER.

```
FUNCTION CHECKWIN (CELL1, CELL2, CELL3 : CHAR) : STATE;
(* DETERMINES WHETHER ITS INPUT LINE IS A WIN                 *)
(*                                                             *)
(*    INPUT PARAMETERS                                         *)
(*       CELL1, CELL2, CELL3 - THREE CHARACTER VALUES IN A LINE *)

BEGIN
  IF (CELL1 = CELL2) AND (CELL2 = CELL3) AND (CELL2 <> ' ') THEN
    CASE CELL2 OF
      'X' : CHECKWIN := XWINS;
      'O' : CHECKWIN := OWINS
    END (* CASE *)
  ELSE
    CHECKWIN := NOTOVER
END; (* CHECKWIN *)
```

Fig. 10.4b Function CHECKWIN.

It is important to realize that the parameter **STATUS** must remain equal to **NOTOVER** in order for any new calls to **CHECKWIN** to occur. If a win is found in the first row, none of the remaining rows, columns and diagonals will be checked. Similarly, the step that checks for a draw will be executed only if a win was not found earlier.

Exercise 10.2: Procedure CHECKOVER is called after each move to determine whether or not the game should continue. Write a Boolean function named VERIFY that verifies that each attempted move is legal. VERIFY should be passed the row and column of an intended move.

10.4   ROOM SCHEDULING

To illustrate further the use of two-dimensional arrays or matrices, we will present a solved problem in which this data structure plays a central role.

Problem 10.2:   The little red high school building in Sunflower, Indiana, has three floors, each with five classrooms of various sizes. Each semester the high school must assign classes to the rooms in the building. We will write a program which, given the capacity of each room in the building and the size of each class, will attempt to find a satisfactory room assignment that will accommodate all the classes in the building. For those classes that cannot be satisfactorily placed, the program will print a "ROOM NOT AVAILABLE" message. A list of unassigned rooms and capacities will also be printed.

Discussion: As part of the data table definition, we must decide how the table of room capacities is to be represented in the memory of the computer. Since the building may be pictured as a two-dimensional structure with three floors (vertical dimension) and five rooms (horizontal dimension), a two-dimensional array should be a convenient structure for representing the capacities of each room in the building. We will read the room capacities into a 3×5 array, CAPACITY, as shown in Fig. 10.5.

Capacity of
room 202   Room number

		01	02	03	04	05
	1	30	30	15	30	40
Floor	2	25	30	25	10	110
	3	62	30	40	40	30

Fig. 10.5   Room capacities for Sunflower High.

By using a two-dimensional array, we will be able to determine the number of the room assigned to each class directly from the indices of the array element that represents that room. For example, if a class is placed in a room with capacity given by CAPACITY [2,4], we know that the number of this room is 204. In general, CAPACITY [I,J] represents the capacity of the room whose number is the value of the expression

$$I \; * \; 100 \; + \; J$$

The data table and level one algorithm for Problem 10.2 follow.

Data Table for Problem 10.2

Constants

COUNTFLOOR = 3, number of floors
COUNTROOM = 5, number of room per floor

Data types

BUILDING = ARRAY [1..COUNTFLOOR, 1..COUNTROOM] OF IN-
TEGER

Input variables	*Program variables*	*Output variables*
CAPACITY: An array used to store the capacities for each room (BUILDING)		The room assigned to each class is printed

Procedures referenced by main program

OUTCAPACITY: Prints the contents of the room capacity table

PROCESSROOM: Reads and processes each room request consisting of a
class ID and a class size. Determines the room number to be assigned (if
one is available) and prints the room number.

NOTASSIGNED: Prints the number and capacity of each unassigned room.

Level One Algorithm

1. Read the room capacity table.
2. Print the initial room capacity table.
3. Process each room request and assign a room if available.
4. Print the number and capacity of each unassigned room.

Only Step 1 is performed in the main program. The program system chart in
Fig. 10.6a shows the data flow between modules. As indicated, the array CA-
PACITY is passed as a parameter to all three procedures. The program constants representing the dimensions of this array are global identifiers. The main
program is shown in Fig. 10.6b.

Steps 2 and 4 of the level one algorithm are fairly straightforward and are
left as an exercise (See Exercise 10.3). Step 3 is performed by procedure PRO-
CESSROOM as described next.

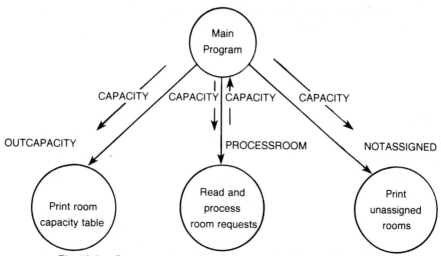

Fig. 10.6a   Program system chart for room scheduling problem (10.2).

```
PROGRAM SCHEDULER;
(* SCHEDULE CLASSES USING ROOM *)
(* CAPACITY AND CLASS REQUESTS *)

CONST
   COUNTFLOOR = 3;
   COUNTROOM = 5;

TYPE
   BUILDING = ARRAY[1..COUNTFLOOR, 1..COUNTROOM] OF INTEGER;

VAR
   CAPACITY : BUILDING;
   FLOOR, ROOM : INTEGER;

(* INSERT PROCEDURES OUTCAPACITY,     *)
(* PROCESSROOM AND NOTASSIGNED HERE   *)
(*$I UCSD5:OUTCAPACITY     *)
(*$I UCSD5:PROCESSROOM     *)
(*$I UCSD5:NOTASSIGNED     *)

BEGIN
   (* ENTER ROOM CAPACITY TABLE *)
   FOR FLOOR := 1 TO COUNTFLOOR DO
     BEGIN
       WRITELN ('ENTER CAPACITIES OF ROOMS ON FLOOR ', FLOOR);
       FOR ROOM := 1 TO COUNTROOM DO
         READ (CAPACITY[FLOOR, ROOM]);
       READLN
     END; (* FOR *)

   (* PRINT ROOM CAPACITY TABLE *)
   OUTCAPACITY (CAPACITY);
```

(continued)

```
(* MAKE CLASS ASSIGNMENTS *)
PROCESSROOM (CAPACITY);

(* LIST UNASSIGNED ROOMS AND THEIR CAPACITIES *)
NOTASSIGNED (CAPACITY)
END.
```

Fig. 10.6b   Main program for room scheduling.

For each room request, procedure PROCESSROOM will read a pair of data items representing the course identification number and class size. PROCESS-ROOM should find a room that is large enough to hold each class if one is available. (The ideal situation would be to find a room whose capacity exactly matches the class size.) For each class, PROCESSROOM will print, in tabular form, the class ID (CLASSID) and size (SIZE) and the number (ROOMNUMBER) and capacity of the room assigned to the class. The data table for PROCESSROOM is shown below, followed by the level one algorithm.

Data Table for PROCESSROOM

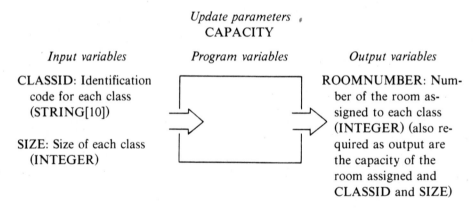

Update parameters
CAPACITY

Input variables	*Program variables*	*Output variables*
CLASSID: Identification code for each class (STRING[10]) SIZE: Size of each class (INTEGER)		ROOMNUMBER: Number of the room assigned to each class (INTEGER) (also required as output are the capacity of the room assigned and CLASSID and SIZE)

Level One Algorithm for PROCESSROOM

1. Read and process each room request.

Level Two Refinements

Step 1

1.1   WHILE more classes to schedule DO
      BEGIN
          1.2 Read each room request
          1.3 Assign a suitable room if one is available
          1.4 Print the description of the room assigned and flag it so
              that it cannot be reassigned
      END

A third level procedure, ASSIGN, will be called by PROCESSROOM to perform Step 1.3. This procedure will search the room capacity table to find a room of size, SIZE, or greater. It will return the subscripts of an assigned room, if one is found, and indicate success or failure by setting a program flag, FOUND, to true or false. The additional data table entries for PROCESSROOM are shown next, along with a description of procedure ASSIGN. The data flow between PROCESSROOM and ASSIGN is summarized in the new program system chart drawn in Fig. 10.6c.

Additional Data Table Entries for PROCESSROOM

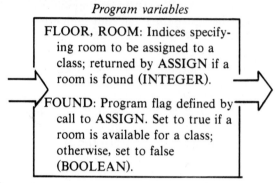

Program variables

FLOOR, ROOM: Indices specifying room to be assigned to a class; returned by ASSIGN if a room is found (INTEGER).

FOUND: Program flag defined by call to ASSIGN. Set to true if a room is available for a class; otherwise, set to false (BOOLEAN).

Procedure referenced

ASSIGN: Assigns a suitable room if one is available

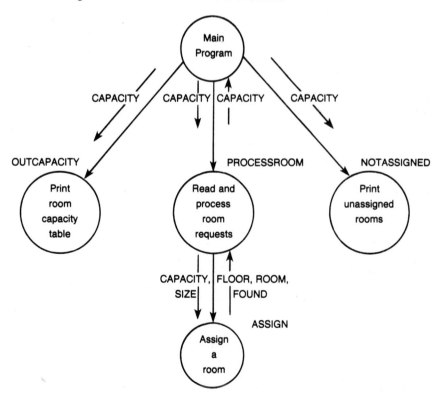

Fig. 10.6c   New program system chart for Problem 10.2.

The refinement of Step 1.4 of **PROCESSROOM** is shown next.

Level Three Refinements

Step 1.4

    1.4.1 IF FOUND THEN
            BEGIN
                1.4.2 Print the room description
                1.4.3 Flag the room so it cannot be reassigned
            END
            ELSE
                1.4.4 Print a room not available message

There are probably many ways to resolve the problem indicated in Step 1.4.3 above. Once a room is assigned, we must ensure that it can't be reassigned to another class. We will provide this protection simply by negating the capacities of each room assigned to a class when the assignment is made. Exactly why this works will become clearer when procedure **ASSIGN** is written. We can now write **PROCESSROOM** (see Fig. 10.6d).

```
PROCEDURE PROCESSROOM (VAR CAPACITY : BUILDING);
(* READS AND PROCESSES EACH ROOM REQUEST       *)
(*                                              *)
(* UPDATE PARAMETER                             *)
(*    CAPACITY - ROOM CAPACITY TABLE            *)

VAR
  CLASSID : STRING[10];
  SIZE, ROOMNUMBER : INTEGER;
  FLOOR, ROOM : INTEGER;
  FOUND : BOOLEAN;

(* INSERT PROCEDURE ASSIGN HERE *)

BEGIN
  (* PROCESS EVERY ROOM REQUEST *)
  WRITELN ('ENTER 0 OR NEXT CLASS SIZE AND ID');
  WRITELN ('AFTER EACH PROMPT');
  WRITELN;
  WRITELN ('SIZE' :6, 'CLASS ID' :10, 'ROOM NO.' :10,
          'CAPACITY' :10);
  WRITE ('? '); READ (SIZE);
  WHILE SIZE <> 0 DO
    BEGIN
      (* READ CLASS ID *)
      READLN (CLASSID);
      (* ASSIGN A ROOM IF POSSIBLE *)
      ASSIGN (CAPACITY, SIZE, FLOOR, ROOM, FOUND);
      (* PRINT ROOM ASSIGNMENT OR "NOT AVAILABLE" MESSAGE *)
      IF FOUND THEN
```

(continued)

```
      BEGIN
        (* COMPUTE ROOM NUMBER AND RESERVE ROOM *)
        ROOMNUMBER := FLOOR * 100 + ROOM;
        WRITELN (' ' :16, ROOMNUMBER :10,
                 CAPACITY[FLOOR, ROOM] :10);
        CAPACITY[FLOOR, ROOM] := - CAPACITY[FLOOR, ROOM]
      END
    ELSE
      WRITELN (' ' :18, 'NO ROOM AVAILABLE');
    WRITE ('? '); READ (SIZE)
  END (* WHILE *)
END; (* PROCESSROOM *)
```

Fig. 10.6d   Procedure PROCESSROOM.

The only step left is the specification of procedure ASSIGN. The algorithm that we will use to find a room for a given class size (SIZE) may be summarized as follows:

Search the array CAPACITY to find the smallest room that is greater than or equal to SIZE and is still not assigned.

This is called the *best fit* algorithm because the unassigned room with the least excess capacity is chosen for each class. (The ideal situation is to find a room that fits exactly.) This algorithm assigns as many classes to suitable rooms as is physically possible without later juggling room assignments. The implementation of this search requires two nested loops with loop control variables ROW and COLUMN. The data table and algorithm for ASSIGN follow.

Data Table for ASSIGN

Input parameters

CAPACITY, SIZE

Output parameters

FLOOR, ROOM,
FOUND

Program variables

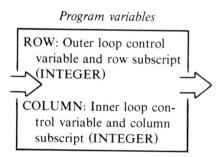

ROW: Outer loop control
variable and row subscript
(INTEGER)

COLUMN: Inner loop con-
trol variable and column
subscript (INTEGER)

Level One Algorithm

1. Initialize FOUND to FALSE.
2. Search for the best fit room. If a room is found, set FOUND to TRUE and define FLOOR and ROOM.

Level Two Refinements

Step 2   *Search for the best fit room*

2.1 FOR ROW := 1 TO COUNTFLOOR DO
         FOR COLUMN := 1 TO COUNTROOM DO
             IF the current room fits THEN
                 IF NOT FOUND THEN
                     BEGIN
                         FOUND := TRUE
                         Make initial room assignment by setting FLOOR and
                             ROOM
                     END
                 ELSE IF the current room is a better fit THEN
                     Change ROOM and FLOOR to the current room

The implementation of procedure ASSIGN is shown in Fig. 10.6e. A sample
run of the program is shown in Fig. 10.6f.

```
PROCEDURE ASSIGN (CAPACITY : BUILDING;
                  SIZE : INTEGER;
                  VAR FLOOR, ROOM : INTEGER;
                  VAR FOUND : BOOLEAN);
(* ASSIGNS BEST FIT ROOM                     *)
(*                                           *)
(* INPUT PARAMETERS                          *)
(*     CAPACITY - ARRAY BEING SEARCHED       *)
(*     SIZE - SIZE OF CLASS BEING PLACED     *)
(* OUTPUT PARAMETERS                         *)
(*     FLOOR - FLOOR OF ASSIGNED ROOM        *)
(*     ROOM - ROOM NUMBER ON FLOOR           *)
(*     FOUND - INDICATES SUCCESS(TRUE)       *)
(*             OR FAILURE(FALSE) OF SEARCH   *)

VAR
  ROW, COLUMN : INTEGER;

BEGIN
  (* INITIALIZE FOUND TO FALSE *)
  FOUND := FALSE;

  (* SEARCH EVERY FLOOR FOR BEST FIT ROOM *)
  FOR ROW := 1 TO COUNTFLOOR DO
    FOR COLUMN := 1 TO COUNTROOM DO
      IF CAPACITY[ROW, COLUMN] >= SIZE THEN
        IF NOT FOUND THEN
          (* 1ST SUITABLE ROOM             *)
          (* - MAKE INITIAL ASSIGNMENT     *)
          BEGIN
            FLOOR := ROW;
            ROOM := COLUMN;
            FOUND := TRUE
          END
        ELSE IF CAPACITY[ROW,COLUMN] < CAPACITY[FLOOR,ROOM]
```

(*continued*)

```
THEN (* BETTER FIT - CHANGE ROOM ASSIGNMENT  *)
   BEGIN
      FLOOR := ROW;
      ROOM := COLUMN
   END (* IF *)
END; (* ASSIGN *)
```

Fig. 10.6e Procedure ASSIGN

FLOOR		ROOM			
	01	02	03	04	05
1	30	30	15	30	40
2	25	30	25	10	110
3	62	30	40	40	- 30
			CAPACITIES		

```
ENTER 0 OR NEXT CLASS SIZE AND ID
AFTER EACH PROMPT
```

SIZE	CLASS ID	ROOM NO.	CAPACITY
? 37	CIS1		
		105	40
? 55	CIS2		
		301	62
? 100	CIS3		
		205	110
? 26	CIS10		
		101	30
? 26	CIS11		
		102	30
? 39	CIS25		
		303	40
? 30	CIS30		
		104	30
? 45	CIS31		
	NO ROOM AVAILABLE		
? 20	CIS101		
		201	25
? 15	CIS120		
		103	15
? 22	CIS203		
		203	25
? 10	CIS301		
		204	10
? 5	CIS302		
		202	30
? 28	CIS324		
		302	30
? 25	CIS330		
		305	30

```
ROOMS NOT ASSIGNED
ROOM       CAPACITY
304            40
```

Fig. 10.6f Sample run of room scheduling problem (10.2).

Exercise 10.3:   Complete the program system for Problem 10.2 by writing procedures OUTCAPACITY and NOTASSIGNED. Your procedure output should be similar to the tables in Fig. 10.6f. Procedure NOTASSIGNED should print the number and capacity of each room whose capacity is still positive.

Exercise 10.4:   Modify procedure PROCESSROOM so that the final contents of the array CAPACITY can be used to determine the number of empty seats in each classroom. Make sure it isn't possible to assign a large room to 2 small classes after your modification.

Exercise 10.5:   The algorithm used in procedure ASSIGN is called a *best-fit* algorithm, because the room having the capacity that was closest to the class size was assigned to each class. Another algorithm that might have been used is called a *first-fit* algorithm. In this algorithm, the first room having a capacity greater than or equal to the class size is assigned to the class (no further searching for a room is carried out). Modify the algorithm and program for ASSIGN to reflect the first-fit algorithm. (You will see that this algorithm is simpler than best-fit). Apply both algorithms using the room capacities shown earlier and the following 15 class sizes: 38, 41, 6, 26, 28, 21, 25, 97, 12, 36, 28, 27, 29, 30, 18. Exactly what is wrong with the first-fit algorithm?

10.5   INTRODUCTION TO COMPUTER ART: DRAWING BLOCK LETTERS

Many of you have seen examples of computer art or calendars "drawn" by the computer. Normally a picture consists of lines of numbers or symbols printed so as to depict a pattern. The pattern is composed of different layers of shading and the degree of shading is determined by the density of symbols printed in a given area. (See Fig. 10.7.) Since the line-printer prints one line at a time, the "computer artist" must organize the picture as a sequence of print lines of constant width.

An array of character strings, or a two-dimensional array of characters, is required to store the lines of the picture. The size of each character string (the second dimension) is determined by the width of the picture.

Example 10.5:   The program in Fig. 10.8 enters a picture into the array PICTURE and then draws a number of copies of the picture. The data table for the program is given on page 384.

```
PROGRAM DRAW;
(* PRINTS A NUMBER OF COPIES OF A DRAWING *)

CONST
  HEIGHT = 100;
  WIDTH = 60;

TYPE
  PICTUREARRAY = ARRAY[1..HEIGHT] OF STRING[WIDTH];

VAR
  PICTURE : PICTUREARRAY;
  COUNTCOPY, LINE, COPY : INTEGER;
```

(continued on page 384)

Fig. 10.7 Computer art.

```
BEGIN
  (* ENTER DATA *)
  WRITE ('HOW MANY COPIES?'); READLN (COUNTCOPY);
  WRITELN ('ENTER EACH LINE OF THE DRAWING');
  FOR LINE := 1 TO HEIGHT DO
    READLN (PICTURE[LINE]);

  (* DRAW COUNTCOPY COPIES *)
  FOR COPY := 1 TO COUNTCOPY DO
    BEGIN
      (* DRAW ONE LINE AT A TIME *)
      FOR LINE := 1 TO HEIGHT DO
        WRITELN (PICTURE[LINE]);
      (* SEPARATE COPIES WITH BLANK LINES *)
      FOR LINE := 1 TO 5 DO
        WRITELN
    END (* FOR COPY *)
END.
```

Fig. 10.8 Program to draw pictures.

Data Table for Example 10.5

Constants

HEIGHT = 100, or height of each picture in lines

WIDTH = 60, or width of each picture in columns

Data types

PICTUREARRAY = ARRAY[1..HEIGHT] OF STRING[WIDTH]

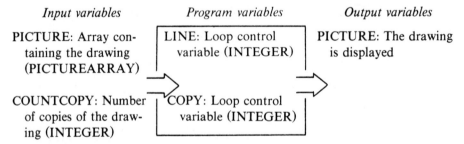

Input variables	*Program variables*	*Output variables*
PICTURE: Array containing the drawing (PICTUREARRAY)	LINE: Loop control variable (INTEGER)	PICTURE: The drawing is displayed
COUNTCOPY: Number of copies of the drawing (INTEGER)	COPY: Loop control variable (INTEGER)	

In the next problem, we will write a program that draws large block letters on the line printer. You may have already seen examples of the output of such a program in signs or announcements printed by the computer. Block letters are sometimes printed to identify the owner of a program listing.

Problem 10.3 Develop a program that prints a sequence of letters, provided as input data, in large block letters across a page. Each letter should be printed as a 6×5 grid pattern of X's and blanks (6 rows and 5 columns). We will skip two print columns between letters. The number of letters that can be displayed depends upon the width of your screen. On a screen with 80 columns a maximum of 11 block letters may be displayed. (11 × 7 = 77).

For example, given the input string

DRAW ME

the program should produce:

```
XXX     XXXX        X       X   X       X X     XXXXX
X   X   X    X    X   X     X   X       X X X   X
X     X XXXX     X     X    X   X       X X X   XXXX
X     X X X     XXXXX     X X X       X     X   X
X   X   X   X   X     X   X X X       X     X   X
XXX     X     X X     X     X X       X     X   XXXXX
```

Discussion. We will use a two-dimensional character array to store all of the block letters. Each line of a letter will be stored as a string of length five in the array BLOCK of type PATTERN. The row subscript of BLOCK will denote the letter being represented ('A'..'Z'), and the column subscript will denote the line stored (1..6).

We will also need a string, INSTRING, to store the input characters. Each letter in the input string will be printed; any other character will be printed as a blank.

The data table and level one algorithm for the block letter problem follow.

Data Table for Problem 10.3

Constants

     MAXCHAR = 11, maximum number of characters per line

     HEIGHT = 6, height of each block letter

     WIDTH = 5, width of each block letter

Data types

     LETTPAT = ARRAY[1..HEIGHT] OF STRING[WIDTH]

     PATTERN = ARRAY['A'..'Z'] OF LETTPAT

     STRSIZE = STRING [MAXCHAR]

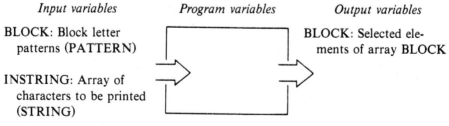

Input variables	*Program variables*	*Output variables*
BLOCK: Block letter patterns (PATTERN)		BLOCK: Selected elements of array BLOCK
INSTRING: Array of characters to be printed (STRING)		

Procedures referenced

     READBLOCK: Reads block letter patterns

     DRAW: Draws block letter patterns

Level One Algorithm for Problem 10.3

1. Read the block letter patterns for each letter of the alphabet.
2. Read the characters to be printed into INSTRING and count them.
3. Print each character in INSTRING in block letter form.

Steps 1 and 3 are performed by procedures READBLOCK and DRAW, respectively. Step 2 is performed in the main program.

The program system chart is shown in Fig. 10.9a. The main program is written in Fig. 10.9b.

Procedure READBLOCK simply reads a collection of character strings. The first six strings represent the block form of letter A, the next six strings represent the block form of letter B, etc.

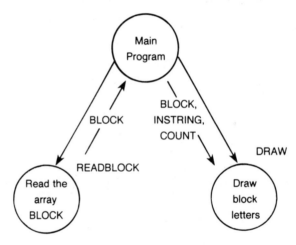

Fig. 10.9a   Program system chart for block letter problem (10.3).

Procedure READBLOCK reads each pattern from a TEXT file. The six strings corresponding to block letter A are first, followed by the six strings for block letter B, etc. The global identifiers HEIGHT and WIDTH are constants defined in the main program. Procedure READBLOCK is shown in Fig. 10.9c.

Procedure DRAW displays the block letter patterns corresponding to the characters in INSTRING. The number of patterns displayed is determined by the length of INSTRING. The first line of all patterns is printed, then the second line of all patterns, etc., until all six lines are printed. Any character that is not a letter is printed as a blank.

The data table and algorithm for procedure DRAW follow; the procedure itself is shown in Fig. 10.9d.

Data Table for DRAW

Input parameters

BLOCK, INSTRING

Program variables

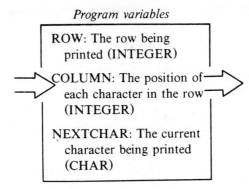

ROW: The row being printed (INTEGER)

COLUMN: The position of each character in the row (INTEGER)

NEXTCHAR: The current character being printed (CHAR)

Level One Algorithm for DRAW

1. Print the block letter patterns corresponding to the letters in INSTRING

Level Two Refinements

Step 1

    1.1 FOR ROW := 1 TO HEIGHT DO
        1.2 FOR COLUMN := 1 TO LENGTH [INSTRING] DO
           1.3 Print the current row of the block letter pattern for
              INSTRING[COLUMN]

Level Three Refinements

Step 1.3

    1.3.1 NEXTCHAR := INSTRING[COLUMN]
    1.3.2 IF NEXTCHAR is a letter THEN
        Print line ROW of its block pattern
        ELSE
        Print a blank string

```
PROGRAM BLOCKLETTERS;
(* PRINTS A LINE OF TEXT IN BLOCK FORM *)

CONST
  MAXCHAR = 11;
  HEIGHT = 6;
  WIDTH = 5;

TYPE
  LETTPATT = ARRAY[1..HEIGHT] OF STRING[WIDTH];
  PATTERN = ARRAY['A'..'Z'] OF LETTPATT;
  STRSIZE = STRING[MAXCHAR];

VAR
  BLOCK : PATTERN;
  INSTRING : STRSIZE;
```

(continued)

```
                  (* INSERT PROCEDURES READBLOCK AND DRAW HERE *)
                  (*$I UCSD5:READBLOCK     *)
                  (*$I UCSD5:DRAW          *)

               BEGIN
                  (* READ THE BLOCK LETTER PATTERNS *)
                  READBLOCK (BLOCK);

                  (* READ THE LINE OF TEXT *)
                  WRITELN ('ENTER STRING TO BE BLOCK PRINTED');
                  READLN (INSTRING);

                  (* DRAW BLOCK FORM OF LETTERS IN INSTRING *)
                  DRAW (BLOCK, INSTRING)
               END.
```

Fig. 10.9b   Program to print block letters.

```
PROCEDURE READBLOCK (VAR BLOCK : PATTERN);
(* READS BLOCK LETTER PATTERNS FROM A FILE   *)
(*                                           *)
(* OUTPUT PARAMETERS                         *)
(*     BLOCK - ARRAY OF BLOCK PATTERNS       *)

VAR
  LETTER : CHAR;
  INFILE : TEXT;
  ROW : INTEGER;
  INNAME : STRING[20];

BEGIN
  (* READ BLOCK LETTER PATTERNS FOR 'A' TO 'Z' *)
  WRITELN ('ENTER NAME OF BLOCK LETTER FILE:');
  READLN (INNAME);
  RESET (INFILE, INNAME);
  FOR LETTER := 'A' TO 'Z' DO
    FOR ROW := 1 TO HEIGHT DO
      READLN (INFILE, BLOCK[LETTER, ROW]);
  CLOSE (INFILE)
END; (* READBLOCK *)
```

Fig. 10.9c   Procedure READBLOCK.

```
PROCEDURE DRAW (BLOCK : PATTERN);
               INSTRING : STRSIZE);
(* DRAWS BLOCK LETTER PATTERNS               *)
(*                                           *)
(* INPUT PARAMETERS                          *)
(*     BLOCK - ARRAY OF PATTERNS             *)
(*     INSTRING - LETTERS TO BE DRAWN        *)

VAR
  ROW, COLUMN : INTEGER;
  NEXTCHAR : CHAR;
```

(continued)

```
BEGIN
  (* PRINT BLOCK PATTERN ROW BY ROW *)
  FOR ROW := 1 TO HEIGHT DO
    BEGIN
      (* PRINT CURRENT ROW OF BLOCK PATTERN *)
      FOR COLUMN := 1 TO LENGTH[INSTRING] DO
        BEGIN
          NEXTCHAR := INSTRING[COLUMN];
          IF NEXTCHAR IN ['A'..'Z'] THEN
            WRITE (BLOCK[NEXTCHAR,ROW], '  ')
          ELSE
            WRITE (' ' :7)
        END; (* FOR *)
      (* TERMINATE CURRENT ROW *)
      WRITELN
    END (* FOR *)
END; (* DRAW *)
```

Fig. 10.9d   Procedure DRAW.

Exercise 10.6:   Prepare the data records for letters 'A' and 'B' (to be read by READBLOCK).

Exercise 10.7:   Modify procedure DRAW so that an error message is printed at the end indicating any characters in INSTRING that could not be printed.

10.6   COMMON PROGRAMMING ERRORS

The errors encountered using multidimensional arrays are similar to those encountered in processing one-dimensional arrays. The most frequent errors are likely to be subscript range errors. These errors may be more common now because two or more subscripts are involved in an array reference, introducing added complexity and confusion.

Other kinds of errors arise because of the complex nesting of FOR loops when they are used to manipulate multidimensional arrays. Care must be taken to ensure that the subscript order is consistent with the nesting structure of the loops. Inconsistent usage may not result in an error diagnostic but will likely produce incorrect program results.

An additional source of error involves the use of arrays as procedure arguments. If the range of a subscript is passed through the argument list, care must be taken to ensure that the value passed is correct. Otherwise, out-of-range errors may occur.

10.7   SUMMARY

In this chapter, we have introduced a more general form of the array. This form is useful in representing data that are most naturally thought of in terms of multidimensional structures. The multidimensional array is convenient for representing rectangular tables of information, matrices, game-board patterns, n-dimensional spaces, and tables involving data with multiple categories (such as that found in the university enrollment example, Example 10.3.)

We have seen examples of the manipulation of individual array elements through the use of nests of loops. The correspondence between the loop control variables and the array subscripts determines the order in which the array elements are processed.

PROGRAMMING PROBLEMS

10.4 Write a program that reads in a tic-tac-toe board and determines the best move for player X. Use the following strategy. Consider all squares that are empty and evaluate potential moves into them. If the move fills the third square in a row, column, or diagonal that already has two X's, add 50 to the score; if it fills the third square in a row, column or diagonal with two O's, add 25 to the score; for each row, column or diagonal containing this move that will have 2 X's and one blank, add 10 to the score; add 8 for each row, column or diagonal through this move that will have one O, one X, and one blank; add four for each row, column or diagonal that will have one X and the rest blanks. Select the move that scores the highest.

The possible moves for the board below are numbered. Their scores are shown to the right of the board. Move five is selected.

1	O	X
2	X	3
O	4	5

$1 - 10 + 8 = 18$
$2 - 10 + 8 = 18$
$3 - 10 + 10 = 20$
$4 - 8$
$5 - 10 + 10 + 8 = 28$

10.5 Write a program that reads the five cards representing a poker hand into a two-dimensional array (first dimension — suit, second dimension — rank). Evaluate the poker hand by using procedures to determine whether the hand is a flush (all one suit), a straight (five consecutive cards), a straight flush (five consecutive cards of one suit), 4 of a kind, a full house (3 of one kind, 2 of another), 3 of a kind, 2 pair, or 1 pair.

10.6 If, in the room scheduling problem (10.2), we removed the restriction of a single building and wished to write the program to accommodate an entire campus of buildings, each with a different number of floors and rooms on each floor, the choice of a two-dimensional array for storing room capacities may prove inconvenient. Instead, it might be easier to use an array of records to store the identification of each room (building and number) and its size. Write a program to solve the room scheduling problem using the 15 class sizes given in Exercise 10.5, and the campus room table shown below.

Room ID

Building	Number	Room size
HUMA	1003	30
MATH	11	25
MUSI	2	62
LANG	701	30
MATH	12	30
ART	2	30

(continued)

EDUC	61	15
HUMA	1005	25
ART	1	40
ENG	101	30
MATH	3	10
EDUC	63	40
LANG	702	40
MUSI	5	110
HUMA	1002	30

10.7 Write a set of procedures to manipulate a pair of matrices. You should provide procedures for addition, subtraction, and multiplication. Each procedure should validate its input parameters (i.e., check all matrix dimensions) before performing the required data manipulation.

10.8 The results from the mayor's race have been reported by each precinct as follows:

Precinct	Candidate A	Candidate B	Candidate C	Candidate D
1	192	48	206	37
2	147	90	312	21
3	186	12	121	38
4	114	21	408	39
5	267	13	382	29

Write a program to do the following:
A. Print out the table with appropriate headings for the rows and columns.
B. Compute and print the total number of votes received by each candidate and the percent of the total votes cast.
C. If any one candidate received over 50% of the votes, the program should print a message declaring that candidate the winner.
D. If no candidate received 50% of the votes, the program should print a message declaring a run-off between the two candidates receiving the highest number of votes; the two candidates should be identified by their letter names.
E. Run the program once with above data and once with candidate C receiving only 108 votes in precinct 4.

10.9 The game of Life, invented by John H. Conway, is supposed to model the genetic laws for birth, survival and death. (See *Scientific American*, October, 1970, p. 120.) We will play it on a board consisting of 25 squares in the horizontal and vertical directions. Each square can be empty or contain an X indicating the presence of an organism. Each square (except the border squares) has eight neighbors. The small square shown in the segment of the board drawn below connects the neighbors of the organism in row three, column three.

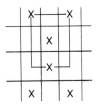

Generation 1

The next generation of organisms is determined according to the following criteria:

1. *Birth:* An organism will be born in each empty location that has exactly three neighbors.
2. *Death:* An organism with four or more organisms as neighbors will die from overcrowding. An organism with fewer than two neighbors will die from loneliness.
3. *Survival:* An organism with two or three neighbors will survive to the next generation.

Generations 2 and 3 for the sample follow:

	X	
X	X	X
X	X	X
	X	

Generation 2

X	X	X
X	X	X

Generation 3

Read in an initial configuration of organisms. Print the original game array, calculate the next generation of organisms in a new array, copy the new array into the original game array and repeat the cycle for as many generations as you wish. Provide a program system chart. [*Hint:* Assume that the borders of the game array are infertile regions where organisms can neither survive nor be born; you will not have to process the border squares.]

POINTER VARIABLES AND DYNAMIC DATA STRUCTURES

11

11.1 INTRODUCTION

In this chapter, we shall see how PASCAL can be used to create *dynamic data structures*. Dynamic data structures are data structures that "grow" as a program executes. A dynamic data structure is a collection of elements (called *nodes*) that are normally records. Unlike an array that always contains storage space for a fixed number of elements, a dynamic data structure expands and contracts during program execution based on the data storage requirements of the program.

Dynamic data structures are used for storage of real world data that are constantly changing. An example would be an airline passenger list. If this list were maintained in alphabetical order in an array, it would be necessary to move all passenger records that alphabetically followed a new passenger in order to make room for that passenger's data in the array. This would require using a loop to copy the data record for each passenger being moved to the next array element. If a dynamic data structure is used instead, the new passenger data can simply be inserted between two existing passenger records with a minimum of effort.

Dynamic data structures are extremely flexible. As described above, it is relatively easy to add new information by creating a new node and inserting it between two existing nodes. We shall see that it is also relatively easy to modify dynamic data structures by removing or deleting an existing node. This is more convenient than modifying an array of records, where each record is in a fixed position relative to the others as determined by its subscript.

11.2 THE NEW STATEMENT AND POINTERS

Since we don't know beforehand the order or number of *nodes* (elements) in a dynamic data structure, we cannot allocate storage for a dynamic data structure in the conventional way (using a variable declaration statement). Instead, we must allocate storage for each individual node as needed and, somehow, join this node to the rest of the structure. The *NEW statement* is used to allocate storage for a new node.

We must also have some way of referencing each new node that is allocated in order to store data in it. PASCAL provides a special type of variable, called a *pointer variable* (or *pointer*), for this purpose. The "value of a pointer variable" is really the address in memory of a particular node. We shall represent a pointer value by drawing an arrow to the node referenced by the pointer.

Example 11.1:   The statements

```
TYPE
  NODE = RECORD
    WORD, : STRING[3];
    PLACE : INTEGER
  END;
  NODEPOINTER = ↑NODE;

VAR
  P,Q,R : NODEPOINTER;
```

define a record type NODE and a pointer type, NODEPOINTER, to records of type NODE. The variables P, Q and R are defined as pointer variables of type NODEPOINTER.

The statements

```
NEW (P);
NEW (Q);
```

allocate storage for two records that are "pointed to" (referenced) by pointers P and Q. Since P and Q are type NODEPOINTER, these new records must be type NODE as illustrated below.

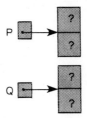

Both fields of these new nodes are initially undefined.

The statements

```
P↑.WORD := 'ACE';
Q↑.WORD := 'BOY';
```

define the WORD field of P↑ (the node referenced by pointer P) and Q↑ (the node referenced by pointer Q) as shown next.

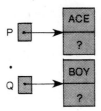

This diagram shows that P points to a record of type NODE whose first field contains the string 'ACE' and Q points to a record of type NODE whose first field contains the string 'BOY'. The second field of both records is still undefined.

The statements

```
P↑.PLACE := 25;
Q↑.PLACE := 37;
```

define the PLACE fields as shown next.

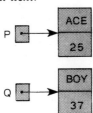

In the example above, we have used two pointers (P and Q) to reference the individual fields of two different nodes. The pointer that references each node was determined when the node was created. We shall demonstrate next that it is possible to change the node referenced by a particular pointer, or to have the same node referenced by more than one pointer.

Example 11.2:   The pointer assignment statement

$$R \; := \; P;$$

copies the value of pointer P into pointer R. This means that pointers P and R now point to the same node as shown below.

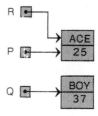

The assignment statements

$$P \; := \; Q;$$
$$Q \; := \; R;$$

would have the effect of exchanging the nodes pointed to by P and Q as shown below.

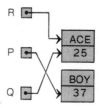

The statement

```
WRITE (P↑.WORD, Q↑.WORD, R↑.WORD)
```

displays the WORD field (a character string) of the records pointed to by P, Q and R. The output printed would be

BOYACEACE

Pointers P, Q and R are similar to subscripts in that they select particular *nodes* or elements of a data structure. Unlike subscripts, their range of values is not declared, and their values (memory cell addresses) may not be printed.

In this section, we discussed how to declare pointer variables and manipulate pointer values. We also saw how to create nodes and reference nodes using pointer variables. These operations are described in the displays that follow. In the next section, we shall see how to connect nodes to form a dynamic data structure.

Pointer Type

$$pointer\text{-}id = \uparrow node\text{-}id$$

Interpretation: The identifier *pointer-id* is defined as a pointer type to elements of type *node-id*.

Procedure NEW

NEW (*pointer*)

Interpretation: The procedure NEW allocates storage for a data structure that is pointed to by the pointer variable *pointer*. The type of data structure allocated is determined by the type of *pointer*.

Referencing a Field Using a Pointer

pointer↑.field-name

Interpretation: The field specified by *field-name* of the node currently pointed to by pointer variable *pointer* is manipulated.

Pointer Assignment

$$pointer_1 := pointer_2$$

Interpretation: Pointer variable $pointer_1$ points to (references) the same node as $pointer_2$. $Pointer_1$ and $pointer_2$ must be the same pointer type.

Exercise 11.1:   The sequence of assignment statements

```
R  := P;
P  := Q;
Q  := R
```

was used to exchange the values of pointer variables P and Q so that P points to the element containing 'BOY' and Q points to the element containing 'ACE'. What would the sequence

```
R↑.WORD  := P↑.WORD;
P↑.WORD  := Q↑.WORD;
Q↑.WORD  := R↑.WORD
```

do? What is the difference between these two sequences?

11.3   BUILDING LINKED DATA STRUCTURES

11.3.1   Introduction to Linked Lists

Linked lists are the most basic form of dynamic data structure. A *linked list,* or simply, *list,* is a sequence of nodes in which each node is linked or connected to the node preceding it. An example of a linked list with three nodes is shown below.

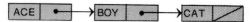

Each node in the list has two fields: the first field contains data and the second field is a pointer (represented by an arrow) to the next list element.

The pointer field of the last list element contains the symbol slash (/). This symbol is used to denote the end of a list. A special pointer value, *NIL,* is normally stored in the pointer field of the last list element. NIL is a predefined constant in UCSD PASCAL.

In order to represent a linked list in memory, it is necessary to define a record type with at least one field that is a pointer.

```
TYPE
  LISTPOINTER = ↑LISTNODE;
  LISTNODE = RECORD
    WORD : STRING[3];
    LINK : LISTPOINTER
  END (*LISTNODE*)
```

The above declarations define a new pointer type (LISTPOINTER) that points to elements (records) of type LISTNODE. Each element of type LISTNODE contains a field named LINK that is also of type LISTPOINTER. (This is a "circular definition" in that the record type LISTNODE appears in the declaration of LISTPOINTER; similarly, the pointer type LISTPOINTER appears in the declaration of LISTNODE. PASCAL requires the pointer type to be declared first.)

Example 11.3:   The procedure in Fig. 11.1 *traverses,* or prints out, the WORD field of all elements of a list. It assumes that the input parameter HEAD points to the first list element and that the last list element contains the pointer value NIL.

```
PROCEDURE TRAVERSE (HEAD : LISTPOINTER);
(* TRAVERSES THE LIST POINTED TO BY HEAD      *)
(*                                            *)
(* INPUT PARAMETER                            *)
(*      HEAD - POINTER TO FIRST LIST ELEMENT  *)

BEGIN
  (* TEST FOR END OF LIST *)
  WHILE HEAD <> NIL DO
    BEGIN
      WRITELN (HEAD↑.WORD);
```

(continued)

```
        (* ADVANCE TO THE NEXT LIST ELEMENT *)
        HEAD := HEAD↑.LINK
    END (* WHILE *)
END; (* TRAVERSE *)
```

Fig. 11.1   Procedure TRAVERSE.

The statement

```
        HEAD := HEAD↑.LINK
```

advances the pointer **HEAD** to the next list element, which is pointed to by the **LINK** field of the current list element. Since **HEAD** is a value parameter, a local copy of the pointer to the first list element is established when the procedure is entered. This local pointer is advanced; however, the corresponding pointer in the calling program remains unchanged.

11.3.2 Creating a List

Let us see how we might create the list described at the start of Section 11.3.1. First of all, we must have some way of referencing the list. This is usually done by establishing a pointer to the first element of the list or the *list head*. We shall declare HEAD, Q and R as variables of type LISTPOINTER and use HEAD as the pointer to the list head.

```
            VAR
                HEAD, Q, R : LISTPOINTER
```

In the discussion below, each statement that defines a pointer is numbered. Each pointer has the same number as its corresponding statement.

The statements

```
        (1) NEW(HEAD);
            HEAD↑.WORD := 'ACE';
```

define the WORD field of a new list element referenced by pointer **HEAD**.

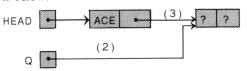

The LINK field of this element must point to the next element of our list. The statements

```
        (2) NEW(Q);
        (3) HEAD↑.LINK := Q;
```

have the effect shown below.

As indicated, a new element is created that is pointed to by Q. The value of Q is then copied into the link field of our first node (3); thereby, connecting the two elements.

The sequence of statements

```
        Q↑.WORD := 'BOY';
    (4) NEW(R);
    (5) Q↑.LINK := R;
        R↑.WORD := 'CAT';
```

completes the linked list. The first statement copies 'BOY' into the WORD field of the second element. The next statement (4) creates a third element pointed to by R. This element is then joined to the second (5), and the value of its NAME field is defined as 'CAT'. The new data structure is shown below.

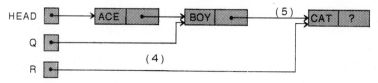

The only ...ing left to do is to indicate that the element pointed to by R is, in fact, the last element of the list and points to no other. This is accomplished by the statement

```
        R↑.LINK := NIL
```

The extra pointers, Q and R, to the elements of this list may be ignored. The final list is shown below.

Obviously, we do not want to go through this process each time we create a new linked list. Hence, we shall write a procedure to do this for us.

Problem 11.1: Write a procedure LISTCREATE that reads a sequence of passenger records consisting of a name, flight number, and number of seats and builds a list of passengers.

Discussion: This procedure will define a pointer, LISTHEAD, to a newly created list. We will find it helpful in future list operations if this list begins with a "dummy" first element. The dummy element will have the letter A stored in its name field. The main program should contain the data type declarations below.

```
TYPE
  SMALLSTRING = STRING[10];
  PASSENGER = RECORD
    NAME : SMALLSTRING;
    FLIGHT : 100..999;
    NUMSEATS : 1..350
  END;
  PASSPOINTER = ↑PASSNODE;
  PASSNODE = RECORD
    PASSINFO : PASSENGER;
    LINK : PASSPOINTER
  END;
```

The data table for procedure LISTCREATE is shown next, followed by the level one algorithm.

Data Table for LISTCREATE

Input parameters	*Output parameters*
(none)	LISTHEAD: Pointer to the head of the new list (PASSPOINTER)

Level One Algorithm

1. Create the first list element (pointed to by LISTHEAD).
2. Read each passenger's data into a new list element and attach it to the end of the list.

Two pointer variables, LAST and NEXT, will be used in the refinement of Step 2. The additional data table entries are described below, followed by the refinement of Step 2.

Program variables

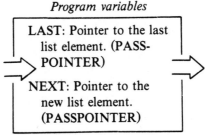

LAST: Pointer to the last list element. (PASS-POINTER)

NEXT: Pointer to the new list element. (PASSPOINTER)

Procedures referenced by LISTCREATE

CREATENODE: Read a passenger's data into a new list element.

Level Two Refinements

Step 2   *Read each passenger's data and attach it to the list.*

    2.1 Initialize LAST to LISTHEAD
    2.2 WHILE more passengers DO
        BEGIN
            2.3 Read a passenger's data into a new list element (pointed to by NEXT).
            2.4 Attach the new list element to the end of the list and reset LAST to NEXT.
        END

Step 2.3 will be performed by procedure CREATENODE. Procedures LISTCREATE and CREATENODE are shown in Fig. 11.2a and b.

As indicated in Fig. 11.2a, it is permissable to use a pointer to specify a record name in a WITH statement. The WITH statement header

WITH LISTHEAD↑, PASSINFO DO

identifies LISTHEAD↑ as the name of a record to be manipulated (the "dummy" node). The field selectors **NAME** and **LINK** inside the **WITH** statement, therefore, are abbreviations for **LISTHEAD↑.PASSINFO.NAME** and **LISTHEAD↑.LINK,** respectively.

```
PROCEDURE LISTCREATE (VAR LISTHEAD : PASSPOINTER);
(* READS A COLLECTION OF PASSENGER RECORDS AND   *)
(* STORES THEM IN A LIST.                         *)
(*                                                *)
(* OUTPUT PARAMETERS                              *)
(*    LISTHEAD - POINTER TO THE HEAD OF THE       *)
(*              LIST CREATED                      *)

CONST
  SENTINEL = 'ZZZ';

VAR
  LAST, NEXT : PASSPOINTER;

(* INSERT PROCEDURE CREATENODE HERE *)

BEGIN
  (* CREATE THE FIRST (DUMMY) LIST ELEMENT *)
  NEW (LISTHEAD);
  WITH LISTHEAD↑, PASSINFO DO
    BEGIN
      NAME := 'A';
      LINK := NIL
    END; (* WITH *)

  (* READ EACH PASSENGER'S DATA INTO NODE *)
  (* NEXT AND ATTACH IT TO THE END OF THE *)
  (* LIST (NODE LAST)                     *)
  LAST := LISTHEAD;
  WHILE LAST↑.NAME <> SENTINEL DO
    BEGIN
      CREATENODE (NEXT);
      LAST↑.LINK := NEXT;
      LAST := NEXT
    END (* WHILE *)
END; (* LISTCREATE *)
```

Fig. 11.2a Procedure LISTCREATE.

The first statement below

```
      LAST↑.LINK := NEXT;
      LAST := NEXT
```

in LISTCREATE attaches the newly created node (pointed to by **NEXT**) to the current end of the list (pointed to by **LAST**); the second statement advances **LAST** to point to the newest list node.

Procedure **CREATENODE** reads each passenger's data into node **NEXT** and initializes the **LINK** field of each new node to NIL. There will always be a sentinel node at the end of the list. The sentinel node will have the string 'ZZZ' stored in its **NAME** field. Procedure **LISTCREATE** is exited after the sentinel node is attached.

```
PROCEDURE CREATENODE (VAR NEXT : PASSPOINTER);
(* ALLOCATES A NEW NODE FOR STORAGE OF THE  *)
(* NEXT PASSENGER'S DATA                     *)

BEGIN
  NEW (NEXT);
  WITH NEXT↑, PASSINFO DO
    BEGIN
      WRITE ('ENTER NAME OR ZZZ: '); READLN (NAME);
      IF NAME <> SENTINEL THEN
        BEGIN
          WRITE ('FLIGHT # '); READLN (FLIGHT);
          WRITE ('NUMBER OF SEATS = '); READLN (NUMSEATS)
        END; (* IF *)
      LINK := NIL
    END (* WITH *)
END; (* CREATENODE *)
```

Fig. 11.2b   Procedure CREATENODE.

Exercise 11.2:   Write a main program that calls LISTCREATE to build a new list and uses TRAVERSE (See Fig. 11.1) to print the list just created.

Exercise 11.3:   Write a procedure that determines the length of an arbitrary list terminated by NIL.

Exercise 11.4:   What are the restrictions on using procedure LISTCREATE?

11.4   DELETING A NODE

We mentioned earlier that one of the reasons for using dynamic data structures is the fact that they are relatively easy to modify. We shall illustrate this by showing the steps required to delete the string 'BOY' from the list segment below. We shall again use two auxiliary pointers, LAST and NEXT, where NEXT points to the node being deleted and LAST points to the node just before it.

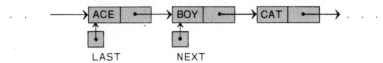

The statement

$$LAST↑.LINK := NEXT↑.LINK$$

performs the deletion by modifying the LINK field of the node pointed to by

LAST. The new value of this field is the same as the value of the LINK field of the node being deleted. The modified data structure is shown below.

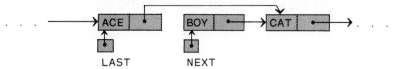

This part of the list now consists of the nodes with WORD field values 'ACE' and 'CAT'. The element with WORD field value 'BOY' is still pointed to by NEXT, but it is no longer considered part of the list. The new list segment is shown below.

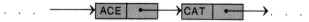

We shall write a procedure to delete a list node next.

Problem 11.2: Write a procedure that deletes an element of a passenger list. Assume that each element is of type PASSENGERNODE (See Problem 11.1) and that the passenger name to be deleted is an input parameter.

Discussion: In order to delete a list node, we must traverse the list until we reach the node to be deleted. In order to start the traversal, we shall need the pointer to the list head as an input parameter. Two local variables, LAST and NEXT, will be advanced down the list. We shall also need an output parameter, DELETED, to indicate whether or not the deletion was performed. The data table and level one algorithm are provided below.

Data Table for LISTDELETE

Input parameters

LISTHEAD: Pointer to head of list (PASS-POINTER)

TARGET: String to be deleted (SMALL-STRING)

Output parameters

DELETED: Program flag that indicates the success (value of TRUE) or failure (value of FALSE) of deletion attempt (BOOLEAN)

Program variables

LAST: Pointer to previous list node (PASS-POINTER)

NEXT: Pointer to current list node (PASS-POINTER)

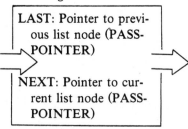

Level One Algorithm for LISTDELETE

1. Traverse the list, starting at the head, until the target string is located or the end of the list is reached.
2. If the target string is located, delete the node containing it. In either case, set the flag DELETED.

Level Two Refinements

Step 1   *Traverse the list until the target is found or the end is reached*

    1.1   NEXT := LISTHEAD
    1.2   WHILE TARGET not found and the end of the list not reached DO
          Advance pointers LAST and NEXT

Step 2   *Delete the target if found and set DELETED*

    2.1   IF TARGET is found THEN
        BEGIN
              2.2 Delete node NEXT
              2.3 DELETED := TRUE
        END
        ELSE
        DELETED := FALSE

The procedure is written in Fig. 11.3. The condition

```
(NEXT↑.PASSINFO.NAME <> TARGET) AND (NEXT↑.LINK <> NIL)
```

is used to control loop repetition. The loop will be exited when either the TARGET or the last list node is reached. If it is exited because the TARGET is reached, the node containing the TARGET will be deleted.

A common error would be to use the condition

```
(NEXT↑.PASSINFO.NAME <> TARGET) AND (NEXT <> NIL)
```

to control loop repetition. The value of NEXT↑.PASSINFO.NAME is undefined when NEXT is NIL.

Note that it should never be necessary to delete the first list element as it is a dummy node rather than an actual passenger. The algorithm would have to be modified if this dummy node did not exist.

Exercise 11.5: Discuss what changes would have to be made to procedure LIST-DELETE if the first list node is not a dummy node.

Exercise 11.6: Modify Procedure LISTDELETE to take advantage of the fact that the character strings are stored in alphabetical order in the list.

```
PROCEDURE LISTDELETE (LISTHEAD : PASSPOINTER;
                      TARGET : SMALLSTRING;
                      VAR DELETED : BOOLEAN);
(* DELETES THE NODE WHOSE NAME FIELD EQUALS TARGET        *)
(*                                                         *)
(* INPUT PARAMETERS                                        *)
(*      LISTHEAD - POINTS TO THE HEAD OF THE LIST BEING    *)
(*                 PROCESSED                               *)
(*      TARGET - NAME BEING DELETED                        *)
(* OUTPUT PARAMETERS                                       *)
(*      DELETED - FLAG INDICATING RESULT OF DELETION       *)
(*                ATTEMPT                                   *)

VAR
  LAST, NEXT : PASSPOINTER;

BEGIN
  (* TRAVERSE THE LIST UNTIL TARGET IS FOUND OR END IS REACHED *)
  NEXT := LISTHEAD;
  WHILE (NEXT↑.PASSINFO.NAME <> TARGET) AND (NEXT↑.LINK <> NIL) DO
    BEGIN
      (* ADVANCE POINTERS LAST AND NEXT *)
      LAST := NEXT;
      NEXT := NEXT↑.LINK
    END; (* WHILE *)

  (* DELETE THE TARGET IF FOUND AND SET DELETED *)
  IF NEXT↑.PASSINFO.NAME = TARGET THEN
    BEGIN
      (* DELETE NODE NEXT *)
      LAST↑.LINK := NEXT↑.LINK;
      DELETED := TRUE
    END
  ELSE
    DELETED := FALSE
END; (* LISTDELETE *)
```

Fig. 11.3   Procedure LISTDELETE.

11.5   LIST INSERTION

11.5.1   Introduction

The next problem in manipulating list structures is that of inserting an element in a list. We shall use two auxiliary pointers, Q and R, to point to the list elements that immediately precede and follow the new element, respectively.

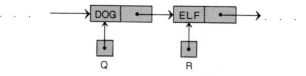

The program segment

(1) NEW (Q↑.LINK);
(2) Q↑.LINK↑.LINK := R

makes the changes shown in Fig. 11.4.

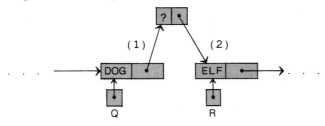

Fig. 11.4   Insertion of a new list element.

As indicated by arrow (1), the new node that is allocated is pointed to by the link field of node Q (Q↑.LINK). Its link field, represented by Q↑.LINK↑. LINK, points to the same node as pointer R (See arrow (2) in Fig. 11.4.). Hence, the new node is inserted between nodes Q and R as shown below.

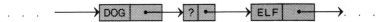

Exercise 11.7:   Write the instructions needed to insert a new node that is referenced by pointer P between nodes Q and R.

11.5.2   Maintaining an Ordered List

Normally, the position of a new list element depends on one or more data fields. In our airline passenger list, we might want to keep all passengers in alphabetical order, in which case the position of a new passenger in the list would be determined by comparing that person's name to the name of each passenger already in the list.

Problem 11.3:   Write a procedure that inserts a new passenger into a passenger list. The names of the passengers should be in alphabetical order before and after the insertion operation.

Discussion: The new passenger's name and flight data (record NEW-PASSENGER) should be passed to the procedure along with a pointer to the current head of the passenger list (LISTHEAD). Pointers LAST and NEXT will advance down the list until the correct alphabetical position of the new passenger is reached.

The diagram below shows the desired location of a new passenger named 'KING'. This passenger must be inserted in front of passenger 'LYNCH' where passenger 'LYNCH' is the first passenger in the list whose name alphabetically follows 'KING'.

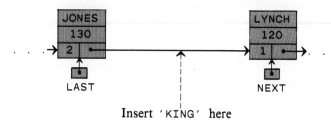

Insert 'KING' here

The data table and algorithm for procedure LISTINSERT follow.

Data Table for LISTINSERT

Input parameters

NEWPASSENGER: The new passenger to be inserted (PASSEN-GER)

LISTHEAD: Pointer to the head of the passen-ger list (PASS-POINTER)

Program variables

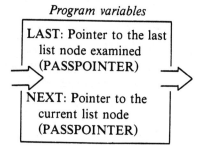

LAST: Pointer to the last list node examined (PASSPOINTER)

NEXT: Pointer to the current list node (PASSPOINTER)

Procedures referenced

INSERTNODE: Inserts the passenger data between two nodes.

Level One Algorithm

1. Search the passenger list to find the insertion point for the new passenger.
2. Insert the new passenger.

Level Two Refinements

Step 1   *Search the passenger list for the insertion point of NEWPASSENGER*

    1.1   Initialize NEXT to LISTHEAD
    1.2   WHILE insertion point not found DO
           Advance pointers LAST and NEXT

The loop repetition condition in Step 1.2 may be written as

```
NEWPASSENGER.NAME > NEXT↑.PASSINFO.NAME
```

Since the sentinel name ('ZZZ') is larger than any passenger name, this condition would be false if the end of the list is reached.

The loop will be exited for one of the following reasons. A name that is the same as the new passenger's is reached; a name that alphabetically follows the new passenger's is reached; the last list element is reached. In the first case above, only the flight number and number of seats for the passenger should be updated (We are assuming it is not possible for two passengers to have the same name.). In the second and third cases above, the new passenger should be inserted just before the node pointed to by NEXT. The refinement of Step 2 below differentiates between these alternatives.

Additional Level Two Refinements

Step 2   *Insert the new passenger*

> 2.1 IF the new passenger is in the list THEN
>> 2.2 Update the flight number and number of seats
>
> ELSE
>> 2.3 Insert the new passenger between LAST and NEXT

The procedure is shown in Fig. 11.5a. The statement

```
INSERTNODE (NEWPASSENGER, LAST, NEXT)
```

calls procedure **INSERTNODE** (see Fig. 11.5b) to implement Step 2.3. INSERTNODE resets the LINK field of node LAST to point to a newly created node; the new node's LINK field points to node NEXT.

```
PROCEDURE LISTINSERT (NEWPASSENGER : PASSENGER;
                      LISTHEAD : PASSPOINTER);
(* INSERT NEWPASSENGER IN THE PASSENGER LIST *)
(*                                            *)
(* INPUT PARAMETERS                           *)
(*      NEWPASSENGER - PASSENGER DATA TO      *)
(*                     BE INSERTED            *)
(*      LISTHEAD - POINTER TO LIST HEAD       *)

VAR
  LAST, NEXT : PASSPOINTER;

(* INSERT PROCEDURE INSERTNODE HERE *)

BEGIN
  (* SEARCH THE PASSENGER LIST FOR CORRECT *)
  (* POSITION OF NEWPASSENGER              *)
  NEXT := LISTHEAD;
  WHILE NEWPASSENGER.NAME > NEXT↑.PASSINFO.NAME DO
```

(continued)

```
    BEGIN
      (* ADVANCE POINTERS *)
      LAST := NEXT;
      NEXT := NEXT↑.LINK
    END; (* WHILE *)

  (* INSERT THE NEW PASSENGER IN THE LIST *)
  IF NEWPASSENGER.NAME = NEXT↑.PASSINFO.NAME THEN
    (* UPDATE PASSENGER DATA *)
    NEXT↑.PASSINFO := NEWPASSENGER
  ELSE
    (* INSERT BETWEEN LAST AND NEXT *)
    INSERTNODE (NEWPASSENGER, LAST, NEXT)
END; (* LISTINSERT *)
```

Fig. 11.5a Procedure LISTINSERT.

```
PROCEDURE INSERTNODE (NEWPASSENGER : PASSENGER;
                      VAR LAST : PASSPOINTER;
                      NEXT : PASSPOINTER);
(* INSERTS A NODE BETWEEN LAST AND NEXT      *)
(*                                            *)
(* INPUT PARAMETERS                           *)
(*    NEWPASSENGER - NEW PASSENGER TO         *)
(*                   BE INSERTED              *)
(*    NEXT - NODE FOLLOWING NEWPASSENGER      *)
(* OUTPUT PARAMETERS                          *)
(*    LAST - NODE PRECEDING NEW PASSENGER     *)

BEGIN
  (* ATTACH A NEW NODE FOLLOWING NODE LAST *)
  NEW (LAST↑.LINK);

  (* STORE NEWPASSENGER DATA    *)
  (* - LINK NEW NODE TO NODE NEXT *)
  WITH LAST↑.LINK↑ DO
    BEGIN
      PASSINFO := NEWPASSENGER;
      LINK := NEXT
    END (* WITH *)
END; (* INSERTNODE *)
```

Fig. 11.5b Procedure INSERTNODE.

Exercise 11.8: Discuss what modifications would be required if the first node was not a dummy node.

Exercise 11.9: Verify for yourself that this procedure works when the new passenger's name alphabetically precedes all names currently in the list. In this case, the passenger should be inserted at the beginning of the passenger list.

Exercise 11.10: How might you solve this problem if the passenger records were stored in alphabetical order in an array?

11.5.3   Creating an Ordered List

The procedure LISTINSERT assumed that it was processing a passenger list that was already in alphabetical order. However, the procedure LISTCREATE (see Fig. 11.2a) that was used to create the original passenger list simply added each new passenger to the passenger list in the sequence provided without regard to alphabetical order. The resulting passenger list would be in alphabetical order only if the passenger records provided as data happened to be in alphabetical order by last name.

The procedure CREATEORDERLIST shown in Fig. 11.6a uses procedure READPASS (Fig. 11.6b) to read each new passenger's data. It also uses LISTINSERT to insert each new data record (type PASSENGER). This will insure that the resulting passenger list is in alphabetical order as desired regardless of the data sequence. Initially, the list consists of the dummy node (pointed to by LISTHEAD) and the sentinel node (pointed to by TAIL) as drawn below.

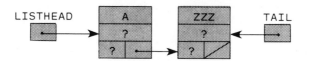

```
PROCEDURE CREATEORDERLIST (VAR LISTHEAD : PASSPOINTER);
(* READS A COLLECTION OF PASSENGER RECORDS AND          *)
(* STORES THEM ALPHABETICALLY IN A LINKED LIST          *)
(*                                                      *)
(* OUTPUT PARAMETER                                     *)
(*     LISTHEAD - POINTER TO HEAD OF THE                *)
(*               LIST CREATED                           *)

CONST
  SENTINEL = 'ZZZ';

VAR
  TAIL : PASSPOINTER;
  NEWPASSENGER : PASSENGER;

(* INSERT PROCEDURES READPASS, LISTINSERT HERE *)

BEGIN
  (* CREATE THE FIRST (DUMMY) AND   *)
  (* LAST (SENTINEL) LIST ELEMENTS  *)
  NEW (LISTHEAD);
  NEW (TAIL);
  WITH LISTHEAD↑, PASSINFO DO
    BEGIN
      NAME := 'A';
      LINK := TAIL
    END; (* WITH *)
  WITH TAIL↑, PASSINFO DO
```

(continued)

```
      BEGIN
        NAME := SENTINEL;
        LINK := NIL
      END; (* WITH *)

    (* READ EACH PASSENGER'S DATA AND *)
    (* INSERT IN THE ORDERED LIST      *)
    READPASS (NEWPASSENGER);
    WHILE NEWPASSENGER.NAME <> SENTINEL DO
      BEGIN
        LISTINSERT (NEWPASSENGER, LISTHEAD);
        READPASS (NEWPASSENGER)
      END (* WHILE *)
END; (* CREATEORDERLIST *)
```

Fig. 11.6a Procedure CREATEORDERLIST.

```
PROCEDURE READPASS (VAR NEWPASSENGER : PASSENGER);
(* READ NEW PASSENGER'S DATA                      *)
(*                                                *)
(* OUTPUT PARAMETER                               *)
(*      NEWPASSENGER - NEW PASSENGER DATA         *)

BEGIN
  WITH NEWPASSENGER DO
    BEGIN
      WRITE ('ENTER NAME OR ZZZ: '); READLN (NAME);
      IF NAME <> SENTINEL THEN
        BEGIN
          WRITE ('FLIGHT # '); READLN (FLIGHT);
          WRITE ('NUMBER OF SEATS = '); READLN (NUMSEATS)
        END (* IF *)
    END (* WITH *)
END; (* READPASS *)
```

Fig. 11.6b Procedure READPASS.

11.6 MULTIPLE-LINKED LISTS AND TREES*

11.6.1 Introduction to Multiple-linked Lists

All the examples seen so far have involved list elements or nodes with a single pointer field. It is possible to have lists of elements with more than one link. For example, each element in the list shown below has a forward pointer that points to the next list element and a backward pointer that points to the previous list element.

---

*This section is optional and may be omitted.

This structure is called a *bi-directional* (or *two-way*) linked list. The statements below declare a list element of this general form.

```
TYPE
  LINK = ↑MULTINODE;
  MULTINODE = RECORD
                .  ⎫
                .  ⎬   data fields
                .  ⎭
      FORWARD : LINK;
      BACKWARD : LINK
  END
```

11.6.2 Introduction to Trees

There is one special kind of multiple-linked list that has wide applicability in computer science. This data structure is called a *binary tree* or *tree*. A sample tree is drawn in Fig. 11.7.

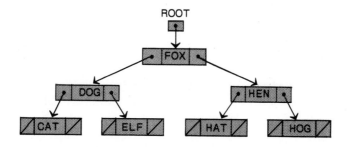

Fig. 11.7 A sample tree.

Trees in computer science actually grow from the top down rather than from the ground up. The top-most element is called the *root of the tree*. The pointer, ROOT, points to the root of the tree drawn in Fig. 11.7. Each tree node shown has a single data field and two pointer fields called the *left branch* and *right branch*, respectively.

The NIL pointer is indicated by a slash (/). Any node with both pointer fields equal to NIL is called a *leaf.*

The node containing the string 'HEN' is the *parent* of the nodes containing the strings 'HAT' and 'HOG'. Similarly, the nodes 'HAT' and 'HOG' are *siblings* since they are both children of the same parent node. The root of the tree is an *ancestor* of all other nodes in the tree and they, in turn, are all *descendants* of the root node.

Each node in a tree may be thought of as the root node of its own *sub-tree.* Since each node has two branches, it spawns two sub-trees, a *left sub-tree* and a *right sub-tree.* Its *left child* is the root node of the left sub-tree, and its *right child* is the root node of the right sub-tree.

The statements below describe the form of a tree node.

```
TYPE
  BRANCH = ↑TREE;
  TREE = RECORD
    WORD : STRING[3];
    LEFT, RIGHT: BRANCH
  END
```

Trees may be used for representing expressions in memory. For example, the expression

$$(X + Y) * (A - B)$$

could be represented as the tree drawn in Fig. 11.8. The left sub-tree of the root node represents the subexpression (X + Y); the right sub-tree represents the subexpression (A − B).

ROOT

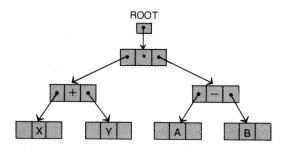

Fig. 11.8   Tree form of expression (X + Y) * (A − B).

Trees are also used to organize related data items as a hierarchical data structure in order to facilitate efficient search and retrieval for a desired item (key). For example, the tree shown in Fig. 11.7 is arranged so that the left descendent of each node alphabetically precedes its parent and the right descendant alphabetically follows its parent. Hence, in searching for a particular key at any level of this tree, the left branch should be followed if the key value is "less than" the current node value, and the right branch should be followed if the key value is "greater than" the current node value. (What if the key value equals the current node value?) This effectively reduces the search space by a factor of two each time since all the descendants (children and grandchildren) in the branch not chosen are ignored.

Exercise 11.11:   Draw the binary tree representation of the expressions

```
X * Y MOD (A + B) DIV C
X * Y MOD A + B DIV C
```

11.6.3 Creating a TREE

The next problem will show us how to create a tree of the form shown in Fig. 11.7.

Problem 11.4:   Write a procedure CREATETREE that creates an ordered tree of character strings. The first character string provided as data should be inserted in the root node. All character strings that are in a left (right) sub-tree alphabetically precede (follow) the string stored in the sub-tree root.

Discussion: Procedure CREATETREE should define a pointer, ROOT, to the root of the tree created. The first character string will be stored in the root. Each subsequent string will be read into NEXTWORD. Its position in the tree will be determined by comparing it to the string stored in each ancestor node (starting with the root) and then following either the left branch or right branch from that ancestor based on the result of this comparison. If NEXTWORD alphabetically precedes the string in the ancestor node, the left branch should be followed; otherwise, the right branch should be followed. A pointer to a new node containing NEXTWORD will replace the first NIL pointer reached.

As an example of this process, we shall create the tree corresponding to the strings 'DOG', 'BOY', 'CAT', 'ELF', and 'BYE'. The first string, 'DOG', is inserted in the root as shown.

The next string, 'BOY', is alphabetically less than 'DOG', so it is attached to the left branch of the root.

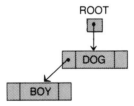

The next string, 'CAT', is less than 'DOG', so the left branch from the root is followed. 'CAT' is greater than 'BOY', so it is attached to the right branch from the node containing 'BOY' as shown below.

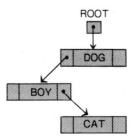

The string 'ELF' is greater than the string in the root; hence, it is attached to the right branch from the root, as shown next.

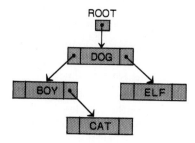

Finally, the string 'BYE' would be compared to 'DOG', 'BOY', and 'CAT' and attached to the left branch from the node containing 'CAT'. (Where would 'FOX', 'DAY', and 'HAT' be stored?)

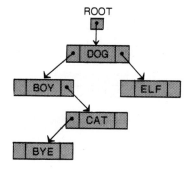

The data types that follow should be declared in the main program that calls procedure CREATETREE.

```
TYPE
   WORDSTRING : STRING[3];
   BRANCH = ↑TREE;
   TREE = RECORD
     WORD : WORDSTRING;
     LEFT, RIGHT : BRANCH
   END;
```

The data table and algorithm for procedure CREATETREE follow. There is only one procedure parameter: the pointer parameter (ROOT) that references the root node of the new tree.

Data Table for CREATETREE

Input parameters	*Output parameters*
(none)	ROOT: Pointer to the root node of the tree (BRANCH)

Constants

   SENTINEL = '/', sentinel value

Input variables	*Program variables*	*Output variables*
NEXTWORD: Each character string to be stored in the tree (WORDSTRING)		(none)

Procedures referenced

   ATTACH: Attaches a new node to a tree
   TREESEARCH: Searches a tree for a specified string.

Level One Algorithm

1. Insert the first string in the root node of the tree.
2. Read each string into NEXTWORD. Search for NEXTWORD (starting at the root node). Attach NEXTWORD to its parent if NEXTWORD is not in the tree.

Level Two Refinements

Step 1   *Insert the first string in the root node*

   1.1   Read the first string into NEXTWORD
   1.2   Allocate a new node for NEXTWORD pointed to by ROOT

Step 2   *Read each string into NEXTWORD and attach it to its parent*

   2.1   Read the next string into NEXTWORD
   2.2   WHILE NEXTWORD < > SENTINEL DO
         BEGIN
               2.3 Search for NEXTWORD and insert it in the tree
               2.4 IF NEXTWORD was already in the tree THEN
                      Print that NEXTWORD is a duplicate entry
               2.5 Read the next string into NEXTWORD
         END

   Step 1.2 is performed by procedure ATTACH. Each new node that is attached must be a leaf node (NIL pointers). Procedure CREATETREE is shown in Fig. 11.9a along with local procedure ATTACH.

Step 2.3 is performed by procedure TREESEARCH. We shall introduce two program variables for communicating with TREESEARCH as described below.

Program variables

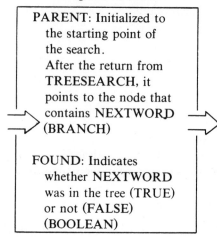

> PARENT: Initialized to
> the starting point of
> the search.
> After the return from
> TREESEARCH, it
> points to the node that
> contains NEXTWORD
> (BRANCH)
>
> FOUND: Indicates
> whether NEXTWORD
> was in the tree (TRUE)
> or not (FALSE)
> (BOOLEAN)

The pointer PARENT corresponds to an update parameter of TREE-SEARCH which may be modified as the search progresses. Since we want to begin the search at the root node of the tree, PARENT should be initialized to ROOT before TREESEARCH is called. If NEXTWORD is already in the tree, procedure TREESEARCH should find it by tracing through the tree until PARENT points to the node containing NEXTWORD. If NEXTWORD is not in the tree, PARENT will eventually reach the node where NEXTWORD should be attached. The pointer from this node will have a value of NIL.

ATTACH (NEXTWORD, PARENT)

attaches NEXTWORD to the tree by resetting this pointer, represented by PARENT, to a new node containing NEXTWORD.

Procedure TREESEARCH should start at the root node and follow left or right pointers until it finds NEXTWORD or reaches the node where NEXTWORD should be attached (indicated by the pointer value NIL). As with many operations on trees, we shall find it easier to implement TREESEARCH as a recursive algorithm (see Section 8.8). The data table and algorithm for TREESEARCH follow.

Data Table for TREESEARCH

Input parameters	*Update parameters*	*Output parameters*
NEXTWORD: The string being located (WORDSTRING)	PARENT: The root of the subtree to be searched (BRANCH)	FOUND: The search result when done (BOOLEAN)

Level One Algorithm

1. If a NIL pointer is reached, then set FOUND to false and insert NEXT-WORD; otherwise, if NEXTWORD is located, then set FOUND to true; otherwise, continue to search the left or right subtree of PARENT.

Level Two Refinements

Step 1

> 1.1 IF PARENT = NIL THEN
> > 1.2 Set FOUND to false and attach NEXTWORD to PARENT
> > ELSE IF NEXTWORD = PARENT↑.WORD THEN
> > > 1.3 FOUND := TRUE
> > > ELSE IF NEXTWORD < PARENT↑.WORD THEN
> > > > 1.4 Search the left subtree of PARENT
> > > >
> > > > ELSE
> > > > 1.5 Search the right subtree of PARENT

The stopping states for the recursion are Steps 1.2 and 1.3 above. Steps 1.4 and 1.5 are implemented as recursive calls to procedure TREESEARCH. Procedure TREESEARCH is shown in Fig. 11.9b.

```
PROCEDURE CREATETREE (VAR ROOT : BRANCH);
(* CREATES AN ORDERED BINARY TREE      *)
(*                                       *)
(* OUTPUT PARAMETERS                     *)
(*     ROOT - POINTER TO TREE ROOT      *)

CONST
  SENTINEL = '/';

VAR
  NEXTWORD : WORDSTRING;
  PARENT : BRANCH;
  FOUND : BOOLEAN;

PROCEDURE ATTACH (NEXTWORD : WORDSTRING;
                  VAR PARENT : BRANCH);
(* CREATES A NEW NODE POINTED TO BY PARENT *)
(*                                          *)
(* INPUT PARAMETER                          *)
(*     NEXTWORD - STRING TO BE INSERTED     *)
(*                IN THE TREE               *)
(* UPDATE PARAMETER                         *)
(*     PARENT - POINTER TO NEW NODE         *)

BEGIN (* ATTACH *)
  NEW (PARENT);
  WITH PARENT↑ DO
```

(*continued*)

```
      BEGIN
        WORD := NEXTWORD;
        LEFT := NIL;
        RIGHT := NIL
      END (* WITH *)
END; (* ATTACH *)
```

```
(* INSERT PROCEDURE TREESEARCH HERE *)

BEGIN (* CREATETREE *)
  (* INSERT THE FIRST STRING *)
  (* IN THE ROOT NODE       *)
  WRITE ('FIRST WORD: '); READLN (NEXTWORD);
  ATTACH (NEXTWORD, ROOT);

  (* READ EACH STRING INTO NEXTWORD *)
  (* AND ATTACH IT TO ITS PARENT    *)
  WRITELN ('ENTER / OR')
  WRITE ('NEXT WORD: '); READLN (NEXTWORD);
  WHILE NEXTWORD <> SENTINEL DO
    BEGIN
      PARENT := ROOT;
      TREESEARCH (PARENT, NEXTWORD, FOUND);
      IF FOUND THEN
        WRITELN (NEXTWORD, ' IS A DUPLICATE ENTRY');
      WRITE ('NEXT WORD: '); READLN (NEXTWORD)
    END (* WHILE *)
END; (* CREATETREE *)
```

Fig. 11.9a Procedure CREATETREE.

```
PROCEDURE TREESEARCH (VAR PARENT : BRANCH;
                          NEXTWORD : SMALLSTRING;
                          VAR FOUND : BOOLEAN);
(* SEARCHES A BINARY TREE                  *)
(*                                         *)
(* INPUT PARAMETERS                        *)
(*      NEXTWORD - THE STRING BEING        *)
(*                 LOCATED                 *)
(* UPDATE PARAMETERS                       *)
(*      PARENT - TREE (OR SUBTREE) ROOT    *)
(* OUTPUT PARAMETERS                       *)
(*      FOUND - INDICATES WHETHER          *)
(*              NEXTWORD IS IN THE TREE     *)

BEGIN
  IF PARENT = NIL THEN
    BEGIN
      FOUND := FALSE;
```

(continued)

```
      ATTACH (NEXTWORD, PARENT)
    END
  ELSE IF NEXTWORD = PARENT↑.WORD THEN
    FOUND := TRUE
  ELSE IF NEXTWORD < PARENT↑.WORD THEN
    TREESEARCH (PARENT↑.LEFT, NEXTWORD, FOUND)
  ELSE
    TREESEARCH (PARENT↑.RIGHT, NEXTWORD, FOUND)
END; (* TREESEARCH *)
```

Fig. 11.9b Procedure TREESEARCH.

Exercise 11.12: What is the purpose of the statement

```
            PARENT := ROOT;
```

in procedure CREATETREE? Why would it not be proper to delete this statement and use the procedure statement

```
        TREESEARCH (ROOT, NEXTWORD, FOUND);
```

to call TREESEARCH instead?

Exercise 11.13: Give at least two sequences of strings that would create the tree shown in Fig. 11.7.

Exercise 11.14: Add the strings 'DOE', 'COY', 'DAY', 'GIP', 'GUN', 'FAT', 'HIT' in sequence to the tree in Fig. 11.7.

Exercise 11.15: Build the tree corresponding to the strings 'ACE', 'BOY', 'CAT', 'DOG', 'HAT', 'HEN', and 'HOG'. What is unusual about this "tree"?

11.6.3   Traversing a Tree

In order to process the data stored in a tree, it is necessary to traverse the tree, or visit in a systematic way, each and every node in the tree. The particular approach that will be illustrated is called an in-order traversal. The in-order traversal is described recursively as:

1. Traverse the left sub-tree
2. Visit the current node (i.e., print its WORD field)
3. Traverse the right sub-tree

where the left subtree of any node is the part of the tree whose root is the left child of that node. The in-order traversal for the tree, shown in Fig. 11.10, would generate the alphabetical sequence

```
    'CAT'   'DOG'   'ELF'   'FOX'   'HAT'   'HEN'   'HOG'
```

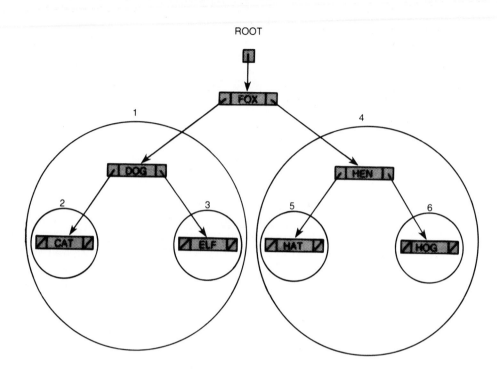

Fig. 11.10   Sub-trees of a tree.

In Fig. 11.10, a numbered circle is drawn around each sub-tree. The sub-trees are numbered in the order that they are traversed. Sub-tree 1 is the left sub-tree of the root node. Its left sub-tree (number 2) has no left sub-tree (or right sub-tree); hence, the string 'CAT' would be printed first. The root node for sub-tree 1 would then be visited and 'DOG' would be printed. Its right sub-tree consists of the leaf node containing the string 'ELF' (number 3). After 'ELF' is printed, the root node for the complete tree is visited ('FOX' is printed) and the right sub-tree of the root node (number 4) is traversed in a like manner.

Procedure INORDER in Fig. 11.11 is a recursive procedure that performs the in-order traversal of any tree. The parameter ROOT represents the pointer to the root node of the tree being traversed. The procedure VISIT would be used to print all data values stored in each node. Procedure INORDER is much simpler than any nonrecursive procedure that might be written to traverse a tree.

```
PROCEDURE INORDER (ROOT : BRANCH);
(* PERFORMS AN INORDER TRAVERSAL OF              *)
(* THE TREE POINTED TO BY ROOT                   *)
(*                                               *)
(* INPUT PARAMETER                               *)
(*      ROOT - ROOT OF TREE (OR SUBTREE)         *)
(*                 BEING TRAVERSED               *)

(* INSERT PROCEDURE VISIT HERE *)
```

```
BEGIN
  (* TEST FOR STOPPING STATE *)
  IF ROOT <> NIL THEN
    BEGIN
      (* STOPPING STATE NOT REACHED - *)
      (* PERFORM RECURSION STEP        *)
      INORDER (ROOT↑.LEFT);
      VISIT (ROOT);
      INORDER (ROOT↑.RIGHT)
    END
END; (* INORDER *)
```

Fig. 11.11 Procedure INORDER.

Exercise 11.16: What can you say about the in-order traversal of any tree created by procedure CREATETREE in Fig. 11.9a?

Exercise 11.17: What would be printed by the in-order traversal of the tree below?

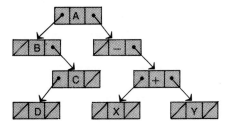

11.7 COMMON PROGRAMMING ERRORS

It is often very difficult to debug a program involving pointer variables since the value of a pointer variable represents a memory cell address and cannot normally be printed. Hence, if a pointer value is invalid or incorrect, there may be no way of finding out what this erroneous value happens to be.

Make sure that the symbol ↑ follows each pointer variable used to designate a particular node or record. The ↑ must always be written when you wish to manipulate a field of a node. If the pointer variable appears without the ↑, the compiler will manipulate the pointer value itself (an address) rather than the node pointed to by the pointer variable.

Another potential source of error involves attempting to reference a field of a node pointed to by a pointer whose value is NIL. This, of course, is illegal since the NIL pointer is a special value used to indicate the end of a list.

An additional error may arise if your program gets stuck in a loop during the creation of a dynamic data structure. In this case, the number of cells allocated may exceed the memory space available in your PASCAL system. This condition will result in a "STACK OVERFLOW" error message.

11.8   SUMMARY

In this chapter, we introduced two dynamic data structures, lists and trees. We discussed the use of pointers to reference and connect elements of a dynamic data structure. The procedure NEW was used to allocate additional elements or nodes of a dynamic data structure.

Many different aspects of manipulating linked lists were covered. We showed how to build or create a linked list, how to traverse a linked list, and how to insert and delete linked list elements.

In addition, the tree was shown to be a special list form with two links. We showed how to create an ordered tree and how to perform a tree traversal. If you continue your study of computer science, all of these subjects will be covered in much more detail in a future course on data structures.

PROGRAMMING PROBLEMS

11.5   Write a main program that first builds an airline passenger list in alphabetical order from passenger data provided on an input file. The program should next process commands read from system file INPUT to modify this list. The first letter of each command indicates what is to be done with any passenger data on that input line (I - Insert, D - Delete, R - Replace flight data, P - Print passengers on a specified flight, Q - Quit). After the Q command is entered, the program system should display the final passenger list.

11.6   Repeat Problem 11.5 only this time use a tree to store the passenger data. When deleting a pasenger, simply blank out the information fields and leave the passenger node in the tree. Use an extra data field to indicate whether a node is still in the tree or deleted.

11.7   There are many applications in which a two-dimensional matrix with large dimensions must be stored in memory. If a majority of the elements in the matrix are zero, the matrix is called a sparse matrix. A sparse matrix may be more efficiently represented using a one-dimensional array of pointers where each element of this array, ROW, points to a linked list. ROW [I] would point to a list whose nodes indicate the value and column number for each nonzero element in row I. For example, if row 3 is (25 0 0 0 −14 0 0), then the third element of this array would point to the list shown below.

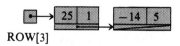

ROW[3]

This list indicates that there are two nonzero elements in the third row of the sparse matrix at columns 1 and 5. Write procedures to read a sparse matrix and store it as shown, to add together two sparse matrices and to print a sparse matrix.

11.8   A polynomial may be represented as a linked list where each node contains the coefficient and exponent of a term of the polynomial. The polynomial $4x^3 + 3x^2 - 5$ would be represented as the linked list

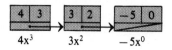

$4x^3$ $3x^2$ $-5x^0$

Write a program system that reads two polynomials, stores them as linked lists, adds them together, and prints the result as a polynomial. The result should be a third linked list. Hint: Traverse both polynomials. If a particular exponent value is present in either of the two polynomials being summed, then it should be present in the answer. If it is present in both polynomials, then its coefficient is the sum of the corresponding coefficient in both polynomials. (If this sum is zero, the term should be deleted.)

11.9 In a pre-order traversal, the root is visited first, then the left subtree and then the right subtree. In a post-order traversal, the left subtree is visited first, then the right subtree, and then the root. Write procedures to perform both these traversals.

11.10 Assume that the registration data for a class of students is stored as the array of records shown below.

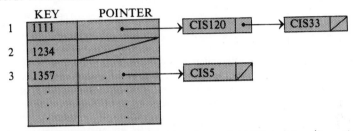

The first field in each record contains the student ID number (four digits) and the second field contains a pointer to all classes for which the student is registered. Write a program system that builds this array from a file of randomly arranged data and prints it out. Assume each data line starts with an I (insert) or D (delete), followed by the student ID and course identification string.

11.11 Write a program system that represents the Morse code as a binary tree. The symbol · should cause a branch to the left and the symbol − a branch to the right. The information field of each node should be the letter represented by the corresponding code. The first three levels of the tree are shown below.

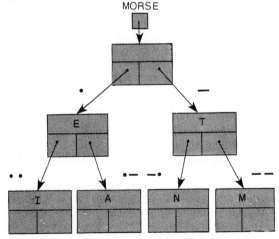

The MORSE code should be read from an input file where each file component consists of a letter, and the córresponding code string. After building the tree, read a coded message and translate it into English.

11.12 A stack is a data structure in which the last element inserted is the first element removed (like a stack of trays at a cafeteria). Represent a stack as a linked list where each new list element is inserted at the head of the list. Write a procedure to insert an element in a specified stack (a PUSH procedure) and a procedure to remove the element at the top of a specified stack (a POP procedure).

11.13 Use two stacks (OPERATOR and OPERAND) and procedures PUSH and POP written in Problem 11.12 to help in "compiling" a simple arithmetic expression without parentheses. For example, the expression

$$A + B * C - D$$

should be compiled as the table:

OPERATION	OPERAND1	OPERAND2	RESULT
*	B	C	Z
+	A	Z	Y
−	Y	D	X

The above table shows the order of the three operations (*, +, −) and their operands. The result column gives the name of an identifier selected to hold the result.

Your procedure should read each character (NEXTCHAR) and process it as follows: If it is a blank, then ignore it; otherwise, if it is an operand (A − F), then push it onto the OPERAND stack; otherwise, if it is not an operator (+, −, *, /), then print an error message. If the character is an operator, then it should be pushed onto the OPERATOR stack if its precedence is greater than the operator currently at the top of the stack (e.g., when * is read in the example above, it is pushed onto the stack because + is on the top) or if the operator stack is empty. Otherwise, a line of the output table should be written by popping the OPERATOR stack and removing the first two elements of the OPERAND stack (two pops). A new symbol is used to hold the result (Z − G), and this symbol is pushed onto the operand stack. The process of generating output table lines continues until the precedence of NEXTCHAR is greater than the precedence of the operator at the top of the stack or the operator stack is empty. At this point, NEXTCHAR should be pushed onto the operator stack. When the end of the input line is reached, any remaining operators and operands should be popped as described above.

In addition to procedures POP and PUSH, you will need a precedence table that gives the precedence value for each of the operators (1 or 2).

APPENDICES

INDEX OF
PROGRAM STYLE DISPLAYS

INDEX OF
PROGRAMS, PROCEDURES
AND FUNCTIONS

APPENDIX 1

Differences between UCSD and standard PASCAL

1. **Case statement**
   In standard PASCAL, an error results when the selector value does not match one of the case labels. In UCSD PASCAL, execution continues with the first statement following the Case statement.

2. **Dispose procedure**
   Standard PASCAL provides the DISPOSE procedure to return dynamically allocated storage cells for reallocation. This procedure is not implemented in UCSD PASCAL.

3. **Compiler directives**
   A comment beginning with a $ is recognized as a compiler directive by UCSD PASCAL but not standard PASCAL.

4. **INTERACTIVE files**
   UCSD PASCAL supports files of characters that are type INTERACTIVE and TEXT. The INTERACTIVE files simplify the handling of interactive terminals. Only TEXT files are supported in standard PASCAL.

5. **Random access files**
   UCSD PASCAL provides the SEEK procedure which enables random access to files. Random access files are not supported in standard PASCAL.

6. **GOTO and EXIT**
   Standard PASCAL allows a GOTO to a label outside the block in which the GOTO statement appears. UCSD PASCAL provides the EXIT procedure for transferring out of a block.

7. **Packed variables**
   Standard PASCAL provides PACK and UNPACK procedures for transferring data between a packed array and an equivalent array that is not packed. UCSD PASCAL does not provide these procedures; however, the STRING data type eliminates much of the need for them.

8. **Procedures and functions as parameters**

Standard PASCAL permits a procedure or function name to be passed as a parameter. This is not allowed in UCSD PASCAL.

9. **Program parameters**

Standard PASCAL requires the identification of all input/output files used in a program as parameters of the PROGRAM statement. UCSD PASCAL does not require this.

10. **String variables and operators**

UCSD PASCAL supports the data type STRING along with a number of built-in procedures and functions for manipulating strings. No such facility is provided in standard PASCAL. Instead, most string manipulation is performed through the use of packed character arrays.

APPENDIX 2

Reserved Words, Standard Identifiers and Operators

Reserved words

AND	END	NIL	SET
ARRAY	FILE	NOT	THEN
BEGIN	FOR	OF	TO
CASE	FUNCTION	OR	TYPE
CONST	GOTO	PACKED	UNTIL
DIV	IF	PROCEDURE	VAR
DO	IN	PROGRAM	WHILE
DOWNTO	LABEL	RECORD	WITH
ELSE	MOD	REPEAT	

Standard identifiers

Constants:

    FALSE, TRUE, MAXINT

Types:

    INTEGER, BOOLEAN, REAL, CHAR, STRING, TEXT, INTERAC-
    TIVE

System files:

    INPUT, OUTPUT, KEYBOARD

Functions:

    ABS, ATAN, CHR, COS, EOF, EOLN, EXP, LN, ODD, ORD,
    IORESULT, PRED, ROUND, SIN, SQR, SQRT, SUCC, TRUNC,
    LENGTH, LOG, CONCAT, COPY, POS, PWROFTEN

Procedures:

    GET, NEW, PUT, READ, READLN, RESET, REWRITE, SEEK,
    WRITE, WRITELN, DELETE, INSERT

operator	operation	type of operand(s)	result type
:=	assignment	any type except file types	
arithmetic:			
+ (unary) − (unary)	identity sign inversion	integer or real	same as operand
+ − *	addition subtraction multiplication	integer or real	integer or real
DIV / MOD	integer division real division modulus	integer integer or real integer	integer real integer
relational:			
= < >	equality inequality	scalar, string, set, or pointer	
< >	less than greater than	scalar or string	Boolean
< =	less than or equal -or- subset	scalar or string set	
> =	greater than or equal -or- superset	scalar or string set	
IN	set membership	first operand is any scalar, the second is its set type	
logical:			
NOT OR AND	negation disjunction conjunction	Boolean	Boolean
set:			
+ − *	union set difference intersection	any set type T	T

Table of Operators

APPENDIX 3

Using UCSD PASCAL

UCSD PASCAL is more than a programming language; it is a complete operating system for creating, saving and retrieving programs as disk files, and compiling and executing these programs. We shall only be able to provide a brief introduction to this operating system. For additional details, see your system manual.

The first step in using UCSD PASCAL is to insert the diskette(s) with the UCSD system into the disk drive(s) and bootload the system. If successful, a message such as

```
WELCOME TO U.C.S.D. PASCAL SYSTEM
CURRENT DATE IS 1-JAN-82
>COMMAND: E(DIT, R(UN, F(ILE, C(OMP, L(INK, X(ECUTE, A(SSEM,
         D(EBUG?
```

will appear on the screen.

The line labelled Command: is a prompt asking what we wish to do. We respond by typing in one of the upper case letters listed. The meaning of some of these letters follows:

E—(Editor) Used to create and modify PASCAL programs

R—Run or execute a PASCAL program

F—(Filer) Used to retrieve, save, or transfer files and for modifying the date

C—Compile a PASCAL program

Before doing anything else, we should enter the Filer system (F) and change the date to today's date as illustrated below. All our responses are underlined.

```
F
>FILER: G(ET, S(AVE, W(HAT, N(EW, L(DIR, R(EN, C(HNG, T(RANS,
        D(ATE, Q(UIT
D
  DATE SET: <1..31> - <JAN..DEC> - <00..99>
  TODAY IS 1-JAN-82
  NEW DATE ? 15-MAY-82
```

After changing the date, we are ready to leave (or quit) the Filer. We type Q and the Command prompt line reappears. We type E to enter the Editor as shown next.

```
Q
>COMMAND: E(DIT, R(UN, F(ILE, C(OMP, L(INK, X(ECUTE, A(SSEMB,
          D(EBUG
E
>EDIT: A(DJST, C(PY, D(LETE, F(IND, I(NSRT, J(MP, R(PLACE,
       Q(UIT, X(CHNG, Z(AP
```

To create a PASCAL program, we must type I for Insert. Each line of the program can then be entered. Whenever the carriage return <CR> is pressed, the cursor always returns to the beginning of the last line entered. To indent more spaces, simply press the spacebar; to indent fewer spaces or to "erase" an erroneous character, press the backspace key. When done with the program, press <ETX> (CTRL C on some systems) and the Editor prompt line will reappear (last line above).

```
I
PROGRAM HELLO;<CR>
<CR>
BEGIN<CR>
   WRITELN ('HI THERE')<CR>
   WRITELN ('BYE')<CR>
END.<CR>
<ETX>
```

In order to correct an error, the cursor must be placed over the first erroneous character by pressing the cursor positioning arrows on the keyboard. Once this is done, the error can be corrected by first typing D(Delete). D is used to remove erroneous text: each time the down arrow key or spacebar is pressed, the character under the cursor is deleted. I is used to insert new text. After I is pressed, the characters under the cursor will be shifted to the right and the new text can be entered. After completing either of these operations, press <ETX>. To cancel either of these operations, type <ESC> (or Break) instead of <ETX>.

Once your program editing is done, you can leave the editor by pressing Q. You will then be presented with a list of choices:

```
QUIT:
    U(PDATE THE WORKFILE AND LEAVE
    E(XIT WITHOUT UPDATING
    R(ETURN TO THE EDITOR WITHOUT UPDATING
    W(RITE TO A FILE NAME AND RETURN
```

Before the edited program can be run, it must first be copied to the system workfile. This is done by pressing U (for Update). After the workfile is updated, the Command prompt reappears. At this time, you should type R (for Run) to cause the program on the workfile to be compiled and executed.

```
>COMMAND: E(DIT, R(UN, F(ILE, C(OMP, L(INK, X(ECUTE, A(SSEM,
          D(EBUG
R
COMPILING .....
WRITELN ('HI THERE')
WRITELN <<<<
LINE 5, ERROR 6: <SP> <CONTINUE>, E(DIT
```

The output shown above appears when a program cannot be compiled because it contains an error. The line on which the error was detected and the preceding line are listed followed by an error message. Error 6 means that there is an illegal symbol (WRITELN) on the last program line displayed. This error is a result of a missing semicolon after the first WRITELN statement shown above. To correct this error, reenter the editor (type E), insert the missing semicolon, exit the Editor and rerun your program (type Q then U and R). If there are no more errors, the program will be executed after it is compiled. This is indicated by the message Running . . . . .

You can stop using UCSD PASCAL at any time and then resume later. When you reenter the system, the most recent workfile will be available for editing, execution, etc. You can also save the workfile as a permanent disk file by using the S (Save) command in system Filer or the W (Write) command in system Editor. The system will prompt you with

```
SAVE AS (WRITE TO) WHAT FILE?
```

You may type in any name of ten characters or less. For example, if the name PROG1 is used, then the workfile will be saved on disk as PROG1.TEXT. PROG1.CODE will be the name given to the file containing the compiled version of the program.

To reuse this file at a later date, you should enter the Filer system and type G (Get) as shown below.

```
G
THROW AWAY CURRENT WORKFILE ? Y
GET WHAT FILE ? PROG1
TEXT AND CODE FILES LOADED
```

PROG1.TEXT and PROG1.CODE will become the system workfile (SYSTEM.WORK.TEXT and SYSTEM.WORK.CODE, respectively). The workfile can then be edited and/or executed as before.

Appendix 4

PASCAL Snytax Diagrams

Program

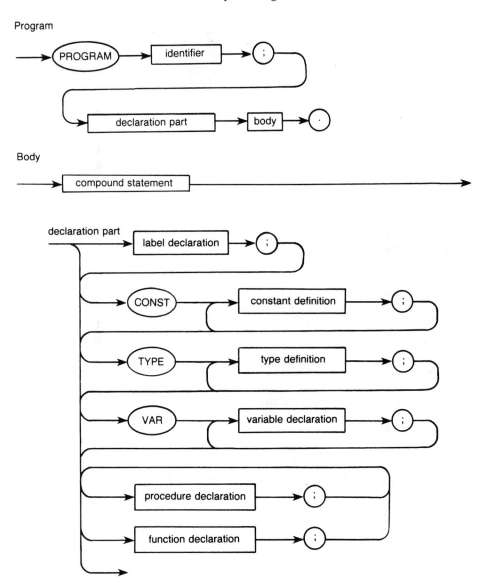

Body

declaration part

Label Declaration

Constant Definition

Type Definition

Variable Declaration

function declaration

procedure declaration

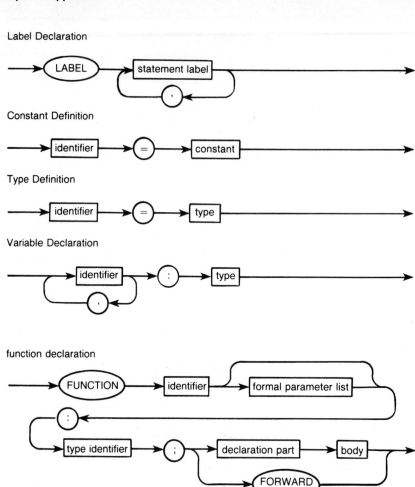

formal parameter list

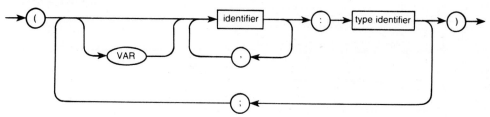

statement label

constant

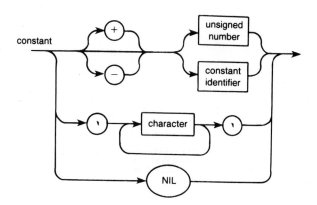

identifier

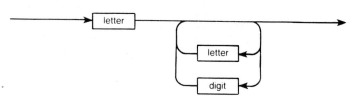

Type

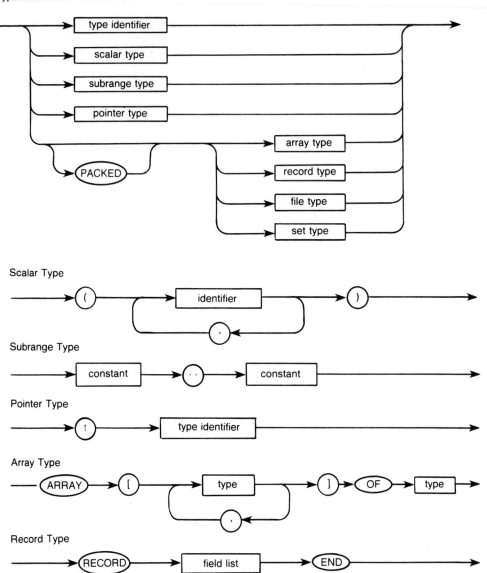

Scalar Type

Subrange Type

Pointer Type

Array Type

Record Type

Field List

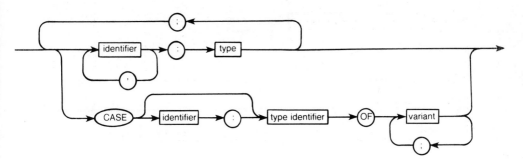

Variant

File Type

Set Type

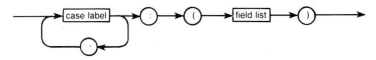

Compound Statement

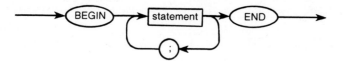

statement

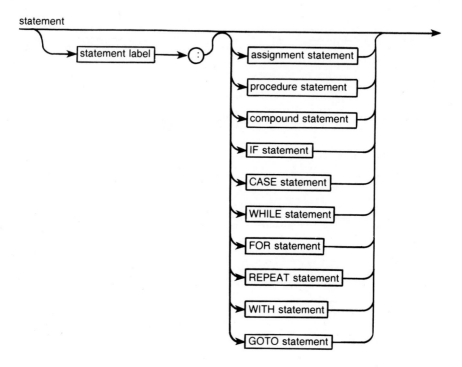

Assignment Statement

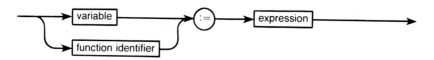

Procedure Statement

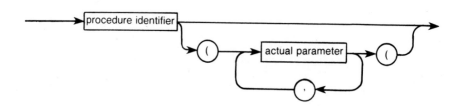

IF Statement

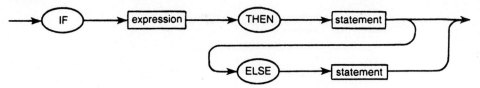

WHILE Statement

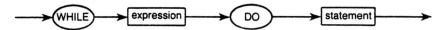

FOR Statement

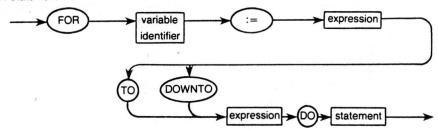

CASE Statement

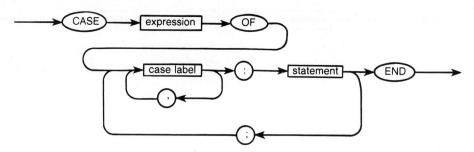

Case Label

REPEAT Statement

WITH Statement

GOTO Statement

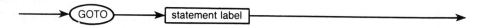

Actual Parameter

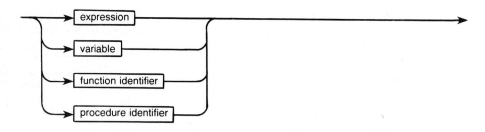

Expression

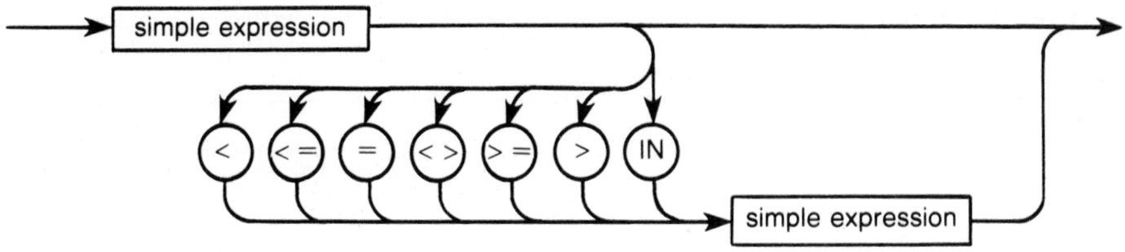

Simple Expression

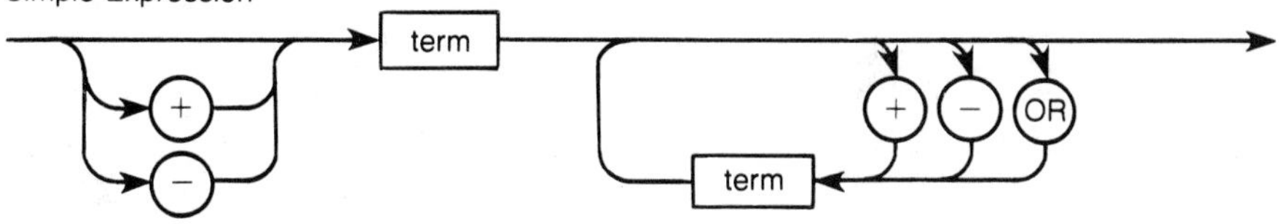

Term

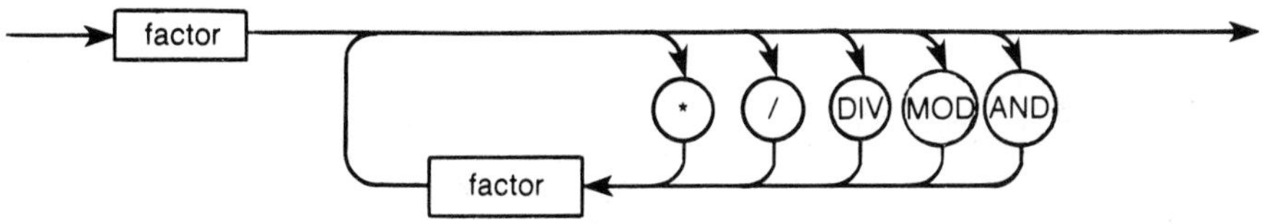

Factor

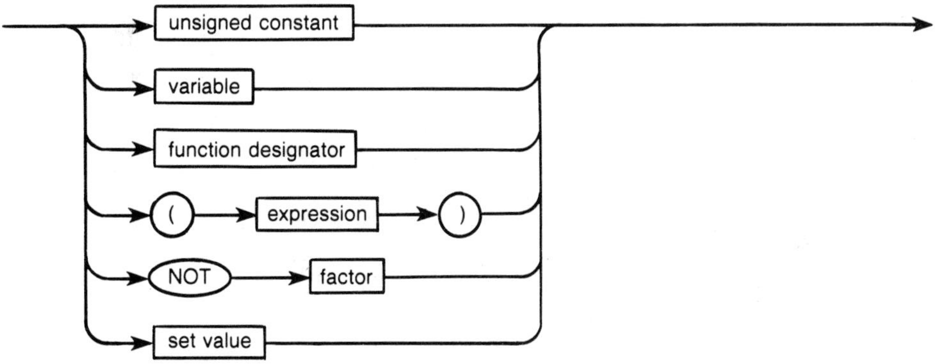

Function Designator

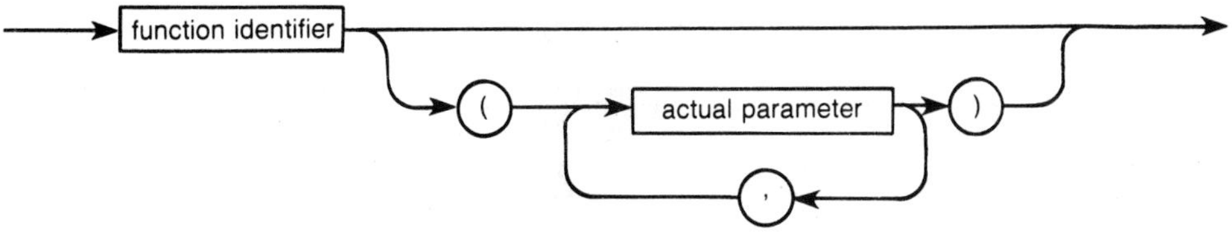

Set Value

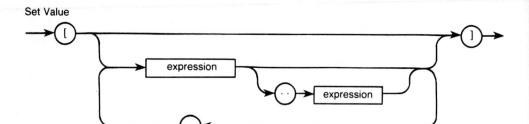

Variable

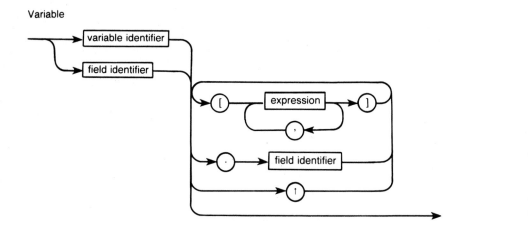

Program Style Displays

Programs, Procedures and Functions

ANSWERS TO
SELECTED EXERCISES

Chapter 1

1.2   12ZIP begins with a digit, P3$ and NINE$T contain an illegal character ($)
       CONST and **PROGRAM** are reserved words

1.3   **WRITELN (HOURS, RATE);** may be moved down

1.5   40.0   16.25   650.0   117.0   533.0

1.6
```
PROGRAM NAME;

CONST
   X = 3.5;
   A = 5.7;

VAR
   Y : REAL;

BEGIN
   Y := X + A;
   WRITELN (A, X, Y)
END.
```

1.8
```
WRITELN ('    I    I');
WRITELN (' X I    I');
WRITELN ('---I---I---');
WRITELN ('   I O I X ');
WRITELN ('---I---I---');
WRITELN ('   I O I');
WRITELN ('    I    I')
```

Chapter 2

2.1

input variables	*program variables*	*output variables*

NUM1, NUM2, NUM3, NUM4: The numbers to be summed

SUM: The sum of four numbers

AVERAGE: The average of four numbers

Level one algorithm

1. Read NUM1, NUM2, NUM3, and NUM4
2. Find SUM
3. Find AVERAGE

Level two refinements

Step 2

2.1   SUM := NUM1 + NUM2 + NUM3 + NUM4

Step 3

3.1   AVERAGE := SUM/4

2.2   a)   IF ITEM < > 0 THEN
            PRODUCT := PRODUCT * ITEM;
       WRITELN (PRODUCT)

b)   IF ITEM > LARGEST THEN
         LARGEST := ITEM;
     WRITELN (LARGEST)

c)   IF X > 0 THEN
         PLUSSUM := PLUSSUM + X;
     IF X < 0 THEN
         MINUSSUM := MINUSSUM + X;
     IF X = 0 THEN
         ZEROCOUNT := ZEROCOUNT + 1

2.5   *Level one algorithm*

1. Store the smaller of NUM1 and NUM2 in SMALLA
2. Store the smaller of NUM3 and NUM4 in SMALLB
3. Store the smaller of SMALLA and SMALLB in SMALLEST
4. Print SMALLEST

Level two refinements

(Steps 1, 2 & 3 have the form below)

Step 3

3.1   IF SMALLA < SMALLB THEN
          SMALLEST := SMALLA
      ELSE
          SMALLEST := SMALLB

2.7

```
IF X > Y THEN
    ABSDIF := X − Y
ELSE
    ABSDIF := Y − X
```

2.8

```
PROGRAM PAYROLL3;

CONST
    MAXSAL = 19000.0;
    TAXRATE = 0.061;

VAR
    SALARY, SOCIALTAX, TAXSAL : REAL;

BEGIN
    (*READ SALARY*)
    WRITELN ('SALARY:');
    READLN (SALARY);

    (*COMPUTE SOCIALTAX*)
    IF SALARY ,< MAXSAL THEN
        TAXSAL := SALARY
    ELSE
        TAXSAL := MAXSAL;
    SOCIALTAX := TAXRATE * TAXSAL;

    (*PRINT SOCIALTAX*)
    WRITELN ('SOCIAL SECURITY TAX = ', SOCIALTAX)
END.
```

2.10   It would be necessary to count the odd numbers being summed and then divide SUM by this count. The steps that would be changed are shown below.

Step 2   Initialize SUM and COUNT to zero and ODDS to one.

Step 3.2   *Add ODDS to SUM and one to COUNT*

     3.2.1   SUM := SUM + ODDS
             COUNT := COUNT + 1

Step 4   *Find and print AVERAGE and print SUM*

     4.1   AVERAGE := SUM/COUNT
     4.2   Print AVERAGE
     4.3   Print SUM

2.11   *Level one algorithm*

1. Read in LAST
2. Find the sum of each pair of odd numbers (PAIRSUM)
3. Find the number of pairs (NUMPAIR)
4. Multiply NUMPAIR by PAIRSUM to get SUM
5. Print SUM

Level two refinements

Step 2

     2.1   PAIRSUM := 1 + LAST

Step 3

3.1   NUMPAIR := PAIRSUM/2

Chapter 3

3.1 a)
```
READ (N);
IF N > O THEN
   POS := POS + 1
ELSE
   NEG := NEG + 1
```

b)
```
READ (N);
IF N = O THEN
   ZERO := ZERO + 1
```

c)
```
READ (N);
IF N > O THEN
   POS := POS + 1
ELSE
   IF N = O THEN
      ZERO := ZERO + 1
   ELSE
      NEG := NEG + 1
```

3.3 a)
```
IF REM = O THEN
   WRITE (N);
```

b)
```
IF PRODUCT = N THEN
   BEGIN
      WRITE (TEST);
      READ (N)
   END
```

c)
```
IF LIGHTS > 25 THEN
   GALLONS := MILES/14
ELSE
   GALLONS := MILES/22.5
```

3.4   2 4 8 ... 1024

3.5
```
POWER := 1;
RESULT := O;
WHILE RESULT < 10000 DO
   BEGIN
      WRITE (' N: ');
      READLN (N);
      RESULT := N * POWER;
      WRITELN (POWER, N, RESULT);
      POWER := POWER * 2
   END
```

3.6

```
(* FIND FIRST PRODUCT BIGGER THAN 10000*)
NUM := 0;
PRODUCT := 1;
WHILE PRODUCT < 10000 DO
   BEGIN
      NUM := NUM + 1;
      PRODUCT := PRODUCT * NUM
   END; (*WHILE*)

(*DIVIDE BY LAST VALUE OF NUM*)
PRODUCT := PRODUCT/NUM;
WRITELN ('LARGEST PRODUCT < 10000 IS',
         PRODUCT)
```

3.7   The value 0 would be printed

3.10   Insert SMALLEST and RANGE as output variables

Step 1   *Initialize SMALLEST, LARGEST and COUNT*

   1.3   SMALLEST := 100

Step 2.4a   *Store the smaller of SCORE and SMALLEST in SMALLEST*

            IF SCORE < SMALLEST THEN
               SMALLEST := SCORE

Step 3   Print SMALLEST, LARGEST, RANGE and COUNT

   3.1   RANGE := LARGEST − SMALLEST
   3.2   Print all output variables

3.11

```
PROGRAM WATER;

CONST
   WEEKUSE = 183;
   STARTUP = 10000;

VAR
   SUPPLY, WEEK : INTEGER;

BEGIN
   SUPPLY := STARTUP;
   WEEK := 0;
   WRITELN ('WATER AMOUNT', 'WEEK' : 10);
   WHILE SUPPLY >= WEEKUSE DO
      BEGIN
         SUPPLY := SUPPLY − WEEKUSE;
         WEEK := WEEK + 1;
         WRITELN (SUPPLY :12, WEEK :10)
      END; (*WHILE*)
   WRITELN ('WATER WILL RUN OUT DURING WEEK',
            WEEK')
END.
```

3.15   PROGRAM FAHRTOCELSIUS;

```
        VAR
          FAHR : INTEGER;
          CELSIUS : REAL;

        BEGIN
          WRITELN ('FAHRENHEIT', 'CELSIUS' :10);
          FOR FAHR := 100 DOWNTO 80 DO
            BEGIN
              CELSIUS := (FAHR - 32)/1.8;
              WRITELN (FAHR :10, CELSIUS :10:1)
            END (*FOR*)
        END.
```

3.17

Step	STARTINV	ORDER	UNFILLED	CURINV	Effect
1	75				
2			0	75	
3.1		20			
3.2					$20 <> 0$ — True
3.3.1				55	$20 < 75$ — True
3.4		50			
3.2					$50 <> 0$ — True
3.3.1				5	$50 < 75$ — True
3.4		100			
3.2					$100 <> 0$ — True
3.3.1			100		$100 < 5$ — False

The trace should continue as shown. The order for 3 widgets will be filled, but not the orders for 15 and 12 widgets. The final values of CURINV, UNFILLED, ADDWIDGETS and SHIPPED will be 2, 127, 125 and 73, respectively.

Chapter 4

4.1   2) 10.0   3) 26.6   4) 2.0
      5) 17.5   6) 13.5

4.2   1) 3   0   1   7
      4) 0   4   4   0

4.3   I is 1, I is 2, X is 2.5, X is 6.28318, X is 2.0, X is 2.5, I is 0

4.4   a) WHITE is 1.66666 . . .
      b) GREEN is 0.66666 . . .
      c) ORANGE is 0
      d) BLUE is −3.0
      e) LIME is 2
      f) PURPLE is 0.66666 . . .

4.5   a) X := 4.0 * A * C   d) K := 3 * (I + J)
      b) A := A * C   e) X := A / (B * C)
      c) I := 2 * (−J)   f) I := J * 3

4.7
```
TIMETOGROUND := SQRT (2 * S/G);
T := 0;
WHILE T <= TIMETOGROUND DO
   BEGIN
      V := G * T;
      WRITELN (V, T);
      T := T + 10
   END (*WHILE*)
```

4.8
```
ROUNDX := ROUND(100*X) / 100.0
```

4.10   If the word stored in string variable **FIRST** precedes the word 'FIRST' in the dictionary; if the word stored in **FIRST** precedes the word stored in **SECOND**.

4.13   Extra blanks would be printed as blank lines. The IF statement should be changed as follows.

```
(*ECHO PRINT CURRENT WORD OR TERMINATE OUTPUT LINE*)
IF NEXT <> BLANK THEN
   BEGIN
      WRITE (NEXT);
      READ (KEYBOARD, NEXT)
   END
ELSE
   BEGIN
      (*SKIP ANY EXTRA BLANKS*)
      WHILE NEXT = BLANK DO
         READ (KEYBOARD, NEXT);
      WRITELN
   END (*IF*)
```

The **READ** statement currently at the end of the loop body should be deleted.

4.14   Remove the ELSE clause in Fig. 4.6.

4.15   Change the IF statement as follows.

```
IF NEXT <> BLANK THEN
   BEGIN
      CODE := ORD('A') - ORD(NEXT) + 26;
      WRITELN (CHAR, CODE :3)
   END; (*IF*)
```

4.16   Change the program body as shown

```
BEGIN
   FOR LINE := MAX DOWNTO MIN DO
      WRITE (CHR(LINE));
   WRITELN
END.
```

4.18   Type a blank space at the end of each data line except the last line.

4.19 a) 1   b) FALSE   c) TRUE   d) 1

4.20 a) 5   b) 5   c) 11   d) 5

Chapter 5

5.2
```
IF ('A' <= GRADE) AND (GRADE <= 'E') THEN
   BEGIN
      POINTS := POINTS + CREDHOUR
                     * (ORD('A') - ORD(GRADE) + 4);
      CREDITS := CREDITS + CREDHOUR
   END
ELSE IF (GRADE = 'P') THEN
   PASSCREDITS := PASSCREDITS + CREDHOUR
```

5.3
```
IF GPA >= 3.5 THEN
   WRITELN ('DEANS LIST')
ELSE IF (GPA > 1.0) AND (GPA <= 1.99) THEN
   WRITELN ('PROBATION WARNING')
ELSE IF GPA <= 1.0 THEN
   WRITELN ('YOU ARE ON PROBATION NEXT SEMESTER')
```

5.4   The compound IF (Step 2.3) should begin as follows.

```
IF (CATEGORY = DECIMAL) AND (NEXTCHAR = 'E') THEN
   BEGIN
      CATEGORY := SCIENTIFIC
      Read NEXTCHAR
   END
ELSE IF (CATEGORY = SCIENTIFIC) AND
        (NEXTCHAR is not a digit) THEN
   BEGIN
      CATEGORY := NONNUMERIC
      Read NEXTCHAR
   END
ELSE IF NEXTCHAR is the first decimal point THEN

         .
         .
```

where SCIENTIFIC is another scalar value for the scalar type CATTYPE.

5.6
```
FUNCTION POWER (X : REAL; N : INTEGER) : REAL;

VAR
   PRODUCT : REAL;
   I : INTEGER;

BEGIN
   (*MULTIPLY X BY ITSELF N TIMES*)
   PRODUCT := 1;
   FOR I := 1 TO N DO
      PRODUCT := PRODUCT * X;
   (*DEFINE FUNCTION RESULT*)
   POWER := PRODUCT
END; (*POWER*)
```

5.8   1)   I2 and R2 are not the same type as their corresponding parameters (FRAC and WHOLE, respectively)

2) Only 2 actual parameters
3) X, FRAC and WHOLE are not variables in the main program.
4) 37 cannot correspond to variable parameter WHOLE.
5) Legal. The fractional part of B would be retained in B; the integral part in I2.
6) Legal. The fractional part of A would be assigned to B; the integral part to I1.

5.9   Main program variable X corresponds to formal parameter FRAC. It is assigned the value 0.632; I1 is assigned the value 25.

5.10 a) `(VAR A, B : INTEGER; C : REAL)`
    b) `(M : INTEGER; VAR NEXT : CHAR)`
    c) `(VAR ACCOUNT, TRANID : INTEGER)`
    d) `(IDNUM : SMALLINT; VAR X : REAL)`

5.11 a) Z (type REAL) cannot correspond to formal parameter X (type SMALL)
    b) Legal. X and Y are type REAL; 8 is compatible with type SMALL
    c) M (type SMALL) cannot correspond to formal parameter A (type REAL)
    d) 25.0 and 15 cannot correspond to variable parameters.
    e) 15 is not compatible with type SMALL
    f) Expressions $X+Y$ and $X-Y$ cannot correspond to variable parameters; Z (type REAL) cannot correspond to formal parameter X (type SMALL)
    g) 4 actual parameters $-$ 3 formal parameters

5.15 a) READHEADER (formal parameter), PROCESS (formal parameter), UP-DATEONE (formal parameter), CHECKACCOUNT (variable)
    b) READHEADER (local variable)
    c) PROCESS (local variable), UPDATEONE (nonlocal variable)
    d) UPDATEONE (local constant)
    e) READHEADER, CHECKACCOUNT, PROCESS, UPDATEONE
    f) PROCESS, UPDATEONE, CHECKACCOUNT

5.16   All identifiers shown in Fig. 5.12 except those that are declared as local identifiers in READHEADER and UPDATEONE.

Chapter 6

6.2   COUNTS[I] is COUNTS[4], COUNTS[2*I] is COUNTS[8], COUNTS[5*I − 6] is out-of-range, COUNTS[I + 1] is COUNTS[5]

6.3   a, c, d

6.4   a) 12.0   b) 8.2   c) TRUE, FALSE   d) TRUE

e)

G[1]	G[2]	G[3]	G[4]	G[5]	G[6]	G[7]	G[8]	G[9]	G[10]
2.0	4.0	6.0	8.0	10.0	4.0	8.0	12.0	16.0	20.0

6.5 a)
```
VAR
    ALPHABET : ARRAY[1..26] OF CHAR;
    NEXTCHAR : CHAR;

BEGIN
    FOR NEXTCHAR := 'A' TO 'Z' DO
        ALPHABET[ORD(NEXTCHAR)-ORD('A')+1] := NEXTCHAR
END.
```

b, c, d)   `VAR`

```
          S, T, U : ARRAY[1..10] OF INTEGER;
          I : INTEGER;

       BEGIN
         FOR I := 1 TO 10 DO
            BEGIN
               S[I] := I;
               T[I] := 11 - I;
               U[I] := SQR (I)
            END (*FOR*)
       END.
```

6.8   `PROGRAM TESTADD;`

```
       CONST
         N = 10;
       TYPE
         ARRAYOFNUMBERS = ARRAY[1..N] OF INTEGER;

       VAR
         X, Y, Z : ARRAYOFNUMBERS;
         I : INTEGER;

       (*INSERT ADDARRAY HERE*)

       BEGIN
         (*ENTER X AND Y*)
         FOR I := 1 TO N DO
            BEGIN
               WRITE ('X[', I, '] : '); READLN (X[I]);
               WRITE ('Y[', I, '] : '); READLN (Y[I])
            END; (* FOR *)

         (*STORE 2*X + Y IN Z*)
         ADDARRAY (X, X, N, Z);
         ADDARRAY (Z, Y, N, Z);

         (*PRINT RESULTS*)
         WRITELN ('X' :10, 'Y' :10, '2*X + Y' :10);
         FOR I := 1 TO N DO
            WRITELN (X[I] :10, Y[I] :10, Z[I] :10)
       END.
```

6.9   a)   Z is not type **SMALLARRAY**
      b)   Legal
      c)   M[1..5] is not a valid actual parameter
      d)   Main program variable X is not type **SMALLARRAY**
      e)   M[2] is not type **REAL**
      f)   X[2] does not exist (X is not an array)
      g)   Legal
      h)   M[10] is not an array (M[10] is a single element)
      i)   M[1] and M[2] are not type **REAL**
      j)   Legal
      k)   4 actual parameters

6.11   PROCEDURE READPIN (VAR M : PINARRAY;
                           MAX : INTEGER;
                           VAR COUNT : INTEGER);

Use this header statement with the body of procedure **READPART**. Make
SENTINEL a local variable.

6.14   VAR
          MONTHNAME : ARRAY[MONTH] OF STRING[9];

Insert the statements

READLN (MONTHNAME[CURMONTH]);
READLN (DAYSINMONTH[CURMONTH]);

at the beginning of the **FOR** loop

        .
        .
        .

Chapter 7

7.1   TYPE
          CATALOGUE = RECORD
            NAME : STRING[20];
            TITLE : STRING[80];
            PUBLISHER : STRING[40];
            YEAR : 1900..1999
          END;

7.2   TYPE
          PART = RECORD
            IDNUM : 1111..9999;
            NAME : STRING[20];
            QUANTITY : INTEGER;
            PRICE : REAL
          END;

7.3   WRITELN ('NAME:', CLERK.NAME);
        WRITELN ('SOCIAL SECURITY NUMBER:',
                CLERK.SOCSECURE);
        WRITELN ('NUMBER OF DEPENDENTS:', CLERK.NUMDEPEND :3);
        WRITELN ('HOURLY SALARY:', CLERK.RATE :6:2)

7.4   If the **WRITELN** was also deleted.

7.8   a) [1,3,4,5,6,7]   d) [1,2,3,5,7]
       b) [1,2,3,5,7]   e) [2]
       c) [1,2,3,4,5,6,7]   f) []

7.12   Change Step 2 as follows

        2.1   IF FOUND THEN
                BEGIN
                  Update the balance for the Ith depositor

(continued)

> IF the new balance is positive **THEN**
> delete element I from the set **OVERDRAWN**
>
> .
> .
> .

Chapter 8

8.1
```
OUTER   1
INNERI  1 1
INNERI  1 2
INNERI  1 3
INNERI  1 4
INNERK  1 4
INNERK  1 3
INNERK  1 2
INNERK  1 1
OUTER   2
INNERI  2 1
```
.
.
.

8.2   Count the number of passes, COUNT. The **FOR** loop header (Step 1.3.1) should be changed to

```
FOR I := 1 TO NUMITEMS-COUNT DO
```

8.3   Use the Boolean expression $M[I] < M[I+1]$

8.5   The procedure body is shown next. **INDEX** and **J** should be declared local variables of type **INTEGER**.

```
BEGIN
  (*STORE NEXT SMALLEST VALUE IN M[I]*)
  FOR I := 1 TO NUMITEMS-1 DO
    BEGIN
      (*FIND INDEX OF SMALLEST VALUE IN REST OF
        ARRAY*)
      INDEX := I;
      FOR J := I+1 TO NUMITEMS DO
        IF M[J] < M[INDEX] THEN
          INDEX := J;
      (*EXCHANGE SMALLEST VALUE WITH M[I]*)
      TEMP := M[I];
      M[I] := M[INDEX];
      M[INDEX] := TEMP
    END (*FOR I*)
END;
```

8.7   Change procedure SORT (Fig. 8.8) as follows

```
PROCEDURE SORT (VAR M : REALARRAY;
                NUMITEMS : INTEGER);
```

Change TEMP to type REAL.

ENTERDATA should be modelled after the procedure with that name shown in Fig. 7.15b.

8.13
```
FUNCTION FIBO (N : INTEGER) : INTEGER;

BEGIN
  IF N = 1 THEN
    FIBO := 1
  ELSE IF N = 2 THEN
    FIBO := 1
  ELSE
    FIBO := FIBO(N-1) + FIBO(N-2)
END; (*FIBO*)
```

This is inefficient because it results in a large number of function calls even for a small value of N (e.g. nine calls for N = 5).

Chapter 9

9.2
```
FUNCTION MARITALCONVERT (MARTIAL : CHAR) :
  MARITALSTAT;

BEGIN
  IF MARITAL IN ['D', 'M', 'S'] THEN
    CASE MARITAL OF
      'D' : MARITALCONVERT := DIVORCED;
      'M' : MARITALCONVERT := MARRIED;
      'S' : MARITALCONVERT := SINGLE
    END (*CASE*)
  ELSE
    WRITELN ('VALUE OF MARITAL =', MARITAL, ' IS
      ILLEGAL')
END; (*MARITALCONVERT*)
```

9.6
```
PROGRAM GRADEFILE;

TYPE
  STUDENT = RECORD
    NAME : STRING[10];
    G1, G2, G3 : INTEGER
  END; (*STUDENT*)
  STUFILE = FILE OF STUDENT;

VAR
  GRADES : STUFILE;
  TEMPNAME : STRING[10];

BEGIN
  REWRITE (GRADES, 'VOL1:GRADES');
  (*COPY ALL STUDENT DATA INTO FILE GRADES*)
  WRITE (' ENTER DONE OR NAME: ');
```

(continued)

```
        READLN (TEMPNAME);
        WHILE TEMPNAME <> 'DONE' DO
          BEGIN
            WITH GRADES↑ DO
              BEGIN
                NAME := TEMPNAME;
                WRITE (' ENTER 3 SCORES ');
                READLN (G1, G2, G3)
              END; (*WITH*)
            PUT (GRADES);
            WRITE ('NAME: '); READLN (TEMPNAME)
          END; (*WHILE*)
        WRITELN ('FILE GRADES CREATED');
        CLOSE (GRADES, LOCK)
      END.
```

9.9   Declare two new data types in the main program.

```
TYPE
  EXPANDSTUDENT = RECORD
    OLDDATA : STUDENT;
    G4 : INTEGER
  END;
  EXPANDSTUFILE = FILE OF EXPANDSTUDENT;


PROCEDURE UPDATEGRADE (VAR GRADES : STUFILE
                       VAR NEWGRADES : EXPANDSTUFILE);
(* ADD A FOURTH EXAM SCORE TO FILE NEWGRADES      *)
(* INPUT PARAMETER                                *)
(*    GRADES-FILE OF NAME AND 3 GRADES            *)
(* OUTPUT PARAMETER                               *)
(*    NEWGRADES-FILE OF NAME AND 4 GRADES         *)


VAR
  GRADE4 : INTEGER;

BEGIN
  RESET (GRADES, 'VOL1:GRADES');
  REWRITE (NEWGRADES, 'VOL1:NEWGRADES');
  (*READ AND UPDATE EACH COMPONENT OF GRADES*)
  WHILE NOT EOF (GRADES) DO
    BEGIN
      (*READ NEW DATA*)
      WRITELN (' ENTER FOURTH SCORE FOR ', GRADES↑.NAME);
      READLN (GRADE4);
      (*ADD FOURTH EXAM SCORE*)
      NEWGRADES↑.OLDDATA := GRADES↑;
      NEWGRADES↑.G4 := GRADE4;
      PUT (NEWGRADES);
      GET (GRADES)
    END (*WHILE*)
  WRITELN ('FILE UPDATE COMPLETED');
  CLOSE (GRADES);
  CLOSE (NEWGRADES, LOCK)
END.
```

Chapter 10

10.1 a)
```
CLASSUM := 0;
FOR CAMP := MAIN TO MONTCO DO
   FOR COURSE := 1 TO 50 DO
      CLASSUM := CLASSUM + ENRANK[COURSE, CAMP, JUNIOR]
```

b)
```
CLASSUM := 0;
FOR CAMP := MAIN TO MONTCO DO
   CLASSUM := CLASSUM + ENRANK[25, CAMP, SOPHOMORE]
```

c)
```
TOTAL := 0;
FOR COURSE := 1 to 50 DO
   BEGIN
      CLASSUM := 0;
      FOR RANK := FRESHMAN TO SENIOR DO
         CLASSUM := CLASSUM + ENRANK[COURSE, MAIN, RANK];
      WRITELN ('STUDENTS AT MAIN IN COURSE', COURSE,
               ' = ', CLASSUM);
      TOTAL := TOTAL + CLASSUM
   END; (*FOR*)
WRITELN ('TOTAL STUDENTS IN COURSES AT MAIN = ',
   TOTAL)
```

d)
```
TOTAL := 0;
FOR CAMP := MAIN TO MONTCO DO
   BEGIN
      CLASSUM := 0;
      FOR COURSE := 1 TO 50 DO
         FOR RANK := JUNIOR TO SENIOR DO
            CLASSUM := CLASSUM + ENRANK[COURSE, CAMP,
                       RANK];
      WRITELN ('NUMBER OF UPPER CLASS STUDENTS AT',
               CAMP, '=', CLASSUM);
      TOTAL := TOTAL + CLASSUM
   END; (*FOR*)
WRITELN ('TOTAL NUMBER OF UPPER CLASS STUDENTS = ',
            TOTAL)
```

10.2
```
FUNCTION VERIFY (TICTAC : BOARD;
                 ROW, COLUMN : INTEGER) : BOOLEAN;

BEGIN
   IF (ROW < 1) OR (ROW > 3) OR
      (COLUMN < 1) OR (COLUMN > 3) THEN
      VERIFY := FALSE
   ELSE IF TICTAC[ROW, COLUMN] <> ' ' THEN
      VERIFY := FALSE
   ELSE
      VERIFY := TRUE
END; (*VERIFY*)
```

10.3
```
PROCEDURE NOTASSIGNED (CAPACITY : BUILDING);

VAR
   ROW, COLUMN, ROOMNUM : INTEGER;
```

(continued)

```
            BEGIN
              WRITELN;
              WRITELN ('CLASSROOMS NOT ASSIGNED');
              WRITELN ('NUMBER', 'CAPACITY' :10);
              FOR ROW := 1 TO COUNTFLOOR DO
                FOR COLUMN := 1 TO COUNTROOM DO
                  IF CAPACITY[ROW, COLUMN] >= 0 THEN
                    BEGIN
                      ROOMNUM := ROW * 100 + COLUMN;
                      WRITELN (ROOMNUM :6, CAPACITY[ROW, COLUMN]
                        :10)
                    END (*IF*)
            END; (*NOTASSIGNED*)
```

10.7   Store these characters in a set (initially empty) and then print out the set.

Chapter 11

11.1   This sequence exchanges the **WORD** fields only of the two nodes shown in Example 11.2.

11.2
```
PROGRAM BUILDLIST;

(*INSERT ALL TYPE DECLARATIONS FOR PROBLEM 11.1*)

VAR
  LISTHEAD : PASSPOINTER;

(*INSERT LISTCREATE AND TRAVERSE HERE*)

BEGIN
  LISTCREATE (LISTHEAD);
  TRAVERSE (LISTHEAD)
END.
```

change the data type of the parameter for **TRAVERSE** to PASSPOINTER.

11.5   It would then be possible to delete the first list node. This would require changing the value of **LISTHEAD**, as shown in the refinement of Step 2 below. **LISTHEAD** would become an update parameter.

IF (TARGET is found) AND (NEXT = LISTHEAD) THEN
    LISTHEAD := LISTHEAD↑.LINK
ELSE IF TARGET is found THEN
                .
                .
                .

11.6   The loop header

```
WHILE NEXT↑.PASSINFO.NAME < TARGET DO
```

should be used instead. This will cause loop exit as soon as the first passenger in the list is reached with a name that is the target or alphabetically follows the target. There is no need to search the rest of the list.

11.7
```
Q↑.LINK := P;
P↑.LINK := R
```

11.8   It may become necessary to change LISTHEAD if the new name precedes the
first list element. LISTHEAD should be an update parameter. Step 2 should be
modified as shown next.

2.1 If the new passenger is in the list THEN
        2.2 update the flight data
    ELSE IF NEXT = LISTHEAD THEN
        2.3 Insert the new passenger at the
            head of the list

                .
                .
                .

New step 2.3 would be implemented as

```
INSERTNODE (NEWPASSENGER, LISTHEAD, LISTHEAD↑.LINK)
```

11.11

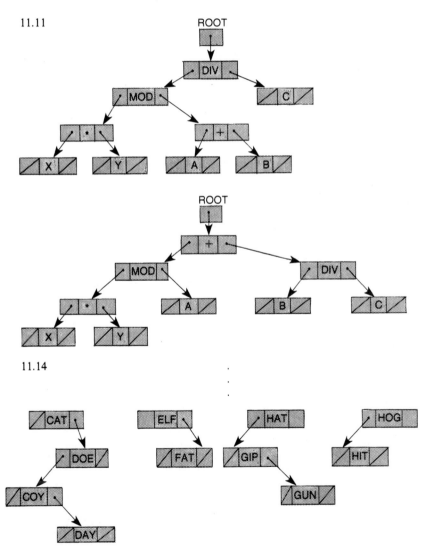

11.14

11.15   The tree resembles a linked list. All left branches are NIL.

11.16   The words will be printed in alphabetical order.

11.17   B D C A − X + Y

INDEX

ABOUT THE AUTHOR

Elliot B. Koffman is a Professor of Computer and Information Sciences at Temple University, Philadelphia. He has also been an Associate Professor in the Electrical Engineering and Computer Science Department at the University of Connecticut. Dr. Koffman received his Bachelor's and Master's degrees from the Massachusetts Institute of Technology and earned his Ph.D. from Case Institute of Technology in 1967.

With Dr. Frank L. Friedman, Associate Professor of Computer and Information Sciences at Temple University, Dr. Koffman has co-authored two other computer language textbooks: Problem Solving and Structured Programming in FORTRAN and Problem Solving and Structured Programming in BASIC.